MORAL DECISION–
An Introduction to Ethics

MORAL DECISION–
An Introduction to Ethics

STEPHEN DAVID ROSS
State University of New York, Binghamton

FREEMAN, COOPER & COMPANY
1736 Stockton Street, San Francisco, California 94133

COPYRIGHT, © 1972, by Ⓕ FREEMAN, COOPER & CO.

All rights to reproduce this book in whole or in part are
reserved, with the exception of the right to use short
quotations for review of the book.

Printed in the United States of America

Library of Congress Catalogue Card Number 71–178770

International Standard Book Number 0–87735–515–0

CONTENTS

MORAL DECISION–
An Introduction to Ethics

INTRODUCTION

THIS INTRODUCTION to moral theory is intended to be unique in two respects, in method and in conviction. In the first respect, this is a study not so much of the abstract tenets of ethical theory as of the specific considerations which influence the making of concrete moral decisions. The book will focus around several specific instances of moral judgment, and explore the considerations that enter into the making of specific moral decisions. In general, I shall emphasize a particular kind of moral decision, that in which an individual stands in some degree of conflict between his personal needs or convictions and the needs or values of others.

In particular, we will study the particular moral relations of men *in*, *of*, and even *against* their societies. One of the most important features of the problems we shall explore is the fact that a decision-making individual is never merely *against* society. He is also a member *of* it, and resides in some degree *within* it. Conversely, we shall see that it is a feature of being an individual never to be quite assimilable to a social norm. Every man is different in some respects from the normal or average person of his society. In the last analysis, his uniqueness will be shown to depend on his function as a maker of decisions. In reaching a moral decision, a man stands at once within and yet apart from the general norms which characterize the groups to which he belongs. Colloquially, this most fundamental feature of the function of individuality within a social context may be regarded as the generation of a tension between individual and social values. We will see, however, that there is an alternative way of regarding individuality—as the flexibility inherent in social organization.

The second feature of this work is its adherence to the principle that the making of moral judgments is fundamentally *open-ended*, and in several respects. It is open-ended in that there are no moral principles which constitute a complete solution to all the difficulties of moral situations. It is open-ended in that there can be no resolution of a moral problem which is equally satisfactory for all men, or satisfactory for all time. It is open-ended also in its dependence on circumstances which are constantly changing in important respects, calling for an unceasing reevaluation of basic values and moral principles. It is the fundamental conviction of this work that moral decisions are always tentative and risky. For this reason, the making of a moral decision is always in part a crisis for a man. A man may blind himself through inadvertence or even cowardice. But blindness never relieves him of the responsibility he bears for deciding what he will do, even when he does nothing.

The organization of this book is no accident. We will begin with several test cases, not to simplify the issues for the beginning student, but because all moral decisions are indeed decisions of how to act in specific situations. The more abstract considerations of ethical theory, which involve the ultimate ground of moral principles or the kinds of knowledge which are relevant to moral judgments, will be regarded as elements essential to the making of moral decisions, not as issues of fundamental importance in their own terms. What this means is that ethics and ethical theory will be viewed as constituents of the making of moral decisions. In return, ethical theory will be treated as the theory of decision-making in moral affairs. From this point of view, philosophical ethics will be regarded as the theory of moral decision which is implicitly called upon in the making of moral decisions. This is in contrast to the current treatment of ethical theory in the philosophical journals, which bears little relation to the decisions ordinary men make. Ethical theory is too often a comprehensive formula which describes the features of moral judgment, but in no way enters into the making of such judgments. We will begin with five specific moral problems, for all the issues of importance to moral theory arise in such concrete problems.

The emphasis in this book and in the moral theory it contains is on concrete moral decisions which arise in particular situations. Two principles are worth mentioning: (1) All moral issues are extremely subtle and complex. Therefore, (2) no theoretical work in ethics can provide advice on specific decisions. At best, a work in moral theory can explain the means of making moral decisions, and study the methods and considerations involved.

I have made no effort to be exhaustive in any area of moral theory. Rather, I have sought to raise the important issues, to explore some of their complexities, and to point in the direction of a solution. I have tried at least to touch on most of the important issues in moral theory and practice. It is my own view that the aim of all studies is to lead the student to more careful and serious thought of his own, not to provide him with simplified answers to difficult problems.

It is a fundamental premise of the moral theory embodied here that a responsible moral agent must be open-minded to ideas and facts. This entire book may be interpreted as a study of what open-mindedness in moral decision means.

Finally, the questions which follow each chapter, and the list of selected readings as well, are not intended to be exhaustive or comprehensive. Both are aimed at stimulating the reader to think upon the issues of the chapter in his own terms. The questions will rarely ask for a repetition of the material presented. Instead, they will usually ask the reader to apply the discussion just ended to new problems. The readings are suggested to cast a new and perhaps more interesting light on the problems dealt with. The conviction of this book is that a thoughtful moral agent—one who lets nothing pass without challenge—is the more responsible one.

I. FIVE TEST CASES

THE FIVE moral problems we shall consider range over a continuum, at least according to most conventional norms of appraisal. They range from problems considered by most people (but not all) to be wholly a matter of individual judgment, to moral problems which most people (but again not all) consider not a matter of individual initiative at all. Some people think that these moral decisions are to be completely dominated by social considerations, such as the welfare of society, God's commandments, or the like. What we shall see is that both types of problems, though thought to be very different by most people who view them uncritically, are very similar when studied in detail, and raise almost precisely the same general types of issues.

The two extremes are defined for us by cleanliness and stealing. In general, most people consider personal hygiene to be a matter of personal judgment alone. Few people would openly call slovenliness a *moral* transgression. On the other hand, it is certainly true that ordinary people are outraged (and no lesser word will do) at bizarre codes of dress adopted by some young people, at their general air of dirtiness, and above all, at their stench. I mention the last because with it we begin to move into areas which involve other people. A person who is unwashed and whose personal odor is very strong can be a compelling source of irritation to other people, especially on a public conveyance. The problem before us is whether a person ought to wash, when he does not wish to, but when his lack of personal hygiene causes discomfort to others. Note that the problem arises whether we suppose personal cleanliness to be regulable by general codes as in the schools, or regard it as a completely private matter subject to no formal coercion. It may be wholly my decision as to whether I dress in clean clothing or not. But a great many people who agree that it is also believe that I have an obligation to consider the feelings of others.

Stealing constitutes the opposite extreme, in that most people consider it morally wrong, punishable by law, and in no way a matter of personal conscience. A man who steals is committing a crime, ought to be punished, and has no right to decide for himself whether stealing is justified or not. In most of these respects, stealing is regarded as a moral transgression. And the prohibition against it applies to everyone equally. Nevertheless, there are countless cases of the stealing of books from university libraries as well as from campus bookstores. Certainly many people regard such stealing as outrageous. But I think it highly likely that many of the students who steal literally do not think it wrong, either for themselves or for anyone else. That is, even in such an obvious case, they would maintain that an individual has the right to decide what is right and wrong for himself. In this respect, the two extremes are alike, in that, for at least some people, the problem of individual acceptance of a social code is a live and burning issue. It is this issue which we will study in the course of this book. We will begin by detailing some of the ramifications of the five problems I have chosen as test cases.

A. Conscription

A young man's country is at war, and he is conscripted into the armed forces. However, it is a war for which he feels little sympathy. In fact, he regards it as a heinous, evil war. He thinks that the men who perpetrated it are either bumbling fools or men of monstrous intent and evil design. Moreover, though he is not truly an expert either on war or on the political affairs of the enemy country, he has become convinced by what he has read in periodicals and newspapers that his own country's officials have lied to their countrymen, and also condoned the torture and murder of enemy civilians. Does this young man have the right to refuse conscription? Even more to the point, as I will show, to what lengths is he justified in seeking to evade the draft, when to join the army is viewed by him as participation in evil?

The problem before us is an extremely complex one, and we will be able to define but a few of the issues which are relevant to it. The greatest difficulties arise with the second of the two problems posed. As soon as we begin to speak of specific actions undertaken in opposition to the war, we raise the entire gamut of problems connected with the effects such actions may have on the surrounding society—that is, on the actions and attitudes of others. Thus, a pacifist who is morally outraged by any and every war may be excused from military service as a conscientious objector. Many people who are not pacifists may even approve of an individual following the dictates of his own conscience in such a case. However, let him begin to demonstrate against the war, carrying his actions to the point of interfering with military maneuvers even at the risk of his own life. Many of the people who approve of the private dictates of conscience will heartily disapprove of the public manifestation of opposition to a patriotic war. Let us consider several of the issues which bear on such a moral problem.

(1) *Principles.* The simplest way to view the moral conflict in its first form is as a conflict between two principles which carry moral weight: (a) a citizen owes allegiance and loyalty to his country, even to the extent of risking his life for her;

(b) thou shalt not kill, under any circumstances whatsoever. The average citizen subscribes to the first of these principles, and accepts the second with an indefinite number of qualifications. He believes in the sanctity of life, but he also believes in capital punishment. He believes that no punishment is more fitting for a murderer than the taking of his life in return. In addition, killing in war or in self-defense is legitimate also. Nevertheless, our acquiescence in the prominent role played by moral principles is so great as to make us fairly willing to accept a man's moral code even where different from our own, particularly where it is more pure or categorical. The patriotic citizen does maintain a firm reverence for life, and is rather uneasy at the qualifications he imposes upon the principle that killing is always prohibited. A man may find little inconsistency in maintaining that abortion is murder, but that capital punishment or bombing is not. Yet a surreptitious respect for moral purity may well lead such a man to a firm respect for a person whose moral principles are totally uncompromised, who believes that all actions which cause the death of others are wrong. A pacifist can be morally respected, even when his actions are considered unwise.

Let us for a moment consider the problem from the pacifist's point of view. He notes correctly that the average person professes to believe in the principle that killing is wrong, and to have a reverence for life not noticeably less than that of the pacifist. Obviously, the pacifist remarks, a man who believes that it is wrong to kill, and yet also supports war and capital punishment, is *inconsistent*. The prominent role played by principles in the making of moral decisions certainly brings before us the whole subject of consistency in the adherence to principles. In fact, it is probably safe to say that a man who does not follow principles consistently does not follow them at all.

This is a logical point, not a moral one. And it is a point worth some amplification, for men find the most remarkable means of rationalizing their departure from rules they claim to live by. There is a good deal to be said about weakness in moral affairs, and the departure of men from the principles to which they claim loyalty, out of cowardice, temptation, or even laziness. But we should note that inconsistency with respect to moral principles is not always a matter of weakness. It may also arise from a more flexible sense of the function of principles in moral decisions. A man may believe it morally wrong to tell lies, and yet not hesitate for a moment before telling an aging movie star that she is ravishing. Only a rather rigid interpretation of consistency with respect to principles would allow us to condemn him for inconsistency.

Nevertheless, we must consider here a fundamental logical point concerning the relationship of general rules, principles, or maxims of conduct to the actions which they presumably guide. A principle is followed only if it guides *all* instances to which it applies. The factual generalization, "all men are mortal," is true for all men without exception. If there existed even a single immortal human being, then the generalization would be false. Just as a factual generalization applies to all instances which come under it, so a maxim or principle of action is accepted as a principle only to the point that all instances which are logically governed by the principle do in fact guide action taken with respect to these instances. If it is wrong to take a human life, then it is always and unquestionably wrong to do so. All too often men are casual about the principles they say they follow. Even a robber may concede that stealing is wrong, but nevertheless steal. Logically speaking—not morally—what he is doing is wrong by his own standards. He is either inconsistent or weak, and in both cases wrong. It is a logical or rational, and not a moral, principle that a man may not make exceptions to the general rules he accepts. Either he follows them without exception, or he does not follow them at all. To follow a rule "often" is still not to accept it fully as a general rule.

Note that there does remain to us the option of keeping a general rule by reinterpreting the instance which falsifies it. We may simply deny that an immortal being can be human, for all human beings are mortal. Though born of man and woman, with two arms, two legs, and all ordinary organs in place, if he cannot die he is another kind of being altogether. Such a device is of great importance in moral arguments. Some people maintain that abortion is the taking of a human life and thus murder. Others simply deny that the life is human (it is *pre*human), that it is yet a life (it is not alive until it is independent), and, therefore, deny that abortion is murder. We will have much to say about this technique when used for the justification of moral decisions.

The same relationship between generalizations and instances holds for beliefs as well as rules. In speaking of accepting or following a moral principle, we are in effect describing a principle a man believes to be good or obligatory, one which ought to be followed. What does it mean to say "I believe"? "I believe 2 + 2 = 4." Could a person have such a belief and still answer the question "what is the sum of 2 + 2?" as "5"? Only if he were joking. A belief commits a man to action in some way consistent with the content of the belief. (We need the phrase "in some way" because all too often we impose from without a specific mode of action, appropriate to ourselves, but not to the agent we thereby condemn.) In the case of moral principles, an action is believed to be an obligatory one or a good thing to do. If an agent generally has that belief, then he will act upon it.

We now return to the pacifist's claim that only he is consistent in his moral beliefs and principles. If a man believes in the principle "thou shalt not kill," then he will be opposed to capital punishment and also to war. If not, either his belief is tarnished or else he is inconsistent. In either case, his morals are suspect.

The pacifist has committed a rather plausible error. And it is one that leads us to an important insight concerning the function of moral principles in moral decision. Indeed it is a logical truth that a man who believes *literally* in the principle "thou shalt not kill" is obligated to oppose capital punishment. However, almost no one accepts moral principles quite literally. Nor is it clear that he ought to, at least not without many qualifications. Consider a variety of qualifications or *caveats* which may be added to the principle "thou shalt not kill." I should not kill anyone, but the state or public executioner may (in support of capital punishment). Men should not be killed *unless* they are in the act of harming others. Men should not be killed *except* during war, riots, crime, etc. There are very few men who accept a moral principle perfectly literally, without qualification, emendation, or ellipsis. The primary qualification is elliptical. There are always exceptions to every general rule.

Unfortunately, if general rules logically permit no exceptions, and if every moral principle has exceptions, we seem to be cast into a highly illogical state of affairs. Can we really maintain that moral judgments look to moral principles, but that moral principles are not to be obeyed without exception? We have arrived at a genuine difficulty in our understanding of moral decisions, and with no very subtle or sophisticated analysis. Some agents do follow moral principles with utmost consistency, but other men not only make exceptions to every principle they believe in, they actually feel that it is necessary and right to do so. They look rather askance on too great a moral purity.

Let us consider a pacifist to be a man who follows the dictum "thou shalt not kill" with no exceptions or qualifications whatsoever. Most men are not pacifists according to this definition, and not merely because they lack fortitude or strength of mind. They think it *wrong* to be too unqualified in the condemnation of the use of force. Sometimes force is necessary—for example, to protect oneself, one's loved ones, or people in general from harm. Force can sometimes lead to death. And it is not always morally wrong for it to do so. Most people would not think it wrong for a policeman to shoot at a would-be murderer or even a bank robber, if that were the only way to prevent him from committing his crime. Most people expect a soldier to kill or be killed in defense of his country. Such people do not believe themselves to have less reverence for life than does a pacifist. Let us try to understand why.

The pacifist is tempted to regard qualifications and exceptions as inconsistencies in adherence to a moral principle. A natural question, then, is whether a pacifist is truly consistent in his actions and beliefs. Consider a policeman with a gun in his hand running into a bank in which a robber is about to kill a witness who has identified him. The policeman has a brief interval of time in which he may shoot the robber, and thereby prevent him from killing the witness. Can he consistently adhere to the principle that life is sacrosanct? We will not address the complex and interesting question of the particular responsibilities to use force a policeman bears by virtue of his position. It can be argued that an ordinary man is not charged with a special responsibility for keeping the peace by the use of weapons, but that soldiers and policemen are. It can be argued in reply that such divesting of responsibilities is only a form of delegation, for which the average citizen still bears significant responsibility—the same he does toward actions performed by his elected representatives. We will return to such issues.

The more important theoretical point is that a man may find himself in a position where his only alternatives are either to take a life directly or to be a witness to murder by another. Only a very narrow and implausible interpretation of the maxim "thou shalt not kill" will justify pacifism in such a case. What a pacifist must do to maintain his consistency is to throw the entire force of the principle onto the first word, "*thou* shalt not kill (no matter what others do)." If other men commit crimes and take lives, then that is *their* evil, and not *my* problem. Such an attitude of mind would also justify a man in washing his hands of Nazi concentration camps and crimes committed by others, maintaining his own sense of purity *precisely because he does not fight back forcefully and effectively*.

We may dramatize this point to an extreme by the following fanciful case. Suppose I am a guard in the War Room which controls the release of five hundred nuclear bombs. There are two of us with the responsibility of pulling the master lever, and of watching each other. Suppose my partner goes berserk, and is running across the room to pull a lever that will kill four hundred million people. I can stop him only by killing him. Is it wrong for me to do so? Have I a choice? Have I even a choice to try to shoot him in the leg, if that would markedly increase the risk of his reaching his goal? Many people would think not. The theoretical point is that the very consistency a pacifist views as a virtue can be so inflexible as to be regarded in some circumstances as an evil. More accurately, a pacifist can achieve only a limited and perhaps even an indefensible consistency, a consistency which may violate the spirit of the principle he considers a good. "Thou shalt not kill" speaks to the evil men do in becoming instruments of the death of others. But we may be instruments in manifold and complex ways. If only a direct killing is to count as proscribed by the principle, then men may follow such a maxim and yet indirectly contribute to the taking of life.

The argument that a moral principle proscribes only direct acts of the agent, and not indirect consequences of his actions, can be countered with a simple though extreme example. I take a pistol, point it at a man, and pull the trigger. But all I directly have done is to pull a small lever. Ah, but the gun fired and killed a man. That is merely an indirect consequence of my direct action, which was a pulling and not a killing. There are only two ways of meeting the force of such an example. Either a moral agent must consider all the consequences of his actions, which is probably impossible. Or, a man is responsible only for the actions he explicitly intended to perform. In pulling the trigger of the gun, I intended to kill a man. A child may pull the trigger of a gun, and cause deaths unwittingly. He is not then culpable. Of course, there is a patent consequence of relying on intentions alone as the objects of moral appraisal. That is, that good intentions too often have extremely unfortunate results. The pathway to hell is paved with good intentions.

Our discussion to this point has been directed to some of the surface issues which arise in the consideration of the function of principles in concrete moral decisions. The burden of my argument has been that principles alone do not enable us to deal effectively with specific moral problems. Moral principles are essentially elliptical, in that they omit qualifications and exceptions. In the logical application of a principle, the ellipses must be filled by interpretation. Unfortunately, it is never a simple or routine matter to interpret a moral principle in its application to concrete cases. For this reason, some recent philosophers have been led to argue that moral principles have no function whatsoever in the making of specific moral decisions. Rather, our inner moral sense, our consciences, our moral intuitions, tell us what we ought to do, regardless of principles or maxims, formulated or not. Either a man believes it is wrong to join the army to fight a war which he believes is unjustified or he does not. A man may accept no principles whatsoever, and still consider an act wrong.

To this point, we have considered the *usefulness* of moral principles in the making of moral decisions. We now come to a very different question, that concerning the *necessity* of moral principles to such decisions. Could we manage with no more than concrete intuitions of right and wrong? It should be noted that all the complex qualifications of principles and maxims of conduct which caused us so much trouble above would no longer be problematical under a view which regarded moral decisions as unprincipled. Unfortunately, there are certain difficulties which arise in the absence of principles. First, even the most rudimentary types and degrees of consistency would be eliminated by the repudiation of principles. A man could regard the same action one day as evil, the next day as noble, and be open to no logical criticisms. As soon as we generalize our moral views, and regard all actions of a certain *kind* as good or bad, we have proposed a principle. It can certainly be argued that all consistency through time and over kinds is due to the acceptance of principles, however implicit they may be. In all reasoning, logical principles are at work, even for children who could not state them. Second, no moral disputes would seem to have any significance where we maintain that the ground of decision is wholly in a moral intuition or a conscience which refuses to generalize its convictions in principles. Either you see it or you don't. But criticism of others and their moral convictions is central to decision-making. So too is the classification of actions into kinds, which are approved or disapproved of collectively. Principles seem central to consistency, criticism, and classification. We do not seem to be able to escape from moral principles all that easily.

The case we are concretely discussing, whether a man should serve in the armed forces or not, literally does not arise where there is no consistent (and in that sense *principled*) attitude to the taking of life. Why not join the army, if you are indifferent to the deaths of others? Well, it might be an inconvenience, even a personal risk. But there are general maxims inherent in both of these notions also. Either personal convenience is important (a vague but frequently accepted principle) or it is wrong to engage in actions which will lead a man to lose his life. Each of these principles requires qualification and exceptions, but it is inconceivable that a moral decision could be called for where there was no general attitude toward actions regarded as good or bad. A man hesitates to join the army because he feels that *killing is wrong*, at least in the situation before him. My point is not the weaker one that moral principles can be found in all cases of moral decision, but

that moral principles are necessary constituents of all moral situations. In our later
discussion, I will define this function of moral principles as a *constitutive* one, for
such principles create the moral problems which call for decisions.

We have pursued this entire discussion—and not to any noticeable conclusion
—with reference to the *second* of the two conflicting principles which defined the
problem of conscription. Let us return to the first of them, at least for a short
space. This is the principle that a man owes allegiance to his country. We will
call this *patriotism*. Now, no doubt there are men who scorn patriotism, and consider it of no value. Probably there can be found civilized men to whom the lives
of others have no value, who consider the principle "thou shalt not kill" to have
only the force of a warning about what other people care about strongly. We will
have something to say about such men in our later discussion. Here, however, we
are more concerned with the conflict which has been generated by a genuine clash
of principles, principles accepted by a single agent. It is far more likely that a
young man brought up within a society which provides for some of his needs will
come to feel a loyalty to his country, and be willing to perform some service for
her. It is far more likely, except in times of extreme social dissolution, that the
same person will believe sincerely that he ought to be patriotic, and yet also that
he ought not to fight in an unjust war. To this point we have discussed a few of
the complexities involved in the following of a single moral principle, when it
conflicts with no other principle of moral significance. The problem before us,
however, is made considerably more difficult by the fact that we have two moral
principles in direct conflict.

We are confronted by the following situation: Our protagonist is a young
man with sentiments of both patriotism and revulsion against what he takes to be
an unjust war. He believes it is wrong to participate in actions which result in the
killing of the enemy. He reveres life, and believes it wrong to kill. But he admits
to several exceptions to the general principle—in self-defense, to prevent crime,
perhaps in the name of freedom and justice. On the other hand, he does feel a
loyalty to his country. A man ought to be willing to serve his country, even to
make sacrifices for her. But just as he cannot quite give all the qualifications and
exceptions to the principle "killing is wrong," our protagonist does not quite
know how patriotic a man ought to be. Ought a man to fight and kill for his
country right or wrong? Comparable to the pacifist's moral purity in never
directly taking the life of another, there is a patriotism which asks no questions
and brooks no qualifications. All we ask is what we can do for our country. My
country right or wrong, but my country.

Patriotism which allows no qualification is a dubious value—dubious not
merely because many quite patriotic men allow qualifications and exceptions, but
because extremes can subvert the very principles they ostensibly support. Recall
that a pacifist can, in his purity, allow another to perform a murder without
forcible hindrance. So too, a man who follows his country's leaders may march
with them into hell *if they are wrong*. Shall we then say that patriotism is strict

obedience and sacrifice, even to what is wrong? Or shall we define patriotism as loyalty to one's country if right, and to leading one's country to the right if it is misled? The general ideal of patriotism affords us the same need for interpretation as does our other moral principle, and the same need for qualifications and exceptions. Should a man be patriotic to a country that has thrown his children in jail? Executed his people? Threatened him with injustice? Starved him? Taxed him? Could not find him a job? Where does loyalty to one's country end, at what degree of personal suffering or moral outrage?

We are led to yet another element which is part of all situations which call for action by an agent—his own personal benefit. What a man decides to do he ought to consider worth doing. In the situation we have been discussing, he must weigh his patriotic loyalties against the values of justice and life. But this is simply not enough. He must also consider the price he himself must pay. He must consider this price in every decision he makes which calls for action on his part—and all moral decisions do just that. A man's hat blows into the street, and it would be nice for me to catch it and give it back to him—but not if I risk being killed chasing it. A drowning man ought to be saved—but not by a man who cannot swim, at great peril to his own life. If the good that can be achieved by certain actions is less than the personal harm which will be provided by the actions, then they are probably not worth doing.

This principle should not be introduced in such a purely negative fashion. It is not harm alone which might prohibit action. Suppose a young man studying medicine should wonder in college and prior to entering medical school if he should join the Church and work to help the poor and downtrodden? Which of us is willing to say that he *ought* to? Shall a man sacrifice himself to others? That is a strong question. The general principle involved is that a man's actions ought to be of benefit to himself as well as to others. Obviously such a principle needs a great many qualifications and exceptions, perhaps to a greater extent than the others we have considered. But it is a ruling principle in moral decisions. This can be demonstrated easily. There are a few men who follow a principle of altruism to its extreme, just as there are extreme pacifists and patriots. Such men give their lives as a sacrifice to an ideal or to other men. But, as always, the extreme has its pitfalls. Sacrifice to one ideal means the neglect of another. Sacrifice to other men can never be a sacrifice to everyone. So one must choose. One must choose when and how to be patriotic, when and how to revere life, when and how to make sacrifices. A physician will benefit both others and himself far more than he would if he had remained a layman. Acting to his own advantage turns out to be of benefit to others also. Surely such a result is preferable to all others. Most men believe that there is a point of personal sacrifice beyond which it is not good to go—where either the sacrifice required is too great, or the benefits achieved are too small.

A word is in order about the opposite extreme from that of sacrifice—that of counting all one's actions in terms of personal benefits. This is often called interests of the agent or others. Sometimes it is maintained that the concern for principles is moral, while the concern for consequences is political. Such a distinction is the basis for the colloquial suspicion of *expediency* as somehow morally wrong. A man may be prudent or moral, but not both at the same time. As we will see, such a dichotomy is usually grounded in a *Kantian* theory of moral decision. There exist other ethical theories according to which such a distinction is far less plausible.

In passing, it is worth noting two difficulties such a dichotomy generates, one a result of applying it in practice, the other a theoretical difficulty we have already remarked on. First, there exists a standard interpretation of the moral qualities of international relations which rests upon the distinction between expediency and morality. A nation owes its first duty to the defense and benefit of its citizens. It exists with the aim of expediency, and will often find it necessary to engage in immoral enterprises in the interests of expediency. Thus, the central problem of this chapter may well arise out of the official conviction that a country may go to war to further its own interests, and that moral considerations are irrelevant to its decisions. Tough-minded men of expediency in fact disparage men of principle as weak, and condemn them for engaging in the sheer luxuries of sentimentality. This is often called "Realpolitik." Morality is a luxury in political affairs. Expediency is realistic. A country may go to war in its own interest.

On the other hand, a particular citizen of a country may consider such a course of action immoral, unjust. The problem we have been considering is what such a man is to do as a consequence of his moral convictions. This problem is rendered totally unresolvable by too sharp a distinction between morality and expediency. If morality and expediency are so defined as to be exclusive alternatives which are not theoretically interrelated, then no intelligible compromise between them can ever be realized. A man may be tough-minded or weak-minded. Or he may be a little of each. But the middle ground can make no sense from the standpoint of either alternative. If consequences are irrelevant to moral decisions, then they may not be considered. If moral principles are irrelevant to expediency, then they may not be considered. We will study these matters later in detail.

The theoretical problem which afflicts the distinction between morality and prudence is a more general one. Since the distinction depends on the differential criterion of concern for consequences, the question we must ask is whether it is in fact possible to make any judgment whatsoever without considering consequences. The problem is whether a factual description of the circumstances, which is certainly necessary to the purest application of moral principles, does not implicitly lead to some or many of the consequences of proposed actions. If a man wishes to follow the principle that stealing is wrong, he must know not only that an object has been taken, and that it belongs to someone else, but also that a sense of loss will be the consequence of its appropriation. If I leave an ugly object in the street and it is taken, it has not been stolen, particularly if I am glad to be rid of it. An earlier example makes this theoretical point more sharply. If a man pulls the "egoism," and we will consider it carefully in a later chapter. Here, however, it is worth making but the same point we have considered with regard to every principle taken in an unqualified sense. Where a man interprets a principle in such a way as to allow him to follow it consistently and without exception, he removes the need for specific decisions on his part. In so doing, he may well find himself an instrument, if only by neglect, of the very evil he opposes. A pacifist may ignore the evil others do. A patriot may injure his country in his zeal. An egoist who acts only for himself may harm others upon whom he is dependent, and thereby injure himself. A selfish man may alienate his wife and torture his children, only to discover too late that he needs them.

The basis for criticizing a moral extreme is not that of principles alone. Rather, it looks to the real state of affairs and the concrete consequences of actions the agent may undertake. We have considered the complex problem of fighting for one's country in terms of the general principles involved in such a decision, and have seen how complex the interrelationships of principles are in concrete decisions. But, even in their complexity, such principles are still not sufficient for the determination of a moral decision. There remain the facts of the case to consider, and the consequences to foresee. We have arrived at our second general category of factors which enter into concrete moral decisions.

(2) *Facts.* Moral principles alone seem quite incapable of providing a basis for moral decisions. Factual information is essential, and in two respects: Facts must be known about the situation involved, both the general fact that it is a moral situation and the particular facts which define the applicable principles. Also, the consequences of actions may contribute to the judgments we make concerning those actions, and such consequences are to be understood as facts concerning the results of real or possible actions. Almost no one would deny that the circumstances of a problem are relevant to a moral decision. Many writers have objected to the consideration of consequences in moral decisions, as if they are somehow irrelevant or specious. The extreme pacifist we have been using as a stalking horse might (though he need not, as we will see) argue that a man can safeguard only his own moral purity, not that of others, and that the only basis for a moral decision is the sincerity of one's own intentions to obey a moral principle consistently. Thus, the *fact* (if it is one) that my refusing to fight the enemy will lead to our being enslaved is totally irrelevant to any moral decision I might make. It is sufficient to consider only the fact that fighting involves killing, that killing is wrong, and that it is therefore wrong ever to use force in opposing even a cruel enemy. The consequences of one's opposition or lack of it are considered morally irrelevant.

So well established is this conception of moral judgment that it has been enshrined in a standard distinction in ethical theory. A judgment is *moral* when it looks only to principles and intentions, and is grounded in an absolute loyalty indifferent to consequences. A judgment is *prudential* when it looks to the consequences of proposed courses of action, and evaluates them in terms of the trigger of a gun and kills someone, he is responsible for that killing. This is not a consequence of a complex theory of responsibility. It is a consequence of the logical principle that any action involves some and often many of its consequences. Shooting a man is not merely pulling the trigger of a gun. It includes also the firing of the gun, the discharge of the bullet, and its impact in the body of the victim. In intending to shoot a man, I necessarily look to some of the consequences of my actions. These consequences are part of my action. Of course, some consequences are distinct from the action itself—such as the name of the doctor who attends the victim after he is shot.

We may make this point even more sharply with a slightly different example. Suppose in a highly charged situation of racial conflict I call a man by a derogatory name. Violence then ensues, and several people are badly hurt. All *I* intended to do was to use an epithet, certainly not to cause anyone a physical injury. But the violence was inherent in the situation in which I spoke, not merely a detached consequence of it. Let me put it this way: my excuse that I only used a word is similar to the excuse that I only pulled a trigger of a gun, and killed no one directly. More accurately, I *insulted* my opponent, I *made him angry*, I induced him to strike out. Some of the consequences of an action are part of it, part of its most rudimentary description. The line between morality and expediency is by no means easy to draw. A country may go to war with the best of intentions. But if war breeds war (if that is an established fact), then the further violence which results is this country's doing. This point too we will come back to in our later discussion. We will now consider some of the factual information which is inherent in the concrete moral situation we have been considering.

(a) We are presupposing a country at war, and the convictions of a young man that the war is unjust. Three overlapping sets of facts are essential to the situation as described. These are the facts relevant to the reasons and activities of the country at war: the enemy attacked first; the enemy tortures its prisoners; the enemy will destroy us if we don't destroy them first; if they win this war, they will go on to take over the world; the enemy violates the rules of international warfare; we are winning; they are winning; a certain number of the enemy have been killed; a certain number of our soldiers have been killed; most of our people support the war; most are opposed to the war; the people will not vote for the party in power unless they end the war; and so forth. There are in addition the facts relevant to the claim that the war is unjust: we attacked first; the enemy violated international agreements; our troops are torturing enemy prisoners; our planes are killing women and children; our bombs and chemicals are destroying the countryside; and so forth. There is also a whole range of facts which contribute to any decision made by an agent who finds himself in the circumstances given, but which are not essential to either of the principles proposed: refusing to be drafted is illegal; the soldiers in the field oppose the war; the press is covering the war in detail and accurately; and so forth. It will be noted that the three categories of facts overlap considerably. Moreover, many of these facts which define the circumstances in which decision is called for look to the consequences of one or another course of action. If the war is continued *this* will happen; if the war is ended, *that* will occur. Finally, the list of relevant descriptive facts is rather long, yet we must always add the words "and so forth."

We may make yet another distinction among the types of facts relevant to the circumstances which call for moral decision: *specific* facts and *general* facts. We have noted several instances of specific facts. The enemy attacked first; so and so many of our soldiers have been killed. It is important to realize that just as we must move from specific facts to principles (they attacked first, and that is wrong), we can use facts in an intelligible way only when we look to general laws of war, politics, history, or human nature. We can argue that our going to war will prevent a political disaster in a foreign country only if (a) we can show that by sheer force we can drive the enemy back; or (b) we will inflict such destruction on the enemy that they will rationally have to concede. The first depends on a causal law relating disparity of opposing forces and victory. The second is a law of human behavior and motivation. These general laws are what link the circumstances of the present to expectations concerning the future. It is a valid causal law that if I pull the trigger of a loaded gun, it will fire. It is not easy to see how any description of a state of affairs can be evaluated without implicit acceptance of a whole range of general laws as well. A compelling argument against a war might be that our country cannot afford both a high level of prosperity at home and a war abroad—a claim which depends on a general principle concerning economic relations, consumption, and production.

We may note here a general principle which many pacifists believe to be true *as a fact*, and which if true strengthens their position considerably. That is, they believe that the use of force always leads to the return of force. Put negatively, if we are to achieve peace, we must begin in peace and always eschew war. To go to war is to engender further wars. Here we have a general law of conduct which is not a moral principle, but an alleged fact. It is either true or false. If true, and if killing is wrong, then we must stop killing, even in defense or for a good cause. For all killing leads to further killing, without end.

(b) These last examples take us to the further type of facts relevant to moral decisions—those facts which describe the consequences of proposed courses of action. If we continue the war, our domestic program will be limited in such and such ways. If we never entered the war, the enemy would have expanded its influence throughout most of the world. If a man refuses to be drafted, he will be sent to prison. If we do not solve certain domestic problems, our country will be in civil war. And so forth. We look ahead to the results of our actions, and we require, not specific information alone, but general laws which link the present with the future, which enable us to take consequences into account.

The use of such generalizations is extremely complex. Let us consider but one example, which generates an argument of great complexity. Our young man is convinced that the war is wrong, and believes that he must refuse to participate in it. He asks himself the question: at what stage of the proceedings must I officially refuse? The reason this question comes up is that he is willing to concede the moral force of the principle that a man ought to obey the law, at least until it leads him to an act in violation of his conscience. There is nothing unconscionable about joining the army, so our young man does so. There is nothing unjust about military training, so he is trained and becomes expert with weapons. There is nothing wrong with being in the enemy country, so he is sent there. There is nothing directly wrong with going on patrol or with serving at a field base, so he does both. Now he is ordered to fire upon the enemy. That is wrong, and he refuses.

But notice what has happened. First, he is about to refuse a direct order in the field, which is grounds for a court-martial and far more risky to him than his refusing induction would have been in the beginning. Second, in the field his life may be in direct danger, and he may find that he must either kill or be killed himself. A strong case can be made that a man must not wait until he is actually called upon to violate his moral convictions, if he knows for a fact that it will be far more difficult and dangerous for him then to refuse. He must refuse to let himself be put in a compromising position. The facts which such arguments depend on are complex, and difficult to substantiate. But they are critical to any justifiable decision which may be offered.

We began this discussion of the facts relevant to moral decisions with the remark that moral principles alone provide no basis for moral decision. Facts are required in addition. But facts are difficult to come by, and seem to have no limit in scope or quantity. Indeed, if we are supposed to look to the consequences of our actions in reaching a moral decision, perhaps we must consider *all* the possible consequences without exception. And we simply cannot do so. We seem to require a superhuman degree of knowledge. There are too many facts which are relevant to any complex moral problem. And justifying these facts seems to be beyond human capacities. Note, however, that the despair which may be engendered by our finite capacities leads easily to a basic form of corruption. I do not know enough, I am not sure, therefore I will do nothing. Governments at war habitually use the ignorance of their citizens to justify their acquiescence in official policies. The same governments also do their best to keep their citizens in ignorance.

Even more interesting than this, however, is the realization that facts alone seem to provide us with no basis for moral decisions. This is a classical principle proposed by David Hume. He argues that the fact that death will result from a given course of action has no moral force unless we feel a revulsion against that death. Perhaps it could be argued that a moral principle with relevant facts ought to provide a secure basis for a moral decision. I think it is important for us to realize that this is not always so. The feelings of the agent are a fundamental feature of moral decisions. Let us consider this matter now.

(3) *Feelings.* Human history is filled with instances of considerable bravery on the part of otherwise ordinary men. Soldiers fight bravely, even die bravely.

Men have been known to resist torture, and to give their enemies no useful information even under extreme duress. While such sacrifices are not, perhaps, so common as to constitute the norm of human conduct, they are not so rare as to define a mere exception to it either. The capacity of men to adhere loyally to a moral principle in the face of arduous difficulties is often quite great. The capacity of some men to follow their consciences, and to remain true to their moral convictions despite the blandishments and threats of others, is almost inexhaustible. In fact, the most obvious feature of the moral convictions of some men, of what is called "conscience," seems to be their ability to resist temptation.

Such examples demonstrate beyond question that men are capable of doing what they think right even at considerable cost to themselves, even if it results in considerable pain for them and for others. Our young man who is considering a refusal to be drafted may be put in jail for his convictions. If he chooses to avoid conscription and to go to jail, then it seems clear that he has made a definite self-sacrifice on the grounds of his personal convictions. He chooses to do what he thinks right even if it causes him and his parents considerable torment. Circumstances can conspire to make a person choose what is right rather than what will benefit him or give him pleasure.

A remarkable feature of the thinking of many people on this subject, however, is that in any group at least one person will be impelled to describe the willingness to go to jail for one's convictions as a sense of *pleasure* derived from such a heroic action. The general principle is adduced that all human actions are performed to the end of personal pleasure. So strongly is this principle believed in that it resists even the most extreme counter-examples. After all, we point out, being in jail is not much fun, especially if we consider what being in jail is actually like today. Or, pushing our examples even further to an extreme, consider the case of the man who resists brutal forms of torture, and refuses to give his captors the information they desire. Surely it makes little sense to describe his bravery as motivated by a desire for pleasure. He would be far better off if he told what he knew and avoided the pain. The argument in return is that unless such a man received pleasure from his bravery, he would not be brave. Unless he feared the pain of a guilty conscience, he would tell his captors what they wanted to know.

We will have occasion later to explore this position in considerable detail. It is manifestly false that men perform all their actions motivated by the goal of pleasure. (Note that we have not even considered the possibility that men *ought* to seek only their own pleasure, which is a very different position.) It is a confused expression of a principle which we have not yet encountered in our discussion. It is not true that men are always motivated by a desire for pleasure. It is probably not true that actions are always motivated by a single desire, or even by any desire at all. It may be possible for men to be motivated to act by no more than a *respect* for what is right, by a *reverence* for what is good. Nevertheless, all motivation has a common trait, be the motive a desire, respect, love, or fear. All motivation rests on feeling. Emotions and feelings are constituents in all actions. Even Kant, who argues that the only unqualifiedly good action is one which is performed from nothing but respect for moral law, must concede the emotive force of this respect in occasioning action. It is false that all action is performed for personal pleasure. It may be true that everything we do has an emotional basis, that feelings are elements of all intentional action. Let us consider some of the types of feeling which enter into moral decisions.

(a) *Respect*. We have already noted a paramount mode of feeling which enters into the making of moral decisions—a feeling of respect for a moral principle, a loyalty to some moral code, a reverence for what is good or worth while. In passing, we have noted also that such a mode of respect may be very different from a desire, particularly one whose object is the gain of pleasure and the avoidance of pain. One always desires something whose attainment will give pleasure. Now, one may indeed *desire* what is right, and gain a feeling of pleasure from doing or receiving it. But, as Kant points out, it is certainly possible for a man to thoroughly dislike doing what is right, and yet do it because he considers it right. A miser may feel nothing but pain at giving up some of his beautiful money to charity, but nevertheless feel that he ought to and must. The feeling of moral obligation can be a compulsion far removed from any feeling of pleasure. But without any feeling at all, it is impossible to understand what motivates a man to do even what he thinks is right.

Our colloquial name for the inclination to perform actions which are believed to be right is conscience. I believe it rather clear in the colloquial descriptions of the workings of conscience that conscience is understood as a mode of feeling. It is his feeling of rightness that enables a man to withstand temptation. In the case we have been considering, it is the belief that the war is unjust, and that killing is wrong, that motivates the young man to consider opposing induction. This belief is not a dispassionate, objective, detached, and cool appraisal of justice and injustice. It is a passionate sense of what is right and wrong. Without its strong passionate qualities, it would never be able to oppose his obvious fears of punishment.

We have been remarking on the point ascribed to Hume above, but which was first stated explicitly by Spinoza: a strong feeling can be opposed only by another feeling, not by reason or knowledge alone. A man considering a major step in affirmation of his personal convictions cannot but fear reprisals. A man beset by a fearful temptation to do something wrong is tempted first of all by his desires. Nothing is tempting in itself, only in the emotional life of the man who wants it. Both Hume and Spinoza agree that feelings do have motivating force, and that nothing else alone has. The fear of jail cannot be overcome successfully by the knowledge that men are being killed, but only by a feeling of revulsion against such killing. In this sense, a man torn by temptation is generally the battleground of warring emotions. Indeed, a far too common case is where a man finds within him a complete opposition of conscience and desire. All his desires oppose his moral convictions. Feelings are opposed to feelings. We may plausibly imagine that the final result of this conflict will be the triumph of the stronger emotions, either of respect or of desire.

It is worth noting the further point that conscience is understood by most men to function not *positively*, as a respect or reverence for principle, but *negatively*, as a fear of the remorse which is the result of doing something wrong. In fact, the entire Freudian theory of conscience is grounded in the reactions which conscience (the *superego*) exerts upon the *ego*. Freud proposes a model in which conscience is understood in the guise of an aggressor. The fear a person may feel for what others will do to him is transformed into a fear he feels internally and with no external object. I do not think the concepts of respect and reverence are to be interpreted in so fearful a manner. But that is a point for later discussion.

(b) *Pleasure.* The principle that everything a man does is aimed toward the gain of pleasure has been criticized for being too extreme. One of the features of so extreme a principle is its continual need for reinterpretation—for example, that a respect for principle brings pleasure. Central to the theory of pleasure, however, is an unavoidable qualification. It is not alone the desire for pleasure which motivates action, but also the fear of pain. Even the most devout adherents of *hedonism* (the view that men should act only for pleasure) admit that the avoidance of pain is even a more fundamental basis for action. I mention this point because no discussion of pleasure is possible without reference to pain. Yet the remarkable thing about theories of pleasure and pain is their inherent confusion on this subject. If men seek to avoid pain, they will be led to a life of rather cool pleasures, for intense pleasures tend to lead to intense pains as well. If men seek to gain great pleasures, then their lives will also be painful. There is no simple way of reconciling these matters, as we shall later see.

Nevertheless, if we ignore the attempt to make pleasure (or pleasure and pain) the basis for all human actions, we must agree that the desire for pleasure or enjoyment is essential to most moral situations. The fear a man may feel for being jailed is a fear of pain or loss of pleasure. In determining what he must do, a man must weigh the very real effect his actions will have on himself and others—an effect which seems to be measurable only, if at all, in terms of the pleasures and pains which result. One of the most critical moral problems a young person faces is the point at which he must strike out to forge his own life, if this means going against the wishes and hopes of his parents. For his opposing them will cause them pain, and cause him suffering as well. Parents tend to obtain pleasure from the accomplishments of their children, and to be hurt by their children's rejection or opposition. Because parents and children are so deeply involved with each other, the pains and pleasures generated by their actions are a vital influence on their respective decisions.

This last example brings us to two kinds of feelings which it is not plausible to think of in terms of pleasure or pain. We can, of course, think of all feelings as desires—respect, for example, as a desire for achieving what is right. But, if so, then not all desires result in pleasure when gained. The two types of feeling we

have not yet discussed may be defined by their *objects* rather than their qualities.
I am thinking of feelings directed toward oneself and toward other people. There
are some feelings which have these objects which are not easily related to pleasures
and pains.

(c) *Self-preservation.* Hobbes and Spinoza make self-preservation the fundamental motivation in all human action. In practice, this concept becomes rather
confused, designating not only a fear for one's life, but also the desire to preserve
one's powers and to attain some consistency in life. In order to stay away from
the complexities involved, let us consider only the danger to life some events can
bring, and the feelings we have toward our own lives. Hobbes and Spinoza claim
that all men desire to preserve themselves—though they both seem to ignore the
fact of suicide. It is sufficient, I believe, to note that men generally do love themselves in a manner which involves their attempting to stay alive, though not
always. Many actions are not thought justifiable if they involve a great risk to the
agent's life.

But it is difficult to view attempts to preserve one's life as motivated by a
desire for pleasure, or even to avoid pain. One may die painlessly. And one may
live even though in pain. Men possess a reverence for their own lives that seems to
transcend pain and pleasure. Perhaps being alive is a precondition of experiencing
pleasure—but it is equally a precondition of pain. What seems clear is that men
possess strong attitudes toward their own lives, attitudes which enter into many of
the decisions they make. If a man refuses conscription into the army knowing
that he will be shot for his refusal, most of us would regard his refusal in a
different light than if he risked only jail for a year or so.

(d) *Others.* As for feelings directed toward others, these are extremely
complex, and not easy to extricate from the feelings we have already discussed.
Insofar as other men are like ourselves, we have feelings toward them which are
virtually indistinguishable from respect for moral principles. For example, we may
respect the principle "thou shalt not kill" on the basis of a violent revulsion we
feel at the taking of another's life. In addition, we may gain considerable pleasure
from being with people we like, and we may be literally pained by their suffering.
On the other hand, there are some men who enjoy witnessing the sufferings of
others. It is easy to understand the view that such feelings call for a different
moral code from the conventional one. It is also easy to understand the view in
return that a moral code exists precisely in order to prevent such feelings from
leading to cruelty. In either case, the feelings we have for others enter into our
moral codes and also into our specific decisions.

There are several types of feeling we may have toward others. One we have
already noted: a *concern* for others. We care about them and what happens to them.
When a man literally has no concern for others, we may find that he shares none
of our moral ideals. There is a type of pathology which consists in the absence of
all ordinary moral standards. A psychopath simply may not sense anything "wrong"
with telling lies, with killing, with hurting others. He literally has none of the

feelings toward others which serve as an essential element in all conscience. On the other hand, he may well possess the feelings toward others of the second type, which is basically a *fear* of them.

Other people may put us in jail, torture us, even kill us. We may fear their disapproval because of what they may do to us, the pain they may cause us by their actions. But there is another attitude toward others which is indifferent to what they do, and looks solely to their approval and disapproval. We want others to like us, to approve of us. We are ashamed before them if we do something wrong. We *suffer* their disapproval. A man may join the army simply because he cannot endure the open or even the tacit disapproval of his friends and towns-people, who expect him to join. Emerson repudiates such conformity, and claims that "truly it demands something godlike in him who has cast off the common motives of humanity and has ventured to trust himself for a taskmaster." We are not at the moment concerned with the rightness of conformity or nonconformity, but rather the strength of the feelings upon which conformity rests. Emerson also notes that "society everywhere is in conspiracy against the manhood of every one of its members." Every man's feelings testify to that conspiracy.

It should be clear that the various types of feeling which enter into motivation in moral decisions are not simply to be acquiesced in, but to be understood and even used in the making of moral decisions. Human feelings are complex, and the decisions which follow upon them are complex also. There is a domain of the feelings which influence moral decisions which we have not touched on, and it is of vital importance.

(e) *The future.* Feelings look to the future. Desires look to the future and the consequences of actions which may result in pleasures and pains. What gives us pleasure can influence our actions only insofar as we look ahead to what *will* give us pleasure and bring us pain. A man looking ahead to being jailed for his beliefs must consider, not the present, but the future consequences of his actions and their results in feeling. What this means is that present feelings are somehow insufficient in the determination of action. We must anticipate our feelings and the feelings of others in the future. A man may fear jail very deeply, and yet find its experience far less painful than its anticipation. Unfortunately, the reverse is equally likely. A man may not fear jail, and may find it quite unbearable. Feelings are themselves difficult enough to get hold of. Yet we must look ahead in time and anticipate our future feelings also. This is one of the reasons why general laws of feeling are important in moral decisions.

But there is a more complex relation the future bears to the present than general laws of feeling can represent. A psychological law is almost certain to assume a considerable degree of continuity through time. That is, a law addresses either similar conditions or at least a single agent through time, and represents expected emotional reactions and actions. But the relationship a living person bears to the present is dynamic. In particular, we must note that the future may change a man in vital respects. Yet it is still his future feelings which must be considered in his moral decisions. For example, a man who is sent to jail for his convictions will be in a brutalizing environment and exposed to influences which often make men even more hardened criminals instead of reforming them. A soldier who joins the army, though he intends at the time to resist orders to kill, may find that the training he undergoes saps his resistance, changes him into a military instrument that carries out orders unthinkingly, and makes him no longer wish to resist. The future is imponderable enough. Yet, if we are to consider consequences, we must consider the consequences which the future will bring for us, in changing the very basis upon which we anticipate such consequences. I will later show that such complexities are what make moral principles so very important in moral affairs. But we have reached a point where a summary of our prior discussion is in order.

Summary. We have seen that a wide and comprehensive range of *facts* bear on the making of moral decisions, facts which define a situation to be a moral one, facts which look to the future and the consequences of action, and general laws of nature and of man which bridge present actions and the future. Among the facts which are to be taken into account are the agent's own *feelings*, which look to what will give him pleasure and pain, which address the future as well as the present, and which define his attitudes to other persons and things. In addition to such facts and feelings, there are also to be found in moral situations *principles* which are essential to all moral issues. A moral agent seeks a degree of generality in his moral decisions, a degree of consistency in action and thought which only principles can provide. Such principles define or express that to which a man bears his ultimate loyalties. The common view that a devotion to some religion is essential to morality reveals at least a partial grasp of the fact that moral principles express the greatest loyalties a man has, the *ideals* he lives by. These emphasized elements of moral decision will provide us with a framework for our more detailed discussion. We will find that they lead to yet further dimensions of moral judgment: the reliance of men on an agent's *intentions* as a basis for judging him; the discovery that men in fact deceive others and even themselves about their intentions, and live in a *self-deception* that makes mockery of moral wisdom; the confusion of men about their *responsibilities*, and the way in which they seek to escape them. Most important of all, we will study how the bonds of society are a vital part of our moral lives. Finally, we will try to put all these components together to arrive at a theory of moral decision.

However, before entering upon a more theoretical discussion of the elements of moral decision, let us look at several other moral problems, as concrete examples of these various elements in relation.

B. Abortion

Our second problem enables us to make a distinction which does not arise plausibly in connection with the problem of conscription. The latter, as we viewed it, was the problem of whether an individual should allow *himself* to be drafted into a war he considered wrong. The problem in general of whether conscription itself is right or wrong never arose—though it is an important problem. The problem of conscience concerning a war is far more a problem of what an individual will do than whether it is right to require military service of young men. In fact, as we posed the first problem, it arose for us only upon the concession of the general validity of the draft, and of general obedience to a draft law.

For most people, however, the problem of abortion is not whether a given woman should have one, but whether abortion should be legalized, and under what circumstances. In the case of whether abortion should be prohibited by law, the issue for an individual is whether to oppose or to support prohibition, and how vociferously. Nevertheless, an important distinction must eventually be made, and now is as good a time as any to begin. There is a major difference between deciding not to perform a given kind of action—for example, undergoing an abortion—and deciding that such an action should be prohibited by law, even that such an action is wrong in principle. In particular, there is a tremendous difference in practical effect between an action a man performs on his own, and an action which legislates a rule which will be enforced to guide the conduct of everyone. A woman may firmly and even passionately believe than an abortion would be thoroughly wrong for her, and yet have no inclination to legislate toward controlling what others may do. All too often we find men unthinkingly equating the moral judgment "this is wrong (for me to do)" with the principle "this is wrong (for everyone)," and even further, "there ought to be a law prohibiting such acts." We will spend many pages exploring the distinction between individual judgments and judgments of principle, especially because certain philosophers have subordinated the former to the latter. Here, however, we will put the issue of principle and law aside. Let us consider only the moral decision of whether a given woman ought or ought not to undergo an abortion herself.

(1) *Principles.* Of course, a woman may accept without qualification the principle "abortion is wrong," and that would settle the matter. Especially, if she is inclined to feel that abortion is *murder*, it is difficult to grasp any argument which could persuade her that having an abortion would be right, for her or anyone. Nevertheless, we recall that one of the fundamental features of all moral principles is an essential vagueness they all possess, which calls for interpretation by the moral agent who appeals to them. A man who disapproves of abortion may argue that abortion is murder. But another may simply deny it—and be in no way *less convinced of the sanctity of human life*. A man may oppose murder so much as to be in favor of capital punishment, quite unconvinced by those who view the death penalty as "legalized murder."

The capacity of a moral principle to serve opponents on both sides of a given question is a very important quality of such principles, one we have noted in passing but not designated by a special title. Yet we will see that it is because of such a capacity that principles can become ideals. Both proponents and opponents

of capital punishment argue from the ideal of the reverence for life which is to be
found also in the commandment, "thou shalt not kill." Both proponents and
opponents of abortion may also argue from the same respect for life. Ideals are the
vaguely formulated guides to action which rule all moral decisions and are central
to the respect men have for what is right. Yet this vagueness means that these
ideals cannot directly guide actions without the complexities of interpretation and
decision intruding. A woman may be convinced of the principle that "abortion is
wrong." That may guide her individual decisions if she accepts such a principle in
its purest form, and without exception. But in most cases we are not easily
convinced of the legitimacy of purity.

For example, what if an incurably insane woman becomes pregnant? Or if a
twelve-year-old girl is impregnated through rape? Of if the pregnancy will almost
certainly mean the death of both mother and child? Or, finally, what if there is
genetic proof that the child will be seriously deformed, due to either genetic
damage or the workings of a drug? In every such case, some people who are
thoroughly convinced that abortion is generally wrong will believe it to be justified
or at least permissible. "Abortion is wrong *except* in the case of insanity, rape, a
major risk to the life of the mother, where the infant will be deformed, *etc.*"
"Abortion is wrong *except* . . ." Again, too great a moral purity is difficult to
justify, and certainly not a popular moral attitude. But what exceptions shall we
allow? The question calls for a decision to temper the given principle "abortion is
wrong." And once we allow any qualification, what is to prevent us *in principle*
from making the specific case before us one of the exceptions? Thus, a woman
contemplating abortion may follow the principle "abortion is wrong" without
qualification, but most people will not share her purity. Yet if she admits qualifications or exceptions, then the principle no longer settles the entire issue of decision.
Shall a married woman not be allowed an abortion just because she is married?
Shall a woman who cannot support her children be permitted an abortion? Shall
an unmarried woman be forbidden an abortion as a form of punishment?

We have before us another extremely complex moral problem, and shall make
no effort to define a solution to it satisfactory for everyone. We are more interested
in understanding the basis on which an individual may make a moral decision for
himself, and guide his own actions accordingly. What we have seen so far is the
inability of a moral principle to constitute a moral decision wholly in itself. In
general, few people regard moral principles so rigorously as to make every one of
their actions an instance of a well-defined general rule. Moreover, most people do
not think it praiseworthy to be so pure in all moral decisions—though they appeal
to purity on occasion. Appeals to purity create problems most obviously by
falsifying the basis on which the people who are being condemned for impurity
make their decisions. In order to show this most clearly, we will define two
simplified models of decision regarding abortion. We have not so far considered the
fact that the decision required is an important one. Generally speaking, a married
woman who becomes pregnant will have the child without even thinking of

alternatives. To think of having an abortion is to raise the possibility that it is right to do so. But this can be so only if another principle can be offered to ground such a possibility. Let us consider two examples of moral conflict among the indefinite range of possible considerations.

(a) First, we return to the ideal of the sanctity of life. This time, however, we interpret the ideal as follows: It is not the mere fact of life that is important or valuable in itself, but the obligation we have to make human life rich and satisfying. Imagine, then, that the decision of whether or not to have an abortion faces a black girl of fifteen who is dreadfully poor, and far from ready to face the responsibility for the child or to marry the father. As for the prospect of putting the child up for adoption, that is merely a theoretical possibility. All too many black children are regarded as unadoptable by those people who can afford to bring up a child. The basis for abortion is a principle which some people feel to carry considerable moral weight: It is wrong to have an unwanted child. It is difficult enough to be a child in today's world. No one ought to be forced to be an unwanted one.

This principle is not the one opponents of abortion usually attack. It possesses too great an aura of concern for others. It transforms the decision of whether one should or should not have an abortion wholly into a moral decision—that is, one in which personal advantage, even selfishness, are of little functional importance. The ruling principle of all moral judgment is that one should not consider one's own personal advantage alone in moral decisions, but one must consider others *as if they were oneself.* The most violent moral attacks against others rest upon the claim that they are being selfish rather than virtuous, that they seek their own advantage without considering others. Unfortunately, such attacks are another example of extreme purity in following a moral principle. Sometimes one's own advantage is accepted to be a ruling factor in moral decisions. Otherwise we would believe it right to give all our possessions to the poor beyond the minimum we may need to stay alive. This is worth considering as part of our second example.

(b) We suppose now that we are dealing with a recent widow, who has borne two children now in high school, and who feels her abilities have been wasted tending the home. She has returned to school and sees ahead a chance of becoming a capable and effective professional social worker. For the moment we will ignore the contributions she may make to others as a social worker. We pose the problem in simpler terms. Suppose that having and keeping the new child will destroy her chances for a career. Suppose that she cannot afford another child, nor even the time and money to cope with pregnancy. Suppose she has felt deprived for most of her life, and only after years of struggle and hard work began to see light ahead— whereupon she became pregnant and immediately thereafter her husband died in the hospital at considerable cost. Of course, she must consider her two children. But let us ignore even this issue. We are concerned only with the harm bearing another child will have upon her. Does there not come a point of personal damage where one must think of oneself? Indeed, if having an abortion is thought of as murder, it is wrong. But that is too pure a position for most people. One must weigh the harm done to oneself against the harm an abortion will have, and make one's decision accordingly. Perhaps, all things considered, an abortion would be the best of the various alternatives. Perhaps all the alternatives are bad.

The two cases we have considered are cases of moral decision, not alone because they involve a moral issue such as abortion, but because they call for a decision based on principle—though the principles differ in the two cases. I have considered the second case to point up the fact that the prevalent attitude that one must never consider oneself in moral affairs simply has no plausibility in some circumstances. Moral decisions arise primarily where principles conflict, and where an individual must look to his own convictions for his final decision. But it is worth noting that even in the cases we have considered as examples, conviction alone is not sufficient, nor are moral principles either. We have not touched on the importance of facts and feelings in connection with a decision concerning abortion.

(2) *Facts.* We note again the two overlapping categories of facts essential to the moral decision called for. First, we have the facts which define the circumstances of the problem. An abortion is a relevant consideration only if a woman is actually pregnant. In addition, also relevant if not quite as central are the facts defining her circumstances: whether she is married or not, whether the father and she will marry or not, how old she is, whether she is healthy, whether the child is genetically damaged or not, and so forth. In case (a) above, certain facts are of particular importance: that the girl is black, poor, young, and psychologically unprepared for the responsibilities of motherhood. This last fact is worth noting. The psychological state of the agent is a fact of great importance, though we will see that what is more important is the future psychological condition of the people involved. Finally, there must be known as well a whole cluster of facts relevant to the consequences in the life of a person who bears an unwanted child. The whole case for abortion depends on the circumstances of being an unwanted child.

But the facts relevant here are not merely the circumstantial ones, but involve also the general or inductive laws which connect the present with the future. What we really need to know is what will become of the unwanted child the girl may have. A central complication is that of determining from her present unwillingness to have her child that she will not want him later. A far greater one, at least from a theoretical point of view, is that our ability to predict future events is quite limited. We need to know specifically that the as yet unborn child will be damaged in certain ways. All we have to go by are general laws of human behavior, laws which at best are of a statistical character, and which are likely to be of a low probability of validity in particular cases. At best, we may have a clear law which states that in 87% of cases like these, the child ends up deprived in certain ways and affected psychologically in certain ways. But we could never prove that any given child would in fact be damaged in any specific way. Such complexities have led many people to the position that facts are simply irrelevant to moral decisions. We have already noted this position. I mention in passing only the example of cigarette smoking, which is defended by some people on the basis of the inadequacy of the evidence linking smoking with cancer and heart disease. Presumably, if cigarette smoking always produced cancer it would be wrong. But it does not, and therefore is not thought wrong by some people.

(3) *Feelings.* We noted in our discussion of some of the facts relevant to a decision concerning abortion that we must know or presume some information concerning the feelings of the mother toward the child in the future. A decision may be founded on the premise that the child will remain unwanted. In example (b) above, it is of vital importance to have some idea of how the widow will feel toward an infant who means the destruction of all her career plans. In all cases concerning advantage, one of the most vital elements to be considered is the feelings of satisfaction or dissatisfaction, of self-righteousness or remorse, that will be engendered by a proposed course of action. In case (a), not only are the mother's feelings relevant, but so are the feelings of the unborn child.

Another aspect of feelings is worth mentioning here. We have been noting only the facts and feelings relevant to the consequences of not having an abortion. In part, we have tacitly assumed the legality of abortion. But abortion has until recently been illegal in most states and countries. An illegal abortion raises very special kinds of issues, facts, and feelings. It is a fact that illegal abortions are risky—though the risk can be defined only statistically. More interesting, however, are the consequences of undergoing an illegal abortion in the feelings and attitudes of the woman involved. There have been cases of girls whose attitudes toward sexual intercourse, toward love, toward men, toward medicine, even toward children have been radically altered by the ugly, distasteful, and painful experience of an illegal abortion. A woman contemplating such an abortion must consider how she will feel in the future toward many things if she takes such a significant step.

Finally, we may note here a central feature of all moral decisions which we have hitherto neglected. This is, the self-deceptive character of the deliberations agents undertake. To this point we have assumed a straightforward if complex sequence of deliberations devoted to reaching a decision. However, let us look again at the feelings involved in moral decisions. It is far from uncommon that a fifteen-year-old may choose to bear her child on the grounds of wanting to be a mother—when what she really wants is to humiliate her own parents. The lessons of psychoanalysis indicate to us over and over again how often people deceive themselves as to their true feelings, and to their true motives. The parents of a pregnant girl may believe they are adhering to moral principle in refusing to help her obtain an abortion—though they may really desire to see her punished. The whole subject of self-deception is a complex one, and requires careful study. I note it only as an additional complexity inherent in deliberations which involve facts and feelings. Men rationalize all too often, and blind themselves to what they are actually doing. But we will leave this matter aside for now.

C. Stealing

The kind of problem we are posing here is not whether stealing is wrong *in general* or in the abstract, but whether in given circumstances a specific individual ought to take what does not belong to him. Many people take the position that if stealing is wrong, then no one under *any* circumstances ought to steal. In our previous discussions, we have considered moral situations where complex decisions are called for because of a conflict among moral principles. With respect to stealing, however, many people would claim *in the abstract* that it is wrong, and should never be done. We move here to a firm moral principle. Unfortunately, we recall that even the principle "killing is wrong" does not withstand the press of circumstances. Indeed, some men adhere to some moral principles without exception. But to others, such consistency is not heroism but insensitivity, a purity that in its disregard for consequences leads to far greater harm than would a more temperate view. Put baldly, it appears to many people that loyalty to a moral principle without qualification or exception is plain wrong.

This can be shown rather clearly by our first example. (a) Imagine if you will that you are visiting a friend's house, that he leaves the house for a while, and that you explore and discover a workshop in which he is obviously building a bomb according to instructions displayed on the workbench. Would it be wrong to take these plans away, in the hope of deterring your friend from a risky and abortive act of violence? Suppose further that he had recently been acting harried and emotionally unbalanced. There is no pretending that the plans are not his. Sometimes one must take from a person what belongs to him. A prisoner always has his belongings taken from him.

Taking a man's possessions to protect him is by no means uncommon. It is most common in our experience in the role parents play toward their children. Quite often a parent will take a child's toy away from him, if it is too dangerous, or as a form of punishment. The usual rationale for such appropriation (few of us would call it "stealing") is that a child is not a responsible agent, nor is the man who is busy making bombs. In the latter case, such a position may not serve, for we should probably try to stop him even if he is perfectly responsible and knows what he is doing. The point of such extreme examples is to show that loyalty to a principle alone does not serve our common conceptions of what is right. Circumstances and consequences must be taken into account also. In fact, the theory of justice developed by Plato in the *Republic* is predominantly centered on the problems we encounter if we think of justice in wholly principled terms. When Plato asks if virtue is *knowledge*, he is concerned, not with knowledge of principles alone, but with determining which actions are best in terms of the consequences of actions undertaken. The problem posed for Socrates in the *Republic* is to show that justice is best, not in terms of virtue in general, but concretely in the lives of men and the order of society. The solution to the problem rests on having as ruler a man who knows concretely what is good, a man with sufficient nobility of character and knowledge of what is good to make correct decisions in every moral situation. In the *Republic*, Plato minimizes the importance of principles, and maximizes the importance of particular decisions. Unfortunately, that proves to be a weakness in the end, as we will see. Principles alone do not suffice for moral decision, but neither do facts alone.

We now return to the consideration of cases of stealing, no longer able to declare stealing wrong under all circumstances. Let us look at two additional examples, one of which will prove to be exactly like those we have already considered, the other somewhat different, yet perhaps truly fundamental to young people. (b) Imagine a man with a crippled child who needs a major operation, for which there is no money available. The man has sought loans everywhere, but to no avail. Suppose further that he works for the government buying supplies for government offices. He can divert several thousand dollars to his own use without difficulty. Should he do so? Of course stealing is generally wrong. But the life of his child is in the balance, while no one in particular would be harmed by his embezzlement. Here we return to the kind of situation we have already considered: the conflict among principles each of which carries some degree of moral weight. A man ought not to steal. But a father also is responsible for doing the best he can for his children.

I am not sure what any of us would do or ought to do in the situation described. All we can do is to look closely at the circumstances and make our decisions accordingly. Even in considering a moral principle about which the agent has no doubts whatsoever, he may find it necessary to make a complex decision, even one which violates the principle. Stealing is wrong, but a father cannot neglect his child. The moral situation before us is defined by principles a man believes in. Unfortunately, however, we may find that our strongest convictions may come into direct conflict. The more important point, however, is that the problem as defined depends on strength, not weakness, of principled conviction. A man who has little respect for private property would have no problem in deciding where his loyalties lie, provided his loyalty to his son is great. But we should also keep in mind the fact that a man with little respect for property is not so likely to find himself in charge of large sums of money. The nature of the moral decision as defined rests in the respect the man in question has for property *coupled with* his obligations toward his child. No problem would arise without moral principles to which he is committed. But the principles alone cannot settle the decision for him.

In addition, he must consider various facts, of circumstances as well as consequences. Is his son seriously ill? Will he be helped by an operation, and how much? Is the operation necessary for his survival or well-being? How likely is the father to be caught? What will happen if he is caught? Are there other alternatives

he has not explored ? How responsive have other people been to the man's plight ?
Men do not always consider the likely consequences carefully, and their actions
may lead to irreparable harm from the best of intentions. One of the most common
choices a man can make is to work very hard to give his children material advantages,
only to discover too late that he has provided them with too great a material
security, that he has not had time to spend with them, and that they have been
spoiled and also deprived of their parent's love.

I have defined the problem as a conflict between principles. It may be more
plausible instead to view the situation as a conflict between a moral principle—
stealing is wrong—and the *feelings* of love and concern a father has for his child.
I think it interesting to note, however, that mere feelings of love do not of
themselves generate a moral obligation. I may love my son greatly, yet have no
obligation to support him when he is thirty years old, nor to spend every waking
moment with him. Feelings and principles do not conflict directly, but do so in
the general forms feelings are given. I love my son, and I am obligated to help him
in many ways if not in others. My feelings endow my obligations with force, a
force which makes the conflict among principles a critical one. A man who loves
his son greatly will feel far more keenly the obligation to help him. A man who
truly believes that stealing is wrong will feel the force of that principle keenly,
and experience remorse afterward also keenly.

(c) However, the sense of the last situation as a conflict between a moral
principle and feelings of love brings us to an even more striking problem, perhaps
the one which it is most important for us to come to grips with. I am speaking
now of the problem of whether a man should steal from another solely to his own
advantage. Most people would think not. That is what is meant by saying that
stealing is wrong. But we have seen that the mere principle "stealing is wrong"
does not of itself tell us what to do. We must take circumstances and consequences
as well as other principles into account. Consider then two ways in which a man
may justify stealing to himself. First, everyone has a duty to himself, an obligation
to seek his own advantage. Everyone accepts this principle, at least where one's
personal advantage does not conflict with the needs of others. Moreover, one can
attack suicide and slothfulness on the grounds that a man ought to make the most
of himself. If, by stealing, a man can develop his abilities and become a better
person, would that not be right ? Second, one's feelings toward oneself may be
very strong. If a man desires something greatly, why is it wrong then to steal it ?

I call this problem an important one for any understanding of moral decision
because it confronts the fundamental question of whether there are any grounds
on which we may show that we ought to be moral. Are there good reasons for
doing what is right ? Plato certainly thinks this question important enough to
merit extended discussion in Book I of the *Republic*. On his view, there is an
intimate connection between the questions "why should anyone do what is right ?"
and "what is good about doing what is right ?" Thrasymachus argues that being
just is foolish, that it is not good or beneficial. Socrates makes short work of

demolishing Thrasymachus' position in Book I, but in the end, it requires the entire *Republic* to deal adequately with the issues Thrasymachus has raised. We will consider this problem in considerable detail.

Here we are interested only in some of the issues that arise in pursuing personal advantage. Let us define the problem in the baldest terms: A man is a teller in a bank, earns enough to live on, but wonders if he should not embezzle a few thousand dollars to live better, or to buy a yacht. What are the considerations which enter into his decision to embezzle the money or not? First, we find a conflict which defines the situation, either between principles—*stealing is wrong* as against *one should act to personal advantage*—or between a moral principle and strong desires. If the man's loyalty to principle is great enough, he will not even think of embezzling. If his desire for gain is slight, he will not be inclined to think of embezzling. Second, there are rather vital facts to consider: Will he be caught? What will happen to him if he is caught? What will happen to him if he is successful? Will he be fearful? Will he really gain very much? Will he feel a need to repeat himself? How will he feel later, pleased or remorseful? Will he be proud of himself or despise himself? Will other people respect or despise him?

There does not seem to be any fundamental difference between this problem and any of the others. Although stealing is wrong, that principle does not of itself settle all problems of moral decision. A man with a powerful conscience will not even think of stealing except in dire emergency. A man with no personal moral convictions will pursue his own advantage without further ado. We may be able to persuade or force him to follow our general moral code by threatening him with punishment if he does not. But he may observe moral principles not from conviction but from fear. The problem, then, is whether the *only* rational ground for obeying moral principles is that of fear of the consequences, or whether there is another basis for loyalty to principle. Unfortunately, we have seen that no principle can plausibly command so complete a loyalty as to permit no questions to arise. And where questions arise, an agent must look to many different places to make a rational decision. Perhaps, at least for men who feel a conflict between personal gain and common norms of behavior, all moral decisions take on the same complex character. The answer to the question "Why, if I do not feel like it, should I follow a moral law?" may be as complex and ramified as the solution to any other moral problem. Certainly the answer "because it is right to do so" is hardly sufficient.

But we may pass from this particular situation with the simple note that men who steal from others are not usually men who deliberate over their decisions in the complex ways which we have been discussing. A young man considering evasion of the draft is quite likely to take everything he can think of into account. A thief is often one who steals because he has thought very little about it, and has not considered various alternatives very deeply. Thieves seldom engage in the complex deliberations which weigh long- and short-range advantages against social norms and personal feelings. Raskolnikov, in *Crime and Punishment*, kills an old woman to no genuine advantage, at most in an act of rebellion to prove that he can. But, of course, if he requires proof of his exceptional qualities, he then does not possess them. He neglects even his own obvious advantage in the act he performs, and discovers this in the end through remorse and confession. As for a man who, in conscience, believes himself justified in stealing from others, we must consider his case a special one.

D. Sex

With this subject we come to an area of decision rather different from any we have heretofore considered. Though in most respects the various decisions involved are quite similar, in one respect the subject of sexual intercourse is rather unique. Let us take for our premise the principle which prohibits sexual intercourse among unmarried adults. What is remarkable about the prohibition is the conjunction of the emotional force it carries for many people, coupled with the extreme difficulty we have in discovering grounds for it. Consider the other principles we have appealed to: "murder is wrong," "stealing is wrong," "a man should be loyal to his country," and so forth. For many people, the emotional power of such principles far transcends the apparent grounds upon which they rest. Nevertheless, killing and stealing clearly cause harm to someone. But it is by no means obvious what harm results from sexual intercourse outside of marriage.

I hope not to be understood to be saying that no arguments can be found for the claim that damage can be caused by unrestricted sexual activities. I am only noting that such arguments involve premises which are far from obvious. One might argue that early sexual relations bring one to lose one's ability to enjoy sexual relations later. But such a claim is most likely false, and certainly without foundation. One might argue that becoming the early prey of predatory young men would make a girl lose her self-respect, even coarsen her. Such claims are not wholly without foundation, but they seem not to have been substantiated by evidence quite to the point of justifying the power of sexual repression in our rather puritanical society. If we ask why stealing is wrong, we may be told, "It just is. It hurts others." But if we ask why sexual relations among unmarried adults are wrong, and we note that they involve no harm to others, we are left with no reply but that "they just are." We seem to have here a principle that does not look beyond itself at all, to have its entire basis in the extreme purity which we have seen is not defensible in other moral decisions. Prohibitions against sexual promiscuity appear to be a residue from a religious tradition in which bodily pleasures are suspect. These prohibitions appear to retain most of their religious force but to have no basis in experience. I wish to show that even were this description of them correct, it would not be defensible to wholly ignore the norms of sexual conduct.

We have not defined the specific moral problem which calls for a decision. Our discussion has been wholly in the abstract, addressed to the ground of the

principle involved. We recall, however, that even a moral principle of utmost force
and defensibility cannot of itself promote a plausible moral decision in all cases.
So, too, the apparent indefensibility of the principle of chastity does not *of
itself* compel a girl to give up her chastity on call—though no doubt it is a feature
of adolescence to pretend that it does.

Let us, then, consider the following almost trite situation: An eighteen-year-
old girl is enticed by her boy friend to make their love real. What possible reasons
are there for refusing? There is an assortment of factual claims we will consider
shortly. The two conflicting principles, however, would seem to be: a woman
should be a virgin until she is married; and, opposed to this, there is nothing
wrong in obtaining pleasures which harm no one. We have already noted that it is
not easy to explain why virginity is prescribed, though for many people today it
certainly is. It is in almost all cases a social or religious prescription which has no
basis in experience. This in no way entails that it should not be followed. The
point is, that disobeying the prescription will harm no one, or at most only the
people involved. Why then not have sexual relations, whenever it will give one
pleasure? We note in passing that doing something because it is to one's *advantage*
is not quite the same thing as doing it for *pleasure*. This will become clearer in our
ensuing discussion.

We turn, then, to the contrary principle: One may do whatever gives one
pleasure. In this form, almost no one would accept such a principle, for one's
pleasures may lead to injury for others. One may do whatever gives one pleasure,
provided it brings harm to no one else. Here too, we have a principle which is
not easily defended, for one's pleasures today may bring considerable harm tomorrow. One may enjoy getting drunk at the party, but if one has to drive home
afterward, one should not. Clearly what is involved here is the consideration of
the long-range consequences of a course of action, even where in the short run a
great deal of pleasure is provided by that same course of action. On the other hand,
we cannot expect the principle, *one may do whatever brings pleasure if it brings no
harm to anyone*, to be very helpful. All courses of action involve at least the harm of
not doing something else, a harm of deprivation. Moreover, sometimes it is
certainly worth performing actions of great moment, though the result is ex-
haustion, even physical pain—for example, performing a heroic athletic feat. As
for whether we can succeed in balancing pleasures and pains, and whether we
ought to, we will consider such issues later. What should be clear here is that it is
not a simple thing to find a principle which addresses human pleasures and yet
defines for us a clear course of action.

A more important point, however, arises if we look again at the general form
of all the principles offered in the last paragraph. "One may do what gives one
pleasure if . . ." Note that such principles do not tell a man what he *should* do,
only what he *may* do. But is this a principle which can prescribe to a course of
action? The girl who must make her decision knows that, in a loose sense, she

may always do what she pleases. What she wants to know is the right or best thing to do. There is a whole middle ground of actions which are neither prohibited nor required. It is not wrong to collect stamps, but it is not right nor even good to do so. One may do so if . . . If it gives one pleasure? But that is exactly the problem we are considering: should a man always do what gives him pleasure?

The question may be put more clearly in the following form: is it ever a sufficient reason to perform an action that it will give one pleasure? Plato and Aristotle argue not. Some actions may give pleasure today and lead to pain tomorrow. Some pleasures are simply not very valuable, and cannot justify a major course of action based on them. There is a shaggy dog story about a man who builds a complex scaffolding on a battleship, of tracks and planks up several hundred feet, tying up the battleship for many weeks while it is being completed. He then drops a small ball down from the top, which goes round and round, and falls into the sea with a "plunk." Even if we assume that the final sound is pleasurable, it cannot justify the actions which are necessary for it. Certainly it is absurd to drive one hundred miles for a stick of candy, *unless the drive itself is enjoyable*. Certainly it is *wrong* to obtain pleasure at the expense of others. It is not entirely obvious that *any* pleasures of themselves justify any actions to obtain them. It is certain that many actions which lead to pleasure are morally proscribed.

Must we then conclude that pleasure is irrelevant to moral decisions? Such a conclusion seems absurd. There is an important thrust to the question, "If pleasure is not the end of human actions, what then could be?" But there are many kinds of pleasure, and of differing intensities, differing circumstances, and differing qualities. A moral decision indeed looks to pleasures, *among many other things*. Pleasures alone suffice for very few decisions—those where the consequences as well as the circumstances are of little importance. It simply doesn't matter very much whether one has a chocolate or a strawberry sundae, so one may choose whichever gives the most pleasure. Wherever our principles and values tell us of greater moral importance, pleasure alone is not a sufficient reason for action.

A further point is worth noting here. There are many kinds of pleasure. For convenience, however, let us divide our pleasures into two kinds: those which are relatively immediate, which require little cultivation or effort to achieve; and those which are complex, sophisticated, and require time, effort, and learning. John Stuart Mill calls the latter "higher pleasures," claiming that everyone who has achieved both kinds prefers the second. He has in mind the intellectual pleasures of learning, of literature and painting, of skillful work, of intelligence and invention. Let us for the moment accept his claim that higher pleasures are preferable, and agreed to be so by almost everyone who has felt them. We have, then, a rather interesting argument to offer against the principle that a man may do what gives him pleasure. Putting all questions of harm aside, and ignoring all moral issues, we may nevertheless find that enjoying the immediate or lower pleasures without further thought may literally stand in the way of gaining the higher pleasures. The pleasant fruits of labor come only upon the effort. Immediate pleasures may be only distractions. Every task which involves a great deal of time for its achievement can be negated completely by an enjoyment of all the pleasures of distraction. Yet no joy may be able to touch that of completing an experiment, a book, or a piece of sculpture, or winning the game. Indeed it is true that writing, sculpting, and playing the game are all pleasures. But if at every moment they must compete with all other possibilities of pleasure, they will never win. For there are always boring moments in all tasks.

The case I am developing here is toward a principle that the greater satisfactions in life come from postponed enjoyments (though not postponed forever). If this is true, and if it is also true that immediate pleasures have a naturally greater appeal for most people, as Spinoza claims, then it follows that men ought *not* always to do what would give them immediate pleasure. The ability to postpone and to look ahead to the future is a skill to be developed as all skills are, by practice and repetition. To a man who believes that pleasure is a sufficient reason for action, the ennui of dedication and the strain of effort will never be appealing. Thus, certain pleasures may be prohibited to children so that they may gain the discipline of having endured temptation without submitting to it.

Yet this entire argument depends on certain *facts* about the way men learn habits of dedication and self-discipline. It may be true that a person who experiences all pleasures without deprivation when young will never learn to deprive himself of a lesser good to achieve a greater one. Yet it may be true instead that deprivation so focuses one's energies on what one cannot have as to blind him to other, more valuable possibilities. One argument is that our eighteen-year-old girl should forgo a minor pleasure as an act of self-discipline. Yet perhaps such a minor pleasure will then take on the aura of a forbidden fruit. Perhaps if she allows herself free rein in sexual affairs, she will discover how unimportant sexual pleasure is compared to other possibilities of pleasure.

These are only a small part of the facts which are relevant to the decision required. A girl considering sexual intercourse must also know something of the risks of pregnancy she runs, of the risk of censure by others, even of a change in the attitude of her lover toward her. One of the most common cliches proffered concerning sexual relations is that men do not respect women who submit to seduction. We cannot rule here on the truth of this claim. Probably some do and some don't. What is important is the relevance of such a consideration to the girl whose decision is called for. If she is simply willing to perform a generous act for her boyfriend, regardless of consequences, that is one thing. If she wishes to gain her own pleasure, that too has its consequences. But if she wishes to increase her lover's love for her, then she must consider the consequences of her actions with respect to his feelings for her.

As for her feelings, they are in a case like this of far greater consequence than in the other cases we have considered. Indeed a person thinking of performing a theft must consider the feelings of others as well as himself. However, the obvious effect stealing will have on others may provide a moral repugnance which settles the decision for him. In the case of sexual relations, however, the harm to others or oneself is rather subtle and diffuse, and not so easy to discern.

There are basically two kinds of feelings involved. First, there is the possibility that a woman who is known to be an easy mark may have ruined her reputation, and will be despised, reviled, even molested by other people. The general prohibition against casual sexual relations works its greatest effect on the feelings of people who accept it. A person considering the violation of a moral law, even one he theoretically rejects, must consider what other people will think and do afterward.

Second, there are the woman's own feelings to consider, of regret or remorse. The peculiar force of prescriptions of chastity seems to stem from a conception that, like murder, a sexual act cannot be undone. Either a woman is a virgin, or not. Conventional double standards have always reflected exactly that view. A fallen woman is fair game for anyone. A gentleman does not deflower virgins. Obviously there is something perverse about viewing sexual acts with the same attitude as acts of murder. But let us not worry about such matters. More important is the question of whether the woman involved, who must make the decision, accepts the conventional view, and how she will feel after she has lost her virginity. She may indeed feel like a fallen woman, sorry for what she has done, but unable to repair the damage. A simple act, seemingly of little consequence, can work the greatest effect on a person's life, especially where his own moral feelings are concerned. In an urban environment, such an issue may be the only one worth considering deeply. How well can the agent live with the decision he makes? Such a question is central to all moral decisions, though of greater weight in some cases than in others.

Sexual problems are extremely complex. Often they are not understood to be so, and thought to be nothing but a matter of pleasure or inhibition. What is overlooked is that sexual relations are a paramount way in which people interrelate in their most intimate moments. The most important feelings toward others and toward oneself are involved. The deepest habits of response and fears of rejection or pain are aroused. The rules for sexual conduct which are established in a given society may be indefensible. But their existence reflects a genuine sense of the importance of interpersonal relations and intimacy. A completely casual attitude toward sexual relations may be part of a completely casual attitude toward other people and even toward oneself.

E. Cleanliness

With this final example of a moral decision, we move to an issue that is not thought by many people to be of any moral significance. Yet, a bit like our last example, personal cleanliness is a subject loaded with emotional implications, whether or not we can find grounds for defending them, or even wish to criticize them. Here, we consider a college student who simply does not want to bathe, to dress neatly, to consider his appearance at all. Let us suppose that a lack of money is in no way his problem. Rather, he is either uninterested in cleanliness, or even thinks it of so little matter that he will be dirty and ragged to demonstrate his contempt for common norms.

The principles which define the problem here are not quite as easy to determine as the others have been. On the one hand, we have the principle that one ought to be clean. No doubt many people keep themselves clean, and have contempt for those who do not. But it is difficult to argue that such a principle carries moral force, or even that it should bear an important weight in affairs of conduct. A person may become so dirty as to smell, and his odor may be offensive to others. Yet despite the blandishments of deodorant manufacturers, who offer the world if one becomes odor free, human odors are not all that awful. At worst they constitute an inconvenience to others, not so great an inconvenience as to compel a person to change his behavior.

We look, however, to the opposing side, and find only two kinds of approaches to justify aversion to cleanliness. One is laziness. It is simply too much trouble to bathe. Second is a firm rejection of the magnitude of concern personal hygiene evokes from so many people. In the first case, the principle is something like: no one should have to exert himself for others. But that is nonsense. It is often morally right to consider others rather deeply. Therefore, the second principle is required. Cleanliness is unimportant, and it is wrong to be deeply concerned about so trivial a matter. In effect, we oppose the principle seemingly maintained by others that one should be clean in dress and person by the negative principle that such a principle is too trivial to merit even our consideration, much less our respect.

But we saw in our discussion of sexual conduct that the mere denial of a principle does not justify actions to the contrary. So too, the fact that the principle mandating cleanliness cannot be defended does not justify remaining unclean. What is required also is a conviction that lack of cleanliness is advantageous, or at least beneficial. To some extent, European mores tend to support such a view. But in most respects and obviously, all the advantage lies with cleanliness. It is better for health, for efficiency, for neighborly relations, and so forth. Certainly lack of personal cleanliness is but a minor impediment to the lives of others— though in extreme form it can become a danger to everyone's health. But, assuming we are not speaking of a man so poor as not to possess running water, the inconvenience of remaining clean is very small also.

The entire issue is a minor one, so minor as to make us wonder at whether it is worth taking the time to consider it. Yet strangely enough, the small issues are often the more powerful ones. The humility which the great problems of life can evoke is dispelled by the rather minor matter of slight inconvenience. "Why should he look so awful?" "Why does he smell?" "Why doesn't he clean up his front yard?" The reaction of other people to lack of cleanliness is a judgment not so much upon the act as upon the person. We have only barely touched on such a mode of judgment in our former examples. Stealing is a critical enough act to overshadow the person involved. But a man who steals is a *thief*, an untrustworthy and dangerous person. A girl who is promiscuous is often thought to be coarse, unthinking, perhaps mentally unbalanced. A man who is filthy and who lives in filth is unfit to live among others. He is inconsiderate, thoughtless, rude, uncivilized. It is so easy to be clean that one must be truly degraded to live in dirt, at least if he can afford the ordinary appurtenances of life.

My description is exaggerated, but for dramatic purposes. There are many more complex possibilities which might lead a girl to sexual acts or a man to disregard his personal grooming. In particular, he may find the hypocrisy of his environment difficult to tolerate, when cleanliness matters to most people so much more than war and killing. So he may let himself be dirty and yet demonstrate against war, to show the world that he knows better than the rest of them what is truly important. However, his rebellion is likely to produce in others, not moral respect, but condemnation of his personal habits. War is a serious matter, and a man should do what he can to oppose it. But he will probably be able to accomplish little. In the little things, however, that make life easier among men who are crowded together and meet daily, we can all accomplish a great deal. The neglect of the little things is often taken as proof that a man neglects the greater things also.

This last point has raised a factual matter which we have not yet considered. That is, whether or not the agent is likely to be effective in the course of action he has undertaken. Among the facts we must reckon with are those which are related to our abilities and strengths. Men often put greater efforts into issues of smaller importance than into international affairs of great moment. This may not be hypocrisy or foolishness. It may be a consequence of the realization that we can be more effective in the lesser affairs, and that they therefore merit our greater attention. Not everyone can bring peace to the world. Everyone can be kind and considerate to the people he meets daily.

F. Laws

There remains a final matter to note before we go on to a more detailed analysis of the various issues that have been raised. Throughout this first chapter, all the examples have been of the form, "what shall I do?" It is worth noting that men often do not raise moral issues in this form, but rather in the form, "what is right?" The latter question, however, is ambiguous. It may call for an answer of the form, "it is right for me to do so and so in these circumstances." It may instead call for a law or at least a general principle. We have seen that general principles alone cannot settle a moral decision. Yet we must often legislate rules, not only for ourselves but for others as well.

Perhaps it is sufficient to note only that legislation is an *act*, that the passage of a law is an act of a legislator, that a letter written in support of a law is an act of a citizen. It follows, then, that we may analyze the request for a law into a question concerning what a man should do in support of or opposition to a proposed law. Thus, in the case of abortion, the more common problem is not whether a woman should *have* an abortion, but whether there should be a law prohibiting abortion. I am suggesting that we consider the latter question to be instead the question of whether a given person should support or oppose such a law, and to what extent.

What is of paramount importance here, however, is that we note the difference between deciding that a given act is *wrong for the agent*, and deciding that it should be prohibited generally. A general prohibition is a rule that carries some weight of enforcement, if only that of the disapproval of others. If we decide to legislate a rule of conduct, we must undertake a process of decision which is exactly like the ones we have considered, except that it looks to the support of a law rather than to a more individual action. A given type of action might be very wrong for a given individual to perform, yet not merit general proscription.

The first case we considered is generally if tacitly understood to make the distinction just mentioned. In general we agree that a man ought to be willing to serve his country, and to be drafted into the armed forces when necessary. Many people also have a considerable respect for those men who condemn all wars, so great a respect as to justify a conscientious objection to war. To many Quakers, it is wrong to become a member of the armed forces, and to participate even indirectly in war. It by no means follows that it is wrong for anyone else, who has no deep religious or moral scruples against all wars, to join the army and to engage in battle. Taking circumstances into account, it seems wrong for one man to perform a given type of action, but not wrong for another. Therefore, we cannot justify a general rule of conduct in such a case, one with no exceptions whatsoever. In fact, the ordinary view is that we need a general law compelling service in the armed forces, provided we allow exceptions for men of sincere objections of conscience.

There are two general questions facing us when we are concerned with the promulgation of a general rule. Is the practice we will legislate by law one which in general men ought to follow, whether or not exceptions are allowed? And, is such a practice of sufficient importance to justify the repressive measures of enforcement which follow upon the passage of a law? A salutary example which distinguishes the two questions is that of the state support of a particular religion. Many if not all devout members of religious sects believe that theirs is the one and only true religion. Everyone ought to follow the one true path, at least if there is one. But the consequences of enforcing but a single religious practice are frightening to contemplate: religious wars, imprisonment, blood and turmoil. Therefore, even men of deepest religious conviction and assurance are convinced of the moral inadvisability of the legislation of rules concerning religious worship. Tolerance in religious affairs is justified by the consequences intolerance may bring.

Clearly men in general consider stealing to be so wrong, perhaps in the chaos frequent theft can bring to pass, that they are convinced of the rightness of a criminal law prohibiting theft, a law with appropriately severe penalities and effective enforcement. In the case of abortion, however, as the current debate indicates, there is considerably more leeway in attitude and also in the conclusions reached. On the one hand, some people consider abortion murder, and would enforce a criminal law prohibiting it to anyone. In return, there are those who believe that no unwanted children should be born. We have already seen that the question of whether a given pregnant woman should undergo an abortion is a complex one. The same kinds of complexities and even more of them bear upon the question of whether a law should be passed prohibiting abortion.

Yet the latter question may be easier to resolve. For the question here is whether those who disagree should be forced to conform to a common rule. Prohibition of alcoholic beverages was repealed, not on the grounds that drinking is a good thing, but on the grounds that enforcement of the prohibition was difficult and also led to unfortunate consequences—bootlegging, disrespect for law, gangsters. Too many women seek illegal abortions where necessary. Illegal abortions are often extremely dangerous. Sex is made fearful. Moreover, those who are impelled to disobey the law may then hold it in contempt. There is nothing in the least inconsistent about holding that abortion is evil, yet also opposing the passage of a law prohibiting it.

The last argument we considered may be worth special mention. One of the vital functions of a moral principle is to generate respect and reverence for a particular course of action. As we have noted, moral problems arise in situations where principles conflict. And they can conflict only where each is held in some degree of respect by the agent. But one of the most obvious features of laws which exist more in the breach than in observance is that they then produce little but contempt in those who break them. Therefore, it can be argued, where a given mode of behavior is too widespread, even if it is harmful, it must not be prohibited by law. Such an argument may be made in favor of ending the prohibition of marijuana, both use and sale. The use of marijuana may be provably injurious (though that has not yet been shown). Yet it would not follow that we should legislate against its use. It might justify rather severe restrictions on advertising and selling it. The existence of a law which many people violate is a hard teacher that laws do not matter. And that is the last thing we wish to teach anyone.

G. Summary

We have done no more than to sketch in a superficial manner the kinds of considerations which enter into the making of moral decisions. We have noted the significance of *facts, feelings*, and *principles* in such decisions, as well as the complex relationship they bear in the making of concrete decisions. We turn now to a more detailed study of these various elements, and to some of the classic insights which have been discovered concerning them.

A last point is worth mentioning, however, before going on. The five problems posed in this chapter all rest on a genuine conflict among principles. To some people, it is obvious that a man should not steal, even if he is in desperate need. Whenever a genuine moral problem is posed, one which is more than an exercise of a man's conscience toward what he always knew was right, there are at least two principles in conflict, or, at least, a conflict among principles and feelings. It is not misleading then to say that there are *two sides* to *every* moral question. There are several ways of interpreting such a claim.

(a) To every moral question posed, we may find a principle which supports both sides, provided that the question allows for reinterpretation. Murder is always wrong. But killing is thought by most people to be right under some conditions.

(b) Since there are two sides to every question, none is more correct than any other. We have here an extreme version of moral relativism.

(c) In making a moral decision, we must look to both sides of the question to avoid error. Therefore, we should not ignore or repress undesirable moral positions.

(d) No method of the making of moral decisions can eliminate the genuine possibility that a decision reached was wrong.

All of these interpretations except that of (b) are justifiable in terms of the problems we have posed. The issues in all of them are complex, and all of them stem from a conflict of moral principles on both sides of the questions posed. In no case can a single principle relieve the difficulty except by a moral purity that is not likely to have beneficial consequences. In all moral decisions, the consequences remain ahead, to show to us our mistakes. As for (b), the making of a moral decision itself proves that some sides are indeed regarded as right, and others as wrong, at least by some people. Yet relativism remains a genuine problem for many moral views.

The twin reefs of blindness and dogmatism, on the one hand, and extreme relativism, on the other, seem to haunt most contemporary thinking on morals. The purpose of this book is to wend a way between the twin disasters, though not necessarily to arrive at any safe port on the other side.

QUESTIONS

Analyze each of the following moral situations in terms of the various elements which constitute it. In particular, define the situations in terms of the principles, facts, and feelings involved.

1. A college student wishes to be independent of his parents, who are quite prosperous. He cannot easily support himself, so he finds it necessary to use food stamps paid for by public taxes. Is it right for him to let himself be

supported by public funds, when his parents could easily afford to support him ? Does it matter how well he gets along with his parents ?

2. A housewife, mother of four children, all under the age of three, wishes to get a job. What responsibilities does she have to care for her children personally ? How relevant to her decision is psychological information concerning the development of young children ?

3. A narcotics addict needs to support his habit to the tune of far more money than he can earn. How justified is he in stealing to support it ? How responsible for his plight are the men who make the laws prohibiting access to inexpensive sources of drugs ? Is the illegality of narcotics a relevant factor here ?

4. A rich young man has received a very large inheritance. What responsibilities has he toward others because of his inheritance ? What responsibilities has he to himself ? Is it right for him to spend his life flitting from one pleasure to another ?

5. A soldier in wartime has captured an enemy officer. He is convinced this officer possesses information which would save many of his fellow soldiers' lives. Is it right for the soldier to torture the enemy officer for this information ?

6. Is it wrong for two men to engage in homosexual acts ? Does it matter if they are faithful lovers or not ? Should there be a law prohibiting homosexual acts ? Is it wrong for two men to kiss in public ?

7. Is the torture of animals morally wrong ?

8. A man with an extremely malicious and penetrating tongue gains a great deal of pleasure from verbally assaulting everyone he meets. Is it wrong for him to do so ? Would it be wrong for us to prevent him from doing so ?

9. The emergency care unit of a hospital costs $50,000 per year to operate. Last year it saved the lives of twelve men who would have died of heart attacks otherwise. Should the $50,000 be spent instead on informing the poor about contraceptive methods ?

10. A man's family are held hostage by a foreign power, and he is asked to obtain documents of a secret nature that are vital to his country's security. Is it right for him to do so ? Does it matter how many children he has, or how old they are ?

SELECTED READINGS

The most interesting and provocative studies of moral problems are to be found in works of literature rather than works of philosophy. Here are just a few:

Sophocles, *Antigone.*

A more modern and simpler version is:

Anouilh, *Antigone.*

F. Dostoievski, *Crime and Punishment.*

    The Brothers Karamazov. Both great studies of moral problems.

A. Camus, *The Stranger.* A very difficult book to interpret morally.

U. Betti, *The Queen and the Rebels.*

Euripides, *Iphigenia in Aulis.* A clear treatment of a difficult moral problem, with its solution.

H. Melville, *Billy Budd.*

Two philosophical works which together represent the challenges of moral thought:

Plato: *Republic.*

Kierkegaard: *Fear and Trembling.* Do not let the religious issues obscure the moral fundamentals.

II. THE BASIS OF VALUE

WE WILL begin in part by retracing some of our earlier discussion, although from a more theoretical vantagepoint. We recall our discovery that the constituents of a moral decision are rather complexly related in any particular case. Neither facts, principles, nor feelings alone seem to provide us with a clear basis for moral decision, at least not in every case. If for convenience we define *evaluation* as the process in which we make a moral decision, or discover the value of something, then we seem to be led to the conclusion that neither facts, principles, nor feelings alone constitute a basis for value. As we will see, such a conclusion leads easily to a form of despair in which we deny that anything truly possesses value. But the claim that nothing has value is not itself a moral decision. It is rather a form of nihilism in which rebellion and destructiveness come to the fore. We have already seen that the judgment that a given action does not possess value does not of itself entail that we ought not to perform that action. Indeed, the judgment that a given action is in principle valuable does not of itself entail that we ought to perform it. A man may love his country, and believe it good to fight for her, and yet refuse when the cause is unjust or harmful to his country's welfare. Nihilism is a despair turned outward into action, though the despair is rooted in the conviction that action is impossible to justify. Obviously, such nihilism cannot itself be defended, nor actions which follow from it. If we are to be clear on the issues relevant to such matters, we must consider first the various grounds which have been proffered for moral decisions.

A. Facts

In his *Republic*, Plato defines the philosopher as a man who loves wisdom, and argues that such a man ought to rule over society, because he knows the Good. It is a major task to interpret any of the important writings of Plato, especially in a treatment which can be no more than a surface reflection upon them. Plato argues that the philosopher's *love* of wisdom will protect him from the temptations ordinary men are heir to. Moreover, his knowledge of the good will also of itself make him do what is right. A fundamental principle of the Platonic writings is that *all men desire what is good*, and fail only because they do not know what this truly is. Knowledge of what is truly good is sufficient as a basis for determining what one ought to do. It certainly seems that such a position depends on a conception of good and bad, right and wrong, as *properties* of things. Once we know enough about the Good, we know which things are good and which are not, and in which respects. What we have done is to establish an analogy between goodness as a property of things and, say, weight or length as properties of things. Certainly if we know about weights and measures, we know what kinds of things possess weight (stones and animals) and which do not (numbers and colors). We also know how to measure the weight and length of physical objects. If the analogy is justified, then just as the length of a rod is a *fact* about it, so also the goodness of a thing is a fact about it.

It is important to avoid a rather common objection which is sometimes offered against the conception of values as facts. We have drawn our analogy by comparing the property of goodness to that of length or weight. The latter, it must be noted, are relatively straightforward properties of things, and relatively easy to determine. But we are all quite aware of the complexity of evaluative judgments. We can look at things and ascertain their colors and their shapes in a straightforward fashion. We can measure weight and length rather easily. If goodness is a property of things, it is of a very different order of complexity. There is no simple way of determining the goodness of things. But it does not follow from the complexity of value properties that we cannot know the facts about what is good and bad.

Consider then two other properties of things, which are certainly factual as we usually conceive them, yet which are akin to goodness and rightness in their complexity. First, we imagine that we have a mechanical system in space which contains eleven bodies moving with respect to each other, each exerting a gravitational influence on the other ten. Even if we neglect the effects of the rest of the universe, no property of this system is very easy to determine at any given time. Consider that we wish to determine the position of a given body at a specific time. Note that even defining the terms in which the position is to be expressed is far from straightforward. We can express the position in terms of any framework we choose. What is far worse, the computations of position are extremely arduous, and take no simple and elegant form. Perhaps goodness is a definite property of things, but so complex are the computations necessary to measure it that no one can be sure of the goodness of a thing in any simple way.

Consider by way of contrast the property of being in good health. Any physician has a rather definite sense of what a well functioning body is, and how it works. He can recognize ill health fairly straightforwardly, yet he must work very hard to determine that a body is in good health. Certainly no physician could tell a layman very precisely what good health is. It involves a complex interrelationship of various parts, each of which must be described and measured separately. A full-scale physical examination, to determine if a man is in good health, is a time-consuming process. Perhaps goodness is a property of similar complexity, determinable but only in arduous and elaborate ways. There are philosophers, in fact, who argue that "being in good health" is not a factual property of things, for it involves comparison with a norm. It is worth mentioning, however, that good health is completely determinable by measurements and physical tests. We might concede that health is not entirely a factual property. But nevertheless, a physician determines the health of a man by facts alone. Perhaps goodness is a factual property in this second sense.

If, however, we return to Plato's own fundamental principle—that all men pursue what they think is good—we are led to wonder about goodness and its rather unique character. Let us suppose that goodness is a complex factual property, and that we have come into possession of the facts. Will we then pursue only the good? One of the remarkable features of human behavior is the frequency with which men do what they believe is harmful, to others and even themselves. A narcotics addict may be completely convinced that taking drugs is bad, yet be unable to stop using them. Either Plato is simply wrong, and we may find ourselves with factual knowledge of the good without using that knowledge to our own benefit (perhaps we act out of weakness or even spite), or else knowledge of the good is not knowledge of facts alone. This last conclusion follows from a principle we have not enunciated formally: that knowledge of facts alone cannot influence us to action. It is this principle which is the basis for the philosophical claim that goodness is not a factual property like weight and length, nor even like good health. It is no surprise for a man to be convinced that cigarette smoking injures his health, yet not stop smoking. But we expect a man to be moved toward what he thinks is good. If so, then goodness is not a factual matter.

The argument that facts and values are distinct takes its classical form in two arguments provided by David Hume. In his first argument, Hume compares the killing of one's children to the shade cast by a tree over its own seedlings. In both cases alike, the progeny die because of the parents. Yet only in one case do we consider this death with moral revulsion. Therefore, Hume concludes, it is the feeling of revulsion itself which underlies the moral judgment that it is wrong for parents to kill their children. Wrongness is not an objective trait of things, but is a property which resides in the sentiments of the observer. We determine the value of things by looking, not to facts about them, but to the feelings of the person making the valuation.

Several points are worth noting concerning this argument. First, the argument depends on the strength of the analogy between filicide and the deprivation of sunlight to seedlings. Certainly there are some important similarities, but there are at least three crucial differences. (a) The parent tree does not *voluntarily* cast a shade over its progeny. Filicide is defined here as a voluntary act. The parent tree has no power to change its position to avoid depriving its seedlings of light. An analogous case is to regard the survival of the mother in the hold of a slaveship as filicide, if she were selected by the owners to be fed more than her children, and if her children would have survived were the mother not there. It is by no means obvious that a mother should commit suicide to save her child in a situation full of such imponderables.

Nevertheless, there is a point Hume stresses which the last example neglects— the horror of the situation and the pain of the mother. A tree has no sense of horror or revulsion at the death of its young. But we may interpret this fact differently from Hume. (b) The cases differ because human beings can and do experience powerful emotions, revulsion and pain, and are also aware of what they do and experience. It is a *fact* about human beings that they are conscious of what they do and feel. Trees are not. Animals are not, at least not in the same ways or to the same extent. We may reply to Hume that it is not the feelings themselves which are crucial, but the capacity for feeling and self-consciousness which makes men moral agents and trees and animals not. But the feelings and awareness of men are facts about them.

Hume's argument in general commits the error we noted just above—looking for facts about values in an oversimplified form. Certainly in the mere death of progeny there is no moral conclusion to be drawn. We must know also the circum- stances of the case, the abilities of the parent, the voluntary nature of his actions, his self-awareness, the extent of his contribution to the situation, and so forth. In particular, we must know something of the alternatives which are available. A parent with enough food for only one child is not to blame if the other dies. Hume's argument can at best show that values are not to be equated with *simple* facts, but not that values are not facts at all.

(c) The more general feature of Hume's argument is its confusion over a distinction that applies to facts as much as values, and that is worth noting here. Consider the properties of things in the following terms: Some properties of things are seemingly independent of everything else, in particular, the observer and his measuring instruments. Some properties depend on the observer, and vary from observer to observer. Examples of the first kind are length, weight, and position. Examples of the second are color and warmth. Locke calls this distinction one between *primary* and *secondary* qualities: qualities which belong to things independent of the observer, and qualities which are relative to some observer. Hume points out himself that if a man has his left hand in hot water and his right in cold, and both hands are moved into the same basin of water at an intermediate temperature, the water will feel cold to the left hand and warm to the right. Hot and cold are secondary qualities. So also is color. Locke was led to conclude that primary qualities are objective properties of things, and secondary qualities are not. Primary qualities are facts. Secondary qualities are merely ideas in the mind. Unfortunately for this view, Berkeley demonstrated beyond doubt that length is relative to the measuring instruments and other conditions of the observer, in effect that *all* properties are relative to the observing conditions. The only difference is that some qualities are relatively permanent from observer to observer, and some are not.

In modern times, this whole problem has been dealt with by introducing the notion of a *dispositional concept*. To say that an object X has property P is to say that under specified conditions C, X will be observed as O. An iron bar is *magnetized* means that if iron filings are brought into its proximity, the bar will attract them. The critical point for our purposes is that assigning a property to an object is a far from simple procedure. Facts are not simple relations among objects independent of observers. The *fact* that an iron bar is magnetized depends on the circumstances surrounding it, including the conditions of observation. In short, factual properties may be assigned to things only in a context which includes observed traits of these things and also certain conditions of observation. The most objective facts involve not a two-term relation between object and property, but a triadic relation among the object, its dispositional property, and the traits observed under conditions specified.

We may now return to Hume's argument. What the argument shows is that a value may be assigned to an action or an object only in a triadic relation among the object, the conditions or circumstances specified, and the person or evaluator. Properly speaking, we may now regard evaluation as a process taking place in a complex context or situation which includes the objects of evaluation, the persons involved, and the circumstances and conditions as well. Hume's argument cannot show that values are not objective traits of such situations, only that they are not qualities of things independent of such situations. Hume's argument suggests that values are not primary qualities of things. Hume's own suspicion of secondary qualities then entails the view that values are not factual or objective properties at all. But recent analysis has broken down the distinction between primary and secondary qualities. It should follow—though it does not for most theories of evaluation—that values may be regarded as complex facts concerning human situations. Let us consider other arguments offered against such a conclusion.

Hume's second argument is the more powerful one, and may be the basis for most of the claims that values cannot be derived from facts alone. Hume argues that reason alone cannot motivate the will. No one would undertake any action at all on the basis of reason alone. Though Hume does not use this terminology, it would not be misleading to represent his position as the claim that knowledge of facts alone cannot lead men to act. But evaluation is directed toward action. It follows, then, that evaluation cannot rest on facts alone.

Before looking carefully at Hume's second argument, it may be worth noting an interesting reply to the entire argument which is almost always overlooked, yet which may have some plausibility. Hume's argument rests on the principle that evaluation is directed toward action, and that a value arrived at has a motivating force on the will. Now motives and the will are very complex notions, as we will

come to see. Would it not clarify our understanding of evaluation considerably to
distinguish evaluation as deliberation prior to action from decision as the final
step in which we undertake to act? Hume's argument then shows only that
decision requires something more than facts. But *deliberation*, which may be the
procedure whereby we determine what is good or what we are obligated to do, may
indeed rest on facts alone. Such an attack has the merit of making intelligible the
common fact that men who claim to know what is right often do not do it, particularly when they do nothing. Men may deliberate at great length to determine
what they should do. But unless they also *decide* to do it, they will not act. The
step of decision rests on some emotion or motivating force. With Kant, let us
define this as a *respect* for what is good and right. The determination of values on
this theory would be wholly a factual matter. But the action undertaken would
not. Men might be too weak, too evil, too depraved, or too capricious even to
follow their own judgments. This approach emphasizes as Hume's cannot that
men are often too weak to do what they are convinced they ought to do. Returning
to Plato's principle that all men pursue the good, we may admit then that all
men seek the good in their deliberations, but they may not act accordingly. We
will study the subject of weakness in a later chapter.

We return here to Hume's second argument. The force of the argument
depends on a distinction we have not explicitly developed. Hume claims that
reason can provide us only with knowledge of the consequences of actions and
events, and not with their import or significance. Factual knowledge, in other
words, is causal knowledge. It provides us with knowledge of causes and their
effects, of circumstances and consequences. But it cannot give us knowledge of
whether what has been produced is good or bad. In Hume's words, "It can never
in the least concern us to know, that such objects are causes, and such others
effects, if both the causes and the effects be indifferent to us." I may know for a
fact that stealing from a man will cause his ruin. But if I am emotionally indifferent
to what happens to him, my factual knowledge can in no way affect my conduct.
Put in a rather gross but modern vein, it is impossible to derive "ought" from
"is." All the facts in the world provide no values by themselves.

Such a conclusion, stated in so bald a form, has its dangers. In particular, it is
imperative to note that Hume claims only that facts *alone* provide no basis for
evaluation. The gross form of the claim that "ought" cannot be derived from
"is" does not stress the word "alone." It is tempting to conclude that facts are
irrelevant to evaluation. Some forms of *emotivism* make such a claim. As we saw
in the first chapter, this position can lead to a pure and extreme conception of duty
as the following of moral principles without regard to the consequences of action.
Morality without concern for factual consequences is thought by most men to be
overly extreme and terribly pure. Facts are indeed relevant to evaluation for Hume.
They are simply not *sufficient* for the determination of values.

Let us make Hume's point in a different way. We define a distinction among
values: there are "intrinsic values"—things which are good in themselves—and

there are "instrumental values"—things which are good because of what they produce. Holding a job is for many men necessary and even good—not in itself, but in what it makes possible. A man receives a fair wage for his labor, and can buy the necessities and even some of the luxuries of life. Things can be good instrumentally and bad instrumentally, in terms of their results. In instrumental evaluation we look to the consequences of our actions. Clearly Hume conceives of reason as being capable of contributing to instrumental evaluation only. Facts are always instrumental relations.

Are there intrinsic goods? The fundamental argument in favor of goods in themselves is a purely theoretical one. Aristotle argues in his *Nicomachean Ethics* that if all goods are instrumental, we are forced into an infinite regress, in which nothing is actually good. If *A* is good because it produces *B*, and *B* is good because it produces *C*, and so on without end, then *A* is never actually good. We must come to an end eventually, and in something which is merely good in itself. Aristotle's conception of an intrinsic good is rather different from Hume's, and we will examine this difference with care. The argument, however, has equal force no matter how we conceive of intrinsic value. In Hume's terms, factual knowledge cannot of itself motivate the will. Yet the purpose of morals is to guide the will. It follows that facts alone do not constitute values, but require emotions as well. The infinite series of instrumental values terminates for Hume in things which are simply *felt to be good and bad*. We are repelled by murder, by pain, by theft. We are attracted to others and want to help them. These repulsions and attractions are the feelings on which evaluation ultimately rests. We will consider them shortly.

The attack on facts as the basis of value comes down in the end to the claim that there must be intrinsic goods, and that facts cannot provide them. Before going on, then, let us consider a few candidates for intrinsic goodness. Kant himself, though he develops a theory of morality akin to a theory of intrinsic goodness, demolishes all candidates for intrinsic goodness we might be tempted to propose. He opens his work on the *Fundamental Principles of the Metaphysics of Morals* with the words: "Nothing can possibly be conceived in the world, or even out of it, which can be called good without qualification, except a *good will*." He then goes on to argue that goods like intelligence, fortune, even happiness are indeed good, but not without qualification. Intelligence in a man of bad character may lead to extremely unfortunate ends. Good fortune and happiness when possessed by evil men are sources of pride and even greater defects of character—smugness and self-righteousness—and appear to us unjust. Kant's argument is that nothing *in itself*—meaning, without qualification—is good without regard for circumstances and consequences except (and this is his unique solution to the problem) a good will. Unfortunately, Kant then defines a good will as one which ignores consequences. His realization that once consequences are to be considered nothing is intrinsically good leads him, not to repudiate all intrinsic goods without qualification, but to carry the principle of intrinsic goodness almost to an obstinate extreme.

Since instrumental considerations cannot provide a basis for evaluation *in them-selves*, we should not consider them *at all*. Kant is the originator of the position that "ought" cannot be derived from "is," and its corollary that facts are quite irrelevant to morals. But the path from Kant to his descendants is not a short one, and we will not embark on it now.

Two other arguments which have been adduced to show that values cannot be derived from facts are worth considering. G. E. Moore attacks what he calls the "naturalistic fallacy" on the following basis: "Good" is like "yellow." It is simple, discerned immediately, and *cannot be defined*. It is grasped or intuited directly. There is nothing we can say "yellow" is which does not presuppose a man with color vision who first can discern and recognize the color yellow. To define "yellow" as a particular wave length of light, perhaps that emitted by sodium under specified conditions, is not a *definition* of "yellow," but is rather a physical fact about the relationship between wave lengths and our prior psychic sense or intuition of the color. It is crucial to Moore's argument that a definition be a logical truth, depending on no facts. We may define a "bachelor" as an "un-married male adult human being." We have here a logical equivalence, what is sometimes called an "analytic statement." The definition may be regarded as giving us a linguistic or logical equivalence, whose truth is unquestionable. But no such definition can be given for "yellow" or "good."

Moore dramatizes the same argument in another form, called the "open question" argument. We may ask, "*Is* a bachelor *really* an unmarried male adult human being?" The question is obviously absurd, precisely because only linguistic and logical relations are involved. The question "does the number five really follow the number four?" is also absurd, to anyone who grasps anything of the nature of numerical relations. Moore points out, however, that whatever we take to the definitional of "good," a nontrivial question may be generated from it. For example, suppose we define "good" as "giving pleasure," as many philos-ophers have done. Drinking when we are thirsty is good because it gives us pleasure. Moore points out that the question "Is it really good to be given pleasure?" is by no means absurd. Men have actually doubted the definition proposed. No one doubts the definition of "bachelor." Therefore, "good" cannot be defined in any way. It is simple and indefinable. We grasp it directly and intuitively, as we grasp the color yellow.

It is vital that we be aware of an important distinction Moore makes. "Good" is simple and indefinable. "*The* good" is not. Moore does not in any way deny the relevance of facts and circumstances to the determination of *the* good—that is, the best course of action among all the competing alternatives. His point is rather that the good is derived, with facts and knowledge of consequences, from what we take immediately to be good. The latter is not definable in terms of facts. Moore's position is a first cousin of Hume's. Facts alone do not give us knowledge of the good, of what we ought to do or seek. In addition, we need emotion, according to Hume, or knowledge of what is good, according to Moore. Moore assumes we gain this knowledge directly and intuitively.

Several criticisms may be given of Moore's argument. First of all, the argument depends on a particular conception of what it is to give a definition of a concept. We may note, however, that there are definitions in various subjects which are not logical or linguistic equivalences in quite the sense Moore assumes. For example, we define an "element" in physics as an atom which contains a given number of protons in its nucleus, or a collection of such atoms. Such a definition is by no means a logical truth, partly because of the complex theoretical terms assumed in the definition, and most obviously if we note that elements were originally defined quite differently. There are definitions which are proposed or stipulated in order to gain knowledge over a particular domain of understanding.

Second, Moore assumes that simple things cannot be defined, as if definitions give parts or constituents of things. Nevertheless, he does assume that simple things can be known. We may feel dubious about even the very notion of a simple thing—noting that yellow is indeed a color, can be charted on a system of other colors, and so forth. Why then call it *simple*, since it is intimately related to other things ? Without becoming involved in complex metaphysical disputes, we may at least wonder at the plausibility of the claim that anything is simple. In addition, we may be even more dubious about whether anything simple can be known, since knowing something involves knowing its relations and its connections. The mere apprehension of yellow, it may be said, is no knowledge. It becomes knowledge when we discover what kinds of things are yellow, what produces yellow, what covers yellow.

Third, we may agree that "good" like "yellow" is immediate, yet deny that it is indefinable. We may use John Dewey's distinction between the mediate and immediate. In a fundamental sense, everything is what it is, even a crusty old bachelor. He is the person he is, and must be recognized or experienced as such. There is a fundamental and individual quality every particular thing has or is. Everything is something in itself, and is not therefore merely what it is in its relations to other things. All definitions, then, concern only relations, and cannot touch the irreducible unity of things. Again, to avoid too sophisticated meta-physical issues, let us look only at our ordinary experience. Is it not true that everything in experience is experienced as just what it is—yellow, good, my house, my child, a boat, etc. ? Yet we can define and understand many things in their relations. Moore's argument shows only that evaluation possesses some appeal to recognition or immediate feeling. But so also do all facts appeal to direct observation and recognition. Moore's argument tries to prove too much, and succeeds in overwhelming us by its case. "Good" cannot be defined, but in the same sense, neither can anything else. "Yellow" cannot be defined. Yet we can know for a *fact* that gold is yellow.

Our final argument to show that facts can be no basis for values is a linguistic one. A. J. Ayer argues that all factual claims can in principle be verified by the collection of evidence. Really *assuming* the validity of Hume's argument that moral statements cannot be justified by facts alone, Ayer concludes that moral statements are therefore not verifiable, and therefore *not statements at all*. If it is true that we cannot verify the statement "murder is wrong," then it is no statement, but rather an expression of an attitude. A man who says "murder is wrong" merely means that he is revolted by killing, or is asserting the imperative "don't commit murder." Obviously, the statement "I am revolted by murder" is a genuine factual claim. Therefore, the imperative form is the only legitimate one. Ayer's position is a version of *emotivism*: expressed evaluations are merely rhetorical devices to affect the emotions of other people and to reveal one's own attitudes. We will return to emotivism shortly. It is worth noting here only that the expressions "abortion is wrong" and "abortion is not wrong" are not, on this view, contradictory statements, since they are not statements at all. Moral disagreements become merely differences in attitude, and varying persuasions, not factual differences or differences in theoretical position.

We conclude this section with the remark that the case for the impossibility of deriving values from facts has not been conclusively made. The argument is often simplistic in its conception of facts or in its understanding of evaluation. What seems quite clear is that the relationship between commonplace facts and conventional values is itself anything but a clear one. A sophisticated conception of both facts and values is called for by a defensible theory of evaluation. It is unquestionable that facts concerning the feelings and intentions of the agent and others are essential to moral decisions. We will look somewhat more carefully at the facts relevant to evaluation and to moral decision in our chapter on such facts. We turn now, however, to the prospect of founding values in human feelings.

B. Feelings

The traditional conception of the function of feelings in moral decision goes back to Plato. In his *Republic*, Plato describes a tripartite soul of man, composed of reason, the appetites, and what some translators call the "spirited element." In a just man, reason and the spirited element together rule the appetites. Such a conception was profoundly welcome to the more ascetic early Christians, who saw the roots of sin in the body, and sought to elevate men to higher, spiritual things. In Kant such a conception of morality reaches its completion: morality consists in following one's duties even against one's feelings and inclinations. For Kant, like Plato, morality consists in obedience to the dictates of reason. For Kant, unlike Plato, obedience to reason may go against all feeling. In this respect, Kant is part of that movement in Christianity whose members went beyond obedience to God, and sought instead to prove their purity by defying their bodies, by repudiating their inclinations, by not only denying but punishing their feelings.

We have, however, noted that twentieth century ethics has moved rather far in the direction of a moral theory grounded in feelings alone, based on the arguments of Hume which we have briefly considered. Holding a related view to an extreme are moral relativists who see the basis of value in the varying feelings of different men, leading to the position that the values of each person are

determined solely by his feelings, and nothing else. It follows, then, that if John
likes something and Paul does not, that same thing is both good and bad, with
no hope of reconciliation. Many young people find moral relativism of this sort
to appease their horror at being continuously judged harshly for what they do.
There is too much condemnation. Our condemnations have no basis other than in
our own feelings, and are valid only for ourselves. The parents of these relativists
are not so happy with domestic moral relativism. Yet they may also subscribe to a
species of moral relativism of an intercultural variety. Norms of society vary from
country to country, tribe to tribe. But individuals should conform to their tribal
norms. Anthropological evidence suggests a great variety of differing attitudes
among different peoples. It is tempting to identify differences among peoples with
differences in values, and to identify these differences in values with differences in
attitudes or feelings.

Nothing we have said so far, however, justifies the view that feelings in
themselves entail differences in evaluation. In fact, Hume argues at length that
moral sentiments are common to all men, and a feature of human nature. To
Hume, the likeness among men engenders in us a sympathy toward others. We
suffer with the sufferings of others, in a type of imitation of feeling. We feel,
Hume argues, toward others who are like us as we feel toward ourselves, though,
it must be admitted, with a lesser intensity. Spinoza too argues that we have a
tendency to imitate the emotions of other people who are like us (which explains,
by the way, why we feel a greater concern for men who are like us than we do for
trees, cabbages, or men who are very different). "Although we may not have been
moved toward a thing by any emotion, yet if it is like ourselves, whenever we
imagine it to be affected by any emotion, we are affected by the same." We are all
human beings and live in like worlds. It is certainly possible that all human
feelings may follow the same laws and be alike also. Hume's claim that our moral
attitudes are generally alike is not obviously ridiculous.

Yet, alike as our general sentiments may be, they do differ at times. The
trouble with Hume's position is that there is no way for us to know what to do
with a genuine difference of conviction. A thief may be reviled by all of us, for
doing something we all find reprehensible. But a man who refuses to fight in a
war is not *merely* reprehensible. He also poses a problem for those who would jail
him. Is it right to do so? He claims it is *not* right. Others find his refusal abominable. He finds the war abominable. Why should we suppose that such an issue
depends on the greater number of people who feel one way or another, or even on
the intensity of their feelings? Here, then, we have made a case for moral relativism.
Bur moral relativism cannot solve the problem either. It simply declares the
difference of conviction to be irreconcilable. Unfortunately for this position, many
differences of moral conviction are reconciled, sometimes by persuasion, sometimes
by compromise, sometimes by a change in circumstances. The views which found
values on feelings make a fetish of differences, as if to make problems of reconciliation vanish merely because feelings have entered the picture. But feelings arise

in specifiable circumstances, arise in particular breasts at particular times, and change under determinable conditions. Founding evaluation in feeling does not seem to solve any problems. Rather, it seems instead to exacerbate them.

Let us return to the three parts of the soul Plato describes in the *Republic*. Consider the distinction between the spirited element and the appetites. Certainly men possess appetites or desires. We have wants and seek to satisfy them. Yet we notice immediately the fact that many appetites are genuinely undesirable. They are directed toward objects not worthy of the emotional force laid upon them. A man may insatiably crave a cigarette when there are none available, and be unable to function until he gets one. Appetites may be directed toward objects which lead to extremely undesirable consequences. A smoker may have a strong desire for cigarettes, though they may cause him cancer of the lung. Worst of all to Plato, some appetites have no limits, are inherently immoderate. The desire for wealth knows no bounds. The desire for power can grow to include the whole world. The trouble with immoderate appetites is that they are unsatisfiable. Nothing we can do can bring us all the money in the world. Are we then to be unhappy? The trouble with the Don Juan syndrome is not that Don Juan succeeds with many women. It is that he constantly is reminded of all the rest he will never conquer.

Appetites of themselves do not bring us goods. Too strong an appetite for an inferior object may distract us from more worth-while goals. A craving for some things may in the end turn out to cause us injury. An appetite which has no limits may lead not to satisfaction but to frustration and the torment of an imagination which overpowers our abilities. In every case, what is required is knowledge: knowledge of what is more important, knowledge of the consequences of activities, knowledge of what is in our power and what is not. For these reasons, Plato is led to claim that it is necessary for reason to control the appetites.

But it is by no means obvious that to *control* the appetites is to weaken them— except, of course, that they must be weaker than the force which controls them. It is far more a Christian than a Greek notion that appetites are sinful, and that we should therefore eliminate our desires as much as possible. It is difficult to imagine either a modern or an ancient Greek defending the view that our blood should run less quickly in our veins. Plato himself defines philosophy as the *love* of wisdom, and makes quite a bit of the emotional quality this love entails—provided it is directed to the right object. The idea of control of feelings suggests the weakening of these feelings only where there is but a single organ of control, and it is not itself a type of feeling.

Plato, however, does not propose that reason should control the appetites of itself. He in fact designs two modes of control. First, the philosopher shall be made ruler of the state, so that he may use the means of social control available: propaganda, manipulation, persuasion, patriotism, even on occasion the truth. Second, we have neglected the spirited element, which works with reason in the soul to control the appetites. The example Plato gives to explain this spirited element looks to a case where we angrily force ourselves to look at injustice to fan the flames of outrage. The spirited element is a form of indignation, perhaps even

what many of us call "conscience." When we feel a strong sense of outrage at
what we know is evil, then reason and indignation work together. Only together
can they control the appetites.

We may summarize this discussion as follows: Plato's view is that the
appetites of themselves are uncontrolled. There is no principle inherent within
them as appetites which could limit them. But reason and conscience together can
control and guide the appetites, not to eliminate them but to redirect them. Plato
uses the analogy of a chariot guided by the strong hand of reason, but propelled by
the horses of appetite. With no desires, how can a man act? But his desires are
alterable. Most interesting of all is Plato's realization that the alteration proceeds
under the guidance of reason, but with the aid of the spirited element *which is
also a mode of feeling*. Desires of themselves cannot produce what is valuable.
Knowledge and outrage are required also.

Plato's moral theory is almost the prototype of a rational morality. Yet we
have seen that it places a tremendous emphasis on feelings. What is fundamental
to Plato's position is the realization that feelings are often in conflict with one
another, and that a reconciliation requires reason and knowledge. In addition,
Plato sees that there are different *kinds* of feelings, which play differing roles in
moral decision. Both our desires and our moral sentiments play a role in such
decisions. But they are not equatable with each other. We may summarize this
last point as the realization that feelings are by no means as simple as they are
often taken to be. They are alterable and changeable. They arise and they pass,
and under specific and knowable circumstances. Until we know more about
the psychology of feeling, we are not ready to treat such feelings as the sole basis
of evaluation.

We will have to look fairly closely at the psychoanalytic theory of feelings
in the later chapters. It is worth noting here in passing but a single feature of
that theory—that feelings are not always conscious. A man may not be aware
of his own feelings. Such a view may strike us as odd, for a feeling of which
we are not conscious hardly seems to merit the name of a "feeling." Let us then
use the words "emotion," "passion," or "desire." The critical claim which
psychoanalysis makes paramount is that men are not aware of what they do nor of
what motivates them to do it. Suppose for a moment we neglect the strangeness of
this view, and simply consider its implications. A man may unconsciously desire to
punish his wife for a slight, and forget an important message which she should
have been given. What is important here is not the mechanism of forgetfulness, but
the problem which unconscious feelings create for evaluation. Remember, Hume's
argument is that only emotions can influence the will. What psychoanalysis
proposes is that unconscious and therefore unknown emotions can influence the
will. If so, we wonder how reason can in any sense prevail over these emotions.
If we literally do not know what moves us, we can hardly seek to correct our
motives and alter our decisions. What Freud has done to moral theory is to add as a
requirement to our knowledge of causes and consequences knowledge of our own
feelings as well, as a prerequisite for moral decision. We do not always know our

own desires. Therefore, one of the most important aims of reason must be to gain knowledge of our unconscious emotions. But we discover that what is unconscious tends to remain so, and to prevent reason from gaining the upper hand. This is a matter for later exploration.

C. Principles

The position that morality rests on a basis of principles alone is held by Kant, who makes a striking case for that position. We have touched on a small part of his argument in passing. Kant argues essentially from three principles. First, nothing is unqualifiedly good except a good will—that is, the *intent* to do what is right. No other conditions or states are good if attached to a man with a malicious intent. An evil genius is more dangerous than a more ordinary man. Happiness, understood by Kant in the sense of contentment or well-being, is the source of pride unless tempered by an intent to do what is good or right. The successful criminal who lives in peace and harmony with his neighbors who think him a successful businessman, but who in secret carries on all sorts of vicious activities, is a mixed bag of values. Even if we grant that his peace of mind is a pleasure to *him*, it is by no means an unqualified good, since it may be the source of many ills to others. A good will is indispensable even for being worthy of happiness. Only a good will is good in itself.

Kant's second and third points are derived from the *form* of moral principles, and the form alone. Consider the principle "thou shalt not lie." The law asserts that (1) lying is wrong *categorically*—that is, without qualification, without concern for consequences; and (2) lying is wrong for everyone without exception. Thus, Kant's second point is that an obligation "must carry with it absolute necessity." The moral law does not say that lying is wrong *if* a man wishes to be happy; that lying is wrong *for those* who are born into Western society; that lying is wrong *if* we wish to make others trust us. The form of the law asserts categorically and firmly that lying is plain wrong. On this basis, Kant can argue also that consequences are irrelevant to morals. For a concern for consequences is at best a concern for instrumental values. But instrumental values can never lead to a categorical obligation—that is, to an unqualified or intrinsic good. Thus, Kant is the source of the principle that "ought" cannot be derived from "is." No facts or consequences could obligate us without qualification to do anything at all.

The third point is that a moral law holds for everyone without exception. If it is wrong to lie, then it is wrong for anyone to lie. A thief may commit a crime, not on the basis that stealing is right, but attempting to make of himself an exception to the rule. But, Kant claims, the unique property of moral laws is that they permit no exceptions. A political law may distinguish between those who have property and those who do not. Only the first may vote. But moral laws are completely impersonal. "Thou shalt not kill" applies to anyone and everyone indifferently.

I hope that it is clear by now what Kant is trying to do. He looks to the form moral principles take when we appeal to them, particularly their imperative character. They are, he claims, always of the form "thou shalt" and "thou shalt not." They impose a categorical obligation which commands an absolute loyalty which brooks neither qualifications nor exceptions. Kant then asks how we can explain so absolute an obligation. It cannot be derived from consequences, nor from self-interest. The strength of Kant's theory is that he seeks to explain what seems so powerful in our moral lives—the imperative demands of our consciences. We will criticize his solution, but we will then be left with no simple explanation of the absolute loyalty we owe our moral principles.

If we cannot look to the consequences of our actions, where is there left to look? Here Kant offers an ingenious solution. It is necessary that a moral principle be binding on everyone. A good will, a will which intends what is right, will intend to follow a principle which everyone ought to follow also. But, Kant argues, not only is this a *necessary* condition of a good will. It is a *sufficient* condition as well. That is, to do what is right, we need do *no more* than seek to follow a principle which everyone ought to follow. Put in Kant's words, "I am never to act otherwise than so that I could also will that my maxim should become a universal law." This is the first formulation of the Categorical Imperative.

How this works can be made far clearer by an example. Take the principle we have used as a model: "thou shalt not lie." Suppose I want to know whether it would be right for me to tell a lie, if by so doing I might win a large inheritance. If it is right for me to lie, then it is right for everyone to lie. And if it is right for everyone to lie, then it must be possible that everyone might tell only lies. It must be possible for everyone to do what is right. We ask, then, would it be possible for everyone to tell only lies?

Now, it is very important that we be very clear as to what we are asking. We are *not* asking, "What would be the *consequences* if everyone told lies?" For Kant, morality does not come from looking to consequences, which cannot bring categorical obligations without exception. Rather, we are asking whether lying is the sort of thing which can *logically* be made a universal prescription. Kant argues that it is not. Lying, he claims, is not merely an error. It is a misrepresentation of the truth. It is a pretense at truth. If there is no truth, there can be no lies. If everyone ought to tell lies, then no one ought to tell the truth. Under such circumstances, lying would lose its meaning. It could pretend to no truth if no one ever told the truth. It would not be unfair to characterize this as a logical point about the concept of lying. It is relative to the concept of truth, and subordinate to it.

The argument so far is quite telling. It would seem that we may reject lying on the grounds that it could not constitute a principle which everyone could consider obligatory, and on purely logical grounds. The next question, however, is whether we can derive by the same mode of argument all our moral principles. Kant claims that we can. It is worth looking to one more of his examples. Consider a man with an exceptional talent. Would it be right for him to ignore it, and to spend his life in idleness and pleasure? Kant claims that it would not. His is a very stern morality of duty. But there is no logical contradiction involved in supposing that everyone might be equally idle and waste their abilities. (The consequences of their doing so would probably be unfortunate. For this reason, John Stuart Mill criticizes Kant for really looking to consequences, though denying that he does so. More of this in a moment.) Rather, Kant argues that a man cannot *will* or *intend* to neglect a talent "given him"—at least, not that such a neglect should be a universal principle of all conduct. Such an argument does not have the force of the first.

This last case brings us to several of the most serious difficulties which Kant faces. Kant's argument, if valid, entails that it is not right to neglect one of our talents and to pursue idleness instead. But what of a man who possesses two first-rate talents, each of which requires a total commitment? Suppose he is a talented pianist and a talented dancer as well. To engage himself in both is to become proficient in neither. The categorical imperative cannot in any way tell a man which talent he should develop. On Kant's argument, he should neglect neither. Yet to neglect neither is to neglect *both*.

We are in fact making a point about the *consequences* of activities, if not quite a clear one. The problem is just what it means to develop a faculty or to build a talent. It is generally true that in a single lifetime a man will not be able to develop many of his talents. We must make choices among our interests and our abilities. If we try to develop too many, we will develop few very deeply or strongly. But the truth we have just noted is an empirical truth, a *fact* if you will. We look to real consequences if we assert that a man may not do everything in a single lifetime. It is logically possible that he might have been able to do so.

We have, then, come to two criticisms of Kant's moral theory. The moral principles which are categorically and universally binding may in some circumstances conflict. To use a modified version of an example Plato gives: if I am asked by a friend who is in a rage to return his gun so that he may kill his wife, I must refuse. Yet in general terms, "thou shalt not keep what does not belong to you." The point is that I have been placed in a situation where the two principles "thou shalt not steal" and "thou shalt not kill" have come into conflict. The first difficulty for Kant's theory is that it in no way tells us how to resolve such a problem. The second is that we note that the problem arises only by looking to consequences—the consequences in this case of my returning the gun I borrowed. This latter difficulty arises especially where we are concerned with notions such as developing talents or with being ungenerous. What is wrong looks to the fruits of such actions, and necessarily.

The third and perhaps most devastating criticism is intimately related to the two we have already noted. We wish to point out that it may be wrong to waste a talent for the sake of sheer pleasure, but not where a greater talent is developed. It may be wrong to tell a lie, but not wrong if it would save a life. We are made uncomfortable with the austerity of Kant's theory, in which principles with no qualifications whatsoever are taken as models. "Thou shalt not tell a lie." Never? Under no circumstances? Kant has been criticized for being too pure and austere, for developing a moral theory at a far remove from the ordinary moral practices he thought he was explaining. Such a criticism merely notes the wide gulf between the categorical imperative and everyday moral decisions.

We may, however, put the same argument in a far more decisive form. We note that the categorical imperative tells us that we must make our maxims of conduct universal laws. Consider a general law of the following form: "thou shalt not lie except to save a life." Is this prohibited by the categorical imperative? Not in any obvious way. We have a general law which could be binding on everyone. It is simply not so general in scope as the principle "thou shalt not lie." But Kant nowhere defines a criterion which relates to scope. We therefore have two alternatives: Either all principles will be as general as possible, with no exceptions whatsoever, and we violate most men's sense of moral practice. Or else we will permit some exceptions as described. Now, if we pick the first alternative, we will find the minor inconvenience that no meaning can be assigned to the phrase "as general as possible." Consider the verb "to lyxed," which I define to mean "to lie except when a death will be the result." We now have the law "thou shalt not lyxed," seemingly of as great a generality as any other, at least in sheer form. The whole subject of generality and scope is a logical muddle, and will not help us very much.

But if we choose the second alternative, and allow some exceptions, then we have destroyed the whole Kantian system. For consider the following maxim: "thou shalt not lie unless your name is Harvey Freeman, you were born on June 6, 1938, in North Platte, Nebraska, etc." Now, such a principle can be universalized, for it applies to one person only. The difficulty here is that there is no logical procedure for specifying the degree of generality required of moral principles. But if we cannot so specify this generality, then we may define principles which have application functionally to but one person.

All of the difficulties we have considered are usually dealt with by looking to circumstances and consequences. In the final analysis, Kant's attempt to found ethics on principles alone is a splendid one, but it fails. Consequences arise and necessarily so in the making of moral decisions. What we must gather from Kant, however, is the importance of an unqualified loyalty in moral decisions. Some principles are worth fighting for, even dying for. Moral decision is something more than a dispassionate calculation of consequences and results. It looks to a total and vitally important loyalty. We have not yet found the source of such a loyalty to principle, at least not in instrumental values.

D. Intuition

One possibility that has been proposed is that we possess an intuition of the good or of what is right. Indeed, it is possible to think of Kant's theory as a form of intuitionism. That is, we in some sense know directly and without calculation or deliberation what is right. The capacity of mind to grasp the categorical imperative is a purely rational and direct capacity. We collect no evidence. Logical analysis of the form of a maxim we are considering is sufficient. Men sometimes speak of our "logical intuitions." Kant's entire theory is founded on such an intuition of the principle of noncontradiction. A principle is a moral one only if it can be generalized without fear of logical contradiction.

The stumbling block for a moral theory grounded on the forms of reason alone is that it provides us with laws of considerable generality, but with no way of relating them to concrete circumstances except in an implausible way. Logical intuitions are inherently general. Moral decisions call for specific and particular choices, in concrete circumstances. An alternative, then, is to suppose that we possess intuitions of what is good or bad, right or wrong, in such concrete circumstances. Such intuitions are so particular that it is by no means implausible that we think of them as inner *perceptions* of what is to be done. We "see" what is right, just as we see our hand before our eyes. Perhaps another analogy may be even more apt. We grasp right and wrong as we remember what we read or what we said yesterday—directly.

It is important to understand the nature of the intuitionist's position. It arises from a dissatisfaction with the other grounds of moral conviction. Facts do not of themselves generate obligations. Principles are too general to provide a basis for concrete decisions. There are no emotions which are common to all men, which might of themselves generate obligations. Nevertheless, there is a fundamental difference between emotivism and intuitionism. The emotivist denies that we *know* right from wrong. On Ayer's view, the statement "lying is wrong" is not a claim which might be true or false. It is merely an expression of sentiments. It is not even a claim about the attitudes of the speaker. Such a theory in effect makes moral conflicts merely a conflict of attitudes, and not conflicts of position. "Capital punishment is wrong" and "capital punishment is right" are not truly contradictory, as they seem to be. They are merely expressions of different attitudes, imperatives to differing effect.

The intuitionist is unhappy with all the grounds of moral decision proposed, but he is even more unhappy with the emotivist solution. He regards it as throwing out the baby with the bath water. He wishes to preserve an objective sense in which lying is wrong and not right, something other than mere attitude. Facts do not substantiate our conviction that lying is wrong. Nevertheless, we do *know* that lying is wrong. The solution can only be to rest our knowledge of good and bad, right and wrong, on an intuition. The attempt is akin to many theories of religious faith. Since religion is supposed to provide knowledge of an inner truth, yet a knowledge insupportable by facts, it is necessary to invent another way to this knowledge.

The problem with all forms of intuitionism is essentially the same, though it can be dramatized in different forms. We may note, for example, that religious intuitions have differed markedly for men in different cultures, and even within a single culture. As William James points out, the varieties of religious experience and of religious belief are considerable. How then claim that there is a particular

religious truth, to be reached through faith or revelation? So also, men differ in
their moral convictions, often quite heatedly, and usually quite sincerely. There
is no way for intuition alone to settle a genuine difference in conviction. But the
intuitionist seemingly is committed to the view that we can know through
intuition what truly is wrong or right. If his position is that our intuitions tell us
only what is right for each of us, and not for others, then we have lapsed into the
relativist position: my claim that capital punishment is wrong does not contradict
your claim that capital punishment is right. Extreme moral relativism has its
appeal, but it cannot be thought of as a theory of *knowledge*. Moreover, as we shall
see, it suffers from some major defects.

The criticism of the last paragraph is a powerful one, provided we assume
that differences of conviction are possible. Certainly there are differences among
men in moral beliefs and in religious convictions. But suppose there were not:
would that justify our belief in moral or religious intuition? In the Middle Ages,
everyone worth mentioning was a Christian. Was there then at work an intuition
which we no longer possess? Obviously there are other ways of explaining agreement than by appeal to intuition. There is a more general criticism of intuition as
a form of knowledge than we have so far considered.

The problem is not so much with the claim that we see, perceive, or grasp
some truths directly. We simply look and see the tree in front of our eyes, that
$2 + 3 = 5$, even that the base angles of an isosceles triangle are equal. But in all
these cases, what we intuit directly is continuous with what we can show by other
means. We can touch the tree, take its photograph, check out its location by asking
others. We can prove mathematical theorems in many different ways. If we are
to make an error in intuition, then we may detect it by using another method of
deriving the same truth. Nothing is more clear about the history of mankind than
that men have believed many false claims on the basis of intuition or direct
perception. Intuitions are not vicious where there exist means of checking them out.

But moral intuitions are in their very nature isolated from everything else.
Sometimes men come to different conclusions about what is wrong or right.
Can the intuition alone provide a test of who is correct? Clearly not. The very
nature of intuition here is to deprive an intuition of a base in evidence and
experience. Imagine that what we really mean by saying that "capital punishment
is wrong" is that it will have deleterious consequences for men in their lives.
Here we indeed may confirm an immediate intuition by looking to see what
happens in the future. But we are not here taking an intuitionist position. We are
rather admitting that we often appeal to an intuition for immediate action—but
the confirmation rests on the consequences brought about by action.

E. Society

To this point we have looked for the basis of value in fairly abstract elements
of human experience—facts, feelings, laws, and intuitions. We should not overlook
a very different approach to evaluation which does not fit easily into the categories

we have employed so far. I have in mind here the not uncommon view that moral principles are derived from social relations, from the fact that men live together in societies. Certainly such an approach looks to facts. Its uniqueness comes from its emphasis on a particular kind of fact—the fact of social relatedness—and from looking to special kinds of principles which are grounded in the relations of men to each other. In its crudest form, this approach denies the legitimacy of moral principles for men who do not live within society. In a more elegant version, it asserts that the facts which matter in moral decision are not facts concerning individuals alone and their feelings or rational faculties, but the facts of relations among individuals.

The position we are addressing often takes a specific dramatic form. We are called upon to imagine a world in which men do not inhabit social relations—a "state of nature." In such a condition, there are, Hobbes tells us, no moral principles at all. Justice does not exist except within a social order. Why ? Because principles of right and wrong are meaningful only where there exists a common power. Completely ignoring personal convictions and the sense of duty which most men experience, Hobbes looks only to the power which *enforces* a moral law. What is implicit here is the conviction that there is no basis for moral decisions other than the power which enforces obedience to common laws. The only ground for a moral conviction is the fear we bear toward the authority which will punish us for disobedience. The only basis for obedience to moral principle, therefore, is the social order and its use of power.

In the state of nature, then, men may follow no moral principles. They seek their self-interest only. But, Hobbes points out, the state of nature is dangerous, chaotic, and fruitless, "the life of man, solitary, poor, nasty, brutish, and short." With no central authority, men must fear each other, for others may attack them, steal from them, even kill them. Perhaps Hobbes has a pessimistic sense of the natural evil of mankind. More likely, he is aware of the unrestrained capacity of men to covet things where no limits are set to their appetites. No single man is so powerful and superior to the rest as to be free from fear. Men must devote so much of their energy to defense as to have none for pleasure or for progress.

The solution, then, is to seek a society in which there exists an authority so powerful as, through fear, to end the preying of men upon each other, and to bring about a stable society. Hobbes seems not to believe that a tyrannical despot could make the conditions of life for most men worse than the state of nature, which Hobbes clearly thinks of as the worst condition imaginable for men. Almost any society is better than the state of nature. Nevertheless, Hobbes agrees that where a man's life is directly threatened, he may operate from a condition of war against the authority of the state—though, if he is alone, much good that will do him. In point of fact, however, if many men are threatened in their persons by the state, they may oppose it and even destroy it. Revolution is not taken lightly by Hobbes, and almost never justified. In this sense, he is a sober conservative.

We must look a bit more closely at the case Hobbes presents. In the state of

nature, there are no obligations, no moral laws, no right and wrong. But the state
of nature is very bad. Men therefore join together in a common cause, and under a
common authority which then both promulgates the law and enforces it. Clearly,
however, the ruler of the state may promulgate foolish and destructive laws, and
enforce them badly—laws which lead to his own demise and even death, for
example. How can we move from a condition of no laws whatsoever to one in
which it is right to obey the laws of the state? It may be smart to follow the laws.
It may be good or beneficial to obey the law. It is not easy to see how we can derive
the principle that we ought to obey the law from Hobbes' premises. If we can get
away with breaking the law, why not do so? Hobbes' argument is basically an
argument from self-interest: it is to a man's benefit to live in an orderly society.
But it may be even more to his benefit to live in an orderly society and to cheat a
bit without getting caught.

In order to avoid such a conclusion, Hobbes is forced to modify his view that
there is no right and wrong in the state of nature. There is, he claims, one right in
that state—the right to self-preservation. Clearly there is no way of deriving this
right from the conditions of the state of nature. Hobbes is forced to blur the
transition from the *fact* that men often desire their own self-preservation, even the
view that it is *good* to preserve one's life, to the position that men have the *right* to
life. But Hobbes is wrong. There is no such right. A stronger man may kill
another and violate no right in the state of nature. A man may kill himself and
violate no right. On the other hand, if the smart thing to do is what a man has a
right to do, then even in the state of nature men would have no right to take their
neighbor's possessions, if that would be injurious to themselves. Hobbes needs
this right of self-preservation, for he argues that in forming a society, men contract
their rights and powers to the sovereign, in return for safety. In the final analysis,
Hobbes' argument is that it is right to obey the laws of the state because it is
right to be secure in one's life.

The upshot of this entire discussion is that we have discovered that the
model of a state of nature without obligations and morals is misleading in a
fundamental respect. If there is no basis for judgments of right and wrong in the
state of nature, there is none within society either. Put another way, if men make
no evaluations when they are alone, they cannot make any in a social context either.
If there were no other men in the world, the last survivor would still ask himself
what he ought to do at any given time, what he preferred for breakfast, whether
he should allow himself to get fat or whether he should exercise regularly. No
doubt he might decide that he ought to do exactly what he felt like doing at any
moment—though if there were wild animals around that could be a risky decision.
But he could avoid all evaluative decisions no more than can a man who lives
among other men. There are obvious consequences of one course of action as
compared to another. There are the benefits of adherence to principle, and the
virtues as well as the risks of loyalty to ideals.

Nevertheless, there is a fundamental difference in evaluative judgments reached in and out of a social context. It is not, however, so obviously a difference in type or even method of evaluation. Rather, there is a critical difference in circumstances. Many of our moral principles concern our relations with other men. Thou shalt not lie to *others*. Thou shalt not steal what belongs to *others*. Of the moral problems in our first chapter, many would simply disappear as irrelevant to the circumstances and conditions of the last survivor on earth. There would be no conscription or army. There would be no one to perform an abortion, no one to steal from, no one to consider sexual relations with, no one to object to one's lack of personal hygiene.

Yet if the survivor were a pregnant woman, the possibility of an abortion would face her with especial poignancy, assuming she could succeed in giving one to herself. Should she bring a child into the final agony of the human race? As for sex, there are private acts which may be worth performing, though frowned upon by many. And a last survivor may find that he preserves his last shreds of dignity only by trying to keep clean. It is by no means true that moral principles have no bearing on the life of a man alone.

Social relations set the conditions of moral decision and are vitally relevant to many of the important consequences of a decision. A man without friends or loved ones may neglect the consequences upon their lives of his committing suicide. A married man with three young children must consider what his suicide will mean to his wife and children—and suicide is a relatively private act. As for the circumstances of his decision, how often does the thought of suicide arise for men whose depression is not enhanced by their encounters with others? The surreptitious and infantile wish to punish one's parents or family by killing oneself is all too well known. In addition, society has taken certain safeguards against suicide, and a would-be suicide must take them into account—though he is usually incapable of doing so. Finally, failed suicide attempts are far more common than successes, on some interpretations looking to the hope that the agent will be given help by hospitalization or therapy.

We must conclude, then, that social relations are among the most vital elements of moral decisions. But they are only a part of decision-making. What is presupposed in the first place is the capacity of men to make decisions and to perform evaluations, which they might do in or out of society—though, of course, to different ends in either case.

F. Norms

Mentioning therapy brings Freud's theory of moral principles to mind, a theory notably akin to Hobbes', but worth noting for its differences. Like Plato, Freud postulates that the soul or psyche of man is to be regarded as tripartite. The *id* consists of the primal source of energy, is mainly unconscious, and seeks pleasure or satisfaction of its desires only. The *ego* is the rational element in man, which must reconcile the obstacles and conditions of the real world with the desires of the *id*. Clearly we have already before us a theory of evaluation. The ego must determine what desires can be effectively satisfied and how. It must endeavor to substitute preferable courses of action for infantile but destructive wishes. The passage from infancy to adulthood is a process of strengthening the ego with respect to the id so that more enduring, reliable, and long-range goods can be achieved.

Like Plato, Freud is led to the conclusion that in principle the ego is not equal to the task, especially in a civilized and complex society. Various prohibitions, derived both from one's parents and one's sense of what is permissible, are internalized powerfully in the *superego*. There are installed taboos against incest, for example, which the ego alone would not be able to defend against the natural desires of a child for its parents and siblings. In other words, the social relations of the developing person, especially within the family, promote the internalization of certain principles—obligations and taboos—and create a sense of guilt and shame. If we identify the restrictions of the superego with moral laws, then moral laws are derived virtually entirely from social relations alone.

However, Freud's is not a theory which tells us how to choose among the variety of constraints within the superego. He is concerned that the sense of guilt men feel in modern societies can become oppressive, even to the extent of destroying the quality of life civilized society is supposed to provide. The superego, however, does not choose its taboos. The ego, then, is given yet another task—to reconcile the demands of the superego with both the primary desires and the realities of the world. The future of civilization rests upon the ability of the ego to meet this obligation.

Psychoanalysis is often ambiguous on some vitally important matters. With respect to the superego, Freud on the one hand wants to do no more than define the mechanisms which explain the sense of duty men feel toward their moral obligations. Like Kant, Freud is struck by the power of our sense of duty, and seeks to explain how it operates in psychological terms. (Perhaps it is no accident that both Freud and Kant were German.) There is no evaluation in such a description of the rightness or wrongness of what we take our duties to be. Freud is merely arguing that the way we *learn* our moral principles is through relations with other people. Of course, we may learn the most vicious as well as the most worthwhile principles in the same fashion.

Freud himself, however, wants to argue that some of our moral convictions are destructive and indefensible, particularly the inflexible regard in which they are held. Here it is not the superego speaking, nor is it a mere mechanism of internalization. It is the rational consideration of consequences which leads Freud to criticize the results of a society that is too repressive in its moral convictions, too inconsiderate of the primary and essential desires. We have, then, a theoretical *description* of how social norms are installed in individual conscience, and in addition an *evaluation* of both these norms and their inflexibility in terms of their consequences for the men who hold them.

A recent trend in the social sciences, however, has been toward a species of *positivism* in which evaluative judgments are no longer considered acceptable. Anthropologists and sociologists see themselves as engaged only in describing and analyzing the norms they find in the societies they study, but as professionally irresponsible if they attempt to evaluate such norms in any way. We find ourselves, then, with a variety of social practices, and, in addition, a fairly elaborate theory of how norms are formed, institutionalized, and instilled in young people. It is tempting to look no further, and to define moral principles as principles which structure behavior and institutions in specific ways. Such an approach leads to the view that values are nothing but the norms of society, as installed in the behavior of individual members of that society. The basis of value now is nothing more than the norms of a society, as they are internalized in the actions of the members of that society.

The strength of this position resides in two facts about the moral decisions men make. First, moral norms do vary from society to society, at least to some extent. Second, most men make their moral decisions in a rather habitual and direct appeal to the principles they and others around them believe in. If we look to no other grounds for evaluation than social norms, then we explain the variety of moral practices as a mere fact of social life, and we also pay due respect to the ordinary sense of moral practice as adherence to a code accepted generally within a society. One of the most striking features of this theory of value is that it affords a means of settling disputes, at least in some cases. We simply appeal to the general code accepted by members of our society. When men speak of "common decency," that is probably what they have in mind.

The weakness of the position is revealed when we find ourselves in a situation where the code is insufficient to provide a decision, where there are genuine differences which the code cannot resolve, or where a youth in the society complains that social norms are at bottom arbitrary. Norms are challenged. Sometimes we find that our society has no clear principles applicable in complex situations. Sometimes we find that we are led at best to a conflict of principles, with no means of selecting among them. The basic problem is that the norms of a society are a set of principles which are at best of general usefulness, but which may be quite unhelpful in a vital situation which requires a decision.

In the end, the positivist position is a species of relativism—though of a social and not an individual character. Like all relativisms, it makes a virtue of differences precisely when what we need most is agreement. Two societies meet head on in a religious war to the death. The problem is not whether each *believes* it is in the right. The problem is whether it is really good to fight to the death over religious matters. The two societies differ in their religious principles. Yet they find themselves in a common situation, and may be able to find a common solution to their travail, one truly better than would be possible if they looked no further than the fact of their disagreement. The consequences of their disagreement may be something they can agree on. They may also agree on the desirability of avoiding them.

On the other hand, moral laws are installed within a society as its most sacred principles. In this respect, social norms are among the most important facts an individual must consider in his decisions—both with respect to circumstances and with respect to the consequences of violating these norms. In addition, there is indeed a process of internalization or socialization in which social norms come to influence individual feelings in vital ways. Further, these norms are usually of a general character, and call men to utmost loyalty to principles and ideals. Finally, these norms do indeed look to and even define the relations men bear to each other within a society. We will not be able to casually dismiss norms as arbitrary, for they enter into every other facet of the making of moral decisions.

G. Religion

We have not yet touched on the ground many people hold is the only one on which moral principles can be based, that of religious or divine law. To many devout people, the dictates of their religion determine the moral principles by which they must live. Either the religion they belong to determines as a social institution certain acceptable practices, or the source of the law is rooted in the divine itself. The confusion surrounding moral principles makes many people desire an absolute and unshakable ground. Only a divine order can be secure in this sense. There are men whose piety leads them to believe that no atheist can be a man of moral principle. Dostoievski has Ivan Karamazov in *The Brothers Karamazov* argue that except for God and divine law, anything is permissible. Yet it is no accident that Ivan's position proves to be one not of piety but of nihilism.

The attempt to ground moral convictions in the tenets of religion may be viewed in two ways. In the first place, we may consider the religion in its function as a social institution. The principles to follow are those which are professed by those who practice the religion. In this sense, religion provides exactly the same ground as the norms of society, and has exactly the same plausibility. Both look to the actual practices and appeals of men who engage in certain private and public practices. The particular strength of the religious basis for morals is the intimate relation in so many religions between religious beliefs and moral practices. It is certainly a fact about religions that virtually all of them maintain a close connection between the profession of piety and the adherence to certain moral standards of performance.

The problems for both views are the same. Social norms and the moral principles of religions differ. There are many different religions, and although they maintain a striking similarity in moral principles, the similarity is not identity. Where religions conflict, we have a conflict which offers no resolution. There is no appeal beyond the authority which has defined the principles to be followed. We may dispute over which authority is superior. But such a procedure is usually in vain. Worst of all, it neglects the genuine moral issues, and addresses only the authority and its right to serve as an authority. Thus, Protestants and Catholics may dispute the moral validity of contraception. But a Catholic who appeals to nothing but the authority of the Pope inevitably must ignore the controversy and the hatred generated by it. Yet many issues which we feel merit a tolerance of differences depend on our understanding that such conflict may be the worst evil of all. Such a conclusion does not easily follow within an authoritarian situation, unless the authority is moved to decree that tolerance will be practiced.

An additional problem is the one we have seen recur in all cases of a strict and principled sense of duty. The moral principles of a religion are often strictly formulated, and of considerable generality. As we have seen, Kant takes as models the commandments from the Old Testament: "thou shalt not lie," "thou shalt not kill." Yet neither are such strictly formulated principles faithful to our wish to remain flexible and responsive to circumstances, nor can they resolve all moral difficulties. Principles often come into conflict. A morality of principle based on authority, especially the unavailable word of God, can resolve neither the question of exceptions nor that of conflict among principles by appeal to the divine alone. It must permit a human being as authority to make judgments out of his own moral capacities. And if he can do so, so can anyone else.

There are people who do not merely base their own moral decisions on religious authority, but are convinced that the only defensible ground for morals is a religious one. It follows that an atheist cannot have secure moral convictions, which is simply false. Unfortunately, the need for a religious ground of morality tends to reflect a deeper conviction that morality is essentially based on fear—the fear of divine retribution, of eternal damnation. Such a conviction is probably itself utterly the opposite of a genuine moral sensibility, which believes that one must do what is right because it is right.

A religion may be regarded in a second sense, not as a social institution, but as a loyalty to the divine. Here, morality is an obedience to the tenets of God, whose infinite goodness has brought him to decree for man the principles he is to live by. Clearly, the problems of conflict and of exceptions will still arise. But an even greater difficulty must be faced as well, which looks to the basis of the values men are to live by. We are supposing here that God's will is being offered as a basis for life and action. We are supposing that we are to do what is right *because* God has decreed it. It is important to realize that the reverse may also be considered: we are to follow the decrees of God because they are right.

Plato's *Euthyphro* is a dialogue which addresses precisely this issue. Euthyphro has asserted himself to be a pious man, who therefore does what the gods love. But, Socrates asks, do the gods love what is good because it is good, or is it good because they love it? Clearly there is nothing about their love which *makes* something good. If the gods loved murder or torture, that would not make them good. Rather, we must suppose that the gods will despise such things because they are evil. We are assuming, then, that goodness comes first and can be recognized as such. Such a conclusion does not entail that we should disobey the gods. It does entail that we understand our obedience either to be without goodness, or to be derived from our knowledge that what the gods wish us to do is itself good.

Kant puts the point in another way. A moral obligation is one which we understand to be intrinsic, which we follow because we ought to, because it is right. But if we obey the principle "thou shalt not kill" solely because it is commanded by the divine, then it is not obeyed from a concern for its *rightness*, but only because we are obedient. In other words, a command given to us by another being than ourselves, even a god, is merely a *command*. But it cannot be a moral obligation, which we can follow only from a sense of its inherent rightness.

This last point may be formulated in yet another way. We may obey the will of God, but only if that will is good and because it is good. This presupposes that we understand the nature of goodness in the first place, and can understand that God is good accordingly. Religion, therefore, cannot provide a basis in itself for our moral convictions. What religion can do is to stabilize and regularize a whole group of norms. But so can any authority, even a society itself without the trappings of the miracles, mysteries, and the authority of religion.

H. Nihilism

The greatest danger inherent in authoritarian moralities, and especially that of religion, is the despair and resignation which are generated by a loss of faith in the authority. "God is dead," we hear men say, in imitation of Nietzsche. But Nietzsche's position was that God as authority is dead, so man must choose. Man must *create* value. Easier said than done! To far too many people, the abandonment of religion is also the abandonment of moral principles one can be sure of. Too often, being sure is nothing other than being obedient. When the authority in whom we place our trust has lost our loyalty or our respect, we may have no other source of conviction. The decline of religion, then, means a despair which is nihilistic. There is no basis for values. Our convictions mean nothing. As Ivan Karamazov is led to say, if God is no longer our fortress, "anything is permissible."

But is *anything* permissible? Ivan comes eventually to see that he has been the instrument of his father's death, though not his direct murderer. His collapse into a coma is no surprise at all, for it is obvious that not just anything is permissible *to him*. He cannot endure the sense of his own guilt. There may be no God Ivan can respect, but it does not follow from this that Ivan is without firm values.

We must be clear in our minds as to what follows from the position that *anything is permissible*. Taken literally, it means that anything is just as good as anything else, that any act is just as good as any other, therefore, that nothing is preferable to anything else. In the *Republic*, Plato has Thrasymachus take the position that "justice is the interest of the stronger." Socrates then asks him whether the stronger may not be mistaken about what is *truly* in his interest. Must not even the tyrannical ruler of the state think about what will truly benefit him? If so, then not anything goes. Even a tyrant must evaluate his actions in some terms. Thus, not even the most blatant interpretation of the maxim "might

makes right'' can be understood to mean that simply *anything* which is achieved
by force is as good as anything else. A war fought and won may be the beginning
of the downfall of the winning side. For this reason, Thrasymachus must deny
that the stronger as ruler can err. He does want to say that any action is as good
as any other in a cosmic sense.

But do we need a cosmic sense ? Do we need God ? If any action or thing is
as good as any other, then we cannot make any choices. We cannot even pursue a
desire intentionally. We simply exist in an unthinking and unspeaking state.
We cannot even try to think, for to think is to form preferences. Even to try is to
have preferences and to form values. A man without values is no man. He is a
mere lump of protoplasm, unable even to act, unable to form an intention *which
is always a preference*. He will move as he is impelled to. But he may question no
impulse, nor substitute one for another, since all is the same.

This condition of valuelessness is not impossible. But it cannot be pursued
or defended. To pursue it is to prefer it. To defend it is to value it. Thrasymachus
cannot defend the position he seems to prefer, because his preference is antithetic
to what he claims is best—to be without preferences.

Valuelessness is not despair. For despair is a sadness that there is no secure
foundation for morals, a sadness that one cannot have what one desires. Nihilism
is beset by a fundamental self-contradiction. It despairs at a condition it abhors—
and then escapes into a denial of all value. Ivan is so unhappy at the suffering in
the world that he asserts that nothing matters. But the suffering does matter!
Evaluation is a fact of human experience. There are better and worse things.
There are even better and worse forms of evaluation. Nihilism is one of the worst,
as shown by its consequences.

Nihilism takes many forms which are not as extreme as the denial of all
values. The most interesting of all of them is the nihilism which leads to relativism.
Here we admit that men have preferences, but we deny that any person's preferences are superior to any other's. Clearly this nihilism has many of the same
problems as the more extreme form. In fact, we do prefer some values to others,
some lives to others, some ways of life to others. The consequences of relativism
can lead to a tolerant attitude to other men, and perhaps be quite good in this
respect. But relativism can also provide no means whatsoever of settling a conflict
between men, even a trivial one. That is not very good at all. All of the problems
of nihilism come down to a simple point: we arrive quickly at a condition where
we have no idea of how to choose what is better. It is difficult to grasp the virtues
of a despairing resignation which induces paralysis in thought and action, or even
worse, a blind striking out where one has no real preferences.

I. Decision

The entire search for a basis of value may be summarized as a search for a
way of arriving at a secure conviction as to what is right and wrong, good and bad.

There is no more telling account of the various ways of securing conviction than Charles Sanders Peirce's description of four ways of "fixing belief." There is the method of *tenacity*, or holding onto a position no matter what. One asks no questions, one seeks no answers. There is the method of *authority*, which is exactly what it sounds like. The method of tenacity often does not serve a man well if he is in genuine doubt, or where there are strong disagreements. Men seek views they can share with others. If many men follow a single authority, they strengthen each other's views. There is the *a priori* method, based on reason or some special insight or intuition. Peirce criticizes this on the simplest grounds: many of the strongest convictions men have held on the basis of intuition have proven false. Nothing is more treacherous than intuition.

Finally there is the method of *inquiry*. This is the only method which looks to evidence, which criticizes its own conclusions, which has room for error. Peirce points out that in fact the method of tenacity is far superior as a method of avoiding doubt to the method of inquiry—if it works. But where we can no longer maintain our convictions tenaciously, then our doubts can be laid to rest effectively only through inquiry. Where we have no doubts as to what is right and wrong, we may proceed tenaciously, following authority, or even by intuition. But if a genuine doubt assails us, then it is rational only to engage in investigation, to look to the facts, to review the principles in light of the facts, to consider our own feelings and the feelings of others, and finally to remember that we live in society, amidst its norms and its members. A moral decision is called for when we are not sure of what we should do. There is no reason to suppose that we will find out easily. Worst of all, there is no reason to suppose that we will not make a mistake in our conclusions.

Here is the strange nature of moral decisions. They are often of utmost importance, where mistakes may have vital consequences. We seek, then, to eliminate the possibility of error. But if we choose the methods of tenacity, authority, or intuition, then we eliminate the possibility of recognizing error while at the same time making the chance of unfortunate results far greater. The man who believes without further thought that he ought to obey laws without question may find himself a party to monstrous crimes, if the laws are made by evil men. Only an open-minded method of investigation into the relevant issues can effectively lessen the chance of error. Yet the method of inquiry depends on the frequent discovery of our own past mistakes. In moral decisions we can tolerate mistakes very little. Yet we have the hope of minimizing the risks of error only through a method which calls upon us to look for errors constantly and to find ways of avoiding them.

Moral decisions, then, are extremely risky. No wonder they make us so uncomfortable. They are risky because they involve extremely complex issues. They are risky because we must keep an open mind. Without open-mindedness, we ignore possibilities which make a great difference. But with an open mind, we frequently cast ourselves into confusion, and undermine our loyalties. Too great a loyalty to principle generates a purity that blinds us to consequences. Too great a concern for the future blinds us to the present and its desperate urgency. All of these issues are the lifeblood of moral decision. There is no one basis for evaluation. There is rather an open method of decision which looks to all the elements we have considered, each in its place.

Having come to this conclusion, we make ready for a new beginning. We look once again at the elements of moral decision, not as determinants in themselves of such a decision, but as facets of a complex procedure for making such a decision.

QUESTIONS

1. Could anyone argue that facts are *irrelevant* to moral decisions? Develop such an argument and criticize it.
2. How would the existence of unconscious feelings affect our moral judgments, and the validity of our decisions?
3. If social norms are not completely determinative of moral decisions, explain what function they serve. Can they be wholly ignored?
4. Suppose it were a fact that basic norms differed from culture to culture. Does it follow that moral principles are relative to different cultures?
5. What are the differences between an intuitionist and a religious theory of the basis of moral values, other than the significance of the divine?
6. How would you argue with a cannibal that cannibalism is wrong? Do you believe such an argument could be decisive or convincing?
7. If there were a war, and complete social collapse, would morality still make sense?
8. Of what moral importance is the feeling of revulsion we may have toward certain actions, such as sexual perversions? What if we lack such feelings?
9. Could a society be founded on the principle that everyone ought to steal from others?
10. If religion cannot serve as a basis for moral decision, does this mean that a religious person who thinks it can is not a moral or good person?

SELECTED READINGS

The readings which are the textual sources for most contemporary thought in ethics are the following:

Plato, *Republic.*

Aristotle, *Nicomachean Ethics*, I.

Hobbes, *Leviathan*, Chs. xiii–xxx.

Spinoza, *Ethics*, III, IV.

Hume, *Treatise*, Book III, Part I.

Kant, *Fundamental Principles of the Metaphysics of Morals*.

Nietzsche, *Beyond Good and Evil*.

G. Moore, *Principia Ethica*, I.

A. J. Ayer, *Language, Truth and Logic*, rev. ed., 1936, Oxford University or Dover.

J. Dewey, *Human Nature and Conduct*, 1922. Modern Library.

and J. H. Tufts, *Ethics*, 1938, Holt.

S. Freud, *Civilization and Its Discontents*.

F. Dostoievski, *Notes from Underground*. A wonderful literary treatment of nihilism.

See also the readings which follow later chapters on special topics of interest.

III. FACTS

OVER THE past decade or so, a growing number of philosophers have become critical of too casual a reference to *facts*. Yet as short a time ago as 1921, Wittgenstein could remark in the opening of his *Tractatus Logico-Philosophicus*, "the world is the totality of facts, not of things." A good part of twentieth century philosophy has revolved around some major contrasts with facts: theories versus facts, interpretations versus facts, beliefs versus facts, and values versus facts. All of these contrasts depend on a well defined conception of facts, and of facts which may be obtained independent of theories, interpretations, beliefs, or values. As we will see, if we look too closely at them, facts begin to blur before our eyes, and merge with what we normally contrast them with.

On the other hand, to deny altogether that there are facts is to lapse into the worst sort of nihilism, if what is meant is that there are no truths which men must accept or else label themselves fools. A growing strain of disenchantment with scientific knowledge has led many young people to a cynical view of knowledge and understanding. They claim that every opinion is as justified as any other, as good as any other. There are no facts to be reported as news. All reporting is interpretation. And with the facts so also seem to go expertness and all forms of skill. Is it really true that any man's opinion is equally good in medicine, in engineering, in repairing a stalled automobile? If not, why suppose that any man's opinion is as good as any other's on economic policy, or on designing a school system? Facts are difficult to analyze and to define. But we must not carry our understanding of such difficulties to such an extreme as to lose all grounds for action and understanding.

Let us postpone this issue for awhile. Certainly for a naive moral agent, and even for a rather sophisticated one, there are facts he must consider in his deliberations. We shall assume that he is correct in his view, and engage at first only to determine the variety of facts of importance to moral decisions, and to categorize them in some definite ways. In the first chapter, I proposed a rather to consequences. Let us begin with that.

A. Circumstances

A man finds a wallet filled with money in the street. The moral problem he poses to himself is whether he should return it to the owner whose name is written inside. In order even to deliberate on such a matter, there are certain facts he must consider, which define the problem for him. First, the man involved has *found* the money. He has not, for example, seen the owner drop the wallet. There is a genuine difference between finding a lost wallet, and watching the owner drop it. A different example will make this clear. Suppose what is found is an inexpensive umbrella belonging to someone from another city. It may not be worth either the expense or the time to send it back to the owner. Yet keeping it or even discarding it would not here be stealing. If we saw the owner drop it, however, keeping the umbrella would be wrong.

Second, the wallet contains a sum of money. The exact sum can be determined in a straightforward manner. It is important to realize, however, that the sum alone is not very helpful in determining what should be done with it. Suppose the man who has lost the wallet is a millionaire, and the contents amount to $11. Suppose also the man who finds the wallet is an extremely busy neurosurgeon. Is it worth his valuable time to return a trifling sum to a man who probably hasn't even noticed the loss? I am not suggesting the physician should keep the money. Perhaps that would be a form of theft. But he might donate it to the nearest poor person, to a charity patient, even throw it back in the street. No doubt in an abstract sense, not returning a sum of money to its owner is a form of theft. But there does seem to be a point of inconvenience at which it is not worth the trouble to make the return.

Third, there are known social norms and moral principles which prohibit keeping what does not belong to one, and also define what does and what does not belong to a person. Contrast the case of the wallet with a similar case, which differs in but a single respect. A man is boating in the ocean and comes across another boat foundering near a reef with no one aboard. He climbs in and learns who the owner is. In such a case, the boat may in part become his, by rights of salvage. The exact rules governing private property and the rights thereto are facts relevant to any moral decision concerning property.

Even where there are no formal laws involved, social norms are significant facts to be considered. Our neurosurgeon may give the wallet he finds to a patient, deeming it not worth the trouble to find the owner. The word gets around the hospital, and the surgeon is thought to be rather cavalier in his respect for property and person, and may find his position weakened in the eyes of his peers. Perhaps it is not the norms which are of critical importance here, but the specific views of one's social group. Suppose a man new to a town should simply not try to return a purse he finds which belongs to the poor widow who has lived in that town for a lifetime, and her parents before her? His reputation would be severely damaged if his neglect became known.

This last point is not a fact to consider concerning the *circumstances* of a decision, but is rather a fact about the *consequences* of a certain course of action. Let us stop here and ask ourselves, can we distinguish sharply between the circumstances and the consequences of a moral situation? Let us return to the very beginning. A man finds in the street a wallet which contains a sum of money. Now we ask, what is meant by the word "finds"? Does he take the wallet away with him? That has the consequence of making it impossible for anyone else to return it to the owner. Consider here a case of finding a wallet in the street, where one may be sure that others will find it if he leaves it there. The problem now is that the next person may keep it. Consider instead finding a wallet in the hedges of one's driveway, 175 feet from the road. If the owner of the driveway does not pick up the wallet and do something with it, it will remain where it is until it rots away.

Are the circumstances the same in the various cases? Clearly not. But the difference rests in the differing consequences of the various courses of action. "Finding" is not even definable in terms of circumstantial facts alone. Later we will see that intentional activities such as finding are even more complex than we are here noting. The point here is that *seeing* is not *finding*. Finding is a course of action which has consequences inherent in it, consequences from which the circumstances of the finding are inseparable. To find a wallet in one place is not the same as finding it in another. A man who finds a five-year-old on his own street and brings him home is not doing the same thing as a man who finds him after three days lost in the woods. The circumstances are very different. But these circumstances are not distinguishable in terms of the finding alone nor even in terms of the place or time. The critical circumstance is precisely that the child is lost in one case and not the other. But what is it to be lost? It is the different consequences which are relevant. If the child is lost and not found, he will perish. If he is not lost, then he will find his way home.

Whether a wallet is lost or not is a fact about the circumstances in which it is found. Whether a child is lost or not is a fact highly relevant to a man who finds him. Merely meeting or seeing a lost child is not finding him. One must know that he is lost. And to know this is to know about the probable results of neglecting him. Negligence cases in courts of law tend to support precisely this conception of relevant facts. An unfenced swimming pool is an attractive lure to young children, and a dangerous one. The very fact of the pool is also the fact of luring and the risk inherent in attraction.

We are forced to conclude, then, that the facts of the circumstances of the case are not as simple as we hoped. We cannot define circumstances without reference to the consequences of various proposed courses of action. We now see what is so absurd about moral theories which neglect the consequences of action.

It is impossible to give an accurate description of a situation to which we may apply a principle without considering the circumstances. And when we consider these circumstances, we necessarily consider consequences as well.

We remind ourselves of Kant's argument that the principle "thou shalt not lie" is sufficient as a guide to right action. Suppose I am an actor playing a part, and my lines involve assertions which I do not believe to be true. Am I lying in speaking the part? Is a man lying who utters a falsehood in irony or jest? Clearly not. For his audience may be expected to understand the falsehood in the appropriate and intended sense. Yet in these cases, we have intentional falsehood. If they are not lies, it is because we expect certain responses from our audience. Suppose a radio station broadcasts a fictional newscast in the time slot in which the news is usually reported. All the audience believes the reports to be true. Shall we say that there are no lies involved, for there is no *intent to deceive*? The point is that an intention looks to the future and to consequences.

Firing a gun is not alone pulling the trigger—though pulling the trigger will cause the gun to fire. Shooting and killing a man is not merely pulling the trigger while the gun merely happens to be aimed at him. The fact that the trigger is pulled, coupled with the fact that the gun is pointed at the man at that time, together do not equal the fact that the man was shot in cold blood. In the latter case, the end and the beginning form a single action. Facts relevant to moral action always involve implicit as well as explicit consequences. We now turn to the consideration of such consequences.

B. Consequences

The traditional conception of consequences is that they are to be understood to follow from given actions in a causal order of relations. The law that a given consequence will follow from a given event is a causal law. Thus, the consequence of striking a piece of glass with a hammer is that it will break. The hammer *causes* the glass to break. In making moral decisions, it is necessary that we forecast what the future will bring. What we require in addition to information about the circumstances before us is knowledge of the future. Such knowledge is given by the causal laws we come to know.

In evaluating a present course of action in terms of its consequences, it is often said that we are evaluating *instrumental* goods. Paying one's income tax without cheating is a good thing, *because* otherwise one may get into a great deal of trouble. The consequences of a course of action are sometimes the major means we use for evaluating such actions.

The question is whether consequences are facts. They certainly seem to be. Is it not clearly a fact that if I borrow money from a finance company, and do not pay it back, they will repossess my furniture which I offered as security? To the contrary, it is anything but clear. There is a temporal gap which is quite problematic. Consider a simpler example: it *is* a fact that there *will be* an eclipse. It is not easy to defend a conception of facts which gives them existence prior to the events to which they refer. In the case of an eclipse, we are inclined to think that nothing could interfere with its taking place. But the finance company may go out of business. They will not then repossess anything—though they might have. Future facts are not facts now.

If so, then consequences are not facts. There is another, even more striking reason why we must reach this conclusion. That is, the consequences we are concerned with are not consequences of an actual course of events, but only of proposed courses of action. What will happen *if* I tell lies to my enemies? Since I have not yet told them lies, the consequence that they will catch me and punish me is no fact.

The fact of such an example, then, cannot be a fact about the actual future, but only of a hypothetical future. Such a view seems absurd. Our only alternative, then, is to think of the facts which look to consequences not as specific, descriptive facts about particular events, but as facts of a general nature about the world. A man who lies is usually caught. The audience of these particular lies is pretty sharp, and likely to catch me in a lie. If I lie, I will be caught. It is the hypothetical statement which is true, and the only candidate for a fact which we have.

But note that we are almost never in a position to make an unqualified statement about the future. Sometimes liars are not caught. At best, we can assign probabilities to our expectations concerning the future. But we cannot in advance know the facts about the future, at least not concerning human affairs. We can see the tremendous appeal of a moral theory which neglects consequences. For if we cannot know the future cold, then moral decisions which look to consequences are very risky, and will prove wrong or mistaken quite often. There is, however, a reply which is worth noting—that a moral theory which neglects consequences does not thereby control those consequences to any greater extent. In fact, by its neglect, it relinquishes its control over the future. In a gross sense, a moral theory which ignores the future works against the attempt to make the world a better place. Unfortunately, however, trying to make the world a better place is a risky and wearisome task.

Nevertheless, if there are candidates for facts which we must know in making moral decisions, they are the laws which govern human behavior and other events. We need to know what generally to expect of other men and of things, if we are reliably to look ahead and make our plans accordingly.

C. Laws

A prevalent view of the sciences is that their goal is the discovery of laws—the laws of nature, of human behavior, of institutions, and so forth. Many philosophers regard the concern for causal laws to be *definitive* of a science. Thus, narrative history is thought to be unscientific, in that it seeks to give unique and unrepeatable explanations for events. From this point of view, laws express

regularities in things, and they do so by stating relations among kinds of objects.
Thus, Newton's second law of motion—force equals mass times acceleration—
expresses a constant relation among three factors. "Litmus paper turns pink in
acid" states a repeatable kind of event. *Whenever* litmus paper is placed in an acid,
it will turn pink.

There are several kinds of laws. Laws differ in generality and in scope.
"Metals expand when heated" is a more general law, and of wider scope than
the law "copper expands when heated." Laws also differ with respect to subject
matter. There are laws of nature—physics and chemistry—which address inorganic
things. There are laws of living things. There are also laws of behavior and of
action, laws of thought and of feeling, and laws of institutions and social movements. The sciences of physics and chemistry are rather advanced, and contain
many well confirmed laws. The sciences of psychology and sociology are relatively
new, and possess few laws which can be asserted with justified conviction.

Which of the various causal or scientific laws are relevant to moral decisions?
Virtually all of them. If we are concerned with the consequences of any course of
action, both physical and biological laws enter into our judgments. Is it right for a
cigarette firm to advertise widely and without restraint? We must know the
effects of growing tobacco on the land. We must know the effects of smoking on
health. We must know the effects of burning tobacco on the environment. We
must know the effectiveness of advertising on the consumer. It is not that we
need to know everything in order to make any particular decision, but that a whole
variety of subjects and information come together in any particular case.

The sheer complexity of the information relevant to any major moral decision,
particularly one that has political ramifications, suggests that no single person
can master all the details and foresee a sufficient number of consequences accurately
enough to make a secure decision. Here we find one of the most striking reasons
why we need maxims of conduct—to guide us where our concrete knowledge is
insufficient. We have here also a compelling argument for the Greek view that
morals eventually fade into politics. No individual can possess sufficient knowledge
to expect beneficial results in his actions. Only men working in concert, each
making a small contribution to both knowledge and action, can achieve large
beneficial results.

Any and all laws may be helpful in the making of moral decisions. Laws of
inorganic nature tell us what to expect from the sheerly physical, and in physical
terms. Yet the most vital of laws which we require knowledge of in our moral
decisions are the least well established—the laws of human behavior and of social
institutions. A politician who thinks of war could use information as to the results
of such a war on the morale and lives of the citizens of his country. A man who
tells a lie could use information on the consequences of his being caught. Raskolnikov, in *Crime and Punishment*, errs in his expectations concerning his ability to
endure the remorse of being a murderer.

Psychological laws look to two kinds of events which are of the deepest importance in moral decisions: actions and feelings. The latter we will take up in the next chapter. Here we will scrutinize the notion of psychological laws and actions. Consider a man who wonders if he should tell a lie to deceive someone else. He would like to know what the consequences of telling a lie will be. What law can be found to relate lying and punishment or outrage? Unfortunately, we at present have no such law, at least one confirmed in scientific psychology. Yet surely we are not without information relevant to such matters. Often lying will provoke anger and lead to distrust. We may even consider the last sentence to be a fact. Yet it involves a basic vagueness that does not assure us of the consequences of lying.

More important even than this, consider the very notion of lying. Lying is inherently a form of deception. A falsehood which is not intended to deceive is no lie. It may be an act, a jest, an irony. A deception, however, is not a simple thing akin to a reading on a galvanometer. Imagine that I have installed an apparatus which turns a wheel when a button is pushed. Now, I push the button, but nothing happens. Perhaps a wire became disconnected. The point is that the event *the button is pushed* and the event *the wheel turns* are conceived as distinct events, related through a complex network of laws and materials.

Compare here my telling a lie and my fear of the consequences. I am afraid of being despised. Can a man tell a lie and not evoke scorn or outrage if detected? Certainly, in a competition of tall tales. But these are not lies! There is no deception involved. The very word "deception" has connotations of intentional misleading, of taking advantage. Could one deceive another effectively and not evoke resentment? Imagine a game in which one man tries to mislead the other, and when he does both laugh. Such a game does not involve lying. The intent to deceive is a qualified one. Where the deception takes on a certain degree of forcefulness, and has serious consequences, then deception does not *by chance* elicit resentment. Deception is the kind of thing which looks toward resentment.

It is time to review this point. We began by looking at a scientific law: litmus paper turns pink in acid. There is a regular and reproducible relationship between placing litmus paper in acid and its color. We have, then, two separate events, and a law connecting them. But in the case of lying, we do not have two separate events—lying and anger—and a lawful relationship between them. Rather, in telling a lie we must inevitably look toward resentment if caught. For that is inherent in the lie itself. A child may lie to escape punishment—but the lie necessarily involves both guilt and fear of further punishment. The very word "lie" means something more than telling an untruth.

We recall Hume's argument that the shadow cast by a parent tree which kills its own seedlings is not filicide, not murder. Murder, however, is wrong. Hume argues that a factual description does not lead to a judgment of value. Such an argument assumes that we can give a factual description of a man lying without mentioning lying or its moral equivalent. But lying is an intentional act of deception which is intended to harm. In such terms, it is wrong.

What are our choices ? To give morally neutral descriptions which neglect the aims and consequences of action, as if only such descriptions are factual. Or, to admit that it can be a fact that a man lies, and that such a fact is not value-neutral. Murder is wrong; casting shadows is not. If it is a fact that a man has committed a murder, then he has done something wrong. Courts of law operate on precisely that principle. But it follows, then, that some facts are heavily laden with values and preferences. The fact that a man has *enough* to eat is itself good. The fact that a man spreads false rumors is bad.

We may now review our discussion. We have discovered that the laws we require in our moral decisions are not merely laws connecting separate kinds of events. They often connect together events which form a single process through time. We saw that defining the circumstances of a situation inevitably leads us to consequences. Now we see that describing the events of a situation inevitably leads us to expectations, hopes, and fears for the future. Now we see why the facts in moral decisions are so complex, and why so many philosophers are convinced that facts and morals do not mix. They conceive of facts as separate and distinct from each other. To quote Wittgenstein once again, "The world divides into facts. Each item can be the case or not the case while everything else remains the same." But the fact of lying is tied intimately to the fact of resentment upon discovery. Therefore, on Wittgenstein's definition, lying and resentment are not facts or states of affairs. Lying is already an evaluative act, the result of a decision. It goes beyond an isolated fact. Put another way, the factual claim that a man is telling a lie is also a value judgment. According to a narrow conception of facts, such claims are more than factual. What we must do is to ascertain whether we can defend a narrower conception of facts which do not go beyond themselves.

D. Causation

Let us consider one of the truly great conceptions of the world—that of Spinoza's *Ethics*. Spinoza asks us to view the events of the world as consisting wholly of effects following from causes. Later events are viewed as consequences of earlier events which are the causes of the later ones. In order to avoid ambiguity, we will call a cause which precedes its effect an *efficient* cause. Striking a pane of glass with a hammer is the efficient cause of its shattering. The gravitational pull of the moon and the rotation of the earth on its axis together are the efficient cause of the tides. Viewing the world as composed wholly of efficient causes and their effects is equivalent to viewing all laws of nature as laws which describe how later events follow from earlier ones.

The Spinozistic conception of the world is very much like the Newtonian world-view and also like all subsequent scientific theories, in that all accept the principle that the world functions according to efficient causes alone. The laws of nature describe regular connections which enable us to foretell or predict the future from what we know of the past. The scientific picture of the world may be regarded as a conception of how things are *made* to happen by what precedes them. Moreover, since the past has already occurred and cannot be changed, laws of nature represent what the future will be because of what the past has been. In this sense, the scientific view also suggests Spinoza's conclusion that what has happened and what will happen *must* happen as they do. In the world of efficient causation, effects follow from causes as they do and must. Things can happen in no other way than they actually do. That is what we mean by claiming that there are laws of nature. If copper is heated it will expand. The heat will cause it to expand. It can do nothing other than expand.

Few philosophers have seriously challenged the picture of the physical world as constituted by efficient causation. It is worth noting, however, that Lucretius, whose theory of the world is of atoms falling in the void in an efficient causal order, introduces a principle according to which atoms swerve in an arbitrary fashion as they fall, as if to say that not everything can be understood in terms of efficient causation. The world is not cut and dried as it would be if everything were a mechanical working of efficient causes. Some of the rich tapestry of the world comes from its totally unexpected character. Twentieth-century physics has also found it necessary to accept a degree of indeterminacy between present and future events. I wish to point out, however, that both Spinoza and Newtonian physics have no such indeterminacy within their world views. Moreover, contemporary physicists, Lucretius, Spinoza, and Newton all agree that the only intelligible mode of relation among things is via efficient causation. The swerve of the atoms is sheer unintelligibility and arbitrariness. Science and explanation in terms of efficient causation are usually taken to be synonymous.

Let us now turn to any of the sciences of man. Contemporary scientific psychology is committed to the principle that all sciences work in terms of efficient causation. Experimental psychology aims at *prediction* and *control*. Human emotions and actions are to be understood in the same terms. Thus, in psychoanalysis we find that virtually all the manifestations of neurotic behavior are to be explained in terms of the early events in the subject's life. The experiences of childhood *cause* a man to act as he does in later life. In behavioristic psychology, the fundamental categories are stimulus and response. A stimulus presented to an organism causes it to respond in certain measurable ways. A rat in a cage with a bar arranged so that he receives a pellet of food whenever he presses the bar will press the bar faster and faster.

We are now ready to make a striking observation. Consider a hungry man who enters a restaurant. We ask him, "Why are you doing this?" He will answer, "To buy dinner." He does not explain what he is doing in terms of the *causes* of his actions, but in terms of his aims or goals. He wants to eat. That is his goal. What is striking is that all desires—and certainly men often act from desire— *aim* at something. We desire food, so we eat. We desire attention, so we make fools of ourselves. If men act from desire, their desires are always anticipations of goals to be attained in the future. If desires cause actions, it is the goal which is the cause. It is the food, or the relief of hunger, which causes a man to enter a restaurant. But in such cases, the cause does not *precede* the effect. It *follows* it. A purposive action looks to the final result. Such a theory of causation is called "final causation." Intentional actions, purposive actions, and actions from desire, all look to what *will* come about. The goal causes the action as a final cause. An explanation in terms of final causation is called a *teleological explanation*.

We may now look back on our discussion of lying from the point of view of efficient and final causation. In saying that lying always aims to deceive, we are saying that deception is the final cause of lying. Unless a man wishes to deceive someone else, he will not lie to him. All evaluation is the appraisal of final causes. A value is what we aim for, or, at least, should aim for. In evaluation, we look ahead to the results of our proposed actions, and the foreseen results guide our present decisions.

Many philosophers, Spinoza included, have found it impossible to understand how efficient and final causes can both be part of the same world. If actions are caused by prior causes, then the results follow lawfully and automatically. It is quite absurd to imagine that something which does not yet even exist can possibly cause a man to act in such a way as to bring it into existence. Final causes do not yet exist. A woman cooks her dinner in order to eat. But the cooked dinner, when it is not yet in existence, cannot cause her to prepare it.

Therefore, Spinoza claims, there are no final causes. There are only efficient causes. It is not the cooked dinner which attracts the action in its preparation. It is the idea of anticipation which *efficiently* causes the woman to prepare the dinner. All purposive action is to be explained as the working of the ideas of the goals imagined as efficient causes. All desires are to be viewed, not as *aims*, but as present ideas which make us act as we do. In other words, the future has no causal efficacy. Only ideas in the present have effective power to make us act. The entire position may be summarized in Spinoza's words as follows: "We neither strive for, wish, seek, nor desire anything because we think it to be good, but, on the contrary, we adjudge a thing to be good because we strive for, wish, seek, or desire it." The goodness of a thing does not make us desire it (final causation). Rather, our desire makes us call it good (efficient causation).

There is no way to disprove the theory that the only causes which can be effective are efficient causes. Nevertheless, there are certain difficulties with this position that are worth mentioning. The greatest difficulty is one of consistency. Spinoza himself is not quite consistent. He has written a book on ethics, which is a treatise to tell men how to live. He advocates a certain way of life as truly better than any other. But if there are only efficient causes, then though he may have been caused to write his *Ethics*, and caused to give advice to others, his advice cannot truly be better than anyone else's. Since nothing is good in order to guide our desires, our desires identify what is good. Spinoza's theory is no better than any other to a man who does not desire to live by it. The whole project of giving advice becomes a strange one if we cannot understand the advice to *aim* at a good. The inconsistency eventually leads Spinoza to define the good in two incompatible ways. At first, the good is what we desire, and no more. But the good is later defined as that which is *certainly profitable to man*. If it is certainly profitable, we ought to do it. And we ought to aim for it as well.

The general position that the only causes are efficient causes makes it necessary to explain future goals in terms of present inclinations. There is, however, a fundamental weakness in the identification of what is desired with what is good. Often we reject even a very strong desire because we consider it unwise. The typical moral conflict which underlies Kant's sense of duty is the rejection of a strong desire to do something wrong, just because we consider it wrong or bad. We certainly often set aside a strong immediate desire in terms of its unfortunate consequences. We do "look ahead," and try to do what is best, even contrary to our present desires.

Psychoanalysis dramatizes the problem in an even more striking fashion. Psychoanalytic theory also regards man as wholly determined by efficient causes. Nevertheless, a man enters psychoanalysis because he is not happy with his desires. He may, for example, desire to sexually molest children. But he knows that it is bad to do so, and seeks professional help. The help he seeks to achieve is a transformation of his desires, to make them better. It is therefore impossible to argue that his desires define for him what he takes to be good. In Dewey's language, the desir*able* and the desir*ed* are not the same.

The greater truth of Spinoza's position, whether or not we accept the validity of final causes, is that an aim or a desire is indeed a present idea. A goal which we cannot form a present idea of cannot move us. A man who does his duty even in opposition to his desires must be able to form an idea of that duty at the time he chooses to follow it. But we form our ideas at least in part from our past experience, even the causal effects of that past experience. Perhaps we may find here a way of reconciling efficient and final causation. Efficient causes bring to us the ideas we have, and the aims we strive for. But these aims may then be critically scrutinized to determine which are truly superior. A goal which is genuinely superior to any other is so whether we are moved to think of it or not. But we will not be able to seek it or even to appreciate it if we have not thought of it first. These are very subtle issues, and will be pursued no further here.

We may, however, understand the problem of facts and values in a different way. Science deals with facts, and science deals with efficient causation. It is a natural conclusion, then, to suppose that facts belong only in a system of efficient causation. Values, as we have seen, require final causes. If efficient and final causation cannot belong to the same system, then facts and values also belong to different systems. This in the end is the most plausible justification of the view that values cannot be derived from facts.

But there is another conception of facts, which also makes it impossible to generate values from them. This is the view that facts are simple representations of what is real, what is the case, something in themselves. Values, we have seen, look beyond themselves to the future. We must now consider facts alone, to see if they can be independent and complete in themselves.

E. Theories

It is worth noting that on Spinoza's view, though it is the most extreme version of efficient causation known, facts do not exist in isolation. Nothing exists in itself. Every finite event in the world follows from an infinite number of other events which precede it. In addition, all events follow from the one substance or God. A similar conception can be found in classical mechanics: all events follow from others, without end. And they follow in accordance with the laws of nature, which form a single system. No fact can be understood in isolation from the entire theory. In fact, Spinoza seems to believe that nothing can be known apart from everything else. Only when we can put every piece in its place, and know all the laws of nature in their role in every event, do we know any one event. To know one fact is to know the entire universe.

Obviously we are not likely to know everything in this generation or in any near future. So rigorous an acceptance of the principle that everything is one leads to the view that we can know nothing. To avoid this, Spinoza seems to accept some kind of intuition into general principles. To avoid the same conclusion, other philosophers have supposed that there are facts which we can know directly, and which involve nothing but themselves. I see a chair in front of me. That is a fact. But perhaps I am dreaming, or am having a hallucination. Well, at least I am sure that a colored patch is in my visual field. But can we consider such a private appearance a *fact*?

Imagine going into a scientific laboratory and looking over the complex array of equipment there. We are told that it is a fact that this equipment measures the flux of a magnetic field. A physicist can simply look and see this directly. Certainly a layman cannot. Looking and seeing are different in different circumstances, and to different men, depending on what they know in advance. Put another way, a man looks and sees what his prior knowledge tells him may happen. He begins with a theoretical conception of what to look for. The night sky cannot even be described intelligently without a prior theory according to which we interpret what we see. There are many points of light floating on a dark background. What is the force of the word "on"? Can points of light float? Can there be such things as true *points* of light? We may interpret the night sky according to the model of a planetarium—points of light on a curved ceiling. Or, we may interpret it in terms of a variety of bodies emitting or reflecting light, and moving in curved orbits. What is impossible is to describe an event without a prior model which gives us interpretations of the basic vocabulary.

Certain contemporary European philosophers describe this state of affairs by the claim that all descriptive knowledge is *transcendent*. It goes beyond any minimum we might aim for. The statement "grass is green" tells us something about grass but also about other things of the same color, which are also green. The very word "green" can have meaning only if it refers to many things of a like color. It is impossible for a word to designate but a single unique and unrepeatable occurrence, unlike everything else in the world. It is a fact that grass is green, but it is a fact which looks to other things, to other colors, to other green things, even to the winter color of grass. For if it is a fact that grass is green, it is not a fact during the winter. On the other hand, if the grass is green today, it will be green tomorrow. There is a temporal element to all factual knowledge.

We have been touching on some very complex matters in the last few paragraphs. It does not seem possible to depend a conception of facts in isolation from each other. On the other hand, without some degree of separation among facts, knowing one thing means knowing everything, and that is simply untenable. The resolution of these difficulties is not part of the study of moral decision, though it is by no means irrelevant to such decisions.

What seems unmistakable is that facts are far from simple. They hang together. They together comprise or contribute to a theory of things. The conception of facts as truths *in themselves*, in many ways relatively simple and separable from other truths, cannot be easily defended. We now remind ourselves of Hume's arguments that knowledge of facts alone cannot create a value. His first argument depends on the analogy between a shadow cast by a parent tree and the murder of a child by his parent. This analogy breaks down if we note the far more complex facts which are significant in the latter case—the feelings of parents and their children, the parent's self-consciousness as well as his awareness of consequences. Once we adopt a more complex version of facts than that provided by the analogy, the whole argument collapses.

The second argument is that knowledge of facts alone cannot influence the will. This argument is but another version of the view that facts are relevant to efficient causation only. Knowledge of efficient causes cannot of itself motivate the will. I may know that telling a lie will cause a man's death, but I may be in-indifferent to that eventuality. Notice, however, that what is omitted from such a description are facts about my desires and ends. Suppose I consider it both right and proper that I achieve my revenge against a man who has injured me. It is now good for me to tell a lie if that will gain my revenge. The criticisms of such an account depend on the view that a statement of aims cannot be factual. All we can describe are the facts about the ideas a man may have in terms of which he forms his aims. But facts do not look to final causes.

Formally speaking, we have the following situation. From the premises, "it is right for me to gain revenge," and "if I tell this lie I will gain revenge," it follows that "it is right for me to tell a lie." From the premises, "I *think* it is right for me to gain revenge," and "if I tell this lie I will gain revenge," it does not follow that "it is right for me to tell a lie." Obviously we have begged the whole question. From efficient causes alone, we cannot infer anything about

intentions and aims. *But*, we cannot describe evaluation in terms of efficient causes
alone either. We have already seen the difficulties inherent in a world view which
looks only to efficient causes for explanation of human actions.

We are led, then, to the remarkable conclusion that if we define facts solely
in terms of efficient causes, we cannot even speak of values and preferences, nor of
aims and intentions. We cannot even describe human actions without reference to
goals and purposes. Men lie and tell the truth. They do not merely utter noises
which just happen to be words which just happen to be statements which are
untrue. The future and its consequences, and the values men bear toward that
future, are a part of a minimal account of what they do.

Either facts are then irrelevant to human beings, and there are no facts
about human actions. In this case, facts cannot generate values. Or else, facts
about human beings are facts about anticipations and values, and involve the
future essentially. In the latter case, it is by no means obvious that values are not
generated wholly from facts, albeit in no simple way.

F. Situations

Let us make a fresh start, though not forgetting the ground we have covered.
John Stuart Mill defines what is good in terms of the pleasure a good action or
thing will produce. He then remarks that there are different levels of pleasure,
which he calls "higher" and "lower" pleasures. The claim he makes is that there
are certain kinds of pleasure which are not more *intense* than others, but which are
preferable. What is the measure of a preferable pleasure? It is a pleasure which a
man who has tried both does in fact prefer. Mill asks, what other test could there
be? Thus, men often do prefer the pleasures of the mind to those of the body. Of
course, men who have not tried both—perhaps from lack of opportunity—will not
be able to make a deliberate choice.

Plato offers a similar argument as to the preferability of the pleasures of
knowledge and of philosophy as contrasted with the pleasures of the body. At the
moment we are not concerned with the validity of this argument, but rather with
its character. The case that higher pleasures are preferable rests on the claim that,
under certain conditions, it is a fact that men prefer one kind of thing to another.
Here is an example of an argument which links values to facts, but to facts of a
very special sort. The facts are about what men will do and feel in certain *situations*.

The *Republic* is in the main an extended development of the position that
justice is not only an instrumental good, but an intrinsic good. We might be able
to argue that justice is an instrumental good in terms of the consequences that
would follow from breaking social rules. Nevertheless, Plato's major argument
that justice is a good in itself depends on the claim that, in a just society, men
would be at peace with themselves and with others, and live according to knowledge
and truth—that is, that they will all be *happy*. Plato does not shirk the problem of

defining happiness. Nevertheless, the argument in the end comes down to the claim that, under certain conditions (those of a just society), men will indeed be satisfied and happy.

There are two important points to be noted in such an argument. The value claim that is being defended, though apparently a claim about what justice is and that it is intrinsically valuable, is not defended by reference to either a distinguishable property of things in isolation from other things or circumstances, nor separated from the preferences and other goals of human beings. Justice is treated as a dispositional property. What this means is that its value is given by the actions of men under specific conditions. The intrinsic value of justice, and justice itself, are to be understood in terms of relations between conditions and circumstances, and the feelings, preferences, and purposes of the men who are in such circumstances.

The first point, then, may be generalized as the principle that evaluation is a triadic relation among persons, objects evaluated, and the conditions or circumstances of evaluation. The entire relation, since it always involves specific persons and objects, may be thought of as a *value situation*. Evaluation is a procedure which takes place within an encompassing situation. Objects do not merely possess value. Their values are values to and for some person who makes the evaluation. In addition, objects are not valuable merely in terms of the responses of the agent. These responses depend on particular circumstances and conditions.

Nevertheless, the triadic complexity of value situations in no way entails the conclusion that values are not factual or natural. We have seen that the property of being magnetized is a dispositional concept, which defines observable traits of magnetized objects under specified conditions. Magnetization too looks to situations which go beyond the immediate object. It looks to conditions and circumstances and to results as well. The property of being magnetized is given in terms of what iron filings may be observed to do under certain conditions. The property of being good is given in terms of what human beings may be observed to do under specifiable conditions.

The second point is implicit in the Platonic principle we have considered several times: every man desires what he thinks is good. The implicit premise is that desire is always for an object, and involves an aim or a goal considered good. In other words, human actions are purposive. And in addition, there are some ends which men do not really desire, though they think they do. Men can be mistaken about what they think is good. There are true ends and mistaken ends. Men discover their errors under the appropriate conditions. They discover that what they thought they wanted they do not really care for. They discover that an anticipated good is not really good at all. Sometimes they may describe such a discovery as one about an untrue feeling: "I thought I was in love, but it was only a passing fancy. Marriage was therefore a mistake."

The Greek approach to morals is in terms of the ends of activities. Plato and Aristotle take for granted that all human activities and all natural processes as well have inherent aims. Today, modern science can no longer support a teleological conception of the inorganic world. We have no justifiable reason to suppose that the universe as a whole, or any part of it, is directed by final causes. The physical sciences all work with a principle of efficient causation alone.

But human actions are not even describable in terms of efficient causes alone. We do not think of a man being moved by neural impulses and muscular contractions. We think of him eating, walking, deciding, even speaking his mind. Each of these activities describes an achievement, a goal, something aimed at and accomplished. Each of them looks to the completed act, not to the efficient causes of the activity. The description of the activity itself is a purposive one.

John Dewey argues that even animal behavior is unintelligible in terms of efficient causes alone. Consider a fox chasing a rabbit. Stimulus-response theory would have us believe that at every instant we are to understand the fox's movements as responses to changing circumstances. Dewey argues that the welter of changing circumstances and stimuli cannot be expected to lead to the continuity of movements the fox performs in chasing the rabbit unless we understand that a ruling aim guides the entire activity—the aim of catching the rabbit. Without the goal, the complex of stimuli and responses will fall apart into a meaningless and discontinuous jumble of elements.

What this means is again that the facts of human action cannot be given in terms of efficient causes alone. Were we to try to describe actions in such terms, the very actions themselves would become unintelligible. The facts about human beings are facts about the circumstances they are in—which we have seen look to consequences necessarily—and facts about the goals or purposes they have—that is, what they are looking ahead to.

But are there facts about aims and purposes? A man scratches his ear: is it not a fact that he intended to do so? A man takes the dead body of his favorite dog, and goes out with a shovel to the field. Is it not a fact that he intends to dig a grave? In Platonic terms, we must also note that the goal in every case is deemed good, if only relative to the available alternatives. What a man chooses to do he considers good. Evaluation and purposive action are two faces of the same activities.

Every parent of an infant is aware of an interesting experience. The child *says* he wants to play with a toy, though somehow it is impossible to find the one he wants. He cries and runs about uncontrollably. The parent concludes that what the child "really" wants is to go to sleep. The child screams in protest for a moment or two, and then goes soundly to sleep. The distinction made is between an apparent goal and a real one, between an imagined good and a real one. The test of a true value is found in the results of activities undertaken under particular circumstances. The Platonic principle is that all evaluation is a factual judgment about real needs and goals.

In psychoanalysis, we find a similar conception of aims. The *id* is the seat of diffuse but very powerful needs, desires, or *aims*. In order to understand what he is doing, and also in order to make an intelligent decision, a man must know his true or hidden needs. "Am I being tactful to avoid hurting someone else's feelings, or to avoid a difficult scene?" Basically, psychoanalysis adds to the Platonic view two additional complexities. First, men engage in a variety of forms of self-deception. They are not merely ignorant of their own desires. They seek to *hide* these desires from consciousness. Second, men are rather complex. In viewing the psyche as tripartite, Freud dramatizes even more than Plato the principle that a given person may have differing and conflicting real goals. Knowing one's true aims will not suffice if at the same time one desires incompatible things. In addition to the facts about his intentions, a man may also have to decide among incompatible prospects.

How, though, is a man to do this? Suppose we do know the conditions and circumstances of our actions, and the hidden as well as the conscious purposes we have. We ask, what do we really want? Unfortunately, we want too many incompatible things. A man nominated for public office may desire at once both time to be with his family and time to serve the public in a responsible position. He cannot have both. How can he choose between them?

We assume that he knows the relevant facts. There are the various circumstantial possibilities of his alternative courses of action and their consequences. He cannot simply do what is good, for each alternative is good in different ways. He cannot easily decide what is best, and for an important reason: to do one thing while strongly desiring the other will dissatisfy him. A decision in a case of conflicting goals must not only involve the calculation of the superior good. It must also bring the lesser goal to have a lesser influence on the agent's feelings. A moral decision may entail a change in what a man really intends. No wonder facts alone do not comprise a moral decision. But it does not follow that any constituents beyond the facts can be found.

We may now see what is wrong with the Platonic principle that all men desire the good. The principle entails that a man who knows what truly is good will do it. The principle omits the change in the person and his goals which "knowledge of the good" requires. Evaluation is not merely a calculation of facts and consequences, nor even of aims and desires. Evaluation is also a choice among alternatives, a choice which literally changes the aims of the person who has performed the evaluation.

G. The continuum of means and ends

The principle that evaluation and actions undertaken change things is fundamental to a view which underlies a good part of the discussion of this chapter. This view, that of John Dewey, is that evaluation is a process which inhabits a continuum of means and ends. All instrumental goods look ahead for their value to goals to be achieved. But, Dewey points out, nothing ever completely ends. All "ends" are but temporary and projected ends. After they have come to pass, the world moves on, and what was in the past a goal, now realized becomes a means to something else. All ends are therefore also means, in that they lead on to new events.

In return, all means are in fact something in themselves, and have a significance as ends also. To ignore the intrinsic value of events is to weaken one's capacity for evaluation. Activities which are merely means are ugly and sterile. Work for nothing but the remuneration it brings is sterile and degrading. Things must be evaluated in terms of their capacity as ends and also as means. Everything must be judged in both terms.

The continuum of means and ends is a very rich notion. It has several dimensions and many important ramifications. Here are just a few:

(a) The continuum of means and ends is in large part a *temporal* continuum. Dewey's point is that with the passage of time, even secure and reliable goals may change their character. A moral decision in a man's youth may no longer be satisfactory in his later life. A moral principle valid at one time may no longer serve a later generation. All consequences of actions pass away, and leave their own consequences to replace them.

(b) Evaluation is always something to be carried on in a place and at a time. And with new circumstances, new judgments and decisions may be called for. Moral principles are therefore only aids to decision. They never in themselves can meet the onset of new circumstances. We have seen the difficulties involved in attempting to settle complex moral decisions by an appeal to principles alone.

(c) In evaluation, we must look ahead to an indefinite range of consequences, immediate and remote. Obviously, we will never be able to foresee all remote consequences of projected actions. If any decisions are to be reached at all, then, they will be in the first place *tentative*, since they look ahead to consequences which no one could anticipate. And in the second place, they are all *risky*, since later events may reveal that an earlier decision was in error. Nevertheless, all evaluation demands from us a long-range view, at least to look as far ahead as we can.

(d) The most important point of all, however, is our realization that events and what follows from them are not mere logical possibilities, but are bound in a close relationship. Means and ends form a continuum in that means look ahead to ends, and ends bear the means which produce them. Put another way, means and ends, if they can be related in expectation, are going to possess common characteristics. A man who steals to obtain enough money so that he can retire from active life *becomes a thief*, with everything entailed by that word: arrest, jail, flight, fear, disrespect for others. A country that goes to war to win the peace engages in juggling with words and fantasies. War engenders war. Violence breeds violence. Distrust breeds distrust.

We should not exaggerate the identity between means and ends. In fact, means are different from their consequences in at least some respects. The continuum, however, demands that we look to the facts to ground our claim that certain means can actually produce our intended goals. Has war brought peace in the past? Have thieves shown themselves to be honorable and generous men?

Facts Are children brought up to strict obedience likely to develop a strong sense of responsibility and personal conviction? In stressing that means and ends form a continuum, we throw the burden of proof on men who would engage in types of action wholly different from the goals they propose. Dewey has little patience with revolutionaries, for example, for they too often aim to destroy in the barest hope that better things will come to pass.

(e) Therefore, a man who would look to consequences must plan very carefully the transitions he has in mind, and must have good grounds for believing that the ends he desires will come about. The most secure way of achieving good ends is by employing valuable means. For then the character of goodness is preserved throughout. A democracy that would preserve itself by restricting freedom of speech destroys exactly what it reveres in its repression for self-protection.

(f) It is in the means, then, that intelligence in moral decision is to be placed. We may not ignore consequences, but we must predict consequences which truly follow from means we respect. We must regard means in terms of what they lead to. We must also seek to achieve an end by incorporating it into our means. It was pointed out in the first chapter that the strongest case a pacifist can make is that the willingness to engage in war is itself a cause of war.

(g) Finally, the continuum of means and ends calls our attention to the principle that facts about human beings are not facts about efficient causes alone, but look ahead to intentions and purposes. Inherent in all means are the ends they will bring about. Inherent in goals truly chosen are the actions which will bring them about. In the value situation, intentions constitute a unity between initial acts and final expectations. A country goes to war intending to win—by killing and destroying. The very act of war has the end of destruction within it. If we do not want destruction, then we cannot go to war. A lie is an intentional deception. It contains within it the seeds of distrust and a disrespect for truth. In the continuum of means and ends, the deception is already inherent in the original intent. And that is true for all human actions.

Therefore, in looking to consequences, we must distinguish the consequences which are wholly unknown, and which cannot be anticipated, from those which are central to the actions proposed. The facts of human action are restricted to efficient causation only insofar as we are generally ignorant of what is to happen. But to a knowledgeable man, the future is part of his prior activities. His knowledge is a fact to take into account. An electrician who runs a wire from an electric socket to his wife's bathtub is doing something very different from what is done by a two-year-old child performing the same wiring.

Typically, men ignore the expected consequences of their actions, as if hoping for a miracle to save them. A common example is that of a school community which turns down a tax increase for the schools. I do not mean to imply that every tax increase should be supported. Rather, I wish to point out that few people who vote against the proposal actually consider the needs of the schools, and the consequences of a shortage of resources. Thus, it is a common consequence that school busing is curtailed, and many children may have to walk to school in dangerous streets. Or teachers are fired, and the school does not serve its intended purposes. Tax increases are not a trifling matter. But they are most impossible where the consequences of various alternatives are neither known nor a matter of interest.

H. Summary

We may now summarize the preceding discussion in schematic form. In evaluation, it is necessary to know the *circumstances* of the situation which evokes the need for a decision, and to look ahead as well to the *consequences* of proposed courses of action. What seems clear is that any description of circumstances looks ahead to consequences, and unavoidably. The facts of moral situations involve relations between the past, present, and future.

Nevertheless, there are two ways of relating events through time—in terms of efficient causes and in terms of final causes. The physical sciences have gained their success in terms of efficient causes alone. From a purely scientific point of view, we may regard the circumstances of action in terms of efficient causes alone. We explain the consequences in terms of prior conditions. We may identify relational facts or laws of nature with efficient causation.

But we cannot explain or even describe human actions in terms of such efficient causes alone. Actions are purposive, and involve intentions and aims. If there are facts about actions, they are facts about purposes and goals. They are facts about real needs and real aims. They take the form of hypotheses about what agents would do, were certain conditions to be met.

The problem, then, is whether we can understand the connection between the inorganic world of efficient causes and the human world of purposes and intentions. The claim that we cannot infer values from facts depends on the identification of facts with efficient causes alone. There is little plausibility for such an identification. Nevertheless, on a fundamental level of understanding, efficient and final causes are not easy to reconcile. The problem for the defender of efficient causation alone is that human actions become inexplicable and also indescribable. The problem for the defender of final causation is to understand the beginnings of aims and their causes—which without efficient causes become inexplicable. Thus, many people who believe in human purposes believe that such purposes do not have efficient causes. Such a view is puzzling to the behavioral scientist. Finally, a man who believes that human actions are both efficiently and finally caused has the burden of explaining how. But that is a problem we cannot pursue here.

What is the point of so theoretical a discussion, seemingly so remote from the concrete issues of moral decision? What we have been studying are the *kinds* of facts which we must look to in moral decision. There are the facts of the case calling for a decision. These are in part given by our descriptions of the efficient causes involved. In deciding whether to try to save a man drowning, we must know the temperature of the water, the distance he is from shore, how quickly we can swim, and so forth. Such facts allow us to envisage the consequences of various courses of action. But these facts are not sufficient for making a moral decision, nor even for the existence of a situation calling for one. We need facts in addition concerning the aims and preferences inherent in the situation. We require knowledge of efficient causes so that we may determine whether we can achieve the final causes we have proposed. To decide whether to give charity to a poor man, we must know what will benefit him, or, at least, what he desires.

To judge a man's actions, we must consider what he has done. And what he did looks to what he intended, or thought he was doing. The facts relevant to evaluation are not themselves value-free. They include the preferences and also the true goals of the agent doing the evaluating, and also of any other person whose actions are relevant. But other men, their responses and feelings, are a major part of all our moral decisions. We then look to the facts about their intentions and preferences, their apparent desires and their real desires. We therefore look to the facts about their values in considering our own.

It is sometimes said that we might know all the facts that the physical and social sciences could give us, and still not be able to determine what is valuable from that. Such a claim is perfectly correct, but the conclusion derived from it is not. The facts of the physical and social sciences, if cast wholly in terms relevant to efficient causation, would tell us nothing of needs and aims. Add now facts concerning the intentions of men, their wishes and preferences as well as their deeper goals. It is by no means so obvious that these facts do not determine what is truly valuable, to and for a particular man.

Nevertheless, there is one point to be cautious of here. That is, that such facts determine what is valuable to a man only where his goals remain constant and are well defined. For a man in genuine conflict, or whose goals change in the very process of making a decision, then the relationship between facts and evaluation is far more complex. That is why facts alone cannot replace a moral decision, even if we grant that facts may be facts about values and aims. But neither feelings nor principles alone can settle moral decisions which involve major conflicts.

It is sometimes said that we can never know the intentions of a man because they are purely internal mental states. We can know only of his actions. Such a view fails to see that in the very description of human actions, we describe intentions as well as motions. Perhaps we are wrong when we describe a child moving pieces around a chess board as "playing chess." But we cannot describe what he is doing without ascribing some purposes to him, if only that of playing with pieces on a board. He *moves* them. He does not merely cause them to move. Our knowledge of the intentions of other men (and, if we accept the testimony of psychoanalysis, even ourselves) is limited. But we depend on it nevertheless.

Let us look again at some of the cases we have proposed as examples in the

first chapter. (a) In the case of the boy who considers the war unjust, there are the
specific facts which define the injustice, be they the historical sequence of events
which led up to the war, the killing and torture, or the lies of government
officials. There are also the facts of his intentions, real and apparent. What is his
aim in opposing the war? Ending it? What if an abrupt termination leads to other
wars? What if an abrupt diversion of resources leads to domestic crisis? What if
open opposition to the war generates chaos and violence? Is that what he really
wants? Perhaps he really is but a coward, who wants only to avoid the risks of
fighting. It is not sufficient to say that he must simply *decide* his goals. We fashion
our decisions from the facts about the world and about our own obscured desires
and feelings. Otherwise, we may achieve our stipulated goal, only to realize that
it was not what we really wanted. Revolutionaries often come to realize that the
fruits of the revolution are not in fact what they intended them to be. In effect, we
look to the deeper good which will in fact prove satisfactory.

In the *Republic*, Socrates replies to Thrasymachus' claim that a tyrant is
happy by showing that the tyrant is really badly off—in terms of Thrasymachus'
own values. Thrasymachus claims the tyrant is fortunate in being able to do and
have anything. Socrates' reply is that in terms of deeper and more basic needs,
which Thrasymachus himself recognizes, the tyrant is a slave to his appetites,
unable to follow the better part of himself. The just man achieves an inner
harmony of soul coupled with knowledge of what is good. The tyrant is a mere
creature of whim, and does not know what is good even for himself. The entire
argument depends on the *fact* that men do indeed seek a harmonious and knowledgeable condition. If that is no fact, then the argument is invalid. A man must
not only *admit* the truth of a premise concerning his ultimate goals. The premise
must be true, or else his actions will eventually prove unsatisfactory. If fear is
really the fundamental impulse of his opposition to the war, the boy will not be
able to tolerate a violent repression against that opposition, and he will come to
regret what he has done.

(b) In the case of deciding whether she will have her child or instead undergo
an abortion, a woman must face the factual questions of motivation. Does she
really want the child, or is she merely punishing herself for her sexual conduct?
We are forced to consider the quality and also the degree of self-deception involved
in such a case. If the welfare of the prospective child is paramount, then she must
weigh the prospects of achieving it when she is uneducated and poor. If her goal
is only to punish herself and others, she may decide that such an attitude can
lead to no good for her child.

(c) A college student steals from the campus bookstore. Does he really need
the money, and is it worth the risks of being caught? He must consider the
attitudes and values of others, but also weigh the risks he himself runs in his
thefts. Often, stealing represents a symbolic defiance of social norms, one wholly
disproportionate to the real risks run and to the real gains possible. Some people
steal small and inexpensive things, though they risk both jail and ruin if caught.

Facts   In all these cases, the consequences of actions look not to the mechanical conditions of movement, but to the intentions inherent in all human actions—intentions which must be detected though hidden, and sometimes inferred though overlaid with rationalizations and self-deception. In all moral decisions, the agent must in effect consider not only what has happened and will happen, but also what he and others really want to have happen—*even where he changes his mind.*

It is worth noting that courts of law make exactly the assumptions we have come to see are necessary. A man is tried for murder only on the assumption that he intended to kill his victim. If he did not so intend, we regard the death as accidental—manslaughter for example. An act of fraud requires an intent to defraud. The only issue before us is whether to regard intentions and feelings as facts or not. But if there are not facts about feelings which look to the objects as well as the goal of such feelings, we have no intelligible conception of the emotions at all. We turn now to the consideration of feelings in the making of moral decisions.

QUESTIONS

1. Discuss the difficulties which face the position that there are no facts, that there is no truth to be known.
2. Is it ever right to tell a lie because it is too much trouble to tell the truth?
3. Is it ever right to tell a lie because other people will despise you for telling the truth?
4. A man finds a wallet in the street. List the variety of scientific laws which might be relevant to his decision to return the wallet. Do you think the variety and number of these laws so great that we should ignore them?
5. Suppose cigarette smoking caused cancer 100% of the time. Should it be prohibited by law? Suppose only 90% of the time. 80%. 1%. Discuss the relevance of scientific information to our moral evaluation of a law prohibiting the sale of tobacco.
6. Can we give a description of a human action which does not look to a proposed goal? Explain how relevant this issue is to moral theory.
7. Can a scientific explanation be given of human actions? Do the causes of an action explain it? Take the case of repairing a leaky faucet as a concrete example.
8. Evaluate an act of assassination from the point of view of the continuum of means and ends.
9. Evaluate working in a factory from the point of view of the continuum of means and ends.

10. A man decides that come what may, he will always follow his moral principles.
Does he thereby eliminate the risk of doing what is wrong? Explain.

SELECTED READINGS

Some interesting works which develop a new and challenging view of the physical sciences:

T. S. Kuhn, *The Structure of Scientific Revolutions*, 1962, University of Chicago.
S. Toulmin, *Foresight and Understanding*, 1961, Harper.
D. Shapere, *Philosophical Problems of Natural Science*, 1965, Macmillan.

Some studies in the relationship between ethics and science.

B. F. Skinner, *Science and Human Behavior*, 1953, Macmillan. A well known behaviorist's position.
J. Dewey, *Theory of Valuation*, 1939, University of Chicago.
"The Unity of Behavior," *Philosophy and Civilization*, 1931, Minton, Balch. and J. H. Tufts, *Ethics*, 1938, Holt.
S. Toulmin, *An Examination of the Place of Reason in Ethics*, 1950, Cambridge University.
A. Gewirth, "Positive 'Ethics' and Normative 'Science,'" *Philosophical Review*, Vol. LXIX, No. 3 (July 1960).
A. Edel, *Ethical Judgment*, 1955, Free Press.

An anthology of readings on intentions and actions:

D. Gustafson ed., *Essays in Philosophical Psychology*, 1964, Doubleday.

IV. FEELINGS

A. Pleasure

The feeling which has been given the most important role in the history of moral theory is the feeling of pleasure—though a pleasure almost always associated with the absence of pain. Several philosophers have based their moral theories on pleasure and pain. Epicurus, for example, claims that the goal of life is the achievement of pleasure. The position that regards all goods as pleasures is called *hedonism*. Strangely enough, from the very beginning certain difficulties haunt those who would defend pleasure as the only good. In particular, we may ask: what is it to achieve pleasure? To achieve a fleeting but intense pleasure, or a continuous but rather mild sense of enjoyment? Epicurus defends the second, and eventually comes to the view that the aim of life is rather a continuous absence of pain.

What happens when such interpretations are given of pleasure and pain is that the surface plausibility which hedonism possesses vanishes. The view that what is good will give us pleasure is a very powerful one, and a valuable antidote to an extreme and oppressive sense of duty. A moral law that leads to no pleasure for *anyone* is a harsh and unconvincing principle to follow. If no one is to be given pleasure by an action, why then perform it? We note, however, that some pleasures are intense but brief, and lead to considerable pain. Like Epicurus, we may look instead for the absence of pain. Unfortunately, a life without pain is not so plausible as an antidote to duty. Hedonism looks to the gain of something *for the agent*. Many people consider a life without some intense pleasures more a bore than an ideal. Moreover, there are some violent and strong pleasures which verge on the very edge of pain. I have in mind not only sensual pleasures such as that of sexual intercourse, but also the pleasure of being emotionally affected by a powerful drama, whose pleasure rests in good part in how much we suffer and are moved by it.

Hedonism is a constantly recurring theme in conventional moral thought.

The oppressiveness of duty and the risks of life seem to make people desirous of a little joy, and to make them consider a life without pleasure as barren of goods. Plato and Aristotle both criticize the identification of what is good with what gives pleasure. At one point, Aristotle dismisses the identification as "slavish." He clearly has in mind the fact that men of good character, men who are conventionally respected for their character, are noble and virtuous, sometimes even to the point of personal suffering. Ibsen dramatizes the nobility of a passion for truth in *An Enemy of the People*, to the point of ruin for Dr. Stockmann's family. Some duties are more important than our own pleasure or even lack of pain. If we look to what men actually do, rather than what a hedonist says they ought to do, we discover that they often think that what is right demands a personal sacrifice of them.

There are two forms of hedonism worth distinguishing. *Psychological hedonism* is the view that the sole motivating force in human behavior is the desire for pleasure. All evidence speaks against this position, yet it persists. We will look at its particular problems in a moment. *Moral hedonism* is not a theory of what men *in fact* do, but what they *ought* to do. In saying that the good is what gives pleasure, a man may mean either psychological or moral hedonism. If the latter, what he means is that the only truly good thing in experience is pleasure. This is the view which Aristotle calls "slavish." It follows from moral hedonism that men ought to do what gives them pleasure, and that only. We will study this position first.

It is important to realize that the identification of the good with pleasure takes both the nature and the character of pleasure for granted. Pleasure simply is. Pain simply is. As soon as we make a distinction between types of pleasure, we have moved to a qualified hedonism subject to Plato's devastating criticism: there are *good* pleasures and *bad* pleasures. Therefore, pleasure is not *in itself* good, but its goodness is an added quality.

As we shall see, the difficulties in the path of equating the good with sheer and unqualified pleasure are insurmountable. We have already touched on the difficulty of ascertaining what it means to have pleasure—whether it means *intense* or *enduring* pleasure. How shall we choose between an intense but brief pleasure and a mild but enduring one? The claim that intense or even enduring pleasures are better cannot be defended on hedonistic grounds alone. If there are better and worse, preferable and less preferable pleasures, then pleasure itself is not what is good.

There are several physical difficulties with unqualified pleasure, inherent within it, which make it seem not itself good. First, pleasure is not continuous, but is basically intermittent. Intense pleasures must be interrupted by rest or they become painful. In return, as Schopenhauer notes, pleasure as a goal is a strikingly unreliable one. To pursue the goal of pleasure is to be in a state of unrest, while to achieve it is to eliminate the desire and therefore also the pleasure. A thirsty man obtains pleasure from drinking. But drinking eliminates his thirst and also his pleasure.

Second, pleasure is unreliable and precarious. It depends on the state of the body and its health, which are not always controllable. Moreover, many of the more intense pleasures are destructive to the health of the body, and to its capacity for other pleasures. The pleasure received from some drugs literally destroys the body, and in effect destroys itself. Pleasure has a habit of changing into its opposite.

Third, as we mentioned before, pleasure and the desire for pleasure are inherently without limits. The pleasure of a miser in his money has no end—he may want all the money in the world, and therefore be unable to achieve his goal. The more we have, the more we want. For this reason too, pleasure becomes pain and leads to dissatisfaction.

Fourth, pleasures are enhanced in anticipation more than in their actualization. The greater pleasures are provided by more than the senses alone, and involve reflective awareness of the pleasure. But the more intense the pleasure, the more does it tend to overwhelm reflective appreciation, and to destroy even the awareness of the pleasure.

Fifth, unqualified pleasure is dangerous, since it does not look beyond itself to its fruits. The consequence of many immediate pleasures is later suffering. We may casually remark that too many pleasures are *unwise*. In looking ahead to later and enduring pleasures, we qualify our desire for pleasure by our knowledge of different kinds of pleasure. The major argument against equating pleasure with what is good is that there are better and worse pleasures, good and bad pleasures. This is Plato's point.

Pleasures may be criticized in terms of their consequences as good and bad. Plato dramatizes this point by an example which provides us with a slightly different argument. There are some pleasures, Plato points out, which are not worthy of any concern. When we itch, we gain pleasure from scratching. Yet a life of the pleasure of scratching is not a good life. Imagine a bird which lives a life of continual pleasure, eating and defecating. Would any of us consider that a life good *for a man*? There are good and bad pleasures, at least for human beings.

This last argument is a very powerful one, though it involves a more critical approach to the nature of the good with which pleasure is to be equated. In claiming pleasure is good, we may simply have in mind an uncritical conception of both pleasure and the good. Suppose we ask, what is good about pleasure? We may interpret this question as follows: in calling something "good," what we mean is that it is something that should serve to guide our actions. It is a justified aim or goal. Things are not *just* good. They are good as they function to be *sought* or *intended*.

We are here giving a functional definition of what is good. Something is good when we should aim for it. Calling something "good" is declaring it a worth-while goal. In asking if pleasure is really good, we are asking whether pleasure is always a worth-while goal. Are there not pleasures unfit to be pursued? Are not pleasures too fleeting and intermittent to constitute viable aims? Finally, are there not pleasures which no human being would regard as worth achieving?

We may dramatize this last point in the following way. Suppose we could place electric probes in a man's brain, and stimulate him to the most intense and continual pleasures, and for his whole life. He would lie in a nutrient solution, tended by machines and titillated electrically. Suppose that this provided a maximal realization of pleasure. Would it be worth doing? Who would choose it over a productive and creative life, though one containing fewer pleasures? It is in this sense that Aristotle condemns the view that the good is pleasure as slavish. Only a broken man cannot imagine something better than the passive experience of pleasure. To Aristotle, happiness or the good is not passive pleasure, but is a mode of activity. The goal of action is part of the action. We intend what will maintain our powers as agents. It is better to be Socrates suffering than a contented pig.

Psychological hedonism is not a theory of what men ought to do or seek, but is rather a theory which attempts to describe what they actually do and what their actual motives are. Psychoanalytic theory, in Freud's version, rests on what he calls the *pleasure principle*: all human activity is to be understood as a quest for pleasure. The plausibility of such a theory is derived from the search for a psychological principle which underlies and explains all action. What *could* motivate a man to act except the desire for pleasure?

We may note almost immediately, however, that men often act as they do where no obvious pleasure can result. A man returns a wallet he finds in the street, though he could use the money himself. A boy is willing to go to jail rather than to be inducted into the army. On the surface, men often do what they think is right *instead of* what will benefit them or give them pleasure.

In order to meet the force of such counter-examples, psychological hedonists must expand the range of pleasures they allow. Thus, the two cases mentioned are explained by the claim that men often obtain pleasure from doing what they think is right—a sense of rightness. Freud explains that the guilt and anxiety generated by a conviction of duty is great enough to make men act according to their consciences to avoid the torment of remorse.

Let us take an even more extreme example. A man is tortured for information, knowing he will be killed as soon as he talks. Can we possibly interpret his refusal to give the information as motivated by a desire for pleasure? If we do, then we have done two things as well. First, we have expanded our notion of the pleasures to include almost anything. Rather than claiming that men do what they do to achieve one of a definite number of pleasures, we are saying instead that anything which a man does we will *call* a pleasure! Psychological hedonism keeps discovering new sources of pleasure, to explain those cases where men ignore the traditional pleasures. The whole position becomes trivial, in the sense that no evidence which could be found would count to disprove the theory.

Second, we must explain the choice of remaining silent as receiving so great a pleasure from the sense of having done one's duty that the extreme pain of torture will fail to matter. The problem here is that, in all obvious respects, the physical pain is great, and the sense of rightness is small by comparison. This brings us to one of the most difficult problems for all forms of hedonism—the comparison of various pleasures among themselves.

The deeper problem which psychological hedonism addresses is that of motivation. What motivates a man to act as he does ? What psychological hedonism does is to assimilate all intentions to desires, and, further, all desires to the desire for pleasure. We may note that a man who acts from conscience may not desire anything except to do what is right. He may have no desire to acquire, to possess, or to experience anything. He may have no concern for pleasure—though perhaps he ought to. His desire, looking to possess no object, is no *appetite*. It may be but an emotional disposition to regard the required sacrifice with reverence and approval. We need a broader study of feelings and desires if we are to understand human motivation.

Psychological hedonism may take two forms: Either men always do what will give them one of a definite number of pleasures—which is obviously false. Or, whatever men do we will call gaining pleasure—which is trivial. Psychological hedonism is on one interpretation obviously false and on the other trivial. In any case, it has the problem of explaining a choice among pleasures. We will study this last difficulty in the context of a discussion of the principle of utility.

B. Utilitarianism

The two most well known utilitarians are Jeremy Bentham and John Stuart Mill. For simplicity, we will consider only Mill's version of utilitarianism. The general principle of utility is that *an action is good or right insofar as it produces the greatest amount of happiness*. The first response of almost every student who reads this principle is, *whose* happiness? The second response is, what is happiness? Mill defines happiness as *intended pleasure, and the absence of pain*. We are, therefore, still concerned with the many problems connected with understanding what is good in terms of pleasure. As for the question of whose pleasure is to be used as a measure, Mill sees no problem here at all. There is no reason why one person's happiness is to be thought of as superior to another's. Therefore, an action is good or right insofar as it produces the greatest amount of pleasure for *everyone*.

The transition from the pursuit of one's own pleasure to considering the pleasures of other men as well is not easy to defend on utilitarian grounds alone. Mill seems to take for granted that any moral principle is of a general nature that transcends any particular man's interests. We may note the Golden Rule: do unto others as you would have them do unto you—that is, *all* others. Moral rules are without concern for specific persons. We recall Kant's first version of the Categorical Imperative: act so as to make your maxim a universal law.

Let us be clear about the issues here. Kant virtually *defines* a moral law as one without particular exceptions. A man's particular interests are morally irrelevant. Mill seems to follow the same path. There is no need to build a case to convince a

man that he ought to think of others in the same terms in which he thinks of
himself. That is what "morality" means.

The word "moral" has two senses, and it is about time we noted them. The expression "it is moral to _____" may mean: (1) it is the right thing to do; or, (2) it is part of the subject matter or field of ethics. "Murder is immoral," means that murder is *wrong*. "A moral law has no particular exceptions" may seem on the surface to assert that making exceptions is *wrong*. But it may also mean that making exceptions is not what one does in moral decisions, *by definition*. It is not uncommon to confuse the second point with the first. That is because disobedience of what is right is often conceived as wrong. There is no room in most people's moral views for the simple *disregard* of moral principles.

The question, "why should we look to the happiness of others as well as ourselves?" is usually given two kinds of answers, and two kinds of arguments in support of them. One is that it is *wrong* to consider only oneself. How can this be shown? To most people, only by an appeal to a general principle such as that of utility or the Golden Rule. The transition from one's own happiness to the happiness of others is not something to be justified. It is rather a fundamental principle of the moral view proposed. The other argument is not a moral one, but is a theoretical or logical argument. The logical meaning of the expression "moral principle" is that of a principle which obligates everyone equally to obey it. A man who asks why we consider other people in moral affairs is asking a meaningless question. Put extremely crudely, it is part of the rules of the game to consider everyone equal before the moral law.

There is a third way of dealing with this issue, to be found in Socrates' reply to Thrasymachus, and in some later passages of Mill's *Utilitarianism*. Socrates argues that justice is a good in itself, and leads to what Thrasymachus himself considers good—knowledge and freedom. Unfortunately, Thrasymachus does not realize this on his own, for his education has not served him well. Mill points out that the ultimate sanction of the principle of utility—that which brings people to follow it—is "the conscientious feelings of mankind. Undoubtedly this sanction has no binding efficacy on those who do not possess the feelings it appeals to; but neither will these persons be more obedient to any other moral principle than to the utilitarian one." In the end, either a man has a conscience or he does not; either he is concerned about others or he is not; either his enlightened personal interest is served in considering others or it is not. A man who lacks certain feelings, preferences, or abilities at deliberation cannot be convinced that certain general principles of morality are justified. In other words, whether men do or do not have moral convictions is a problem for moral education. It is not a problem of importance to moral theory. The only problem is a practical one—how to engender in men what we take to be right.

We have been discussing the general problem of whether moral principles can be given an ultimate justification. We will put this issue aside for now.

Feelings   Nevertheless, the problem of others can be regarded as a problem for utilitarianism even from a different standpoint. The problem here is not of justifying our considering the happiness of others. Let us suppose that we wish to do so. The question is, can we succeed in doing so on the basis of the principle of utility? On this principle, we must calculate the greatest amount of happiness for everyone.

But is it really possible to perform such a calculation? How does one compare several men slightly inconvenienced with one person given many good things? The issue is not whether the calculation is arduous or not, but whether it makes any sense at all to speak of *amounts* of happiness. It is difficult enough to draw the line between happiness and unhappiness. It is certainly problematic to consider the tremendous range of alternatives to being either happy or unhappy which fall between these two states.

Does Mill's explanation of happiness in terms of pleasures and pains lead us in the direction of a solution to this problem? Not obviously. First of all, can we compare an enduring mild pleasure with an intense but brief one? How can we tell which is superior? In particular, how are we to tell when only one of the two will ever be experienced in the particular circumstances involved? Second, how can we compare the varieties of pleasures and pains among different persons? There seem to be no grounds for setting up such a calculation.

An individual person has considerable difficulty choosing among pleasures and deciding that some are greater. Spinoza points out that we always prefer the nearer pleasure, though in fact the later one may be far more intense. Can a man really choose between not going to college and having the pleasures of earning money and free time, or becoming a physician with the pleasures of success and dedication—and choose on the basis of greater amounts of pleasure? How are these amounts to be calculated? And if we cannot make sense of amounts of pleasure for one man, how can we do so for many? One of the more compelling arguments in favor of a freer and less rigid society is that no one can determine to any degree of precision what is more valuable to others and even himself. We must therefore allow people room to try out alternatives and to change their minds.

The most striking problem, however, is sharply revealed in our example of choosing to attend medical school or not. A student must choose between two courses of action which will have complex consequences for him over several years. Such a choice is in itself extremely difficult. But in addition to the number of consequences he must consider, each course of action will change him and will change also what will give him pleasure in the future. How can a boy of eighteen choose among alternative styles of life, where they each involve major changes in what he will become, and in what will give him pleasure? What we do changes us. We cannot calculate amounts of pleasure under these circumstances. Here is another reason why principles are so necessary to evaluation—to generate some degree of uniformity amidst the complex affairs of human experience.

If we have not yet faced a sufficient number of problems, Mill himself provides us with another. We need, *in addition to* a calculus of pleasure, a distinction

between higher and lower pleasures. Higher pleasures are those a man of experience
prefers. Lower pleasures are preferred only by men who have not experienced the
higher ones. Mill argues, as we have in the last section, that "it is better to be a
human being dissatisfied than a pig satisfied; better to be Socrates dissatisfied
than a fool satisfied." That may be true. But it destroys the last vestige of
plausibility a calculus of pleasure can be said to have. Pleasures are not preferable
on the basis of quantity or intensity alone.

To this point, we have considered only the difficulties inherent in the very
conception of the principle of utility. There remain several other difficulties for
Mill's version which are worth noting. First of all, the principle of utility defines
the test of an *action* in being right or wrong. We look to the amount of happiness
the action will produce. Suppose we put all our prior criticisms aside, and assume
a general measure of benefit. Would it be right to do what makes most people
happier? In *The Brothers Karamazov*, Ivan Karamazov asks his brother whether it
would be right to torture a child now, if that would bring paradise for everyone
else tomorrow? Is it right to harm one person, if by doing so many others are
benefited? In a more plausible example, would it be right to throw an innocent
man in jail to relieve the anxieties of the crowd? Most of us would think not.

The application of the principle of utility to *acts* is called *act utilitarianism*,
and is susceptible to the kinds of criticisms just proposed. A well known alternative, which Mill himself touches on in his discussion of justice, is to apply the
principle of utility to *rules*, not acts. This is called *rule utilitarianism*. We ask,
which *rule* will bring about the greatest happiness to everyone? Would a known
rule that we ought to punish the innocent when it will benefit men in general be
conducive to general welfare? Certainly not, for it would generate fear and anxiety,
disproportionate to the relief of anxiety hoped for.

The distinction between act and rule utilitarianism is a very important one,
as we will see in our discussion of moral principles. It is unbelievably difficult to
evaluate actions in themselves, and isolated from the rules proposed to govern
them. When young people challenge the norms of their society, and fail to replace
society's rules by alternative principles, they make their decisions much more
difficult. Rule utilitarianism is far more defensible than act utilitarianism. One
hypothesis to consider as a consequence is that moral decisions should look to the
determination of rules and principles even more than to specific actions which a
man may perform.

There is one last point concerning Mill's version of utilitarianism which is
worth mentioning, as extremely relevant to our study of feelings. Mill argues that
the principle of utility can be given a *proof* or justification as follows: The only
test of something being desirable (or good) is that it is desired. Mill argues that
desirability is analogous to visibility. The test for visibility is *being seen*. The test
for being desirable is *being desired*. Pleasure, then, is the only goal of action, in
being the only thing desired.

Mill here commits the same error we ascribed to psychological hedonists—

that of equating all desires with the desire for pleasure. His fundamental error, however, is far more interesting. That is, of equating the desirable with the desired. John Dewey has attacked this equation forcefully, arguing that not every thing desired is desirable. There are some desires we come to discover are dangerous, fleeting, ugly, precarious, and so forth. There are steps to be taken from what we desire to what we *ought* to desire. Dewey accepts Mill's fundamental premise—that we must in some way look to what we do desire in order to determine what we should desire. But no simple equation will do. We will now explore this issue more deeply.

C. Emotivism

The emotivist position has many refinements which are not worth elaborating here. We will consider only its most general characteristics. The fundamental principle of emotivism is that moral statements are *not* factual claims, nor are they genuine ascriptions of properties to objects. A moral sentence is therefore a rather odd linguistic item. Its function is not to provide information, but to affect the feelings and attitudes of others and even of the speaker himself. When a parent tells a child, "that was a bad thing to do," the result is to condition the child's *attitudes* toward such actions.

The emotivist theory has many strengths. Its greatest one is that it calls our attention—if too strongly—to a feature of moral expressions which we have hitherto noted only slightly. Moral expressions are heavily laden with emotional attitudes. We will avoid an elaborate analysis of attitudes. It will suffice to note that men possess attitudes in the sense that they are moved for and against things. And among the most striking of our attitudes are our moral feelings. Our moral convictions are precisely for and against certain actions and events. To say that a man "ought" to do something is to betray a rather strong attitude in favor of that action. To say that something else is "wrong" is to reveal an attitude against it. What we call "good" is also something we incline toward in our feelings and attitudes. What we consider "bad" we are moved against.

All ethical language is heavily laden with feeling, and in two respects. First, the language expresses the speaker's own attitudes, sometimes very strongly. To call an action "evil" is to condemn it as strongly as we can. It is as violent an expression as a man can use. When a principle such as "murder is wrong" is used in moral discussions, we know that not only the speaker but most other men are strongly moved against acts of murder. Finally, we certainly know through experience that men are often moved to punish or at least censure actions of which they strongly disapprove. An element of apprehension is therefore present in anyone who hears a violent expression of moral outrage.

The second and most striking quality of moral language is its ability to move the attitudes of those who hear it. From the very beginning, a child is conditioned by words like "good," "bad," "right," and "wrong." His mother uses such a word, and hugs him and smiles, or frowns and raises her voice. The aspect of personality which psychoanalysis calls "internalization" is another way of representing the same process: the charging of both language and actions with attitudes pro and con. And an important feature of the growth and spread of attitudes is that a man who has been conditioned to certain emotional attitudes then acts in ways which foster similar attitudes in others. The emotivist theory provides a powerful explanation of the strength of our moral convictions, and the uniform character they take on in a given society. Social norms are not merely prevailing and common modes of activity. They are common *attitudes* possessed by men who live together and speak together, and who influence each other strongly.

To this point we have given only the premises on which emotivism rests, premises which are so obviously true that all moral thought must accept them. Emotivism, however, takes an additional step. Not only does moral language express attitudes; not only does moral language influence attitudes; but, emotivists claim, that is *all* it does. Moral sentences assert no facts, and make no claims. To give reasons, arguments, or any sort of explanation for an ethical position is not to support it logically, but only to influence the attitudes of the listener. Facts are indeed referred to, but only so as to change and reenforce given attitudes. In that sense, reasoning in morals is viewed as different *in kind* from reasoning in science. Using a classical distinction, ethical discourse aims at best to *persuade*, while scientific evidence is given to *prove*.

It should be clear how naturally emotivism follows from the premise that facts do not alone justify moral beliefs. For then giving facts cannot be a mode of proof. It can be understood only as a mode of persuasion. However, emotivists seem also to regard all other forms of moral argumentation as merely persuasive also. One cannot derive any moral conclusions from any moral premises as a form of proof. Certainly such a view is not defensible on logical grounds. From the premises, "not paying taxes is a form of theft" and "theft is wrong," it follows that "not paying taxes is wrong." But, the emotivist may ask, what can possibly justify the premises? Facts alone cannot. Intuition is unreliable. Therefore, moral premises are merely formulated attitudes, and arguments from them are no proofs —only devices for persuasion.

The greatest problem for the emotivist theory is its view of the factual character of moral language and also of the relationship of moral language to other facts. The extreme and rather pure version of emotivism we have considered so far makes ethical language only expressive and persuasive, not assertive of facts at all. Facts merely enhance the rhetorical force of ethical pronouncements. The consequence of the extreme view is that two people who are engaged in a moral dispute do not genuinely disagree, but are merely trying to persuade each other. How then can we explain the fact that the discovery of one or another fact may settle the controversy? The extreme emotivist can claim only that the fact persuaded one of the disputants to the other's view.

Suppose a mother and her daughter are engaged in a dispute over whether a suitor for the daughter's hand is "a fine young man." The mother is convinced that he is not, because he has not held a steady job. Suppose her information is wrong, and the mother is shown that the boy has indeed worked steadily and been promoted several times. She may now agree that he is indeed "fine." Has she merely been persuaded by the fact? Or, rather, has she not been looking to such facts from the beginning?

In order to meet such an objection, some emotivists develop more complex interpretations of the relationship between ethical language and facts. Some admit that not only does the sentence "capital punishment is wrong" express the speaker's attitudes, it also *asserts* them. That is, the speaker at least in part is telling the listener what the speaker in fact believes. In addition, if the speaker is known to consider the consequences of actions in arriving at his moral beliefs, then we may also infer the fact that he thinks that capital punishment will have unfortunate consequences—perhaps in generating fear, or in leading people generally to a disrespect for life.

In a further step, emotivists may admit that a given speaker may literally *mean* by an ethical word certain specific properties. A man may literally mean by saying that capital punishment is good that it is an effective deterrent. Thus, it is a fact for him that capital punishment is right because it effectively deters men from murder. Emotivists may then admit that sometimes or often men may be *asserting* in their ethical discourse their concern with certain facts.

But, to avoid a position of ethical naturalism, which maintains that ethical beliefs look to facts alone, emotivists always conclude that the attitudes are fundamental and uneliminable. Suppose a man *means* by saying that capital punishment is good that it is an effective deterrent to murder. A naturalist might say, then, that a factual dispute alone would settle the issue of the value of capital punishment. The emotivist, however, would deny this. For a man can always change what he means by a moral term, since it does no more than represent his attitudes. Suppose a man finds that he approves of capital punishment in the case of a particularly brutal murder, but has been shown that capital punishment is no deterrent. He then simply changes his attitude toward the deterrence, and re-interprets what he finds wrong about murder so that it entails capital punishment. Ultimately, what the emotivist does is to rest his entire position on the principle that facts alone do not constitute a moral argument.

Yet it is worth nothing that we have not included among the facts worth mentioning by the emotivist the facts of the agent's own attitudes and feelings. It is not easy to see why these would not settle the issue. From facts about others plus facts about oneself, and one's own goals and attitudes, can we not determine what is good or bad? And if a man's attitudes change, then so may what is right and wrong for him. But facts about these attitudes do seem to be able to settle the issue. We must put such concerns aside for now.

Emotivism has great strength. It explains the fact that disagreements among men on moral issues often seem unsettleable. It explains the strong force of the

motivation which most men have to do what they think is good or right. It stresses
the persuasive character of ethical language, which is central to all moral education,
and to the effectiveness of social norms in generating conformity. A weak form of
emotivism which maintains that the function of ethical language *in part* is to
persuade seems irreproachable.

However, the weaknesses of emotivism are equally great. In general, men are
convinced that moral disagreements are genuine disagreements, and can be settled
in a genuine fashion. In particular, when a man changes his moral beliefs, he does
not view his former belief as merely another attitude. He thinks of it as *mistaken*.
Contrast such a conception with a change in *taste*. A man used to like peanut butter
when a child; now he abhors it. His former preference for peanut butter was not a
mistake. A man who once loved Beethoven and now prefers Mozart may not regard
his earlier preference as a mistake, but as a change in taste or attitude. A further
contrast is worth noting. A man may decide that Tchaikowsky is a second-rate
composer. He used to think that Tchaikowsky was a great composer, but changed
his mind. This is somewhat different, for it looks to standards of judgment and
to facts about Tchaikowsky's music.

The example of art points up another problem. It is perfectly intelligible for a
man to say, "I do not like Rembrandt, but I can see that he is a great artist." So
also, it is not absurd to say, "I do not approve of this war, but I can accept it as
justified." Either we need an elaborate theory of how a man's attitudes may
conflict with each other—for they do—or we must view such examples as showing
that a man may find that his own emotional attitudes support a position he
believes on other grounds to be wrong, and the reverse as well.

A further point is that moral *questions* become difficult to understand on the
basis of emotivism. If a man asks, "is capital punishment right or wrong?"
whom is he trying to persuade? And when he looks to facts to justify his conclusion, is he trying to persuade himself? Rather, he appears to be interested in
determining which attitude he *ought* to come to have, on the basis of the facts
available. Here is the mortal weakness of emotivism. Since its fundamental principle
is that ethical language expresses attitudes, then where no definite attitude can be
found, as in a genuine moral conflict, ethical language seems inappropriate. True,
we may regard a moral conflict as ambivalence, or a conflict among attitudes. But
in seeking a resolution of the conflict, we do not look merely to the formation of
some attitude, any attitude. We seek the preferable or best position to take. We
look to facts and circumstances, to consequences, and to our own expectations.

To paraphrase once again Peirce's four ways of fixing belief: where we do not
know what is right, then we may indeed decide arbitrarily and on no grounds
whatsoever, appeal to some authority or our intuition, or we may intelligently
look to facts and investigate the situation to determine the answer. Emotivism
cannot justify the only method among these which uses intelligence—the method
of inquiry. The greater questions of ethics concern not what we *do* prefer, but what
we *ought* to prefer. Our given attitudes we may ourselves recognize to be un-

desirable, in terms of what they lead to. The most fundamental act in morals is an intentional change in attitudes. None of this makes sense within the confines of emotivism.

D. Relativism

The emotivist theory leads naturally to a relativistic theory, though one which may take several forms. Let us suppose that emotivism is correct. It would follow, then, that different men might have different attitudes toward a given action, and that *there would exist no justifiable method for reconciling their attitudes*. Put another way, when two persons make contradictory ethical claims, each is as justifiable as the other. If one man believes that cannibalism is wrong, and another believes that cannibalism is right, then as long as each is unpersuaded by the other, there is no justifiable procedure for reconciling their differences. Moral beliefs are relative to the person who possesses them. They are right *for him*. This position I will call *strong relativism*.

Strong relativism is an instance of a more general position which may be called extreme scepticism. All extreme scepticisms suffer from a fundamental weakness: they are self-stultifying. Protagoras, whose principle that "man is the measure of all things" is regarded as entailing both strong relativism and extreme scepticism, is taken forcibly to task in Plato's *Theaetetus*. The central problem for all scepticisms and relativisms is that they require extremely sophisticated interpretations. The reason for this is that the premises they are challenging in their scepticism turn out to be necessary to their own expression. For example, extreme scepticism is sometimes formulated: "No statement is true." If so, then this last statement is not true either. Consider another version, "nothing can be known." Then neither can the truth of this claim. If we make exceptions of such claims, then we cannot be given any justification for doing so, since justification would require other statements and claims, which would also have to be known.

The basic problem is that an assertion is and must function as a claim to truth and also as a means of communicating knowledge or information. Therefore, we cannot *assert* that no information can be communicated. We cannot *claim* that no claims are true. Plato attacks Protagoras' principle for being senseless. Either Protagoras knows the principle to be true, or there is no point in asserting it. Put another way, a man who makes a claim in effect functions as an authority with regard to that claim (though he may be wrong). Protagoras, for example, would teach others the truth of his principle—though if it is true, then what they believe is as true a measure as his teachings. An extreme sceptic might try to weasel out by claiming that although no statements are truer than any others, some are of greater practical value. Plato's reply is to note that at least, then, it must be *true* that some claims are more useful than others. The conclusion we must come to, then, is that either no claims of any sort can be made, or that when made they may be true and authoritative—true in the sense that all statements to the contrary are *false*.

In the case of moral beliefs, extreme scepticism fares no better. If every man's moral views are exactly as good as any other's, then moral disputes make no sense whatsoever. Such disputes collapse immediately into mere attempts to persuade— and, it is worth remarking, without a hope of success. For if a man accepts strong relativism, then he knows that his antagonist's views are no better than his own. Even the most absurd advertising rests on the implicit premise that the claims made by the advertisement are true. Though they may not be, something *is* true. It is simply impossible to maintain strong moral relativism as an intelligible position.

Does this mean that it is a false position? Indeed not. We cannot prove to a sceptic that scepticism is false. We may only point out the consequences of maintaining it. They are complete silence and avoidance of judgment. If no belief is true, then we may believe *anything*. No grounds exist even for our own beliefs. Evidence becomes meaningless. We end up in total chaos and groundlessness. Nothing can be said, nothing can be done upon grounds. So too in the case of evaluation; if all normative beliefs are as good as any others, then all evaluation becomes meaningless. A man then cannot even choose, for that is to have a preference. Every whim becomes an end to pursue. Extreme scepticism degenerates into silence and valuelessness, a mere passing of time without choice or appreciation. Worst of all, we cannot even regard this position as good or valuable, at least not if it is consistent with itself.

If we need a model, we may imagine a man transformed into a rock, without consciousness or desire. Here indeed no preferences are had. No alternatives are better, none are worse. Or imagine him instead an amoeba, without consciousness, but with attractions and repulsions. Life is here simply what it is, neither good nor bad. But as soon as we add a consciousness of values and choices, then we are committed to what is *truly* preferable and genuinely good.

We turn then to some forms of weak relativism. The most obvious way to escape the self-stultifying character of extreme scepticism is to move from the principle "no claims can be known to be true," to the principle "all statements and conclusions may be false." The analogue of this position in morals is that all our moral beliefs may prove to be mistaken. Therefore, when two men differ, we cannot be *sure* which one is right. Such a relativism is a very modest one, promoting, one would think, a very tolerant attitude toward moral differences.

Strangely, it is rather difficult to maintain so modest a scepticism. It tends to be attracted to the two extremes, and for good reason. Either the modest scepticism which admits the permanent possibility of error changes into "all claims may be mistaken, but mine are really correct." Or else it degenerates into extreme scepticism: "all claims may be mistaken, therefore no position is more justified than any other."

The reason for this is not hard to discern. Such modest scepticism is merely a form of caution. It warns us to beware of hasty conclusions, and of acting on them before the evidence is in. Or, even when we are convinced, to realize that new evidence may come in, calling for us to alter our beliefs. In the case of moral relativism, a modest scepticism urges us to consider others and their beliefs, and to look to both sides of every question. But the very modesty of the position gives it no cutting edge. It is an affirmation no more of relativism than of absolute morality. It is merely an expression of an attitude which all open-minded men ought to have. But open-mindedness is the antithesis of ordinary morality, which demands strong loyalties.

Therefore, the moral imperative of open-mindedness—and I shall argue later that it is an imperative, and that open-mindedness and a modest scepticism are among the greatest values in human life—tends to undermine its own forcefulness. It degenerates into other positions where moral fervor sits more easily. It is difficult to be strongly in favor of letting your enemies speak, and strongly in favor of considering the possibility that your most cherished beliefs may be wrong.

The greatest difficulty with modest scepticism is that it attaches to any position whatsoever. We can always be asked to be open-minded, whether relativists or not. In this sense, modest scepticism is not a true form of relativism. We turn then to yet another version of weak relativism.

Here we qualify strong relativism not by the word "may" but by the word "some": some moral beliefs are justifiably different for different persons. Sometimes it is supposed that men differ in their *ultimate* values. Sometimes what is meant is that *in fact* men differ in their moral beliefs. We will consider three interpretations and explanations of this form of weak relativism.

(1) It is a fact that different societies have differing moral customs. Cannibalism is considered not merely acceptable but even a good in some societies, where it is believed that certain virtues are transmitted by ingestion. Many anthropologists are convinced that norms and customs are relative to different social groups and societies, and that what is thought right and wrong is to be understood simply in terms of what members of different societies actually do.

Unfortunately, it is far from clear how far anthropological relativism can be pushed on the basis of the evidence adduced. The observable fact is that men in different societies differ in what they consider right and wrong. But we have not shown that there is not a fundamental agreement on the most important values, which would permit an agreement on the more specific issues if all the relevant facts were known. For example, cannibals may believe that honor and bravery are transmitted by eating the flesh of a brave man. This appears to be a factual matter, and perhaps a rigorous study of the results of cannibalism would permit agreement among cannibals and noncannibals.

For many years, the sheer differences among societies and their norms seemed to dominate anthropological thinking on moral values. More recent evidence, however, has suggested that in fact there is a rather definite agreement throughout most societies on what may be called *basic* values—involving fairness, the responsibilities of parents toward children, and the value of knowledge and the arts. There is a tremendous variation among other more superficial values. But if it were true that superficial values are tested in terms of basic values and factual

information, we might well find almost total agreement among all men on even
superficial values once the facts were known. We cannot disprove this first form
of weak relativism. But we cannot regard it as proved either.

(2) The most common argument for weak relativism notes merely that it is a
logical possibility that men may differ in their ultimate values. And if they do,
then we must acknowledge that some values could differ among men, and that
we would have no way of reconciling them. This is either a version of modest
scepticism, or it is akin to position (1), with merely an argument grounded in
possibilities.

For example, we find that men differ in their concern for animals, and
especially in their attitudes toward the suffering of animals. What could possibly
convince us of the correctness of the position and beliefs of an animal lover, as
contrasted with a man who is emotionally quite indifferent to animals?

A fundamental error has been made in such an argument which is worth
explicit notice. We recall that the problem with emotivism is that it gives us no
way of settling a dispute among men in a genuine conflict. They simply differ in
their attitudes, and that is that. Unfortunately, we have returned to the same
position, though now on the level of ultimate values.

The model used here is the following: We possess a range of differing moral
beliefs and associated attitudes, and we test the more superficial ones in terms of
the more fundamental values. But in the end, if men differ in their most fundamental values or attitudes, there is no further appeal. Such a conception is akin
to the view that we understand the world in terms of some first principles—and if
men differ in their ultimate scientific or metaphysical principles, then no further
appeal can be made. Obviously, in science at least, this view cannot be supported.
First principles are abandoned, as physicists have abandoned Newtonian mechanics.
We keep reverting to the premise, still as yet unproved, that science and morals
are fundamentally dissimilar.

But is there a way of changing ultimate values? Indeed there is, in fact two
ways, for there is a central ambiguity involved. We may change values through
persuasion and education, by a psychological method in which attitudes are
manipulated and directed. Thus, we may in our society seek to instill in all men a
common concern for animals and their suffering. And if we succeed, then there
will be a uniformity of attitude, not a variety. And weak relativism would then be
invalid.

But, the relativist replies, that is not the issue involved. Rather, we wish to
know if we can *justify* changing a man's fundamental attitudes through educating
him. Obviously we do think we should in many cases. Children are taught the
norms of their parents, and we think it right that they are. Otherwise they will
form no moral attitudes of their own. Is it not a perfectly good reason to teach
people a common concern for animals, that we will then have a more secure and
stable society, that we will have generated a greater mutual respect among men?

We are making a point central to the continuum of means and ends. Calling a value "ultimate" installs it in a hallowed place, where it is untouchable. But all values may themselves be evaluated in terms of where they lead. A man may have no respect whatsoever for cleanliness, and find that others have contempt for his filth. It would not be foolish of him to endeavor to develop the habit of cleanliness, simply to gain the respect of others—a habit which would mark a genuine change in his values. The mere fact that some men love animals deeply, and despise others who are indifferent to animals, may justify the development of a general attitude of concern toward animals. At least, it could justify a common practice toward animals, if, for example, we legislate that men who harm animals will be punished.

The point here is that there are no specific values which come labelled "ultimate." We possess many values, some in conflict with others, and we evaluate our values in their relationship to each other. If it is true that men value the respect of other men, then that alone may disprove the second form of weak relativism we have been considering.

(3) The last form of relativism we shall consider is the most interesting. This is the position that some moral decisions are bound to differ from person to person *because the agents differ*, because the societies differ in which the agents live, because the circumstances of decision differ. In general, this form of relativism seems perfectly compatible with almost everyone's moral views. We often agree that circumstances matter, and that different actions are right in different circumstances. The problem, then, is whether the sheer fact of having different agents making their decisions constitutes circumstances different in important respects.

This position collapses into strong relativism if we assume that *merely* because all men differ from each other, the relevant circumstances are different. Two men, each evaluating similar situations, must come to different conclusions because the men are different. Such an argument overlooks the fact that men may differ in some respects, but they may be alike in all *relevant* respects. The same kind of argument could lead to the conclusion that men cannot even talk to each other intelligibly, since their experiences differ, and therefore so will their understanding of the words they use. Such an argument stresses differences, and overlooks real and important similarities among men and in their circumstances.

The question, then, is whether there are some features of moral decisions which are highly relevant to such decisions, and yet which differ from person to person. I think it should be clear that this is not a question which can be satisfactorily answered at this time. We simply do not have enough information. Men are remarkably similar in their wider aims and their ideals. In the same society, they possess many attitudes in common. They are influenced by each other also, as they live in the same society. All of these similarities tend to explain why there are common and important moral principles which men in a common society and a common environment tend to accept.

Nevertheless, amidst all the similarities inherent in moral decisions, there is a principle of differentiation which is worth noting. Let us suppose there were to be generated in a society a complete uniformity of moral attitudes, convictions, and beliefs. Let us now place two men in rather similar circumstances concerning a fundamental moral distinction—say, one involving civil disobedience to an unjust war. We have presupposed that both men agree on the nature of the conflict. The war is unjust. But a man ought to obey the law. The facts are collected. Both consider the future. Both look forward to jail if they commit civil disobedience. Would we not want to consider it important whether a man could endure jail? If jail would destroy his capacity as a moral agent, should a man risk it? If so, then it may be right for one man—stronger in some forms of endurance—to commit civil disobedience, and wrong for the other.

I wish to emphasize one feature of this discussion. Both men agree as to what is right *in principle*. But principles do not in themselves settle moral issues. The decision called for may be different because the men involved are different, in their characters, personalities, and emotional dispositions. One of the problems of emotivism is that it stresses only the attitudes of men, and not the way their emotional characters enter into their decisions, and ought to be considered in their decisions.

This third form of relativism is not a relativism of principle, but a relativism inherent in decision and action. Men may agree on what is ideal, yet differ in what they do. I consider this type of relativism central to moral decisions, and will return to it. First, however, we must examine the function of emotions in such decisions in greater detail.

E. Affections

It may be of interest to attempt a reconstruction of the development of a person's values, beginning with his infancy and proceeding into adulthood. Such a reconstruction affords us the possibility that certain conceptions of feelings and attitudes will be shown to be somewhat naive. In addition, the function of principles and consequences may be established in a clearer fashion as well. In effect, we will attempt an idealized and simplified account of the formation of values. It will be idealized in particular because we will ask not only how a person forms his attitudes, but whether that particular method is a good one.

In beginning with an infant, we avoid the peculiar problem of not being able to separate a person's values from his desires. Clearly we should not identify every desire as a value. A value is something we deem valuable and therefore desir*able*. But we desire many things which are not themselves desirable, not valuable, not, therefore, values. There is more to evaluation than the formation of a desire. Desires are often merely passive, and arise involuntarily, while evaluation is deliberate and a matter of choice. Beginning with a state prior to evaluation in effect enables us to make some important distinctions in a simple fashion.

We begin with an infant who has no values (as we shall understand them), for he cannot consider consequences or conditions, principles or goals. He cannot even form intentions of a significant character. Nevertheless, an infant, from the day of its birth and even before, has preferences and differential responses. Let us call a favorable disposition or emotion toward an event or action an "affection": a person has an affection toward things which move him positively. If he is negatively moved, we will call the emotional response a "disaffection." Affections and disaffections are simple feelings, toward or away from an activity.

There is no reason whatsoever for us to suppose that affections are pleasures and disaffections pains, at least as we understand such words in adult experience. And there is a major reason not to. Some activities are pursued because they eventually lead to a pleasurable activity. But the disposition to pursue the activity in the first place, though an affection, is no pleasure—though it usually will become one. A newborn child does not yell because the yelling produces pleasure, nor to avoid pain. Only if he is encouraged to throw tantrums does this kind of behavior come to give him pleasure.

The fundamental principle of experimental psychology is that activities are learned and repeated with the presentation of a stimulus which is *reenforcing*. A rat will press a bar more and more frequently to obtain pellets of food. The bar is a stimulus, the pressing the response, and the food a reinforcement. We are here calling the food the source of an affection which leads to the development of an affection toward the pressing of the bar. The latter affection is learned and can be extinguished, in particular by withholding food.

Our first principle, then, is that affections can generate other affections, toward other things. Our second principle is that all affections, but particularly those secondary affections which have been acquired through learning, can be changed—eliminated or even redirected—by the consequences of actions under-taken toward the objects of one's affections. An affection for pressing a bar may show itself to be without value where no food is provided, or where pressing the bar induces an electric shock.

Affections may come and go, reinforced and extinguished, without thought or deliberation. An affection takes on a special quality not when it is responded to in terms of past learning alone, but when the consequences of acting on it are appreciated in advance. Here we have the beginnings of a choice to act in one way or another. Here we have the beginning of the formation of an intention, which involves the consideration of the future.

The future can be considered only where objects take on at least sign properties if not full-fledged meanings. An object in the present must be a sign of a future object or one not present in order that intentions can be formed. Some philosophers have argued that intentional behavior can exist only within the confines of language. We will not consider such matters here. But it is worth noting that without significatory relations, intentions are impossible.

The first stage of evaluation, then, is not a mere affection or disaffection, but a test of an affection in terms of foreseen consequences. The affections and disaffections provide the initial impulse toward action. But the consequences which actions have engendered provide a means for the transformation of affections and the redirection of energies. Evaluation is not sheer impulse, but impulse directed toward intended and appreciated results.

The first step in all learning, then, is the initial stage of evaluation. Evaluation is the central mode of learning in all organic development. Values are not mere preferences, for even an infant has preferences—for food rather than for noise. But an affection takes on evaluative characteristics when it has been submitted to the test of consequences and future affections. In this early stage, evaluation is the judgment that a given affection is not desirable or valuable. Such a judgment is easy to come by for a secondary affection. It is rather difficult to learn for primary affections, and even more difficult to learn that disaffections can lead to valuable results. Nevertheless, the fundamental stage of evaluation is the distinction between an affection and a value, between an uncriticized emotional disposition, and one tested by the consequences produced—though the consequences themselves are useful in evaluation only insofar as they are affections and disaffections themselves.

Thus, a child learns to value bodily warmth and also the step of his mother, for it foretells feeding and cuddling. On the other hand, some glittering objects are painful. And an infant's natural curiosity, which is a generalized affection toward everything, is tempered by the pain which results from the close scrutiny of painful things. All in all, a child learns to transfer affections into disaffections fairly easily. He also is influenced by reinforcement to transform disaffections into affections. This stage of evaluation is one many people never learn to perform well.

To this point, our model conforms both to the branch of experimental psychology called "learning theory" and to psychoanalysis. An infant is from the first disposed toward certain things and away from others. He learns to repeat activities which are associated with affections, and to avoid activities which are associated with disaffections. These repetitions and avoidances are the result of secondary affections and disaffections. In general, a child learns *habits* of response, habits intimately conjoined with his affections. The habits are formed as the result of the interaction of primary or initial affections with the world. The initial fund of affections and disaffections is transformed by contact with reality. This is what Freud calls "the reality principle."

The formation of habits can be directed or undirected, the result of fortuitous circumstances alone or intentional activities devoted to gaining the objects of our affections and avoiding what produces disaffection. In both cases, it is the *facts* of individual experience which generate habits, and therefore lead to the generation also of new affections and disaffections. However, where habits come to be formulated and studied, and men generalize habits into guiding principles, we have the first stage of critical control over our affections and the objects that provide them. Habits of response lead naturally to the development of maxims of conduct or principles which guide conduct.

A fundamental principle of both psychoanalysis and experimental psychology

Feelings is now worth explicit mention. This is that although many habits of response are formulated in principles of conduct, many habits are never so noted, never formulated, and therefore never an object of deliberate thought and examination. A rule for achieving objects of affection may be consciously scrutinized for its success in achieving its goal. But a mere habit is extremely unlikely to be an object of thought. The *unconscious* in psychoanalytic theory may in an oversimplified way be thought of as the fund of habits which have never been formulated or brought to consciousness. Psychoanalytic theory maintains, however, that such habits are not merely unconscious: they are kept out of consciousness by mechanisms of repression. Whether or not we accept so strong a view of repressive mechanisms, there is always much to personality and to the habits which govern human conduct that is not formulated, not conscious, not then fully open to deliberation. The problem of self-deception will be discussed in detail in a later chapter.

It follows from the very existence of unformulated habits that formulating them provides a gain in controlling them. Only with respect to known maxims can we examine their fruits and evaluate their results. Evaluation proper begins only with at least partly expressed principles of conduct. We generalize our habits, and formulate the ways in which affections can be achieved and disaffections avoided. An object chosen as an object of affection in the light of what may be experienced in terms of its consequences is a value. An object pursued as worth while through a means of achieving it is also a value. The relationship among objects as means and ends, in terms of affections and disaffections toward them, is expressed in maxims of conduct, and these maxims become guides to conduct.

Up to this point, our maxims function solely as generalizations of means to objects of affection and disaffection. It should be noted, however, that the maxims have a double purpose. They formulate instrumental values, as means to ends we are favorably disposed toward. But they also formulate the procedures which are necessary to achieve aims proposed. A means toward which we feel extreme disaffection may not be worth using to achieve an end toward which we feel only modest affection. We have here a genuine continuum of means and ends, in that extremely disaffectionate means are generally rejected even when they lead to worth-while ends, while moderately disaffectionate means are often extremely desirable as they lead to strongly desired ends. As we operate by habit within this continuum, we discover that affections transfer, from means to ends and ends to means. Thus, if we use extremely disliked means to a desired end, the latter may take on the character of disaffection by transfer. The formation and dissolution of secondary affections and disaffections is a constant process throughout a man's life.

A striking characteristic of human experience, however, is that the principles which are to guide conduct toward the achievement of affections can themselves become objects of affection and disaffection. As they are themselves repudiated or desired, we move into the moral realm, where it is not the goals which constitute our ends, but the principles to which we appeal in defining our conduct. The first step toward loyalty to moral principle is the development of an affection for that principle.

Two additional elements of experience contribute to the formation of such loyalties. Both involve relations among persons, which we have neglected to this point. It is unquestionable that, at least in early stages of life, human beings are affected very strongly by their relations to others, and in several ways. First, infants are dependent on their parents for sustenance, and develop strong affections toward them for what they do as providers. Second, such affections have a powerful effect on the development of more complex habits of response, and of secondary, tertiary, and even more remote affections and disaffections. A child acquires the habits appropriate to pleasing his parents, though often in highly subtle and obscure ways. Third, children play with others, and are influenced by them. Unless a child is very strongly discouraged by his parents from responding to his peers, he will acquire strong affections toward them, and learn from them. Fourth, and worth separate mention, there is a class of activities and principles which other people feel very strongly about, and which a child picks up quite early.

The two major elements here are: (1) the genuine affections and fears most children have toward other people, which enable them to learn to please others and to avoid causing them anger; and (2) the very strong attitudes which people have toward certain activities, attitudes which constitute what we usually call mores or social norms. As Piaget has pointed out, principles of equity and fairness are initially rules for pleasing one's parents, but they later become rules for managing effectively with one's peers, developed in play. In the latter stage, they are fully acknowledged by the child to be *his*—that is, to be maxims or ideals toward which he feels a personal affection.

In a brief review of the model we are developing, a human being grows in his experience through the generation of secondary affections from primary affections, the formulation of maxims of conduct which promote satisfactory achievement of objects of affection, affection toward such maxims themselves, and also toward principles involving conduct toward other people. Now, it is true that the strength of loyalty to social rules can be very great. Yet the very strength of a principle can make it useless and even destructive in the achievement of other goals. Superstitions are habits of behavior that can be crippling in extreme form and useless otherwise. What psychoanalysis considers pathological behavior is the result of habits which are unformulated in principle, yet also unmodifiable by experience. What psychoanalytic therapy provides is a means for rendering implicit habits explicit, as a further means to the modification of these habits.

The same principle seems imperative for any intelligent morality. The principles a person has come to feel a very strong affection for may in fact be extremely destructive in his own life. The principles which guide his life would seem to require modification insofar as they do not lead to satisfactory results. On the other hand, in an adult human being, some of his strongest affections and disaffections are associated intimately with the moral principles he considers obligatory. Therefore, any test of one principle is bound to evoke violent emotional responses related to others.

For this reason, genuine moral decisions are called for in an adult life only when principles which command loyalties separately come into conflict—whether they are both moral principles, or principles of self-interest as opposed to principles which look to others. And when there is a violent opposition of principles, we must look to facts, to consequences, to conditions, and also to other principles which are relevant.

Freud defines a healthy person as one whose primary impulses and moral taboos are reconciled with each other and with the facts of life in a satisfactory accommodation. In terms of our model, a satisfactory moral decision requires an accommodation of the objects of one's primary affections, the facts which are relevant in terms of one's secondary and tertiary affections, and the maxims or principles which guide one's life and toward which one also has affections. Where a man could have achieved objects of far greater affection than he actually does, then there is something wrong. It may be the external conditions of life—a lack of food or money. It may be that the agent's emotions have been warped by earlier experiences, and nothing would satisfy him. Or it may be that his maxims of conduct are inappropriate to the real conditions of his life.

The decision that it is a man's moral principles which are at fault is by far the riskiest decision—though ironically, it is the one many young people today seem to leap at. It is risky because it incurs the wrath of others. It is risky because it often involves ignoring their needs and interests. It is risky because moral principles constitute a means of social unity, and if repudiated can promote chaos. But most of all, it is risky because the very existence of moral principles and their endurance through a hundred or so generations suggest that they have indeed provided a satisfactory accommodation with the needs of men over thousands of years. The norms of a society represent the greatest loyalties men ought to have within that society. We should at least consider the possibility that the reason for this is that our moral principles do indeed represent a viable set of guidelines for human life, having been tested through hundreds of years. This subject will be discussed in the following chapter.

F. Emotions

The term "affection" of the previous section was chosen to afford a sharp distinction between certain kinds of feelings and others. In particular, we should not confuse desires and inclinations, which are merely emotional movements toward or away from things, with full-fledged *emotions* such as love, hatred, anger, envy, sympathy, or boredom. It is by no means plausible to view any of these emotions as affections or desires, for it is not always possible to define an object of such desire—though some desires may be associated with all emotions. Treating love as a form of desire trivializes it, and is not worth further discussion.

It would be absurd to attempt to provide here a full-scale analysis of the emotions, and probably irrelevant. I will present only three schematic views of the emotions, mainly to note some of their complexities. The critical problem of the emotions is the fact that men often regard themselves as moved almost wholly by their emotions. A man commits murder in a rage. Another tells lies out of fear. A third tells the truth because he is fearful of being caught in a lie. A fourth spreads rumors out of spite. A fifth follows the dictates of his church in the hope of avoiding damnation. In all these cases, the emotion which moves a man is not an attitude—pro or con—but is far more complex. One of the greatest weaknesses of emotivism is its superficial theory of the emotions which inspire conduct.

(1) A common and perhaps plausible conception of the emotions is that they are merely states of mind. Anger is a felt quality "in the mind." Such a view tends to regard emotions as essentially (a) passive—in arising through no intentions or actions on the part of the agent; (b) detached from any action, in the respect that emotions are merely in the mind; and (c) detached from any content, merely *feelings*.

If emotions are passive, and if they are strong elements in moving men to act, then it would seem that we are mere creatures of emotion, especially where they are strong, quite unable to help ourselves. An angry man, overcome by his fury, is a mere automaton. If we are to avoid such a view, we must find a way to influence the emotions, in effect to understand them in an active sense.

If emotions are detached from any action, then it becomes unintelligible how they lead to action. Descartes' famous mind-body dualism rests on the premise that a mere idea, which is located nowhere and has no physical dimensions, cannot intelligibly move the physical body. To understand how emotions have a motivating power, we need to relinquish the isolation of emotion from action. A natural theory is then to regard an emotion as a disposition to act in certain ways. An angry man is disposed to shout, to become tense, to stress his consonants in his speech, and so forth.

If emotions are detached from any content, then they tend to float freely, attachable to any content in their vicinity. There are indeed such free-floating emotional states. An angry man may act angry and even feel angry at everything. Nevertheless, an angry man is usually angry at something. He *believes* something objectionable to have occurred. When we treat emotions as motivations, but as contentless, then we may conclude that no facts are relevant to such emotions. But if emotions always have a factual content, in which something is believed to be the case, then facts may bear directly on the emotions and transform them.

(2) Spinoza attempts to meet these objections to the first conception of the emotions by defining an emotion as "the modifications of the body by which the power of acting of the body itself is increased, diminished, helped, or hindered, together with the ideas of these modifications." He goes on to remark, "If, therefore, we can be the adequate cause of any of these modifications, I understand the emotion to be an action, otherwise it is a passive state." He also treats passive emotions as confused ideas. His theory is extremely complex, and cannot be completely unravelled here. Nevertheless, some points are worth noting.

First, emotions are always to be understood both as characteristics of the body and as characteristics of ideas. In particular, the ideas we have during emotions are ideas of how the body can act. An emotion always looks to the powers of the body to perform actions. A man angry at another is disposed to act toward him in some fashion, and his ideas within the emotional state are about how he may act. Thus, an angry man is quite likely to imagine all sorts of things he might do to the other person.

Second, most emotions are confused ideas, in that we do not know exactly what caused them, what they arose from. There are two important points involved here. One is that emotions are indeed ideas about the body, and therefore always have a content. However, such ideas are never quite complete and clear. An angry man may believe that the person who made him angry cheated him in some way, but may not be quite clear as to exactly what he did.

Third, a confused idea is passive, in the sense that it is caused in the agent by other things, and is the result of external causes. An emotion is an action only when it is self-caused. Spinoza's view of self-causation is rather complex, but depends on knowledge of both ourselves and our place in the world. A man when made angry is made so by someone else, and is a passive agent only. An emotion is active only when associated with full knowledge of what is going on. Perhaps this will be clearer if we add a further point:

Fourth, all our ideas are ideas of the body, and conjoined with bodily modifications. Therefore, when we know what we are doing, and act accordingly, we will experience emotions—but very different emotions from passive ones. All our common emotions are passive, and caused in us by external things. But when we act under knowledge of what we do, then there are emotions present which are active and powerful.

Fifth, there are many different kinds of emotions, even of those with the same name. Since all emotions are partly beliefs, as our beliefs change, so do our emotions. In addition, the character of the agent is part of his emotions. A hot-tempered drunk who is angry feels a different emotion from the anger felt by a cool and deliberate man.

Certain important conclusions follow from such a view of the emotions. First, emotions can be changed, by changing the environment and the surrounding conditions, and also by gaining knowledge of oneself and the world. Second, it is superficial to assume that emotions are even approximately the same in different men. Rather, we should consider one of the goals of morality to influence men's emotions as well as their actions. Third, it follows that one of the things a moral agent must consider in making a moral decision is the effects of his actions on his own emotions and the emotions of others. A college student who steals becomes a thief, not alone in his reputation if caught, but in his emotional views of property and other people. Most professional thieves are men of no sympathy whatsoever, who steal from people poorer than themselves.

(3) Both Freud and Sartre have theories of emotion which resemble Spinoza's in some important ways. In particular, psychoanalysis maintains that there are

both unconscious and conscious emotions, both of which influence conduct, and that the goal of psychotherapy is to gain in knowledge of the unconscious emotions, and thereby to change them. It follows that the emotions experienced by a healthy person are genuinely different from the emotions experienced by a neurotic one. Finally, insofar as emotions are unknown, they are out of our control, and we suffer them without being able to do anything about them. Psychotherapy is itself a means by which the patient may gain control over his actions and become an active agent instead of a passive one.

Sartre has a rather strange theory of the emotions. He regards them all as actions, for he repudiates any aspect of human actions which is merely passive. The emotions are active transformations in imagination of the world, when we cannot cope with it realistically. A man is angry and defines someone as his enemy in order to escape from his real problem, which is to find a practical and effective way to act. We are not angry in the conventional sense at being insulted if we can effectively repudiate the insult.

This entire discussion of the emotions leads to a single conclusion. Men are usually motivated by emotions. But such emotions are usually confused and are often destructive. A fundamental goal in action, and therefore in developing both techniques and principles of action, must be the improvement of the emotions, through knowledge of what we are doing and what we most deeply desire. Affections cannot be eliminated, nor should they be. Life would be pretty meaningless without them. But the complex emotions we often experience may in fact stand in the way of our gaining the objects of our greater affections. Certainly this is true for all pathological behavior.

Emotions themselves, then, become objects for study and for change. Evaluation is not merely the study of means to goals towards which we have an emotional attachment in the first place, but looks also to the redirection of feelings and affections. In this respect, all evaluation rests ultimately in affections and disaffections; but no affections are themselves ultimate and final. This is what is wrong with speaking of "ultimate goals," as if they cannot and should not be changed. Everything we do involves either the diminishing or the enhancing of our prior affections, and therefore may change even our ultimate goals. Evaluation can achieve at best a balance or harmony among the variety of competing affections.

G. Sensitivity

The critical importance of emotions in evaluation requires an additional quality in order to be successful—an awareness of the emotions and feelings of others, even when unvoiced. For some reason, this *sensitivity* to the feelings of others is overlooked in most discussions of evaluation, though it is far more important in most respects than logical rigor and rational deliberation. There may be some few men who are genuinely indifferent to what other men think of them and also to their joys and suffering, though if such men exist I would guess that they were made so indifferent by their early experiences of other people. All the rest of mankind suffer the disapproval of others deeply, and even more, respond emotionally to the emotions of others.

Hume virtually bases his entire moral theory on the sentiment of *sympathy*, the reproduction of the emotions we sense in others. Spinoza too is convinced that a fundamental principle of human emotions is the tendency to feel the emotions others feel. They are like us, and the more like us they are, the more do we experience the emotions which we take them to have. We suffer when we see a man in pain. We are joyful at another's joy. Thus, Hume argues, we tend to avoid making others suffer, and seek to make them happy, for it is in our own interest to do so.

Such a theory of sympathetic response is too simplistic. Some men are spiteful. Others are envious. There are men who are pleased at the sufferings of others. In fact, there is a well known psychological view that we laugh at others' misfortunes, just because they are not our own.

Though men may be indifferent and even pleased at the sufferings of most other people, there are always some people whose emotions are important to us. The emotions of a child's parents are vital to him, and he is important to his parents as well. The opinions and attitudes of the community affect the reputation and the well-being of any individual who lives there. Perhaps if men were other than they are, the opinions of the community would not matter. But men must live with the facts of their own needs and dispositions.

Therefore, sensitivity is vital for an agent to be able to anticipate how others will react to his actions. A married woman who has an abortion without consulting her husband must have a pretty good idea of what his reaction will be. An adolescent who ceases to keep himself clean certainly ought to know how other people will regard him.

But many of our emotions are covert and barely grasped. If so, we cannot tell others of them. We can only betray them indirectly. Sensivitity is required because it is not believable that human beings will be able both to know their deeper feelings and to openly express them. Human life is social. The feelings of others, though they may not themselves be aware of these feelings, affect us deeply. Any hope of success in anticipating the future depends on a greater sensitivity to others' feelings than most men are capable of.

Sensitivity is so vital a factor in moral judgment that a person who possesses a sensitive concern for others—the Good Samaritan of the parable—may require no other ground for his moral decisions. Obviously there can be a sensitivity which is no concern, an alertness to the feelings of others in order to enjoy their suffering or from fear of them. But out of sensitivity, a very persuasive moral view can be formed.

Where sensitivity is lacking, the most rigid adherence to duty may fail to satisfy the imperatives of moral decision. The consequences of telling the truth may shatter another person's self-esteem, though sheer duty compels obedience. Often the consequences which matter most in human life are the ones which depend on the responses of others to what we do, and call for a deep sensitivity to them. Thus, a goal of moral action is not only to change our own emotional states, but to capture a sensitive awareness of the feelings of others, as they will feel in the future in addition to their feelings in the present. Here the importance of psychological knowledge as well as sensitivity is beyond question.

But psychology is as yet a weak science, and human sensitivity is rather unreliable. Poets and playwrights reveal to us the world of feelings also, but in an unclear fashion. If morality and goodness waited upon all men caring for others and sympathizing with them, we would be in dire straits. Here we come to another of the important functions of moral principles—to regulate a uniform order of expectation within human experience. Where certain moral principles are installed as social norms, then we may expect most men to follow them, and to react emotionally in terms of them. The norms themselves foster attitudes which perpetuate those very norms.

Moral principles in common use are therefore a substitute and even a crutch for sensitivity. They represent important emotions, formulated in general rules of conduct. We may legitimately expect other people to be outraged when their moral convictions are flouted, and to have developed moral convictions in accordance with general norms. Sensitivity is not usually required upon every subject, and at every moment, but rather plays a lesser role—that of tempering justice with mercy.

Moral principles tell us of the feelings of others because they play a major role in the formation of such feelings. Where a society is in a period of transition, to such an extent that no particular rules are effective generally, then there seems to be insufficient stability to allow any sensitivity to function. Sensitivity has a significant role to play for most men only within a society with stable norms. Sensitivity here serves to temper the rigidity of principles with an awareness and a concern for men who are injured by the rules. Sensitivity can also make us aware of men who are unreliable in their convictions, who are not trustworthy or dependable.

Sensitivity in practice—though not in theory—is the other face of duty, and leads us beyond a moral principle to its effects. We wonder what the results of obedience to law will be, in our feelings as well as the feelings of others. Sensitivity is required. It is now time that we turned to the major face of moral decision—principles and rules.

QUESTIONS

1. Discuss the equation of the good life with a life of pleasure. What kinds of qualifications must be made? What difficulties does hedonism have?

2. What is pleasure? Discuss some of the interesting aspects of this question.

3. What kinds of arguments can be given against a man who claims that it is good for him to assault other people, because he enjoys doing it? Can we say anything more than that he is wrong for doing so?

4. Discuss some of the ambiguities which are involved in calling an action or thing "good." Especially distinguish the Aristotelian and Platonic conceptions of what is good from the uncritical conception.

5. Explain in some detail a variety of motives which could lead a man to die for his country. Are some of these morally superior to others? Can you develop a criticism of hedonism from your analysis?

6. What kinds of answers can be given to the question, "why should I do what is right?"

7. List some of the higher pleasures, and explain why and in what sense they are higher. If you do not think that there are higher pleasures, explain why.

8. A college student plans to steal some items from the college bookstore. His roommate tells him that it is wrong to do this. Analyze the situation in terms of the emotions and attitudes of the people involved. Explain how the theory of emotivism might be applied in such a case. What are its difficulties?

9. Critically evaluate the statement, "right you are if you think you are."

10. Do men have "ultimate" values? Explain.

11. Do men have "value systems"? Explain.

12. Two men have decided that one of them should run for public office to oppose the corrupt incumbent. In what sense is it morally right for one to become a candidate and not the other?

13. In what sense can conventional moral principles be thought of as a form of wisdom? In what sense not?

14. To what extent is it true that a man should not worry about his inner feelings, but only about what he does? If he acts rightly, is that enough?

15. To what extent can we ignore the hidden feelings of other people in our own moral judgments? How are such feelings made manifest to us, if they ever are?

SELECTED READINGS

Works on utilitarianism:

J. S. Mill, *Utilitarianism*.

J. Rawls, "Two Concepts of Rules," *Philosophical Review*, Vol. LXIV (1955).

C. L. Stevenson, *Ethics and Language*, 1944, Yale University. The most influential work on emotivism.

S. Freud, *Outline of Psychoanalysis.*

H. S. Sullivan, *Conceptions of Modern Psychiatry*, 1947, Norton.

J. Dewey, *Human Nature and Conduct*, 1922.

J. Piaget, *The Moral Judgment of the Child*, 1948, Free Press. An important work on stages of moral development.

Spinoza, *Ethics*, III, IV.

E. Fromm, *Man for Himself*, 1947, Rinehart. The moral theory of a well known psychoanalyst.

A variety of works on relativism:

Plato: *Theaetetus* 151–186. Still the best criticism of relativistic theories of knowledge.

R. Brandt, *Hopi Ethics: A Theoretical Analysis*, 1954, University of Chicago.

E. Westermarck, *The Origin and Development of the Moral Ideas*, 1906, Macmillan.

R. Benedict, *Patterns of Culture*, 1934, Houghton.

R. Linton, "The Problem of Universal Values," in R. F. Spencer, ed., *Method and Perspective in Anthropology*, 1954, University of Minnesota.

The last two are works of influential anthropologists.

V. PRINCIPLES

THE FUNCTION of principles in moral decisions is complex. This complexity has engendered a variety of theories of moral action, each of which stresses one aspect or function of principles to the exclusion of others. Thus, utilitarianism maintains that an action is good only if it is of maximal benefit to men as contrasted with its alternatives. A rule is valid if it is superior to all conceivable alternative rules, in providing benefits generally to mankind. Such a view looks to the consequences of legislating a principle. The function of the principle is to achieve goods and to avoid ills. This function I shall call the "substantive" function of principles. The substance of a moral principle is a kind of wisdom—knowledge that by following the principle, men will achieve the best possible results.

On the other hand, Kant's theory of duty rests on the conviction that conformity to principle is the sole basis for morality. A man should not break his promises, even if by doing so he would manage to achieve beneficial results. This is no more than what is meant by the principle that it is right to keep one's promises. The function of moral principles in settling among the competing alternatives inherent in a decision I will call the "regulative" function. Moral principles regulate the decisions we come to as moral agents. Kant in effect argues that the very form of moral principles is regulative. "Thou shalt honor thy father and mother," without exception or qualification, no matter what happens. We have noted that men generally make exceptions and look to consequences. Yet they also appeal to principles as if such an appeal ought to settle certain moral issues.

Can the substantive and regulative functions of principles in moral decisions be reconciled? Take the case of promising. If we consider the substantive function alone of the principle "thou shalt keep thy promises," then only the results of following the principle seem to matter. The rule is intended to achieve beneficial results. Where it will not, a man is justified in breaking it. If we consider the regulative function of the principle alone, then we may never break our promises, regardless of consequences. Promises are made to be kept.

The problem is rather clear. Almost everyone, except for purists of one variety or another, senses the appeal of both the substantive and the regulative function of principles. Promises are made to be kept. But where the results of an action will be very bad, we should not perform it. How can such very different conceptions of the function of moral principles be combined in a single view? Either principles are to be judged in terms of the consequences or they are not.

The notion of reconciliation is an ambiguous one. Some antithetic principles are reconciled by being combined in a single principle. The two principles "matter can neither be created nor destroyed" and "energy can neither be created nor destroyed" may be reconciled by combining them in the single principle "the total sum of matter and energy in a system is constant." Some antithetic principles are reconciled by the understanding that each is a partial truth, and that the whole truth involves both of them. The reconciliation may be accomplished by explaining that each principle has a different domain of application. Thus, the principles "metals expand when heated" and "metals melt when heated" are both true, but in different ranges of temperature.

The problem of reconciliation may therefore be viewed as one of determining where the substantive function of principles is primary and where the regulative function is primary instead. But that is precisely what we cannot determine. Consequences are *always* relevant—though if not of sufficient benefit or harm they are ignored. Principles are *always* regulative, in that they are appealed to in settling issues of right and wrong—though where the consequences of following a principle too closely are sufficiently undesirable, the principle will be modified or abandoned.

There is yet another possibility of reconciliation—though by no means as satisfactory by rational standards as the others. Here we reconcile antithetic views when we can manage to steer a path among them, taking them all into account yet not overemphasizing one over the others. A political leader must reconcile the conflicting demands of the members of his constituency by a form of compromise, by considering them all and wending his way among them. A policy which ignores the needs of a large bloc of voters will probably lead to his fall from office.

This latter reconciliation accedes to the possibility that the conflicting positions may be formally opposed, and permit no combination in a larger principle. Yet there is a mode of practice which achieves a satisfactory compromise among them. It is the theory of this book that a moral decision achieves this last sort of reconciliation. And, just as different politicians manage their accommodation with their constituencies in different ways, different men may be led to different moral decisions on the same principled grounds. Nevertheless, it is worth emphasizing that politicians often make their choices and fail. So, too, a moral decision carries no guarantee within it of success.

The nature of a moral decision, in achieving its reconciliation of opposing constraints, will be discussed in a later chapter. Here we will consider only the variety of functions of principles in contributing to such decisions. There is a third function we have not yet mentioned, which follows from its regulative function. Once we have installed a set of moral principles which serve to settle moral disputes, then we may distinguish problems of evaluation which involve none of these principles from those problems which do. Thus, the decision of what to wear to a job interview, though perhaps of vital importance in a man's life, has no *moral* significance. No moral principle is relevant to such a decision. Such a conception of principles treats them as *constitutive*. Principles serve a constitutive function when they generate the need for moral decision.

We now turn to a discussion of each of these functions of moral principles.

A. Substantive

The substantive function of principles rests upon the view that such principles are in fact the most beneficial principles we can find to live by. Thus, men often argue that capital punishment is good because it strikes fear into the hearts of evil men, and deters them from committing murders or acts of treason. And the counter-argument, that capital punishment is bad, points out that it achieves no effective deterrence, and is not administered fairly. Black men are executed for minor offenses, white women are almost never sentenced to death. Therefore, capital punishment does not achieve its aim of deterrence, and also exacerbates the fears of minorities that justice is not even-handed.

These are not the only arguments which are given to support capital punishment. Some people believe in the principle that the punishment ought to fit the crime. Such a principle is often regulative, for we may not know how to determine its substantive value. Yet, in recent times, most criminal laws have been defended in the main on substantive grounds. Thus, laws prohibiting the use and the sale of marijuana are justified on the grounds that marijuana is a dangerous drug. The newspapers have been filled for the past several years with evidence on both sides of the question of the exact dangers involved in the use of marijuana. Many communities have instituted coercive public health measures, on the grounds that the general benefit achieved by compelling people to submit to inoculations which will prevent epidemics far outweighs the disadvantages of the costs and the types of compulsion required. Even these measures are not as straightforward as some public officials pretend. A case in point is the oral vaccine against polio, one stage of which turned out to be the cause of the disease in a small number of adults.

The appraisal of social laws on substantive grounds is very well established. Yet many people are made uncomfortable when they are asked to regard moral principles in the same light. We should not look to the benefits and the injuries which the stricture against lying produces. Lying is just plain wrong.

Yet we have seen rather clearly that some cases of lying are not in the least wrong. Physicians tell their patients who are dying that they are not very ill,

from kindness and to maintain the patients' will to live. Such lies aren't *really* lies,
we may say. White lies are not wrong; only lies to benefit oneself. The point is
that we distinguish good from bad lies solely on the basis of the consequences.

At this point we must emphasize the distinction proposed earlier between act
and rule utilitarianism. It is important to distinguish the view that a given *action*
is to be judged in terms of its results from that of judging a *rule or principle* by its
consequences. In all the cases mentioned, we appraise a given *instance* of lying in
terms of its consequences. Consider instead the question of whether lying in general
and as a rule has beneficial results or not. Is it a good thing *in general* to tell the
truth? It promotes trust and mutual respect. As Hobbes argues concerning con-
racts, without a reliable means of engendering trust, men would find their lives
unstable and fearful.

We must make a second distinction. Contrast the following claims: *it is
usually a good thing for people to tell the truth* and *it would be a good thing if people usually
followed the rule that people should tell the truth.* The first is a general substantive claim
that telling the truth usually has beneficial consequences—though there are
exceptions. The second is a substantive claim *about the benefits of making a principle
a regulative principle.*

The important thing to realize about the substantive function of moral
principles is that such principles are not regarded as merely generalizations about
what will have beneficial results. Rather, the claim is that installing such principles
as regulative guides to conduct will be beneficial. The same distinction can be
found in many people's views of criminal laws. During the legislative consideration
of a proposed bill, the question asked is whether it would be a good thing *to have
a law,* not merely, would it be beneficial if most people acted in a particular way?
The point is that many people feel it a moral duty to obey the law, so much so
that if they oppose it, they will still obey it while they work to have it repealed.

The regulative function of moral principles has been intruding on our entire
discussion of the substantive function of such principles. It is important to realize
why this is so. Let us revert to the model of evaluation we developed in the last
chapter. Evaluation is the appraisal of things in terms of achieving maximal
satisfaction in terms of primary and secondary affections. We recall that among the
most important objects of affection in human life are principles of conduct.

We reformulate our model as follows: a principle is a general claim about
what will lead to objects of strong affection and avoid objects of disaffection. All
human beings develop implicit habits of action which their past conditioning has
led them to think will promote satisfactory results. Some of these habits are
formulated as principles. Then, through practice and also through the reactions of
others, these habits themselves take on very strong affective and disaffective
qualities.

What is now true is that in seeking to judge a principle as to whether it leads
to beneficial results, a man also reacts with affection or disaffection to the principle
itself. If the strength of his affection is very great, it will overbalance most incon-

veniences which result from obedience to the principle. What he *is* evaluating, then, is not alone the consequences of acting according to the principle, but also the consequence of *having* and *obeying* the principle, especially if that principle is a social norm and involves others. In other words, among the relevant consequences to consider in evaluating a principle are the principle itself, and the agent's loyalties to it. Such loyalties lead directly to the regulative function of that principle.

In evaluating the substantive function of moral principles, we look to see if such a principle is a beneficial one in terms of its consequences. Yet what we have seen is that we in effect must include our own loyalties to that principle in looking to its consequences. But if we are loyal to that principle in the first place, how can we evaluate its results objectively in the second place? Obviously we cannot. But this is by no means the problem it appears to be.

Let us compare substantive evaluation with confirmation in a scientific investigation. We walk into a scientific laboratory to examine the experiment in progress. What we see is an array of electronic instruments, wires, dials, slides, and all sorts of paraphernalia. We ask, "What's happening?" Obviously, unless we are scientists ourselves, we won't understand the reply. The reason for this is that the apparatus used to test a scientific law presupposes the truth of many other scientific laws if it is to work at all. Now suppose we have a so-called "crucial experiment," to test whether one or another general theory of electricity is correct. The apparatus for the test would have to be built according to the specifications of one or both of the theories. We cannot test a scientific theory from scratch.

We may make this point in a different way. A scientific theory consists of several general principles, and a large number of laws which follow logically and mathematically from the first principles. The laws may be arranged in order of descending generality. Finally we come to laws which are so specific that they can be used to directly guide experimental results. An experiment will use instruments built upon some of the laws of the theory. To test a part of a theory, we presuppose the rest. In addition, if we disconfirm a lower-level law of the theory, we can save the theory by changing only a part of it. But since a lower-level law usually follows from the conjunction of *all* or many of the first principles, there is no obvious way to tell which of these first principles must be modified.

In effect, then, a scientific theory is tested *as a whole* in every experiment. Moreover, the theory defines the experimental means to be used for its own test. Nevertheless, theories are abandoned upon severe disconfirming evidence. The point to keep in mind is that no simple relation can be found to exist between any part of a theory and any particular body of evidence.

In addition, it is worth noting that the part of a scientific theory which is appealed to in the design of an experiment is in effect *regulative* for that experiment, and *constitutive* for it as well. It is regulative in that there is no way for that experiment to challenge its own design. It is constitutive in that without first presupposing the truth of some scientific laws, a scientist could not even begin to design an experiment. Euclidean geometry was regulative in classical physics, in defining essential properties of space. Yet the theory of relativity has abandoned Euclidean geometry, and on adequate grounds. A scientific theory can abandon regulative principles, due to their unsatisfactory functioning as such regulative principles.

There is some degree of analogy, then, between the substantive appraisal of moral principles and the testing of scientific theories by the collection of evidence. Scientific theories are tested by the observations they lead us to expect to occur. Under substantive appraisal, moral theories are regarded in a utilitarian fashion, as generating the greatest degree of benefit of all competitive moral alternatives. A scientific theory is tested as a whole. A moral system must be tested as a whole.

Nevertheless, there are obvious and extremely important differences between scientific theories and their confirmation, and moral systems and their substantive appraisal. First of all, a scientific theory forms a rigorous logical system. A moral system is loosely knit and not rigorous at all. Second, the several first principles in a scientific theory are compatible, and together entail specific laws. Moral laws come into conflict, and seem to do so necessarily. Third, the observations which confirm scientific theories can be extremely precise and controlled. The affections which as a whole test a moral system are diffuse and almost inchoate. Fourth, a scientific experiment can be designed so that a single observation can count as confirmation or disconfirmation. But moral principles are designed to achieve maximal benefit, where we have no measure of single benefits, nor a way of calculating a sum of them.

These are not minor differences. They are quite fundamental. Substantive evaluation is very much more loose and vague than confirmation. It is so vague that we can never be fully assured that a moral principle has substantively failed, especially where it looks to benefits for many people. We can at best point out obvious shortcomings, and propose alternatives for eliminating them.

This explains the incremental quality of moral judgments. We begin with a general principle which is rather vaguely conceived, and which has exceptions which are as yet unformulated. "Killing is wrong." But then we discover relatively clear cases where the principle if followed has deleterious consequences, and the principle is amended, a bit here, a bit there, in small increments. Under some circumstances, a general maxim of conduct may be repudiated entirely. The principle of individual combat to preserve honor existed in Renaissance Italy and France, and on the American Western frontier. We no longer consider this principle of substantive benefit. In general, however, we tend to preserve the same general moral principles, and resolve their inadequacies by amending them through exceptions.

More than any other principles of moral force, sexual mores have come under attack in recent times for their substantive inadequacy. The regulative force of the principle of chastity has been weakened considerably. Many young people consider sexual restrictions to have no substantive worth at all. The burden is thrown heavily onto those who would prohibit by law or even by custom premarital sexual relations, homosexuality, or even communal sexual activities. The burden is to show that there is any basis *in fact* for any sexual restrictions at all, where the result to be expected is no longer a large number of unwanted children. Ironically, venereal diseases are spreading at an unbelievable rate. But they are not in themselves adequate ground for sexual restrictions.

In the end, it is probable that sexual norms will be evaluated wholly in substantive terms. The general question is not difficult to define, though it is as yet very difficult to answer. Is an early and relatively uncontrolled range of sexual experience beneficial in leading young people to deeper feelings, deeper intimacies, more profound relationships, greater trust in others, and greater respect for themselves and their abilities? Or is the postponement of sexual experiences, and their restriction to a degree, a more reliable road to depth of feeling, to productive activities, to trust and self-respect? The evidence is not now sufficient for a decision, and may not be for a long time. But it is difficult to see why sexual norms should be grounded in any but substantive considerations.

We have noted that substantive appraisal is inherently loose and incomplete. Moral evaluation cannot ever be made as rigorous even in its substantive dimensions as scientific inquiry. This entails the need for a particular type of action, which is the making of a moral decision. In addition, the fundamental vagueness of moral principles is not wholly a liability, and it is a central characteristic of such principles. In particular, moral *ideals* are and must be vague. That is one of their *virtues*. Nevertheless, the vagueness of ideals, when coupled with their importance, does indeed make substantive appraisal a nebulous affair. Yet where obedience to moral principle has nothing but disadvantageous consequences to *everyone*, it must be mistaken.

The case for substantive evaluation can be made beyond a chance of doubt by the simple point that a moral principle which hurts everyone is not worth having. An action that harms everyone is not worth performing. This is the extreme case. But it makes substantive appraisal necessary.

We turn now to the regulative function of principles.

B. Regulative

The regulative function of moral principles is the one which generates the tension between the alternatives of morality *or* expediency, of adherence to principle *or* the calculation of tangible benefits, of duty *or* self-interest. A man must not sacrifice his principles to expediency, or his sense of duty to a concern for himself above others. To some people, the essence of immorality can be found in a man who calculates every action in terms of its consequences, and ignores all moral principles in doing so. There is much to be said for viewing an exclusive concern for consequences as immoral, since it reveals the absence of regulative control by moral principles over a man's actions. There is an important aspect of moral decision which depends upon an almost unrestricted loyalty to principle.

Nevertheless, there is considerable confusion in the alternatives just presented. They are not all equivalent. We have seen that there can be a choice required between loyalty to principle and consideration of consequences. Yet such a choice may not have anything obviously to do with expediency or with self-interest. For example, a physician who tells a child that she will recover from a crippling illness when he knows she will not may be acting wholly out of kindness. Many of us would have no trouble in viewing his action as right and good, even while we continue to accept the principle that lying is wrong (most of the time).

A substantive principle which claims that an action will usually have beneficial consequences, but on occasion will not, may allow exceptions. But a regulative principle which asserts that lying is wrong may have no exceptions while it continues to regulate actions which come under it. It may, however, allow *qualifications*. And it may be reinterpreted. Thus, we may say that lying is wrong unless it is intended to avoid unnecessary suffering. Or, we may say that an untruth told to avoid pain is no lie.

In all cases where a moral principle serves a regulative function, and where we choose to qualify or reinterpret the principle as if to allow an exception, we are led to oppose the first regulative principle by a second. Lying is wrong, but so is harming an innocent person unnecessarily, *even by the truth*. Where we look to the circumstances in which action is called for, and look to the experienced consequences of such action, we may find ourselves forced to make a choice among regulative principles. The trouble with the view that we should look to principles and not to consequences is that the consequences may lead us to confront other principles.

On the other hand, we may feel outraged at a man who considers only how to increase his fortune from one million dollars to two million, ignoring all principles in doing so. Or course, we are just as likely to condemn him for ignoring the consequences of his actions for the widows whose investments he manages to take for his own. What seems essential is that *some* regulative principle be found which grounds an obligation, and against which sheer calculation of consequences is mere expediency. There is no regulative principle which many people accept as obligatory or even worth while which justifies a man in increasing his personal wealth when he has enough.

We may now return to the tension with which we began this discussion. The alternatives of morality or expediency, principles or consequences, duty or self-interest are oversimplified, since principles too may conflict. Therefore, where consequences are not relevant, it is because they lead to no regulative principle. Where self-interest is not right, it is because it involves no regulative principle. Expediency is wrong only where no regulative principle is involved. Where telling a lie will save a man's own life, he should tell it. It is foolishness to believe that a small lie is wrong if one's life is at stake. Here one regulative principle may be repudiated in terms of self-interest, though a self-interest which has the regulative sanction of the protection of life.

To say that the regulative function of moral principles is essential in all moral decisions is to say that a special and rather deep loyalty (or affection) must be directed to such principles. In all regulative functioning of principles, what is entailed is that in all circumstances where no other regulative principles are involved, either in the circumstances or in the consequences, then the right thing to do is to follow the principle which is relevant. Unfortunately, this version of the regulative function of principles is very weak, because human life is rather complex, and because regulative principles are so often in conflict with each other. Certainly in all political decisions there are an almost indefinite number of conflicting issues of a moral character to consider.

In our prior discussion of principles, we noted Kant's attempt to found moral decisions on principles alone. More accurately, Kant sought to ground moral decisions in the regulative function of principles alone, neglecting the consequences of actions, exceptions to principles which are made necessary by conflicts, and also that degree of self-interest which is morally justified and obligatory. For example, it is right to preserve one's life in a prisoner of war camp by cheating one's captors. The regulative function itself rests on no secure basis other than a substantive ground, though it is not reducible to it.

The greater plausibility of rule utilitarianism is worth noting once again. A general principle may be considered right if it is the principle of action which will have the most beneficial consequences, taking everything into account. Note, however, that what is being tested is the advantageousness of the principle when it functions as a *regulative* principle. In other words, rule utilitarianism offers a substantive means for evaluating a regulative principle. We are committed in the first place to regulative principles which determine the rightness or goodness of actions, and seek only to determine the best regulative principles to follow.

Shall we ask, then, what grounds can be given for accepting any regulative principles at all? This question is very close to the question of whether there are any grounds for morality. It would seem that there are only two kinds of answer that can be given to such a question. The first is wholly substantive. We ask, is it on the whole more advantageous or not to live by rules, and also to be able to expect other men to follow such rules? Hobbes argues that without rules of morality—which he views as inspired wholly by fear—the life of man would be nasty, brutish, and short. Certainly a strong case can be made that the consequences of being without any regulative code of morals would be disastrous, for social order, for trust, for progress. *Some* moral principles are necessary to a good life, and morality is thus substantively justified. Our only remaining question concerns the exact principles to follow.

The second answer is not an argument. It merely notes the *fact* that men usually do become attached to principles as objects of very strong affections, which take on a regulative role. Perhaps men ought not to have such attachments—the first argument is a reply to that speculation. But strong moral attitudes are a genuine fact of human life—though so also is human weakness.

The two answers together provide a strong ground for morality. The consequences of having no regulative principles would be unfortunate. And we may rely also on the workings of human psychology to provide a means for social norms to become disseminated widely, and to lead to reliable expectations of uniform conduct. The regulative function of principles is inherent both in the nature of man and in his experiences where regulative principles have generally collapsed.

I have criticized John Stuart Mill somewhat harshly in an earlier chapter. Yet I should note in passing here that the basis for morals set forth in the last paragraph or two is almost identical with the one he offers for the principle of utility. Schematically, Mill's argument for the principle of utility is that we can evaluate principles only in terms of what men do in fact desire. Unfortunately, he moves too rapidly from what they do desire to what is desirable. We have seen that there is a more complex relationship between primary affections and regulative principles.

In addition, Mill defines what he calls "the ultimate sanction of the principle of utility"—that is, the means whereby men are brought to obey that principle. This is nothing other than "the conscientious feelings of mankind." Either men are in fact psychologically motivated to form regulative principles and to develop ultimate loyalties, or they are not. If they are not, then no persuasion or argument can convince a man that he ought to. If they are, then and only then may they seek to determine substantively which regulative principles are of greatest benefit.

In Plato's *Republic*, Socrates argues that justice is an intrinsic good because it brings about an inner harmony of soul which rests upon knowledge. Plato appears to offer no more than a substantive defense of justice, and to ignore entirely the regulative function of principles. On the other hand, his argument can also be interpreted to show that a just man will discover (substantively) that his obedience to regulative principles of justice is truly a good.

The arguments given above can only show that regulative principles are *generally* beneficial, and also that men form such principles. Nevertheless, it might pay a brilliant criminal, in a society governed by moral principles, for him alone to disregard such principles on occasion. But then we have raised a problem not of justifying regulative principles, but of *moral education*.

If a man lacks all sense of regulative principles, then his education has been at fault. At best, we might be able to show that it would be to his benefit to pretend to revere the same principles as everyone else. But no argument can ever prove that it is *always* disadvantageous to violate a moral law, especially where no one else knows of it. It simply has to be acknowledged that a man might benefit financially from keeping a wallet he found. Only when he has come to sense the force of regulative principles himself will it be disadvantageous on the whole to seek financial gain at the price of his sense of rightness. A man's conscience has been well formed and can be effective only where principles have become regulative.

A man with a very strong conscience, and a firm commitment to some regulative principles, may disapprove of a particular principle which others find to have regulative force. Some very virtuous people have little respect for chastity. In some societies, religious practices are obligatory. Yet a man might have a strong sense of justice and a weak sense of reverence for God. Here too is a problem of moral education. But also, such variety may be on the whole a good. Genuine disagreement concerning some principles makes the few regulative principles which are virtually unanimously accepted even more compelling. They take on the special character of ideals.

It is important to preserve a clear distinction between lacking a sense that a principle has regulative force, and having that sense but nevertheless disobeying the principle. The latter may be the result of weakness, of a mild conscience, or merely so great a sense of self-importance as to make one an exception to a rule. A college student may genuinely think that stealing is wrong, yet steal a book for a lark, to prove his cleverness, because the world owes him something, or even in a half-stupor of self-destruction. Conceding the validity of a moral principle, yet making an exception of oneself, is a special kind of decision, which we will study in a moment.

C. Constitutive

The regulative function of principles is almost inseparable from their con-stitutive function. In fact, if principles were not regulative at all, but merely general guides to gaining advantage, then they could not be constitutive either. If men had no strong loyalty to principle, then all cases of evaluation would do no more than to look to tangible benefits achievable through a variety of actions.

Where moral education has failed, and some individual men possess no personal experience of the regulative function of some principles, their mode of evaluation is wholly in terms of personal advantage. Severe deprivation can produce men of little conscience, some of whom become criminals. Such men are likely to be motivated by a strong desire for gain tempered only by a fear of being caught. Narcotics addicts, who need a continual source of funds to feed an uncontrollable habit, are often men whose consciences are literally demolished by the force of their need, and who steal almost without restraint except for the fear of arrest.

A striking point to keep in mind is that such drug addicts are motivated by so narrow a conception of personal advantage that they often fail to achieve their own long-range benefits. For example, they may be impelled to steal where apprehension is certain. They may lose their jobs because of their activities, and so forth. As Spinoza points out, the temptations of immediate pleasures are far stronger than the attractions of remote goods. A man with the ability to look to the long view, and to set aside an immediate affection for a long-run gain, possesses a good part of what a conscience can provide—a known principle which becomes habitual in guiding action.

A narcotics addict with an extreme habit is already laboring under a per-manent problem of evaluation. He must always be finding ways to get his next fix.

The commandment, "get drugs," and its correlative, "get money," govern his life at almost every moment. Almost everything he does is regulated by these two imperatives. And they are genuinely normative principles, though they are neither justifiable in the long run nor moral principles.

We may contrast three different situations. First, a man of ordinary moral sensibilities who finds in the street a wallet which contains both the name of the owner and a large sum of money. Second, our narcotics addict who steals in order to support his habit. Third, a man who lacks all regulative moral principles, but lacks any strong desires as well.

In the latter case, we have no regulative principles or constitutive principles. We may suppose the person involved to have affections and disaffections, though of a mild sort. He is interested in personal advantage, but in a rather diffident fashion. A great many opportunities will pass him by, for the situations in which he finds himself are not constituted by normative principles. He will generally tell the truth, for it is too much trouble to think up lies which matter so little. He will generally pay his debts, for he dislikes the consequences of owing money. If he finds a wallet in the street, he will probably keep it, more from indifference than eagerness. Except for some urgent crisis, such as an automobile accident or a lawsuit which directly threatens him, such a man will often avoid making normative choices, especially moral ones. If he hears a woman being killed outside his window, he may look out from curiosity, but do nothing, for it is too much trouble to become involved. A man can become indifferent to things to such an extent, though he still possesses mild affections and disaffections, as to ignore their evaluative aspects. For such a man, nothing *constitutes* the situations he is part of as value situations. Nothing evokes evaluation from him. Nor is it clear how anything of less importance than the threat of jail or loss of his job would constitute an evaluative situation for him.

The two other cases are indeed constituted by normative imperatives. In the first case, the moral principle rules that one should not keep the property of others. In the second case, the addict is governed by a need that makes him view every situation as an opportunity to acquire a new fund of drugs. In both cases, evaluative situations have an imperative quality.

Value situations are constituted by imperatives which call for decision. Life situations do not come of themselves calling for urgent action unless they contain an imperative to such action. Personal advantage of itself is not an imperative—though it is for some people, and can be for others. The point is that all regulative principles are such imperatives where they are felt to be regulative. And where no moral principles are sensed to serve a regulative function, it is impossible to envisage what could constitute such a situation as one which requires a moral decision.

A striking example of the constitutive function of moral principles is given in Kierkegaard's *Fear and Trembling*. Kierkegaard takes the story of Abraham, who is instructed by God to take his only begotten son Isaac to Mount Moriah and to sacrifice him there. Kierkegaard then carefully points out that the situation is thoroughly constituted by regulative principles, and that Abraham is admirable only insofar as such principles are assumed effective. Thus, Abraham is generally obedient to God, yet also loves his son and realizes that filicide is monstrous. If Abraham did not love his son or care about his death, he could obey God and there would be no problem. If Abraham were a rebel, he could defy God and there would be no problem. The particular situation Kierkegaard postulates is one constituted by two irreconcilable and opposed principles. This is the closest one can come to a purely constitutive role of principles. The regulative function is virtually suspended in the opposition of principles.

The easiest way to describe the constitutive role of moral principles is to say that they levy *prima facie* obligations on a man who accepts them. All the moral principles we believe in are *prima facie* obligations. What this means is that they define a problem of evaluation for us. They define what we ought to do. But because *prima facie* obligations may conflict, and we may be able to meet only one of them, we distinguish the *prima facie* obligations which constitute a problem of decision from the *over-all obligation* which is the obligation we accept as the result of decision.

In such terms, the man who believes that it is wrong to fight in an unjust war, and yet also that it is obligatory to obey the laws of his country, is faced with two conflicting *prima facie* obligations toward a war he believes is wrong: the obligation to avoid the draft, and the obligation to obey the law. The obligation he comes to accept as the result of his decision is the over-all obligation. He may, of course, leave the country, and conform to both *prima facie* obligations, at least to the letter if not in spirit.

Some moral theorists provide a simplified model for moral decision based on *prima facie* and over-all obligations. They claim that it is sufficient for moral decision to have a system of *prima facie* obligations and also a hierarchy among them, which settles any choice among obligations. Such a model rests implicitly on the view that a regulative principle alone determines what a man should do. As we have seen, one of Kant's major problems was the inability of his system to settle between conflicting imperatives. Moral theorists who would ground their views in duties alone, ignoring consequences, suggest that by adding to a pure system of principles of duty a hierarchical order among these principles, all problems may then be resolved.

In effect, such a system rests on two levels of regulative principles—the *prima facie* obligations, which constitute moral situations, and the ordered priority among them, which defines the over-all obligation where conflicts arise. The constitutive and regulative functions of principles are sufficient for any decision.

But we have seen that principles are inherently vague, and function more like ideals than specific rules for action. In particular, whenever courses of action involve risks of injury to other people, we must come to some judgment of *how much* risk is involved, and *how much* injury is likely. Such questions require us not only to look to consequences, but to have a way of calculating among a variety of risks and probable disadvantages. The hierarchy required for judgment where principles conflict must include a calculus of benefits and disadvantages as well. Such a system goes far beyond a simple ordering of regulative and constitutive principles. The procedure whereby we choose among *prima facie* obligations does look to an ordering of priorities among such obligations, but to consequences, feelings, and long-range goals as well.

D. Expediency

The contrast between morality and expediency is one of the central oppositions in all moral thinking. A man who acts from a concern for his own advantage alone is thought to be *immoral*. Sometimes this view is pushed so far, as it is in some versions of Christianity, that every vestige of self-interest is thought to be evil. Nietzsche was so horrified at the idea of a morality that would lead men to ignore their feelings and desires that he turned firmly to the opposite extreme. To him, morality calls for a strength of character and a heroic quality that is incompatible with self-denial and Christian humility. Humility degenerates into mediocrity. Greatness is always an assertion of *oneself*.

The subject of expediency is rather a confused one, and there are several types of confusion. For example, it is considered wrong by some people for a man to place his own interests ahead of the interests of others. Yet it may be considered right by the same people to place their country's interests ahead of all other interests in the world. In addition, it would be absurd for a man to be willing to die so that another might collect a few hundred dollars in insurance. It is wrong to ignore the interests of others. It is equally wrong to sacrifice ourselves to benefit others in small ways.

What is expediency? The tension between expediency and morality might suggest that any gain which is not morally right is expedient. But this is absurd. A narcotics addict is not acting expediently if he steals to support his drug habit. We are not tempted to call a foolish action "expedient." All men must learn to distinguish immediate from long-range goods, and we understand that an action of only immediate value is not truly expedient.

But if we mean by expediency the pursuit of long-range advantages to oneself, then we at least acknowledge the possibility of discovering that, in the long run, actions in conformity to principle are generally advantageous, at least in a society which reveres principles. No doubt some criminals have never been caught, and have lived comfortably to a ripe old age. But this is the exception, not the rule, and we cannot form guides to life on the basis of the exceptions.

Let us suppose the principle "crime does not pay" to be *generally* true— that is, most criminals are not made wealthy by their crimes nor contented. It could then be argued that, as a rule, crime is inexpedient. Conformity to ordinary moral principles and expediency would coincide, at least for most people. There might indeed be some exceptions. But such exceptions are more of a statistical character. To escape detection is often a matter of chance. It is not wise to plan to gain by a life of crime.

In general, I suspect the truth about life in most societies would support such a conclusion. Let us be very clear about the point being made. It is directed at the probability of a satisfactory life of crime. It looks to the statistics of crime and of detection, and the genuine circumstances of life in society. We have a substantive argument exclusively, that the principle that one should avoid crimes is generally expedient. We may take this principle as a guide to action. It may then become a moral principle.

Nevertheless, there are some exceptions—though we usually do not know who they are. In addition, we can *imagine* a criminal living a rich and satisfying life. Shall we rest the case between morality and expediency on such imaginary grounds? It seems that the conviction that substantive considerations alone do not justify obedience to moral principles rests on the supposition that a man *might* be benefited by disobedience.

The major confusion in the opposition of morality and expediency is that of misconstruing entirely the substantive function of moral principles. Expediency presumably looks to advantage, not duty. On a Kantian moral theory, duty and advantage are always opposed and in tension. But wherever substantive considerations are allowed, at least general advantages are taken into account. Both morality and expediency look to advantage. If they can be distinguished, there remain only two possibilities. One is that moral principles look to the general advantage of everyone, while in expediency we look only to personal advantage. This is an equation of expediency and egoism. We will consider egoism separately in the next chapter. Here we may simply note that, in political affairs, men often look to general benefit, and think of that as a matter of expediency not morality. The second distinction is that morality may be thought of as concern for principle, while expediency is a repudiation of principle in the name of gain or advantage.

We recall that in substantive evaluation, consequences can be used to evaluate the rightness of *actions* or the rightness of *principles* which are then to be accepted as at least *prima facie* obligations. A man may try to determine the advantages or disadvantages of keeping a wallet found in the street. Or he may try to determine the advantages and disadvantages of having a rule which men will be obligated to obey that no one should keep property that is not his. An action which is thought to be advantageous without concern for principle is expedient. An expedient act is one which is beneficial to the agent, but which comes under the rule of no regulative principle.

There are many regulative principles, so many that we might think that nothing would be prohibited as merely expedient. For example, may not a person keep a wallet on the grounds that his children are starving and he can obtain the money no other way? We might be hesitant to condemn a man in such a case. May not a person keep a wallet on the principle that it is right to seek one's own benefit? Certainly it is wrong to deprive oneself of benefits, at least if one has no reason to do so. We drop the qualification, and we have now a justification for all acts of expediency: a man owes it to himself to gain advantages and to live well. If one can be happy, one ought to be happy. Such a principle certainly should be regulative in a man's life, probably in everyone's life.

But if we now endeavor to test this rule by its consequences *as a rule*, we see that it requires qualification. It would generally be harmful if men sought to be happy by stealing from others or killing them. Rule utilitarianism has a fundamental point which we have incorporated into substantive judgment: we test rules as regulative principles in substantive evaluation. There are indeed principles which men take to be regulative, and which look to their own personal advantage. But such principles may be indefensible as rules which everyone ought to follow, indefensible in terms of the harm that would result to almost everyone. If in fact they are principles which would be generally advantageous as regulative principles, then they are moral, not merely expedient.

A moral principle is a regulative principle which is well substantiated in terms of the benefits it provides men in general, and substantiated as a principle for guiding conduct. An expedient act is one which looks to personal advantage regardless of the general principles which militate against such an act. Nevertheless, there are some moral principles which are vitally concerned with personal advantage. It is wrong to sacrifice oneself for others, where they will gain little. It is sometimes morally right to seek one's own benefit, not merely expedient. Expediency is a departure from regulative principle. Morality is adherence to such principle.

We may now summarize our discussion. Expediency may be distinguished from substantive appraisal as follows: expediency is the evaluation of an *action* solely in terms of its benefits for *the agent*. Substantive appraisal is the evaluation of a regulative *principle* in terms of its benefits for *everyone*. In general, regulative principles, if substantively grounded, are the best principles for men to live by. What a man who acts from expediency does is to make an exception of himself, *even though he needs the regulative principles as much as anyone else!*

Now we see what is so outrageous about expediency. It undermines a principle which is of general benefit, and required by everyone. For example, a thief may depend on the stability of property as much as anyone. If everyone took from everyone else, without restraint, he might himself suffer. Yet he pretends that on grounds of expediency he can flout the general rule which he wishes others to obey.

Expediency has its major applications, not in ordinary life, but in political affairs. It is a common view that the freedom of one's country is so paramount a value that no merely moral considerations should be allowed to conflict with it. In foreign affairs, anything at all in the interests of one's country is justified. Morality is thought of as a value only within a society, and not among societies.

Such a view is fundamentally a Hobbesian one. Hobbes argues that men are obligated to obey moral laws only where there is a central authority strong enough to enforce such laws, and to generate fear in men who would disobey them. A national government is such an authority. But in foreign affairs, no such authority can be found. Unfortunately, Hobbes does not develop his own argument far enough, for if it is beneficial to have such an authority within a state, to avoid chaos, it would seem beneficial to seek such an authority internationally as well, for like reasons.

The view that international affairs are to be ruled by expediency and not morality is one which rests upon all the confusions we have already discussed concerning the notion of expediency. It rests even more on a fundamental contempt for moral principles, as if they are blind and indefensible rules men follow with no grounds or aims. In particular, it completely overlooks the substantive function of such principles. And it overlooks as well the continuum of means and ends.

Let us take the example of an international treaty among nations. Sheer expediency should suggest that a country has the right to make or break treaties at will, provided that such actions are in its interests. Such a position is limited, in that it fails to look to the actual function such treaties serve. A perfectly analogous case can be made for a man making and breaking promises at will, if doing so is to his interest. The point is that the rule of promising—promises are made to be kept—is a regulative one because the trust and good will generated by such a regulative principle are extremely beneficial. Certainly it must be conceded that a regulative principle that treaties ought to be kept would improve relations among nations considerably.

The important point is that breaking a treaty, though perhaps beneficial in a short run, may be extremely disadvantageous over all. If we use means that involve distrust, we will not accomplish the end of mutual trust and respect. Nothing is more absurd than the *principle* that a country will gain peace by waging war. (It may be true as a rare exception, in very special circumstances.) Building weapons looks to the use of such weapons. At the very least, they will be sold to smaller countries and used in their wars.

It is simply undeniable that the regulation of foreign affairs by ordinary moral principles of trust and respect for life would be a tremendous improvement. The problem, then, is not one of justifying expediency on the whole over morality but of finding a way to achieve sufficient trust to allow for further trust and loyalty to principle. In domestic society, men generally do not steal. The few who do are usually caught. These two facts reenforce each other. But if stealing were common, and thieves almost never caught, that would be Hobbes' state of nature, and only a fool would follow strictures against stealing. Yet it would still be desirable to eliminate such stealing.

The continuum of means and ends makes it clear beyond doubt that the trust required for adherence to principle and the possibility of enforcement must come virtually together. We gain trust by acting in trust. A child is made responsible by being given responsibilities. The fundamental problem with advocating sheer expediency in international affairs is that this very expediency weakens the possibility of mutual respect and trust, and makes the development of regulative principles less likely.

Let us look back to the example given above. A country may break a treaty at will, if in its interests. So, too, a man may break his promises at will if in his interest. But is such a general practice likely to be of benefit? Obviously not. On the other hand, a man who generally keeps his promises may find that he will be attacked by a lunatic if he keeps his word, and feel justified in breaking it. Other considerations, some of which involve personal advantage, may come in conflict with a regulative conflict. This does not make the principle any less moral, nor make expediency more justifiable.

There is no fundamental difference between the function of regulative principles in international affairs and in ordinary life. But the circumstances are different. The scale of judgment is larger in political decisions. The consequences are more vital. The security is often less. Therefore, political decisions will often require a careful deliberation on the advantages of certain courses of action, since the harm in error could be very great. Most conventional moral decisions are of little consequence except for one or two people. In political decisions, the results of actions undertaken may be momentous, and must be considered in the decisions made. It is far more accurate and desirable to recognize the existence of regulative moral principles in international affairs, and to deny the value of expediency, but to admit that circumstances may call for the application of one principle rather than another, and that political decisions are both difficult to make and extremely insecure.

Most people admit that it is sometimes right to break one's promises, sometimes right even to cause another person's death. There is nothing expedient about such actions. But a deep purity makes us hesitate to admit this. The result has been an oversimplification of political affairs, and a view that is not only incorrect, but damaging to the relations among nations. A national leader who thinks that he must be expedient will have little impulse to seek trust and respect. In all too many cases, his expediency will be no more than shortsightedness. If he were required instead to reach complex political and moral decisions, keeping his country's welfare well in mind, then he might very well gain in long-range benefits also.

It follows from this entire discussion that expediency and morality are not contrasts in types of principles. Rather, expediency is a principle which claims that it is right to break moral principles when it is advisable to do so. Expediency is either absurd, in being a principle which asserts that it is right to be loyal to no principle, or else merely an acknowledgment of substantive considerations in the making of moral decisions. Where a person appeals to expediency to justify obeying no regulative principle whatsoever in a particular case, he contradicts himself by asserting a principle to justify obeying no principle. In addition, the open disregard of regulative principles tends to encourage their further disregard, and makes morality even less justifiable than it would be.

The greatest danger of expediency, and its greatest confusion, rests on mistaking an immediate interest for a true interest. If the substantive function of moral principles is well established, then accepting *prima facie* obligations of a moral character is in fact beneficial. If it is not, then we may wonder truly at the ground for doing so. If regulative principles ought to be followed, then they should be followed in international affairs also. And if they are, then the greatest long-range benefits may be achieved thereby.

Nevertheless, circumstances must be taken into account in political decisions, and such circumstances have their special character. A war may nullify all long-range prospects. Political decisions are extremely difficult and complex. But it is by no means clear that they are different in kind from any other moral decisions. This subject will be considered again in connection with crises and emergencies.

E. Ideals

The most important function of moral principles to this point has been mentioned only in passing. This is their capacity to serve as ideals. The vagueness inherent in moral principles which allows us to interpret them in different ways, and to be unsure as to how to apply them in particular circumstances, is a vagueness essential to principles as ideals. Ideals are ultimate principles, ultimate in that men tend to avoid to as great an extent as possible giving them up. But if we are not to relinquish our ideals in times of crisis, they must be vague enough to allow us to reinterpret them where necessary.

The principle that life is a paramount value is an ideal. It marks a reverence for the miracle of life, and an unwillingness to be party in any way to the destruction of life. It can lead to a respect for one's own life, and the principle that since a man has only one life to live, he should not waste it. It can lead to capital punishment, as justified retribution against those who do not respect human life. It can lead to the repudiation of capital punishment, as evil in terms of the ideal.

The principle "thou shalt not kill" represents only a part of the ideal that life is something to be preserved. Yet the ideal often lurks within the narrower principle. The respect we have for physicians, for example, is not based on the moral principle in its narrower form, but on the ideal to which they contribute. Public health measures, such as inoculations, always involve a general interference with the lives of individuals. Yet the ideal of preservation of life obligates us to such measures with their relatively minor inconveniences.

There are a great number of ideals, all of them to some extent vague, and all of them capable of eliciting great passions and loyalties. Life, beauty, knowledge, individuality, freedom, democracy, love, all are qualities which are considered intrinsically good, and of an ideal nature. The ideal aspect is what makes people willing to die for any of them, although they are so vague that it is difficult to know what follows from them. All regulative principles are part of or a sign of an ideal. Stealing is wrong because a man has an ideal right to his possessions, inherent in the ideals of security and enjoyment. Lying is wrong because the truth constitutes an ideal to be preserved. Where regulative principles conflict, often the ideals behind them aid us in settling the difficulties which arise.

Ideals have regulative, constitutive, and substantive functions as do moral principles. In that respect there is no central difference between them. If there is a difference, it is that ideals are wider and more important than are moral principles. Moreover, ideals are always vague, and for that reason difficult to formulate.

The most striking approach to ideals can be found in Aristotle's *Nichomachean Ethics*. Aristotle postulates that all human actions aim at some good. But if there were no highest good, then we would have an infinite number of actions leading to each other with no end, and nothing good *in itself*. Therefore, Aristotle argues, there is a highest good, and he calls this *eudaemonia* or happiness.

But Kant argues that happiness is no unqualified good, since happiness in an evil man can bring pride and self-righteousness. Either Kant and Aristotle disagree on the goodness of happiness, or they have a different conception of such happiness. To Kant, only a good will is unqualifiedly good, only the motives or intentions. Happiness is no good if it comes without being accompanied by a good will.

What sense can be given to Aristotle's definition of happiness as the highest good? It is the good for which all human actions aim. Obviously, well-being or contentment are not always pursued by men. We will interpret Aristotle as follows: whenever a man performs an intentional action, he is doing so for a reason, to achieve something he considers good. If there is no final or complete end, a good in itself which can make all actions which lead to it good, then no action can be thought of as good. In short, we are looking for an ultimate reason for doing anything, a reason complete in itself. Put another way, we are looking for a complete and self-sufficient ideal for human life.

We can now understand Aristotle's casual dismissal of men who think happiness is pleasure. He calls them "slavish," for their ideal is too shallow. A life of pleasure is not the best life a man can postulate as an ideal. We have already seen that a life of pleasure through dreams produced by probes in the brain is no ideal. No one would consider such a life worth pursuing on an ideal level—though it might be better than dying painfully of cancer.

What then is an ideal life? Clearly it must contain a moderate number of worldly goods. But would a great deal of wealth in a life of stupidity be ideal? Clearly an intelligent and rational life is superior to a foolish one. In the end, Aristotle is led to conclude that a life of excellence in accordance with reason is the ideal life for man. The ideal life is to be productive, rational, and, most important of all, *active*. Aristotle argues forcefully that all states of being—such as peace of mind, wealth, pleasure, or satisfaction—are risky and transitory, capable of being destroyed by external circumstances. Happiness must be as complete a condition in itself as possible, if it is to be an ideal. Therefore, happiness is to be understood as an activity, as a way of life, not as a passive state of being. It is useful to interpret Aristotle's position as that the ideal for man is doing things well in accordance with reason. Reason is essential because it is man's unique and highest capacity.

How can we justify such an ideal? We can appeal to the variety of values in human life, to what men have said and done, to deeper feelings and patterns in life. But, in the end, the justification rests on the *fact* of whether we do or do not find such an ideal plausible in terms of the rest of our experience. The point is that we are speaking of an ideal, which is more than merely good. It is the highest imaginable condition of human life. Consider a thief. Does he steal because he is poor, because he owns very little himself, because he has been cheated by others, because he cannot get a job, because he cannot do anything else well? These may or may not be good reasons for stealing. But with respect to the ideal, we ask, if he could imagine the best possible life for him, would he still be a thief? Is there something ideal about stealing, lying, hurting others? Is there something ideal about working on an assembly line, emptying septic tanks, or collecting garbage? Or is not an ideal human life one of rational knowledge, or productive activities and important work, from which a man derives enjoyment and a sense of fulfillment?

In our society, many men are thought to desire to escape work, and to do nothing but loaf and play. Is this because they consider play ideal, or because the work they can find is degrading and inhuman? If men were able to choose what they would do with their time in terms of their own ideals, would they choose to do nothing productive? Or would they not seek to learn to do many things, intelligently and well?

In his early writings, Karl Marx reveals a deep humanism which rests upon his perception that capitalist life is inhuman, degrading, destructive to the nature of man. Marx's revolutionary call is directed toward the achievement of a more ideal human life. He views the end of capitalism as the abolition of work with no excellences, and the beginning of a life in which men can live as they ought to, in terms of some sense of the ideal. Instead of living in a uniform way for their seventy years or so, devoting most of their waking hours to ugly and demeaning labor in factories, men will live varied lives of excellence, excelling in a variety of gifts and abilities.

There is no way to justify an ideal to a man who lacks it even after he has engaged in its substantive appraisal. Moreover, the details of our ideals vary, as they must. Nevertheless, each of us might do well to ask himself whether his ultimate ideals are not shared with his friends and neighbors—that kind of life we would choose to live above all others, if we could so choose after we had gained some experience of life and the world. This is a factual matter, and is capable of disproof. But it may well be that where ideals are defined as Aristotle defines them, then virtually all men share ideals which are remarkably alike. And where such ideals differ, it may be because men have led different lives, learned different things, and differ in the quality of their imaginations also. It is at least plausible that, as John Stuart Mill also suggests, all men of wide experience and understanding will have the same ideals.

The striking part of Aristotle's ethical theory, however, is his conviction that our ideals must define for us our sense of what is good, and tell us how to act. He argues that ethics leads eventually to politics—and we can easily see why, for an ideal life is impossible on an individual level alone. An ideal life calls for a political as well as a moral solution.

Nevertheless, our morals seem to Aristotle dictated by our ideals also. He has a very striking point. We do not live in an ideal society, and the circumstances of our real lives certainly will make a difference in how we act. But if we can envisage an ideal, and it is an ideal which involves actions which we can perform now, are we not both obligated and wise to undertake such actions? If an ideal life involves the development of our mind and the pursuit of knowledge, then we should begin now. If an ideal life involves trusting people, we should begin by developing that trust now, and by trusting others *as much as possible*. If the ideal life involves respect for the property of others, then we should begin with that now.

The continuum of means and ends entails that our activities which aim at a certain result must incorporate those results as much as possible in the activities which are means. Aristotle's point is that insofar as we postulate an ideal we truly respect, then what we do must be aimed at trying to bring it about. But the only way to accomplish a goal is to begin by acting in ways that will realize it—ways which usually involve acting in as ideal a manner as we can.

This point can be made complete by defining two kinds of ideals. There are ideals whose sole function is to set a contrast with the present, and to reveal the inadequacies of the real conditions of life. Such an ideal does not serve to improve life nor to guide action. There are also ideals which serve as guides to action, which direct and improve actions, which draw a man's thoughts and intentions to themselves.

The first kind of ideal is *unrealistic* in two senses. It is unrealistic in that it has no roots in the present, and it is unrealistic also in that nothing can be done to realize it or bring it closer. The omnipotence and omniscience of God are unrealistic ideals, in that nothing a pious man can do will bring him to a total power or knowledge. The doctrine of grace postulates an unrealistic ideal in God, for nothing a man can do will bring him closer to God. Grace is a bequest from God to man. In Dostoievski's *The Brothers Karamazov*, Ivan is angered because the ideal of eliminating suffering seems unrealistic in God's world, for suffering seems to go on without end, no matter what men do. The doctrine of original sin, which postulates that men are sinful from the beginning, and cannot be saved by means of their own efforts, makes all ideals unrealistic. Where ideals are conceived in unrealistic terms, we have what Hegel and Marx called "alienation." A man is alienated when his ideal of what is good forces him to conceive of himself as evil, even to become evil, and unavoidably. Under capitalism, the ideal of many men is to be free as owners of machines. But, Marx argues, both the owners and the tenders of the machines tend to become mechanical themselves. Capitalism makes men commodities, to be bought and sold in the marketplace. The factory worker dreams of freedom from the machine. The only hope he can realize is to own the machine, and therefore to become even more dependent on it.

The second kind of ideal is *realistic* in two senses. First, it is realistic in being achievable. Second, it can be achieved in part, at least, in the means which might lead to it. The ideal of life can be realized only by having a respect for life from the beginning. In this respect, a pacifist is *more* realistic than the soldier who believes that through war and killing we may develop a reverence for life. The ideal of a responsible electorate can be achieved only by giving the people the right to vote, even before they are ready for it. Here is a fundamental lesson for moral education. Children will become responsible only by being given responsibility. Of course it is risky, but there is no other way.

Aristotle's ideal of happiness is defined, not as a goal to be reached through activities distinct from it, but as a complex mode of activity itself, containing several types of excellence in conformity with reason. Such an ideal is completely realistic, for it is both a goal we might be able to achieve through effort, and an ideal which can in part be incorporated into the activities which lead to it. Aristotle's point is that the way to happiness is by living up to its ideal character to the greatest extent we can.

From this point of view, regulative principles are components of the ideal life. If such regulative principles are substantively grounded, they represent rational judgment looking to the consequences of action. If the principles are regulative, they represent a loyalty to what is excellent. In addition, such principles represent the way men adjust to each other, their mutual needs and concerns. Morals then becomes politics, as Aristotle argues, because men can live well only with and among others. A good part of the basis for conventional moral principles is the need men have for each other, to live well.

Ideals represent the ultimate reasons men have for what they do. Often, however, men act without any ideal intent, hoping to get through the next few days or weeks without disaster. We have been considering the fact that to neglect a realistic ideal is to prevent its realization. Therefore, there is something misguided about ignoring one's ideals if they are realistic and genuine. A man who respects life, but who ignores cries for help from his window, makes it more difficult for others to respect his own life. Indifference perpetuates indifference.

A man may ignore his ideals for two reasons. Either he does not know what they are, or he is too weak to pursue them in the face of temptation and obstacles. Ignorance as to greater ideals is extremely common. Men are caught up in immediate affairs, and take no long-range view. They are concerned with the immediate, and ignore the consequences. A common example of this is the appeal to emergency police measures in a democracy to secure it against external threats—measures which may lead to its own downfall. We strengthen the police to make ourselves secure. But the police then become the enemy.

Weakness is even more common. Men vaguely sense a greater ideal than they conform to, but are tempted and fall, or are frightened and submit. A woman may be awaiting a deep and trusting love, but fall in love with a man who is cold and superficial. She is afraid to wait any longer. Her impulses and needs are too strong. Yet in some hidden part of herself, she may know that she has not kept to her own aims.

In this sense, our ideals represent our *true* aims, though we may be misled by ignorance and weakness. Aristotle's position is that moral decisions are to be made in the light of what men *truly* want—the truth as it would be revealed if they ceased deceiving themselves. The exercise of admitting to ourselves what we truly hope for, and would consider ideal, is taxing and even frightening. For often we do not know what we want. Even more often, we pretend to ourselves it is not our wish. One of the most interesting features of psychoanalytic therapy is that it endeavors to uncover the patient's hidden goals, and to end his self-deception.

Is Aristotle's conception of the ideal the only defensible one? Aristotle tends to view the ideal life as a life of rational contemplation, the life of the philosopher. Yet we can imagine other lives of an ideal character—the poet, painter, inventor, athlete, naturalist, or politician, for example. There seems to be a variety of styles of life with an ideal character—though all share the moral virtues in common. We may well find that a plurality of ideals is essential to human life. If there is a man who finds nothing ideal in cooperating with some other men, it is not easy to see how to convince him that he should. In the end, appealing to an ideal for mankind depends on what men actually revere. And if they revere different things, Aristotle's argument is not convincing.

Nevertheless, the distinction between the two kinds of ideals is a fundamental one. Ideals govern many human actions, especially moral decisions. Where ideals are unrealistic, they can paralyze action and even lead to destructive conclusions. Ivan Karamazov is led to the conclusion that anything at all is acceptable. The main reason for never forgetting substantive appraisal is to make sure that ideals remain realistic. The continuum of means and ends is acknowledged as a real force in moral decisions only when incorporated into realistic ideals. Whatever ideals we have, we must be able to come closer to them by our actions in the present. Such ideals are realistic. From Aristotle's point of view, what we ought to do is precisely what brings to pass the ideals we set for ourselves as human beings.

QUESTIONS

1. Take each of the ten commandments. Give a speculative substantive justification for each of them. Discuss some of the problems which remain in each case. Try to judge how well justified each of the commandments is as a moral principle of substantive import.
2. What are the substantive considerations which are relevant to evaluating moral prohibitions against early sexual experiences?
3. Explain why loyalty to principle is important in moral decisions. Are there good grounds for demanding such loyalty?
4. Explain the importance of exceptions for each of the functions of moral principles.

Principles 5. Is it morally right to seek your own self-interest? Is it obligatory? Explain.

6. "In the last analysis, whether a man follows moral principles or not is a matter of moral education." Discuss this claim.

7. In what ways can disagreements over regulative principles be beneficial? Or should we seek principles which everyone will accept?

8. If a man believes a moral principle is right, must he obey it?

9. When would it be right to be expedient?

10. Give the constituents you think are essential features of an ideal human life, and explain each of them.

SELECTED READINGS

Kant, *Fundamental Principles of the Metaphysics of Morals*. The most important work on moral principles ever written.

J. S. Mill, *Utilitarianism*.

S. Kierkegaard, *Fear and Trembling*. A challenge to Kant, among other things.

Nietzsche, *Beyond Good and Evil*. Another challenge, from a different point of view.

J. Dewey, *Human Nature and Conduct*, Part III. A completely different approach.

R. M. Hare, *The Language of Morals*, 1952, Clarendon. A modern study.

VI. SOCIETY

THROUGHOUT OUR discussion of the various facets of moral decision, we have recurrently touched upon the relations among men in a society, the considerations which arise either in a concern for certain other people or with regard to society as a whole. Morality certainly involves social relations, duties which individuals owe to others as well as benefits they receive from others. To many people, morality is addressed solely to social relationships.

Aristotle claims that "man is a social animal." Such a claim is a complex one with a variety of dimensions. It ranges over the fact that men are born into a world which includes other people. It refers also to the obligations men have to consider the needs of others. The facts of social life are complex. The duties commonly assigned to individuals which they owe to others are complex also.

The duties we owe to others are often viewed as confining, particularly during late adolescence or early adulthood, when a person first becomes responsible for himself. Family responsibilities may hinder personal enjoyment. Obligations to one's parents may interfere with one's own free development. A child experiences the obligations imposed on him by his parents as arbitrary controls. But he is powerless and conforms to these obligations because he must. Given the greater control over his own life that comes with adulthood, if he still views his social responsibilities as arbitrary and without foundation, he may come to question the entire basis of social obligations.

In one respect, to question duties is to raise meaningful questions about the substantive basis of certain rules, with the intent of modifying them and making them more effective and beneficial. Some moral obligations may be rejected because of changing circumstances. The duties of grown children to aged parents have changed over the past few generations, due in part to changing family structures, to a greater mobility among families, and to the general increase in life expectancy. Unfortunately, changes in norms have not alleviated the problems of old age. If anything, they have exacerbated them.

It is also possible to question the entire basis of social responsibilities. In effect, we question whether a man owes any duties to anyone besides himself. Egoism and altruism are posed as alternatives. The egoist claims that a man is obligated only to himself. Since conventional moral duties are considered strongly altruistic, egoism is often regarded as immoral and evil.

The posing of an opposition between egoism and altruism is unfortunate in several respects. It tends to suggest that we must look either to our own advantage alone or to the general advantage of other people. It tends to obscure the fact that consideration of others is often to a man's personal advantage. It also obscures the far deeper principle that a man is indeed in a privileged and unique position with respect to himself. There are some matters which a man can decide only for himself. Egoism tends to degenerate quickly into a narrow and unintelligent self-interest. Altruism tends to call for virtually complete sacrifice to the interests of others.

We will open our discussion of such matters by formulating the extreme versions of egoism and altruism, scrutinizing the arguments which may be given for them, and then moving to more moderate positions. We will see that an enlightened and moderate egoism and a moderate altruism are not very different in important respects.

A. Egoism

In the *Republic*, Plato seems to be arguing that justice is a good in itself only to the extent that it is of benefit to a just man. Though Plato develops an extremely rich conception of what is of true benefit to a man, he does seem to acknowledge the force of egoism. Hobbes too argues from egoistic premises that men ought to obey the laws of their country, for it is in their interest to do so. I mention Plato and Hobbes to avoid a conception of self-interest so narrow as to be obviously unwise. There is no point at all in defining a view of egoism that a man should do what he *thinks* is to his personal advantage. Egoism and relativism are different positions. A man may err in his understanding of what is to his own advantage. If egoism is defensible at all, it must depend on a distinction between enlightened self-interest and ignorance of what is to one's true advantage.

Thus, Hobbes and Plato argue that obedience to established principles of moral virtue is of personal benefit. They argue from egoism to altruism. We will study such arguments in a moment. The point is that egoism is not to be equated with selfishness, which often works out to harm the selfish man. Many philosophers have argued that we may derive most of the principles of conventional morality from enlightened self-interest.

Nevertheless, cases come easily to mind which seem to call for a choice between others and oneself. A member of the French Underground during the Second World War, being tortured for information, seems forced to choose between protecting his compatriots and suffering pain. Egoism would entail that he look to his personal advantage, and ignore his friends.

Egoism is the position that a man *ought* to do what is to his own personal advantage, provided he knows what that is. It is important to realize that the egoistic position is not easy to defend, though we are all aware of its temptations. Can we maintain that it is true *by definition* that a man ought to do what will make him happy? The very fact that men often construe their duties to oppose their own interests shows that the problem is not merely one of definition. Kant's whole moral theory is founded on the principle that duty and self-interest are not and should not be connected. Even if Kant is wrong, the position he takes shows that duty may theoretically be separated from personal advantage. They are not connected by definition.

An alternative argument is that men are in fact motivated solely by a concern for their personal benefit. This is a psychological argument, somewhat akin to the argument used by Hobbes. However, once again the facts fail to support the force of the claim made. Some men simply do pursue their duties even when they conflict with their own interests. If they do so, then they are able to do so, and their motivations are more complex than psychological egoism can explain. The superficial facts fail to support egoism as a factual theory about human behavior.

The implicit psychological theory of egoism is that men act solely from desire, and that all desires when realized bring satisfaction. In other words, psychological egoism is a version of psychological hedonism, and is open to the same criticisms. In particular, though a man may indeed desire to do what he considers right, and though doing so brings some satisfactions with it, the result may be extremely painful and disadvantageous to him. The small satisfaction he receives from his virtue is quite swamped by his suffering. Yet men do succeed in performing the actions which they consider right, even when the result is pain or death.

An argument may be derived from the Platonic principle that "all men desire the good." We interpret the principle as "all men desire what is good for themselves," not "all men desire what they believe is good." We may associate duty and the good, and maintain that men *ought to do* what is truly good (for themselves). Yet it still does not follow that men ought to pursue their *personal advantage*. It may not be truly good to do so. Only where we associate what is good for a man with what is advantageous and beneficial in a narrower sense are we led to egoism proper. For example, the Platonic and Aristotelian conception of the good is that it is the ideal life for man. A man ought to do what is truly good for himself in the sense that it brings him as close as possible to an ideal human life. But an ideal human life may be conceived as virtuous and heroic, as excellent in a moral sense. Is it right, for example, to flee in battle from cowardice, or is it not nobler and more ideal to be brave and courageous—though not, of course, foolhardy? Egoism would make Falstaff the noblest of men, which is not easy to defend.

There are several arguments which may be offered against egoism. First, it may be maintained that egoism is paradoxical and self-stultifying. An egoist may not promulgate his egoistic position, since to do so will work to his disadvantage. In particular, if other people look solely to their own interests, they will not benefit the egoist by their actions. This argument has two flaws. It assumes that a man cannot hold a moral position which he would not openly proclaim. But an egoist is not prevented from maintaining the egoistic position silently.

Even more interesting, the argument assumes that a society where everyone looks after his own interests alone would be less advantageous to a given person than a society like ours in which but a single person acted from egoism. Yet a society in which everyone were rationally and intelligently self-interested might be far less restrictive and more beneficial in the long run than a more conventional one. Nietzsche argues that a community of men who are self-interested and strong-willed enough to be egoistic would be superior for mankind as a whole. We have returned to the possibility that we may be able to argue from egoism to a general welfare. An egoist may truly believe that egoism would be generally beneficial if accepted by everyone. The only question we have here is whether he believes in egoism because he is altruistic, or is altruistic because of his egoism.

This last seeming paradox is the fundamental problem of egoism. Egoism is a *strange* doctrine. It is not *selfishness*, for then the argument would rest on the belief that everyone ought to work for the *egoist's* advantage. The pursuit by others of their interests may be harmful to the egoist himself. On the other hand, egoism is not *benevolence*, for the pursuit of one's own interests may in some cases harm others. The strangeness of egoism when taken very literally makes it very unlikely that anyone really regards himself in an egoistic light. For men are in fact deeply concerned about what others do, and are affected by them. Egoism pretends to ignore the actions of others, though they may hurt us very deeply. It also over-emphasizes an individual's personal actions, as if they can be isolated from the actions of others.

What then is the appeal of egoism? It is twofold, being grounded on two different levels of analysis. First, egoism looks to the ultimate ground of duty, and notices correctly that the substantive ground of moral decision entails that a right action is advantageous to someone. An action which benefits no one and hurts everyone cannot be right. There is an intimate connection between duty and advantage. The error egoism makes is to assume that the connection is between the *agent's* duty and his own advantage. The more fundamental error is to assume that the agent's actions and interests are separable in fact from the actions and interests of others. A man who will not talk under torture sees his own interests in the future of his friends. It is his interest in his friends which enables him to refrain from giving information which will harm them. His interest in others is disadvantageous to him.

This can be explained easily in terms of our model of affections. A man forms secondary and tertiary affections toward his principles and also toward the men he works and lives with. These affections develop out of primary affections which indeed are self-directed. But it is a psychological fact that derivative affections, out of which a man forms his desires and makes his decisions, may become stronger than primary affections. A man can fast for many weeks to purify his

soul, though the desire for food is primary. He can also disdain his own sufferings
to help others.

Shall we argue that the beginning or primary affections are what men ought
to satisfy? If we do, then we are taking the position that the initial stages of life
are the model for later life. Higher learning, deeper awareness, the arts and the
sciences are of no fundamental importance in the development of the person.
We leave man closest to his primitive state, more animal than human in that
mind has not yet developed. With the development of mind, men form goals and
aspirations based on derivative affections. They look ahead to greater pleasures
and to higher feelings. They learn to set immediate goals aside by forming affections for the future and for what can be known. This is the deeper problem of
egoism. It degenerates into narrowness and inhumanity.

Egoism can be derived from the sense that moral principles which emphasize
the sacrifices men make for others lead eventually to a society which is repressive
and destructive to everyone. In other words, egoism may be derived from an
altruistic position, even that of rule utilitarianism. It would be better for everyone
if each person stopped worrying about others, and pursued his own maximal
satisfaction. Nietzsche's egoism seems to be basically of this sort, though it has
relativistic aspects as well. Mankind moves inevitably to mediocrity if altruism
is all that is accepted as good. Greatness is individualistic and egoistical.

There is much to this argument. A repressive society is precisely one which
sacrifices the welfare of individuals to a larger purpose—that of the society as a
whole, or of the national state. A fundamental premise of democracy, especially of
democratic liberalism, is that individual happiness matters very much, and that
men must find their happiness for themselves. A fundamental counter to repression
is the position that society exists for individuals, and that if each man sought his
own advantage only, we would have a better world.

Nevertheless, the position is limited, for it sets aside conflicts among interests
and the harm such conflicts can generate. The egoism which is based on altruism
or general welfare is a very complex one. Indeed it is true that individual satisfactions are important in evaluation. But sheer egoism is an unlikely way to
maximize individual satisfactions. Egoism is a form of altruism only within a
simplistic theory, where wishes become more important than plans.

B. Altruism

Altruism is susceptible to so extreme a formulation as to have no obvious
defense. This is that we should never consider our own personal interests at all in
making a moral decision. A man should do what is beneficial for others, never for
himself. In some strains of Christianity there can be found a morality of service
which is close to self-sacrifice. The view that personal interest is sinful permeates
some religious sects, leading to service and austerity. Patriotism too tends to lead
to a view that bravery is a sacrifice of oneself.

It is difficult to know how to defend such an extreme altruism, though it must be conceded that men have throughout history sacrificed themselves to greater goods—be it the will of God, an ideal of freedom, or even the benefit of their country.

Nevertheless, there is an important ambiguity in the version of altruism we have posed. In saying that a man ought not to consider his own interests, do we mean that his interests are to be *totally* disregarded, that they are completely irrelevant to a moral decision of his? Or do we mean that his personal interests are of no greater importance than are anyone else's? Wherever Christian asceticism may have led, the most well known Christian duties are the Golden Rule—do unto others as you would have them do unto you—and its equivalent—thou shalt love thy neighbor like thyself. In both cases, it is assumed that a man loves himself, and pursues his own interests. Morality, it is claimed, consists in considering others to exactly the same extent as we consider ourselves. All interests have the same moral weight.

The difference between the two versions of altruism is that the first makes self-sacrifice an essential quality of all moral action. To act morally is to repudiate one's own advantage. The second version preserves the importance of the agent's own aims, but raises all other interests to the same level of importance. Self-sacrifice may be necessary according to the Golden Rule, but only occasionally, and only because we live in an imperfect world. The second version of altruism leaves open the possibility that, in some world, all interests will harmonize, and self-sacrifice will never be required. Plato's argument in the *Republic* is that a just man in a just society will live virtuously and also advantageously. A just society provides benefits for everyone, and demands sacrifice from no one.

The more extreme version is the mirror-image of extreme egoism, and suffers from similar faults. It is basically a strange view, and lacks even the natural basis of egoism in self-love. If one's own interests are truly irrelevant to moral decisions, then other people should not consider such interests either. Yet the principle of altruism is that a man should consider all the interests of other people. It is a strange benevolence that has a man consider the interests of another when the latter is forbidden to consider his own.

The conception of altruism worth discussing, then, is the one which maintains that, from a moral standpoint, all individual interests are equivalent, and carry equal weight. There are several arguments worth considering in defense of this kind of altruism. It will be noted that all of them are arguments we have considered in other contexts, particularly with respect to the general justification of moral principles. The reason for this is simple. Morality is often thought of as a counter to self-love. A justification for morality is therefore one which shows that we should act from other than self-love. Arguments for altruism and arguments for moral principles are taken by many people to be identical.

Of course, this is an error. There are many moral principles which are not altruistic, and many moral decisions required which do not involve the interests of other people in a central respect. For example, the principle "lying is wrong" is not obviously an altruistic principle, since we should often tell the truth even where it will be painful to others. The decision of whether to commit suicide or not is a moral one, whether or not others will be hurt by it. The decision of whether to develop one's abilities through study and work, or to live in play or indolence, is thought by many people to be a moral decision, even where it involves only the agent himself.

All moral principles and moral decisions presuppose the need for a choice among conflicting alternatives. These alternatives are either two *prima facie* obligations, or a *prima facie* moral obligation and a temptation or personal desire. If we take as paradigm the latter case, then a moral decision always involves the repudiation of a personal temptation. But the moral principle involved need not involve others. It may, for example, involve a choice between an arduous and an easy path, a choice which a man must make regardless of others. The obligatory choice may be trying—as is telling the truth in some circumstances.

Having considered these preliminaries, we turn now to several arguments which may be given in defense of the second type of altruism.

(1) The argument Kant gives that the Categorical Imperative is the ground of all duty is in effect an argument for altruism. The Categorical Imperative is a formal version of the Golden Rule. "Act so that your maxim can be made a universal law." A moral law is equally binding on everyone. We recall that Kant's argument is founded on the principle that the only unqualified good is a good will. All other goods are qualified goods, since intelligence, knowledge, and wealth in the hands of a man of evil intent are themselves evils. But a good will is nothing but obedience to a categorical principle, a principle which refers to no particular person and applies to everyone.

All *hypothetical* imperatives—that is, imperatives which look to some end—are obligatory only for a man who accepts the end. They are of the form, "if *A*, then *B*." If you want to be educated, then you must attend school. No hypothetical imperative can provide a categorical rule of the form, "thou shalt not . . ."

In other words, Kant's argument depends on the *form* of moral principles. They are categorical. And no categorical principle can make an exception of a particular person. Therefore, duties must be indifferent to persons, and of general form. In effect, Kant's argument is that moral principles and duties are categorical imperatives *by definition*.

Now, can an egoist make the egoistic maxim a universal law? Clearly he cannot, for he is interested in achieving his own advantage by a law which will make everyone else look to his own advantage, not the egoist's. The Categorical Imperative makes an even stronger case against egoism than the argument we gave above of a similar nature. The reason for this is that the generalization principle inherent in the form of the Categorical Imperative which we have considered is wholly indifferent to the interests of any particular person. A good will for Kant is one which performs its duty totally without reference to any interests *whatsoever*, including that of the agent.

So strongly does Kant accept this dichotomy between duty and advantage that he argues that the purest form of a good will has an especially noble quality. A man who tells the truth from fear of being caught is not good in the interest of duty alone, but is motivated by desire. We cannot call his will good without qualification. He may be primarily motivated by self-interest. A good will in its purest and most praiseworthy state is one which is not adulterated by any interests of any sort.

The fundamental principle for Kant is indeed that duty and interest are completely distinct. All aspects of interest generate hypothetical imperatives—of the form *if* you do this, then that will happen. But morality is not hypothetical but categorical. Therefore, interest of any sort is irrelevant to morality *by definition*. And all interests are, from a moral point of view, of the same weight—that is, none.

The conception of moral principles as general and categorical is one of the greatest insights in moral theory. Some kind of generalization principle operates in morals, which transforms a duty for one man into a similar duty for another in like circumstances. If an action is right for one man, then a similar action is right for any other man in the same circumstances.

But there are unresolvable problems which remain. No two men are ever in exactly the same circumstances. Whether the differing circumstances are relevant or not is not to be settled by the Categorical Imperative itself, but by consideration of consequences. Kant's position is so pure, and so removed from the consequences of action, that an action which conformed to the Categorical Imperative would be thought right if it harmed everyone in the world—which is truly an absurd result.

In addition, there is something disagreeable about the attempt to settle genuine moral disputes by definition. The dispute between the egoist and the altruist is in some forms a genuine one. It is genuine where both egoist and altruist take the position that the general result of one or the other rule will have beneficial consequences. The egoist cannot prove his case easily. We have criticized various arguments which seek to justify egoism as obvious in some sense. Neither egoism nor altruism are true by definition or in an obvious fashion. The tension between individual interests and the interests of others is the very heart of moral decision, and it is not to be erased in any trivial manner.

The fundamental reason for this is somewhat different from the prosaic and extreme arguments we have already considered. The fundamental reason why a man cannot but be torn between his own needs and the needs of others is that he stands in a unique position with respect to his own needs. There are some and even many goods which only he can obtain for himself. Almost all pleasures involve some activities and decisions on the part of the man who would experience them.

All goods a man may utilize must be acted upon by him. This is the force behind the old saw, "You can lead a horse to water but you cannot make him drink." If we are to gain any benefits at all, we must drink them ourselves—though others may lead us to them.

If this is true, then although we may agree that in some abstract sense all human interests are equal, they are not so from the concrete point of view of the individual agent. If he does not obtain certain benefits for himself, then no one else will be able to do so for him. I have in mind here actions like marrying the woman he loves, passing an examination, or accepting a job. Abstract acts are acts anyone might perform, with equally abstract consequences and benefits. But concrete acts generate direct benefits for the agent, but often only *possible* benefits for others.

A bird in the hand is often worth two or more birds in the bush. Suppose a man is in love with a woman he considers perfection itself. Should he refrain from marrying her because someone else would be deprived by his doing so? That would be absurd. Yet if his interest is no greater in any respect in such a case than anyone else's, such a conclusion may follow. The point is that altruism is too abstract. It overlooks the important difference that an agent makes to his own advantages as compared to the interests of others. It follows that any formal justification for altruism will prove vain as a guide to concrete decisions.

The tension between individual interests and the interests of others is a permanent tension because the greater ability of a man to gain his own ends always tugs at the moral obligations he may have toward others. "Thou shalt love they neighbor like thyself." Love is merely an emotion. Perhaps such a principle can be followed. "Do unto others as you would have them do unto you." That too is a genuine possibility. But it is *not* possible for us to act toward others as we act toward ourselves, or even to view others as we do ourselves.

This, I would argue, is the greater truth of egoism. Egoism starts from the true premise that a man views his own aims and interests in a special way. This premise is itself a refutation of the kind of altruism which views particular persons as irrelevant to moral decisions. But egoism then concludes that all altruism is unjustified, and that only self-interest can be obligatory. This does not follow.

We turn now to a more modest altruism. Is it ever right for a man to perform actions which will benefit others and harm himself? The modest version of altruism maintains that *sometimes* it is right to sacrifice one's own interests for others. There are two arguments to support this claim, both of which we have already considered as grounds for regulative principles.

(2) Men live in society, surrounded by other men. The model of development we have considered notes the psychological *fact* that most men become attached to habits and principles of conduct and also to other people. Hume describes the emotion of *sympathy*, or the feelings men have in response to the feelings of others. The more like us other people are, the more we feel exactly as they do. If they suffer, we suffer. Therefore, we will often act to benefit them.

Far more important, men become deeply attached to each other both in fact and because such attachments are valuable. Parents love their children, and that love is a fact and also a great boon in human relations. Yet that love can be so strong as to bring a father to run into a burning building in even a vain hope of saving his child. It is impossible to deny that such strong feelings exist. Moreover, it is difficult to see how we might argue that such feelings are unfortunate, and should be eliminated if possible.

Our first argument, then, for the modest altruism which maintains that it is sometimes right to sacrifice oneself for others is founded on the psychological fact that men come to have such strong attachments to other people, to their country, to mankind in general, that they are led to an act of sacrifice as a natural result of their feelings. The soldier who dies in battle may do so gladly, in the sense that his love for his country has made him willing to protect her when he can, even at personal expense.

We need not conclude from the existence of such strong loves and loyalties that all acts of self-sacrifice are justified. A man may be led to self-destruction when he can benefit the recipient of his noble deed very little. The man who dashes into the burning building to save his child is wrong to do so if it is too late, or if the child is already out. The point is that the strength of human feeling is great enough so that a man's personal interests are sometimes not as valuable to him as the interests of someone else. And he should then do what he can to realize the latter, not his own.

What of men who lack these greater loves and loyalties, even, in Mill's words, "the conscientious feelings of mankind"? Clearly such men are not easily led to self-sacrifice, nor is it clear that they should be. I know of no argument to convince a man indifferent to the plight of another that he should help him, if it means his own death. There are times of stress when we need men of heroic moral strengths and dedication. But if men are emotionally indifferent during such times, it is the fault of moral education, not of the individual men who lack certain feelings.

The argument that men have duties because of their greater feelings is an argument which is grounded in the fact of such feelings. Where such feelings are absent, we may conclude that the duties are absent also. More rationally, we would do better to lay the blame for the absence of loyalties on the conditions of moral education. And that is often what we do. Nevertheless, we should not overlook the fact that moral duties exert an educational influence on the feelings of men who follow them.

(3) The other argument for modest altruism is a version of rule utilitarianism, though from personal advantage. Hobbes argues that egoism entails altruism. That is, it is to everyone's benefit that there be certain rules of conduct which everyone will follow—rules which promote stability and trust. It is of general benefit that promises be kept, that trials be open and honest, that men help each other when in dire need. In a complex society, men are so dependent on each other for many

things that it is of general benefit—to *every* person—that a benevolent and helpful attitude toward others be encouraged in all individuals.

In other words, the feelings toward others and general regulative principles which generate trust and mutual benefit are aspects of social life which are advantageous to everyone. They are advantageous, however, only where they are strong, and followed by almost everyone. There is little benefit from a rule concerning promises which is often broken. There is little advantage in a parental love which is often weak and unprotective. It is of little advantage that patriotic feelings in a country in mortal danger be sporadic and feeble.

This argument, then, is that modest altruism is generally beneficial to everyone, when strictly conformed to. People stop and help others in distress. And they should, because everyone is benefited by such a practice. The point again is that the benefit depends on strict conformity to the altruistic principles.

(3a) A variation on this argument depends on the conception of ideals presented in the last chapter. A modest altruism is a position which is consistent with most people's ideals. It involves less hypocrisy and inconsistency than egoism, and a far more tangible sense of benefit. A man is aware that modest altruism is beneficial to everyone. He now finds himself in a position where the altruistic principles will lead him to death. Argument (3) is that he must be consistent with his principles because what is beneficial is precisely a willingness to make such sacrifices if the principles demand it. Argument (3a) is that the general practices of altruism in his society, and the rewards which have accompanied such practices, make the sacrifice closer to the ideal than cowardice or self-denial would be.

Both of these arguments are substantive. Consideration for others with respect for their needs is a beneficial characteristic for any person to have in social life. Therefore, consideration and respect are installed in feeling, in regulative principles of conduct, and as ideals to which a moral person conforms. A man who then denies the imperatives of self-sacrifice in such circumstances may violate his own feelings, will be hypocritical and inconsistent, cowardly and ignoble.

Such arguments leave completely open the determination of when self-sacrifice is obligatory, and under what circumstances. The moral decision to engage in action is still required. A man may agree that, in the abstract, self-sacrifice is sometimes obligatory, and yet never believe that a time has come for such a sacrifice on his part. None of our abstract considerations can substitute for a moral decision. All we can do here is to study the elements which enter the making of moral decisions. We will now consider further the details of social existence.

We began by noting Aristotle's claim that "man is a social animal." To this point, we have barely touched the surface of the complexity of man's social nature. We may gain a somewhat sharper sense of this by a scrutiny of several ways in which individuals are affected by the social nature of their lives. We shall look to the *benefits* men gain from social life, the *feelings* which are aroused by others, the *regulatory mechanisms* of society, the function of *social disapproval*, and the nature of *moral education*. As for the liabilities of social life, they have no particular character of their own, but are inherent in the variety of functions which social mechanisms serve.

C. Benefits

The view that society provides benefits or ills for individuals is inherently confused. Aristotle's claim that man is a social animal means in part that men cannot choose to live in society or not. They do not choose to be born, but their birth necessarily involves others. They do not choose to be brought up, but they grow up in the company of other people and learn from them. Society is not something apart from a man, but is composed of men and includes each of them. Society is not *for* individual men any more than individual men are *for* society.

It is absurd in a similar way to ask what good a man's liver is, or what good a man is for his liver. We can determine the function of the liver in the body, and even decide that it is diseased. In extreme cases, we may resort to surgery, as we cut out a diseased appendix. Some organs can be removed without death, though not the liver. It is not possible to destroy the man and to preserve the functioning of his separate organs, except in a trivial sense.

Yet a body can be diseased and require a cure. And a society can be ill and require major changes. The point is that the relationship between individuals and the total society is far more intimate, and far more *organic*, than is commonly thought. We cannot eliminate a society while keeping its members intact. We cannot even transform a society without changing its members and their lives. Nor can we change the individuals within a society without changing the society as well.

It follows also that the tension between individual and social values is often misconstrued. One man's values may differ from another's, or from the values of most people. But his society includes him and his values. Usually societies contain many and partly conflicting values, and social norms are only vaguely and confusedly defined. A society encompasses the variety of individuals within it.

All of this suggests that the distinction between a man and his social surroundings is not easily drawn, and that men do not serve their societies so much as they live in them, and societies do not provide for men so much as they constitute the collective ways in which men live. Many diseases of men are diseases of the entire body, with or without a focus in a particular organ. So also, the benefits a society provides are not merely the tangible receipts of funds and services, but the interrelationship of individual men and what they do. A government might do little for its citizens, yet they may cooperate with each other and live well together. Another government might provide all manner of services, yet discourage mutual respect and trust.

In looking to the benefits of social existence, then, we would do best to look to the variety of ways in which men relate to each other. There seem to be three fundamental types of relatedness: a dependent relation, a cooperative relation, and the organic relation we have been referring to.

(1) The fact of individual dependency on others is the fundamental root of social ties. When we are born, we are unable to fend for ourselves, and would die without the care others give us. Infants are weak and defenseless. They are also malleable and educable. Dependency is an initial fact, but its consequences are of paramount importance in men's lives.

From the beginning, infants are tended by adults who provide them with food and warmth. We have had occasion to note the natural consequences of so intimate and dependent a relationship. Children develop a love for their parents, and desire to be near them, to have their approval, and to emulate what they do. Each of these natural and emotional reactions has consequences of greatest importance in social life. Each is inherent in the primary state of infant dependency. We can modify the conditions of such dependency—for example, by providing many different adults to imitate and love. But there is no way to abolish it.

(a) The beginning of life, unless it is brutal and debilitating, generates a natural bond between child and adult. One of the oddest notions in all moral theory is the view that men somehow might be indifferent to others. In fact, from their earliest years, human beings are far from indifferent. They care about what happens to their parents and how they feel, for their feelings affect their children. They care about obtaining the approval and avoiding the disapproval of their parents. The concern for some other people, to the point of playing a dominant rule in a child's life, is a fundamental condition of all infancy. If such concern disappears by adulthood, it has been negated by other conditions of life.

It is quite true that earliest feelings directed toward others are selfish. A child regards his parents as providers, who give him what he desires. Yet every child, however spoiled, comes to be aware of his parents' own desires, and the multiplicity of tensions which life with other people involves.

(b) A dominant element in infancy is the strength of parental approval and disapproval. Children may test their parents, and try different means of getting attention. Yet the stern face of disapproval is always painful to them, and parental approval is very pleasant. Through disapproval, parents exert their authority, and also convey the force of their moral convictions. A child is a sensitive reflection of parental responses, and often is mutely aware of unvoiced disapproval and approval.

In earliest years, children learn of both the existence of parental attitudes and what these attitudes entail. The emotions and affections of other people are inherent in earliest infancy, and are not merely learned of in later life. A child's dependency has an important formative effect on his own feelings, expecially as these are influenced by the feelings of his parents.

(c) In addition, children imitate their parents. Few of the responses of a child are wholly original with him. What he finds his parents doing around him he also does himself if he can, and he tries when he cannot. He imitates the actions of his parents. He also imitates their language, their emotional reactions, and their modes of approval and disapproval.

The latter two aspects of dependency are of utmost importance for education.

Society   Approval and disapproval and imitation are the fundamental elements of all teaching. However, it is important to realize that a child growing up is always learning, whether it is what others wish to teach him or not. Since his early life is so bound up with what others do, especially his parents, he learns from them, explicitly or implicitly. The prevailing customs of society, insofar as individual persons conform to them, are instilled in earliest childhood by imitation, by emotional reactions, and also by explicit instruction.

So intimate and profound is the dependency of an infant on others that its need for care literally *means* that the child will be formed by that care, and will in good part reflect what others do around him. The habits of early life are in large measure the habits instilled by others. Society provides early care, and, in so doing, brings the child into the social order, in emotional make-up, in imitation, and in values. A person who in adult life is fearful of others has been taught to be so in his early years. A person who loves no one but himself has had his earlier trust in others proved false.

(2) In later life, though long before adulthood, a child comes to see the importance of cooperation. There are games which require many participants. There are tasks which require many persons to perform. It is often a great boon to efficiency to divide the tasks of life, and to have each person work on a specified task. Men together are stronger and more secure than men apart. Men together can create leisure time for a few which enables them to add to the store of beauty and science in the world. The great human achievements require that some men be supported to think and invent, a prospect realizable only in larger social groups.

Hobbes argues that the state of nature—understood to be devoid of co-operative endeavors—is the worst condition of mankind. His position is far more plausible when turned around. Mutual effort is one of the crucial requirements for a good human life. The life of a hermit alone in the wilderness must be primitive and devoid of comforts. Only if we engage in a type of false imagination, and pretend such a hermit has access to social instruments, can we begin to give him ease and a gracious life. A man shipwrecked on even a lush desert island will be hard put to live well by any standards, unless we suppose that the tools of the ship, his clothing from the ship, with various and sundry items produced at home, land with him.

The benefits of a cooperative existence, as contrasted with the life a man can manage wholly alone, are incomparable. Unfortunately, the very social organization which brings about cooperative endeavors also generates considerable strain. At times men find these strains beyond endurance, and cry out for relief. The relief which consists in an end to social cooperation is simply absurd. Yet we find that, in any generation, people exist who would get away from it all. Thoreau withdrew to Walden Pond for three years, as if to escape the social constraints which surrounded him.

But Thoreau did not terminate his social existence, even at Walden. Walden represents the possibility that a man might get along with *less*, even much less than is imagined. Knowledge of this possibility can lessen some of the strains of social life. The benefits of cooperation can sometimes be completely offset by the strains of compromise and the needs of others. A man has to determine for himself a satisfactory manner of life, where the gains from cooperation are sufficiently greater than the general oppression to be worth the effort. Thoreau shows that, for a man like him, few compromises are justifiable. But that is because he lacks many of the needs for the company of others, and also the desires for the benefits of cooperation, which other people possess.

Some forms of cooperation are easy to come by. It is quite easy to find a companion to play chess—though not always a man worth knowing in other respects. It is more difficult to find a man to help build a house or clean out a sewer. Elaborate social customs, mechanisms, and institutions exist in many societies to facilitate cooperation. In particular, we should note the system of justice, both rules and institutions, and the system of power developed by societies to encourage and even compel cooperation. So complex are all these mechanisms, and so obvious are their faults, that we may wonder if they are necessary or even worth while.

A common device for obtaining the cooperative benefits of social life is that of specialization. Men accept different tasks within the larger social order. Plato argues in his *Republic* that through specialization a greater efficiency is obtained in work. Certainly an expert in a task will accomplish it more quickly and more skillfully than anyone else. In some professions, only an expert ought to be allowed to function—physicians or airline pilots, for example.

Specialization in occupations leads naturally to a specialization in responsibilities. This is worth remarking because it introduces a dimension to obligations we have not yet touched on. Men differ in the duties they possess by virtue of their position. Policemen are obligated to interfere with criminal activities where other people are not. It may well be argued that an ordinary citizen ought not to try to stop a thief by shooting at him. But a policeman may have a duty to do so. Duties of position have the great merit of placing obligations on men which they are particularly well equipped to meet.

But specialization has its major drawbacks. Two of them are worth noting. First, though specialization in some professions seems unavoidable, a life devoted to but a single type of activity may be tedious and inhuman. Plato assumes that extreme specialization will be an obvious benefit. But Marx seems to believe instead that, where men have the opportunity to live ideal lives, such lives will be varied and diversified.

Second, specialization tends to parcel out responsibilities. The obvious consequence of this may well be a tendency for men to disavow any obligations which are not clearly part of their professions. Thus, the ordinary citizen may feel that he has no obligation whatsoever to respond to crime, to injustice, even to political corruption. He casts his vote, and that completes his duty. He hears screams in the street, but they are none of his concern. It is the business of the police to deal with such matters. Specialization in understanding, in activities, in competence, and in responsibilities can lead to a social life of half-men. There is so much with which they have nothing to do that their moral responsibilities to the events around them are crippled and incomplete.

The issues touched on by such considerations are complex. Let us note only two. On the one hand, a society as it becomes more complex has the capacity to provide many more goods for many more people. But the complexity of the cooperative means within a growing society is also increasing, and becomes more delicate. For example, the logistics involved in the distribution of food to large cities are considerable. The mechanisms for ensuring that all necessary steps are taken grow in complexity also. Where we cannot or do not simplify life, or cut back on population, it appears necessary to maintain a bureaucracy with powers at its disposal and elaborate procedures it must use.

On the other hand, complex organizations tend to generate further complexities out of their own internal imperatives. Parkinson's Law, though humorously conceived, is the principle that bureaucracies breed further bureaucracies. Once a certain degree of complexity is reached in institutions and rules, even more complexities are required to keep the system going. At some point we must reconsider the whole system, and even decide to start again from the beginning. The friction in the wheels requires a daily dose of new energy and new wheels to keep running, which increases the need for energy, and so forth *ad infinitum*.

If there is a simple way of resolving such tensions, I confess I do not know it. We will discuss shortly the fact that many people respond to the bewildering complexity of social life by pursuing simplified solutions that have no possibility of success. On the one hand, a large society requires a certain degree of complexity in its institutions, which leads to certain compromises. On the other hand, too large and cumbersome a bureaucracy can steal all possibility of action from individuals, and make no beneficial solutions possible. It does not seem possible for us to abandon all cooperative ventures while we make up our minds. Yet we sometimes feel that we cannot continue in the path we have been following up to this point.

There are two extreme solutions. One is to ignore all need for cooperation, and to withdraw to a more rural and primitive existence. Unfortunately, it would not be possible to support a large population at any level of affluence by such means. The second calls for a rapid and wholesale transformation of social institutions, on the principle that things cannot be made worse than they are. Unfortunately, they indeed can become worse, especially where the rapid change has no hope of meeting all the needs which exist, which the current system meets by having slowly evolved to that purpose.

If there is a sensible solution, it must lie between the extremes. On the one hand, we must seek to maximize cooperative efforts, and to repudiate all efforts to eliminate mutual endeavors. On the other hand, the institutions which are supposed to provide stability and cooperation may require a complete overhaul.

The exact path to be followed is not easily discernible. But then, we are speaking of political affairs, which never have easy solutions.

(3) The main point, however, is that in weighing various courses of action, it is necessary not to oversimplify individual and social relations. In growing up in a society, a man is made what he is by that society, for good or ill. He may plan to act on a variety of alternatives, but he cannot plan to be something wholly different from what he is. The organic relationship between an individual and his society makes it clear that changing the conditions of life requires changes in social institutions, and also in the ways in which individual men act.

In this respect, it is rather naive for a man to look for benefits from his society. Rather, a man can only seek to live better than he is living. But there is always a variety of possibilities which may bring him to a better life. And also, if there is a way to a better life, it is through the options which are available in the surrounding world.

It is this last point which I wish to emphasize. It brings us back to the distinction between realistic and unrealistic ideals. In condemning society for failing to provide him with goods, a man engages in a type of hypocrisy that is self-destructive. A version of it is the claim by a student that the schools teach him nothing—a claim usually backed up by arguments and facts obtained through his schooling. So also, if society is all bad, then criticizing it cannot possibly make it any better. Rather, our criticisms must pick out the good from the bad, and find a way within the means available to what is better.

We may put this point in a different way. Individuality and sociality are not opposing forces, but two aspects of a single process. Individuals work and plan, and change their relations with each other. Their prior relations with each other govern individual life. There is no path from individual suffering to individual happiness which will affect many persons that is not a social and a political one. Morals and politics are two faces of the same enterprise, which is the betterment of human life. And both can succeed in their aim only where genuine goods are available, to be harnessed through effort.

D. Love

We have had occasion to note several times the sentiment of sympathy which Hume takes to be the basis of all morality. In our discussion, we have noted the principle of *identification*, where men literally imitate the feelings of others, especially of men like themselves. Insofar as we tend to have the same feelings as other people, we cannot harm them and make them suffer without suffering ourselves. We have also noted the fact of dependency in human life, and the feelings which are generated by the early need of an infant to be cared for, feelings of love and a concern for what other people think of him. The emotion of love is a fundamental one for all social life and for all morals as well.

The fundamental moral principle of the teachings of Christ is that men should love their neighbors like themselves. We have explored some of the problems which are connected with *acting* in a way that makes all human interests equal. We have in no way looked to the problem of awakening in men an emotion of love or concern for others.

It seems a central feature of all human life that men should love *some* other men. Admittedly, there are a few people who lack all qualities of concern for others, and we are tempted to say of such men that they lack all *human* feeling. The intimate emotional tie men bear to each other is not so universal as the Christian principle would have it, but it is far stronger than such a disinterested principle could itself provide. And it is a love which is found among virtually all human beings who have had contact with other people.

There is a great variety of types of love, especially if we distinguish them by deeds as well as feelings. There is erotic love, possessive love, destructive love, self-sacrificing love, and many others. All of them have in common the quality that the lover subordinate his own interests to someone or something else. A seducer will go to inordinate lengths to capture the maiden of his lusts, even to the point of self-destruction. Love for other people is proof positive that men do not and probably should not live according to their own personal interests alone.

The principle of love is that emotions can be transferred from a narrow self-interest into a concern for other people that may totally transcend all self-interest. True, there are loves which seem no more than a violent desire for possession—the yearning of a seducer for a woman. We have noted, however, that the strength of even such a passion can transcend any ordinary sense of self-interest. A man driven by lust may neglect his work, lose his job, and destroy his family. Rarely can the gain of his desires make all his destructive actions justifiable. Rather, the lust is an overwhelming passion, which swamps ordinary and in this case beneficial self-interest. Love as irresistible lust is the replacement of a desire for possession by a desire to act in some way toward one's beloved.

Sartre argues that all forms of love are contradictory, since we want to be sure of being loved in return, and at the same time want our beloved to be a free agent. If our beloved is a captive and we can control her love, then it is worth little. Only where love is freely given is it valuable. But if it is freely given, it can be freely withdrawn, and we are necessarily insecure with respect to it. Sartre views all love as a self-contradictory power struggle.

The point we may draw from Sartre's description is that love is not always a possession, and may never quite be truly possessive in any sense. What does a seducer want to possess? He cannot own the woman's body, for she is not his literal slave and cannot be. Slavery is not the aim of love. Love aims at the accomplishment of something whether or not it is beneficial to the agent. The better forms of love are beneficial. But they are beneficial because they improve the character of the lover. A lover is more generous, less surly, more trusting, on his best behavior. This is one of the most important features of love Plato describes in his *Symposium*.

There is a narrow form of desire which is not usually thought of as love—
the desire to have sexual intercourse, to flaunt a beautiful woman, to have a
domestic servant. Where desire for another person is wholly a desire to have that
person act toward oneself in certain ways, it is not usually thought of as love.
Love is an emotion which brings the lover to act toward his beloved in ways which
look to her interests, sometimes even more than his own.

Sexual love is not the only type of love, nor even the most important.
There is love between parents and children, between friends, love of a man for
country, and love for some ideal. All such loves are a form of giving. A lover's
personal advantage is subordinated through the power of the emotion of love to the
interests of someone or something else.

It is unnecessary to seek a proof that love is universal or at least common.
There are few men who love no one or nothing. Therefore, virtually all human
beings have exercised their emotional capacity to subordinate their own needs to
the interests of another person or group. They may not do so well or intelligently,
nor may they be clear in their minds as to their deeper feelings. But they are
certainly in no doubt that the accommodation to the needs of some other people is
both human and good. Here is a thorough refutation of extreme egoism.

But how far does the love for some other people take us? Freud argues that
love for another person is natural in all human life. But, he points out, morality
demands that we love *everyone*. Nothing could be more unnatural. That is one of
the reasons why morality is so difficult, and why we pay so great an emotional
price in our inner lives for a strong conscience.

Freud may be correct that love for mankind is rare because it is unnatural.
But it may also be rare because it is so natural and overwhelming in its implications.
Once we have come to understand the emotional force of love in bringing us to
care for other men, we may recoil from the responsibilities which love of all men
would levy upon us. Love brings a man to run into a burning building at great
risk to his own life. There are fires all over the world. Shall our love for men who
are suffering everywhere make us sacrifice ourselves for them?

Freud's conception of love is essentially a selfish one. We love someone whose
love in return gives us pleasure. Yet we have seen that in principle love overwhelms
selfishness, and makes a man quite willing to make some sacrifice for his loved ones.
Let us take the generous and self-sacrificing aspect of love as fundamental, and
note that virtually all men are capable of loving at least one other person in a
generous way, a way that makes them at least sometimes cease looking to their
own personal advantage.

But once love is no longer selfish, then what limits it and keeps it from being
extended to all mankind? A man loves his son and would help him at any cost to
himself. The love is narrow, and perhaps was originally a selfish one. But it ceases
to be selfish once it reaches a certain level of intensity. What then keeps it from
reaching out to all men? Why should not this man love everyone? In part,
because he knows only a few men in the world. Why does he not love all of them?

The presence of love is not the only thing which requires explanation. Its absence does as well.

One answer is that he must not, for he would then sacrifice himself to them all and help none of them. A universal brotherhood levies an awesome and cruel responsibility. Only a saint can love all mankind, not because it is difficult to have a feeling of love, but because it is almost impossible to avoid being destroyed by it. That is the burden of Dostoievski's *The Idiot*.

The emotion of love as a generous concern for others postulates an ideal of mutual concern and assistance. But, like so many ideals, it cannot be realized fully in the world we live in. A man who loved all men in universal brotherhood would be destroyed for that love, and succeed in assisting few people. Therefore, the ideal can be realized only in part, in relations with only a few people, those close to us in association and proximity. Men often keep looking for friends they can trust—and this trust is a kind of love. It is a bitter lesson for a young person to learn that friends whom one can count on are rare.

A final note in defense of this view of love. Very young children are often thought cruel, and seemingly without love. They are too young. But college students and graduate students are well known to make more attachments, both transitory and of an enduring nature, than at any other time of life. One possible explanation of this is that their general desire to love and be loved is, in fact, not narrow and specific as we usually suppose, but undifferentiated and general. Only hard experience can teach a man the peril of attempting to love unwisely but too well.

A recent study has provided some evidence which runs counter to the view presented of undifferentiated love. Subjects were placed in an experimental setting where they were divided essentially arbitrarily into groups, We and They. They were then offered the opportunity of winning points for themselves, for their team, or for everyone. In general, even where the classification into Us and Them had only an arbitrary basis, the subjects chose to maximize their team's score and also to minimize the score of the other group. They did so even where generosity would have led their own group to a higher gain over-all. The experiment seems to demonstrate beyond doubt that, in at least the contemporary United States, there is a strong rejection of *others*, and a strong loyalty to one's *own kind*, even where such classifications are almost random.

In any case, it is unnecessary to believe that any man's love is general and unspecific in order to grasp the importance of love. Love toward a particular person is always a stance of generosity and concern which overcomes narrow self-interest. Our emotional make-up is such that most people can and do overcome self-interest and selfishness, whether out of generosity to some other men or generosity toward everyone.

In consequence, social life is not alone a matter of balancing interests, but of balancing group and family loyalties also. One of the most interesting features of social life is coping with extreme loyalties and loves, patriotic or personal. We have spent this time to make clear that emotions toward other people are funda- mental in human life and in moral decisions. We now turn to the institutional means whereby the various tensions and loyalties in a society are brought into a common accord.

E. Politics

The political organization of a society, its legal system, and the variety of. implicit expectations we call "custom" seem together to constitute the organizational structure of a society. Each of them may be examined from the point of view of four types of aims which it serves, and each of them can be rather successful in accomplishing all of these aims. Yet the remarkable fact about the organization of a society is that the political, legal, and customary aspects of this organization may be quite different and even conflict. Particularly in a period of turmoil, the legislative decisions of political leaders may look to major modifications of both laws and customs, in a society where laws and customs tend to have different subject matters. In some societies, matters of dress and courtesy may be ruled by very strong customs, which have no connection with political decisions or laws. Yet they work a major influence on the members of the society and what they do.

Politics, law, and custom—though they usually overlap—are thus distinct to the extent that they may have exclusive spheres of concern or even conflict with each other. Yet all of them may be regarded from the standpoint of four aims to which they look: management, the exercise of power, their beneficial results, and their educational influence. We shall consider the three modes of organization separately in their accomplishment of these aims.

In general, politics is the arena in which collective decisions are made for the welfare of a society. The legislative branch of government studies the needs of the society, determines the changes which are required in the system of laws, and enacts them so that they take on the force of law. In effect, the legislative branch of government is the means for the changing of laws, and in this respect politics and law overlap. Yet even here, we may distinguish the enactment of law from the effective influence of the body of law itself. The decision to amend laws usually belongs to the political order.

The executive branch of politics organizes and arranges the resources available to the government, and makes the decisions necessary to achieve postulated results, implicit either in law or in some wider sense. All governments have a nominal head, representing the fundamental fact that politics involves the making of decisions, and that all decisions are in the end personal and individual. A divided decision is no decision at all.

When the political structure of a society involves election by the citizens of the country, there is a mode of decision-making which is reserved for determination by vote. It may be limited in that few issues are brought before the electorate. It may be limited in that few alternatives are offered. In a country where political parties are very similar, and politicians are virtually indistinguishable in significant respects, few options are left for decision by the vote of the citizens of that country.

The complexities of political organization are forbidding. Yet there are four aims or functions which all political systems serve. Let us consider them one by one.

(1) *Management.* All governments manage the affairs of the state, in the sense that they disburse the funds available to them, enforce the laws, and organize the affairs of the country in a workable fashion. All governments engage in the making of decisions, decisions which are essential to the functioning of society. As important as individual members of a society may be, there are certain decisions which have a collective quality, and must be made for everyone.

There are many ways of arriving at collective decisions, and a variety of political organizations. A single person may be delegated the authority to make decisions for everyone. A system of representative democracy allows for a majority vote of elected representatives to make fundamental decisions. The town meeting, where everyone may appear and vote, where the majority decision is the effective one, is yet another procedure. Each of these methods has its virtues and its faults. In some larger sense, every political organization is in constant test as to its effectiveness and beneficial accomplishments. The decisions as well as the procedures for making political decisions are neither sacred nor perfect, and call for a vigilant regard for excesses and for results which are beneficial to but a few people.

It is unbelievable that a society larger than the family could manage without a political organization, and it is important to realize that even a large family has a customary procedure for the making of major decisions. Whether we are conservative or liberal, democrat or monarchist, we must concede the vital need for coordination and organization among the units of a society. The management function of politics is not one that can be denied.

Nevertheless, there are some issues of importance which are not resolved by the mere acceptance of political decision-making. One is the question of the most efficient and responsive means for making decisions. In recent times, the model for management has been the hierarchical bureaucracy: a system of codes and rules, in which decisions are made in a formal and predetermined fashion, yet where the ultimate decision rests at the top. The striking features of such a bureaucratic system are the specific roles each individual plays within the system, the size and complexity of the system, and, finally, the dependence of the head of the system on the bureaucracy as a whole, and his insulation from the particular requirements of almost all decisions.

In a large society, centralized decision-making is essentially bureaucratic. The very number of decisions required prevents any one person from dealing with them responsibly. Yet the delegation of authority requires bureaucratic controls throughout to prevent malfeasance as well as bumbling. The only alternative to bureaucracy, then, is through the decentralization of management, and the making of important decisions on a local level.

At first blush, local and even individual decisions have a tremendous advantage. They are made by the individuals directly concerned, who will be affected by the decisions. There is an obvious advantage in having the parents of school children in a district decide what level of support shall be provided the schools, and even what will be taught.

But at second glance, decisions on the local level automatically fail to meet the requirements for political decision-making. Let us begin with individuals. In the extreme case, we may imagine no management decisions made on any but an individual level. Each individual will make the decisions for himself alone. The difficulty is that almost no individual decision fails to affect other people. A man's decision not to cut the grass on his empty lot creates an eyesore in the community. A man's decision not to work has economic consequences. A man's decision not to educate his children affects both the children—who are not, after all, mere possessions of his—and the subsequent generation, which may be deprived of trained personnel.

Clearly what is required is a means of political management which achieves two results simultaneously: it provides a collective policy which harmonizes the variety of different interests and aims of individuals; and *also*, it is generally beneficial to the individual involved. A compromise at the severe expense of a small number of individuals may be far less defensible than a compromise which is not so advantageous to some, but hurts no one very much.

In practice, centralized political decisions tend to achieve uniformity and even considerable fairness, but often overlook the vital needs of small groups of people. On the other hand, decentralized methods of management tend to gain some individual ends to a far greater degree, but neglect wider consequences of a collective nature. Here is a fundamental tension. I doubt that it will ever be stably resolved. At best, we will achieve a dynamic equilibrium. A given method of decision-making will be carried on until its faults become evident. Collective management will then revert to local control. Later on, the faults of local control will become significant, and control will be preempted by the larger political structure. At any time, there will be men who object to the prevailing trend.

Severe problems enter this process where the dynamic alternation between local and central decision-making is interrupted, and a particular method of decision-making is perpetuated far beyond its effectiveness. Such a result can occur with a national emergency, where the centralized means of meeting the emergency continue even beyond the success of the decisions arrived at. It can also be the result of an ideological bias toward the glory of the state, as in fascism, where decision-making is centralized to an extreme, or of a bias toward an individuality understood as a selfish disregard of others. Political decisions are always collective to some extent, and can be crippled by too arbitrary a rejection of collective relations within society.

Another fundamental question which concerns the making of political decisions is that of the *means of enforcement* which political organizations have at their disposal. Anarchists do not so much question the need for collective decisions as the powers which are given to governments to enforce their decisions. The army, police, penal system, as well as the variety of laws and weapons which are in the hands of a government and usually forbidden to its citizens, are awesome. This brings us to the second function of political organizations.

(2) *Enforcement.* The most striking characteristic of political organizations is that they possess and exercise power. It is this particular quality of governments which many people find so reprehensible. All governments clearly have a managerial function, and would have one whether their method of enforcement were inherent in power or custom.

Many people are convinced that the effectiveness of government rests on the powers which are available to it, powers which are rooted in force and violence. Government is to many people synonymous with the police and with punishment. There are two reasons why governments require the use of force, internal and external. Hobbes accepts both as central to an effective government. National states stand with respect to each other in an antagonistic relationship, and require at least means of defense and sometimes means of offense as well (especially if one accepts the principle that the best defense is offense). Within every society, Hobbes argues, men act solely from personal advantage (or, at least, many people do), and a means is required to force them to conform to principles of morality and justice. The only effective means for this is fear of being caught, and of the consequences of being caught. Ultimately, internal stability in a society is grounded in the fear of the force which the state can use against individuals. Hobbes carries this argument so far as to claim that where a state is so weak as not to inspire fear through its powers, it is too weak to survive and has failed its responsibilities.

The anarchist critique of government is an interesting one, and worth careful note. As I have indicated, anarchists are not truly dubious about the managerial function of government, nor that collective political decisions can have beneficial consequences. It is the use of force and exercise of powers which anarchists are set against. Their fundamental principle is the famous one: *power corrupts, and absolute power corrupts absolutely.* But they do not merely understand by this that the politician who has power is himself corrupted by it. Rather, they note as well that the entire fabric of social life is corrupted by the use of force within it.

Let us review the arguments for the general exercise of power and force. In international affairs, nations are always in what Hobbes calls a "state of war." Under such conditions, only superior force can protect a country from destruction. But at least one consequence of the exercise and use of this force is the perpetuation of the state of war. The imminent violence present in relations among countries tends to perpetuate further violence. Smaller countries fear extreme sanctions when they go to war far less when (1) they can buy their armaments from the great powers, and when (2) these great powers themselves frequently resort to war. The interests of world peace, the anarchist says, are in fact *not* served by the use of ever greater force and violence. Rather, we risk more and more violence, and further wars. Force breeds force. Violence breeds violence. A country which resorts to war easily demonstrates its contempt for the individuals who are killed. Soldiers and even children learn from the fact of war that lives are not of very great importance.

The use of extreme force always has two consequences. It demonstrates that such force is sometimes a good—and other men may then be tempted to resort to force themselves, as in vigilante groups. It proves also that human lives are not as important as the well-being of the state, or some national purpose. It follows from both lessons that men learn to be prepared to harm others, sometimes rather easily. The readiness to use force is a moral corruption.

In internal affairs, the use of force is defended by Hobbes to cope with natural selfishness. Men must be coerced to obey the law for their own good as well as for the good of others. The anarchist reply is once again that the exercise of force generates additional force, and is itself the greater evil. Men learn that violence is not always unthinkable, and thereby become violent themselves.

Consider a group of people who are singled out as specific objects of violence in a society—blacks, for example. They are harassed and beaten by police, convicted more often than whites on similar charges, and executed more often for capital offenses. There are only two lessons such a group can learn from their collective experiences. Either they come to believe that they deserve such exceptional treatment, because they are somehow exceptional—and violence is justified against them. Or else they become convinced of their oppression and persecution, and make ready to reply to violence in kind. The only way for violence to be eliminated is a general agreement that it will never be tolerated, by anyone, except under extremely rare and dangerous circumstances. But where the state exercises violence and uses force, it literally instructs men in the techniques and results of such violence.

The anarchist view is that men are not initially or naturally selfish or vicious, but become so in a society which fosters competition and uses violent means. The anarchist condemnation of state power is twofold. First, the exercise of violence and force is not beneficial, but destructive in its consequences, destructive in its nature, and productive of both fear and hatred in men. Almost all men agree that a government which is unjust and unresponsive to the needs of its citizens may be overthrown. Where such a government is violent, the means used in return will be violent. Second, the use of violence is a great educator, and teaches men to be violent themselves.

The two features of political life just mentioned are worth considering—the responsibility of political organization to achieve beneficial results, and the educative effect of all social institutions.

(3) *Benefits.* It is not too much to say that the sole justification in the end for a government is the benefits it provides for its citizens. It is true that on occasion there have been men who have maintained that the national state serves no one but itself, and that such a state is more important and valuable than any or all

of its citizens. Hitler credited Germany with a national destiny, through which each individual would achieve his own status and value. But if such a claim is not to be interpreted as that of gaining benefits for some future generation of individuals, then I find myself unable even to comprehend it. A present generation may be justified in sacrificing itself to a future generation. But where sacrifice is called for, but no *person* will be benefited, then I am simply bewildered.

The idea of a government is a complex one. In particular, if we take the principle that a government is to be judged by the benefits it provides its citizens, we must distinguish a particular administration and its officials from the general system or method of government, and the general structures, laws, and institutions which comprise it. Both may be judged by what they accomplish, but the results of condemnation would be very different. A government which is blind to the needs of its people might be voted out of office, recalled, or even overthrown. Yet the general *system* of government might be considered a good one. On the other hand, the view that a particular system of government is inherently or on the whole disadvantageous might lead to a total revision of the methods and procedures of political decision-making.

We are describing substantive appraisal with respect both to the form of government and to a specific set of officials. The judgments and the kinds of considerations involved in both cases are very similar, but the results of condemnation are very different in the two cases. What is important is to realize the *level* of judgment involved, and also the alternatives which might be offered to replace what is judged inadequate. A particularly corrupt group of men in office may be thought worth eliminating, yet the general mode of government might be thought good. In condemning a group of men, we may be able to find many other men to replace the first. An important if not critical consideration is whether it is possible to replace one group of men by another within the existing political organization. If the corrupt officials control not only the government offices but all the political parties as well, the whole system may come under attack.

Where the entire system is condemned, the alternatives to be offered are of crucial importance, and so are the means whereby the system will be changed. Here we come to one of the most difficult aspects of revolutionary thought. A revolutionary is committed *both* to a complete change in a system of government (and considerably more, I might add), and *also* to the use of violence to accomplish his ends. It is not difficult to understand the grounds for judging a government and its entire structure evil. It is far more difficult to justify replacing it through revolution. For the alternative must be well conceived, clearly better than what exists at present, and the violence must be justified as a means as well. Yet most revolutionaries—anarchists, for example—stand committed *against* violence. One of their most virulent criticisms of the system they would overthrow is its violent character. These issues of crisis morality will be discussed shortly.

Several things stand against a clear appraisal of governments in terms of the beneficial results they achieve. First, there is a prevalent inertia in human life to keep what we have rather than to pursue something new. Second, the implicit customs of a society tend to perpetuate not only themselves, but the official practices as well, and to increase the force of inertia. Third, political issues are extremely complex, and it is often almost impossible to define alternatives clearly. Political criticism is often extremely simplistic, even sloganistic. Perhaps that is not always so bad. A community may vote down a proposed increase in taxes, not because they know of a better way to achieve the required goals, but in their desperation. It is not the responsibility of the ordinary taxpayer to discover alternatives, but of the professional politician. And it is also his responsibility to convince the taxpayers of the justification of the alternatives proposed.

But there is remarkably little effort on most politicians' part to explain issues to the citizens of their country, and perhaps such citizens ought occasionally to stick in their heels and rebel. On the other hand, too frequent rebellion of this sort can stand in the way of any accomplishments whatsoever. The complexity of political decisions makes the average person feel incompetent, and makes him defer to the views of the experts. Finally, fourth, a patriotic loyalty is instilled in the citizens of a country which often makes them follow most critical decisions of their government without serious question.

When a society does enter a domestic crisis, inertia, blind patriotism, and a sense of incompetence tend to work in the opposite direction, and to prevent the clear thinking necessary to resolve the difficulties. Automatic responses in favor of one's government can easily turn to equally automatic responses against it. Here is the fundamental weakness of all systems of government which depend on secrecy and the knowledge of experts. Citizens who have had little practice in thinking critically and making responsible decisions are ill equipped to understand the imperatives of a national crisis. Where a country depends on a faith in authority, then a crisis in respect for that authority may become a major one, a repudiation of a system of government rather than of a particular group of men.

It would appear that the open scrutiny of political decisions in terms of the benefits they achieve is not only a necessary aspect of politics, but one which should be further encouraged. Politics is the making of complex decisions on a national scale, and requires both open and clear thinking and the devotion of as much thought as possible to the development of alternatives. Unfortunately, the political loyalties which patriotism and fear generate tend to militate against open criticism. In the long run, a country may suffer badly for its own blindness. This issue will be returned to in a later discussion.

(4) *Education.* The practices and institutions of government always exert an educational influence on individuals in a society. Sometimes this can have an inertial quality, where governments rule in secret and by authority. Sometimes the ideals generated in the discussion of political issues lead to criticisms of other decisions.

Of the four functions of political organization, education may be the least prominent, except in the respects already noted. Citizens of a country learn about the exercise of authority, the practice of violence, the value of life, fear, and justice. But the educative influences of political organization and practices should not be overlooked among the variety of other factors. In appraising a government for its results, we should also look to the ideals taught and the feelings engendered in individual men by political practices. All too often, we judge a government by its tangible benefits, when they may be of lesser importance on the whole.

Consider here the government of the Soviet Union. Let us suppose—though it is far from true—that wealth is distributed equitably to everyone in the society. Yet the use of police methods of censure, of generating fear, of arbitrary arrest, can create an educational climate of dogmatism, of closed-mindedness, of fear of risk, and the like. The results here are not alone the direct political and economic consequences, but consequences affecting the various arts, the social sciences, even medicine and biology. Tangible equality in consumer goods is a gain which may be wholly offset by the emotional climate generated by political means. All too often the consumer mentality is made of exclusive importance in judging the successes of a society, when its cultural achievements, its innovations in thought and the arts, and even the emotional qualities of everyday life are of vital importance also. The connections between political decisions and the various cultural features of a society are both economic and educational.

Most of all, governments exert a considerable influence on moral education. We will consider this topic in detail in a later discussion.

F. Law

The legal system serves exactly the same functions as does the political system, though in different ways. Many people do not distinguish the legal from the political. Yet since they can oppose each other in a given society, it seems to me far more advantageous to discuss them separately. There are three aspects to a system of law: the legislative, the judicial, and the law itself. The first two, based as they are on political decisions, I will classify with the political aspect of social life. Here I will discuss only the law itself, in its character apart from the political decisions it depends on.

(1) *Management.* Laws serve the function of management in an obvious fashion. They prescribe certain actions and prohibit others. In this respect, laws represent two phases of decision-making. They represent the result of decisions enacted into law. They also define the prescribed limits for the making of decisions by individual members of a society.

It is tempting to suppose that the sole basis of law resides in force, and the fear that is generated by enforcement. Hobbes in fact argues that the existence of a law prohibiting a certain action is no infringement on a man's liberty. He may break the law and suffer the consequences if he chooses. Hobbes is mistaken in thinking that a threat is no weakening of liberty at all. But he is correct that a

man may always choose to break the law. Hobbes' major error is overlooking the
direct and indirect influence a law exerts on the activities of most people. A law
may theoretically be broken. But for many men, a law should not be broken.
Speaking practically, laws do define limits for individual actions.

It follows, then, that custom is necessary to the functioning of laws. We
could abolish all enforcement of laws, and yet it would be necessary to formulate
regulations which would be *in fact* binding on most people, at least if the collective
organization of a society is to collectively act. A government functions by law
and by regulation. Its effectiveness resides not in its enforcement of laws, but in
the willingness of people to obey regulations where there is no enforcement
involved. On the other hand, if law were reduced entirely to custom, we would
be unable to change customary practices easily. Custom is slow to change and
deeply implicit. Law is the only instrument we have for altering custom directly.

There is an intimate connection between the management function of governments and their laws. There is an essential relationship between decisions for a
society as a whole and the enactment of laws, whether or not enforcement is an
essential component of the laws. Regulations are the means whereby a government
makes its decisions effective. Sometimes regulations are enforced, and we have
laws in the conventional sense. But no society could enforce any laws without men
who obey laws regardless of enforcement. In this sense, enforcement is not the
primary aspect of laws.

We conclude that a society without laws could not easily endure, except in a
rather simplified form. We will discuss enforcement in a moment. Here we are
noting only that a complex society requires the promulgation of general regulations
which virtually everyone will conform to. We are not concerned with the number
of such laws or their content. The point is rather that laws are required for a stable
social order which people will follow *as laws*—that is, merely because they are
laws. A man who questions whether a law should be followed defeats its purpose
as a law. If it is a bad law, it should be repealed. If it is a good one, it should be
obeyed, with or without sanctions, with or without enforcement. A driver who
stops at red lights only when there is a policeman visible is in opposition to the
whole notion of law—unless he believes that there should be no law requiring
drivers to stop at a red light, which is unlikely.

In his *Republic*, Plato represents a society apparently without laws. The
philosopher-king will be obeyed without question, on the basis of his superior
wisdom. Plato builds a political order on the model of a ship, where each member
of the crew has his particular role to play, but defers to the superior competence of
the captain. This is all well and good on a small boat, but even on a large ship,
the captain can rule only through well defined regulations and channels of command. In *The Laws*, Plato describes a society under the rule of law. Many com-
mentators have understood the change in viewpoint as a capitulation to hard facts.
If so, the facts are no more interesting than that an expert and wise ruler can be

effective only through general regulations. No ruler of a large society could make every critical decision and transmit it rapidly. The best he could do would be to define general limits within which individual men would make their decisions.

Some anarchists manifest amazement at the loyalty of other men to law. This is a confusion on their part, and one incompatible with their general position. They would do better to respect loyalty to regulation, and to despise obedience through fear. Reverence for law is a necessary feature of social life. Without it, no political decisions could be enacted except through force, which is extremely disadvantageous and also impossible in principle.

I emphasize that the question of how much loyalty and to which laws has not been broached. Some laws are extremely unjust and ought to be disobeyed. Many should be opposed though obeyed. But society requires that some laws be obeyed out of sheer respect and custom.

(2) *Enforcement.* Nevertheless, the most obvious quality of laws is that they are enforced. Indeed, it is the system of enforcement which is called the system of *justice.* The enforcement of laws of the state is the primary characteristic distinguishing them from moral laws or rules of custom. All laws demand both loyalty and a general conformity. But laws of the state are enforced, and involve penalties, police, courts of law, and penal institutions.

Is it worth considering the question of whether laws *ought* to be enforced? We have already discussed some of the problems which enforcement generates. The use of force to engender fear and to bring about conformity to law also spreads a willingness to use force and brings men to tolerate violence. When we think of the horrors involved in the enforcement of laws, we may truly wonder if the anarchist repudiation of all force is not a superior position on all counts. The police carry guns and use them. Penalties are often assigned arbitrarily. Prisons are horrible, and seem always to be getting worse. Minority groups suffer excessively under the law. The evils of enforcement seem almost without end.

Hobbes' argument is that without fear and enforcement of law, society would collapse. The state of nature which would result is the greater evil. The anarchist looks at the whole array of evils generated by enforcement of law, and doubts that anything could truly be worse. These are the two extremes, and a more plausible position is almost certainly to be found between them. The major thrust of the Hobbesean position is psychological. Without enforcement of laws, people would not obey them. Most people would probably agree with the truth of this psychological generalization. Yet there is no evidence whatsoever to support it. In fact, the effectiveness of custom is so great, and the pressures toward conformity are so successful in the world today, that the evidence to the contrary is impressive. Most people tend to conform to each other, and might do so in the case of law even without enforcement.

The most striking argument against most forms of enforcement is a moral one. Exactly how do we justify killing a man, even one who has killed another? How do two wrongs nullify each other? What could justify putting a young man in a prison where he will be associated with hardened criminals, and prey to a variety of degradations? What can justify stealing several years of his life? Only the likely chance that his experiences would rehabilitate him, and improve his character. But everyone agrees that prisons seldom achieve rehabilitation.

The view that a man ought to be punished as an act of retribution for what he has done in the past is a difficult one to defend on moral grounds, unless we can show that the punishment has benefited him. Plato argues forcibly that it is never right to harm a man. Punishment is legitimate only where it benefits the person punished. But our entire system of enforcement at best protects society from criminals, and at worst merely makes some men suffer without benefiting anyone.

The worst result of law enforcement is its promulgation of the view that an individual man, even a criminal, can be made to suffer for the welfare of society as a whole. Such a view leads easily to the position that individuals matter relatively little, and supports both war and oppression.

Most of us would not be willing to abolish entirely the enforcement of law. Hobbes' argument has too much force—and, besides, how would we survive the period of chaos which would result during the transition? It does not take very many men who feel no moral scruples or respect for others to create chaos and make life fearful. The enforcement of law allows the ordinary man a degree of security. Against this we must weigh the strong arguments against the use of force. Here is one of the most compelling areas where we may judge the benefits which a social institution provides.

(3) *Benefits.* We have touched on several of the benefits of law throughout our discussion. It is important to keep in mind, however, that laws must be evaluated not in themselves alone, as regulations, but also in their results when enforced, if they are to be enforced. The tendency of men to look at only one side of a question is strong. Laws as laws play a very important function in social affairs. But we may find it necessary to reconsider certain laws if their enforcement is extremely harmful. In fact, Hobbes' argument depends on treating the beneficial aspects of laws wholly independent of the beneficial or harmful nature of the modes of enforcement of such laws. It can be argued in reply to him that as soon as the enforcement of law becomes disadvantageous to many people, they should seek to change the law, even where the laws have the appearance of justice.

The beneficial results of law are rather obvious. A system of law provides four important qualities for social life: stability, uniformity, cooperation, and justice. No doubt law alone can achieve none of these. But its contributions to each of them are considerable.

(a) *Stability.* A social order requires at least two types of stability for its existence. First of all, and most questionable, is a stability through time, the preservation of social relations with some degree of consistency. Conservatism reflects an inherent truth not only about human societies but about all collectivities: a larger unit composed of separate elements possesses a character through time, a certain degree of stability and coordination. The United States relies for a good part of its identity on geographical and historical features. But the Constitution represents also a legal stability that is of utmost importance to the identification of a goal as "American." The fundamental feature of law is *precedent*, and precedent provides a genuine legal tradition and an order through change. A society has a historical tradition which is a fundamental aspect of its members' loyalties to it. The law represents a central feature of that tradition.

The second aspect of stability which law provides is reliability of expectation. When there are established laws, a man knows what he can expect from his fellow citizens in relevant respects, and also with respect to the authorities. The criminal law is a system of rules which not only provide a means for the apprehension of men who break the law, but circumscribe the procedures which the government must follow in arrest and seizure. Civil law defines the procedures which are required for legal status with respect to property, contracts, and all sorts of other relations among individuals and within institutions.

To a great extent, the more pervasive is law throughout a society, and the more social relations regulated by it, then the more stable is the society and the more reliable are expectations of men as to how others will act *if they obey the law*. This latter qualification shows that law can never replace custom, especially the custom of conformity to law (which cannot itself be wholly regulated by law). When law is extended to all domains of life, wholly replacing custom and tradition, it exerts too great an influence on life, especially in producing too uniform and inflexible a society. On the other hand, the greatest virtue of law is that it achieves an explicitness of utmost value in social relations, prevents arbitrariness and caprice, and makes clear what is demanded of individual men. Custom alone cannot accomplish such ends.

(b) *Uniformity.* The fundamental feature of law is the formulation of a *general* regulation binding equally on all men who fit the conditions prescribed. The principle that all men are equal before the law is a central feature of all law, not alone of a democracy. Of course, no society can achieve total equality before the law. The wealthy have access to special advice and other benefits. The principle of equality is a functional ideal. Societies differ to the extent that they implement the ideal in practice, and also to the extent that they impose qualifications on types of men who are legally held to be equal. Thus, in one system all property owners may be equal before the law. In another, all members of the nobility may be equal before one law, and all commoners before another.

Uniformity is a central feature of stability, of cooperation, and of justice or fairness. This is the essence of the principle of equality before the law. A stable and well ordered society requires uniform procedures for regulating activities and for rectifying imbalance. Men must be told by formal law that activities are prescribed and proscribed. Where cooperation in a larger sense is sought, a stable and uniform reliability of expectation must be achieved. Automobile drivers cooperate at intersections via the laws which regulate right of way. Finally, the urge toward justice which is shared by all men, even those who reject some laws, requires legal implementation if it is to be reliable. Justice is achieved only through law—though not through law alone, as lynchings show. And a central feature of justice is the principle that different men will be treated the same, by law and by the authorities as well.

Some degree of uniformity is an essential feature of social life, and necessary for the benefits which society provides. Yet not all men are alike in all important respects, and all men differ in some respects. Law provides a vital uniformity for social relations, but it may impose too great a uniformity on them. One of the greatest dangers in law is that too much will be regulated, and too great a uniformity achieved. The value of society depends on some achievement of uniformity. But a complete uniformity would stifle all difference, all creativity, all originality. In addition, laws often achieve the wrong kinds of uniformity. For example, a law protecting the ownership of private property may in practice work to keep the poor poor and the wealthy rich.

It follows, then, that uniformity is no simple goal for a society or for law. It is probably impossible to determine a precise degree of uniformity acceptable to all men or acceptable even for several generations. It would appear that law too must operate in a dynamic tension, ranging from too great to insufficient uniformities in a variety of ways in social existence. There are periods when it is necessary to legislate on moral issues, and other periods when such legislation is confining. It is one of the greatest values of laws that they can be changed, sometimes fairly quickly.

(c) *Cooperation.* A society can be beneficial to its members only where it achieves cooperation among them. If all activities were wholly individual within society, then the society would offer nothing to its members that they could not achieve for themselves. In fact, it would exact the usual price for social life without compensating benefits.

There are two types of cooperation, direct and indirect. Direct cooperation is a mutual effort of men with similar goals who work together on a common project. Such cooperation does not depend directly on law, since it may arise from sheer generosity or shared feelings. Men gather in a park on the weekend to play ball, which is cooperative, without the direct influence of law. It is worth noting, though, that the ball field is likely to be supported by tax revenues and maintained by local government.

Indirect cooperation is the participation of men in activities which together produce valuable and beneficial results, though there is no obvious common project. Every large organization has hundreds of different men engaged in different activities which together contribute to the organization and its functioning. Such a mode of cooperation always depends on regulations and rules, though many may be implicit and customary rather than legal. Nevertheless, law provides a vital organizing force in cooperative ventures. It would be impossible for exchange and possession of property to be as smooth as they are in many countries without laws regulating the flow of money, the procedures for the exchange of property, and so forth.

(d) *Justice.* To many people, the system of justice and the system of law are the same. This is somewhat inaccurate, for there are civil laws which serve only to regulate and organize, and have no relationship to justice. Nevertheless, the close ties between justice and law are obvious.

It is worth careful note that justice as we understand it is only partly achieved through legislation. In order that men be treated justly, it is essential that laws be enacted prior to accusing men of breaking them, and that such laws be clear and definite, both with respect to prohibited actions and with respect to specific penalties. But in addition, systems of arrest and of trial are required, and they must be clearly defined and well organized. And even further, there must be effective and fair enforcement of the law—an enforcement which is not itself wholly regulated by law. A prosecuting attorney always has the option of whether to prosecute a given case or not. The police may overlook some crimes and not others.

A fundamental feature of justice is the uniformity or equality before the law a just system requires. In one respect, justice is wholly a mode of *fairness*, the treatment of everyone equally before the law. Although we have noted that some aspects of equality before the law look to custom more than to the law itself, justice as fairness is deeply related to legislation, to the enactment of law and its enforcement.

But justice also involves something more than the law alone. It is just that a criminal be punished. But exactly how severe his punishment should be is also a matter of justice, and requires that we look to his particular circumstances and needs. A man who steals a small sum of money with no aim but his own benefit is different from one who steals because his child needs an operation. Circumstances matter in moral judgments and also in matters of justice. The maxim that justice should be tempered with mercy should not be interpreted as if justice looks only to the law and mercy looks only to circumstances.

This is an important point, and beset by unending controversy. There are indeed men who believe that laws are to be followed strictly, and that all departure from obedience is to be punished. Of course, it is within the province of a jury or a judge to consider the circumstances of a crime and to consider them as extenuating. Shall we consider this second step as a departure from justice? This is akin to the moral purity we have noted several times. Should a man follow a moral law strictly and without considering the consequences? He can do so, but only by maintaining a purity that may have extremely unfortunate consequences. The strict adherence to law is often disadvantageous. If substantive appraisal is accepted at all, then it follows that consideration of circumstances and consequences is part of all moral decisions. Likewise, though we can apply criminal laws automatically, we may eliminate the value of such laws by too great a strictness. It follows that the consideration of circumstances and goals is a fundamental part of the system of justice, even a system of justice founded on law.

We come here to the disadvantages of law, each of which is an extreme form of a benefit. Law contributes to stability, to uniformity, to cooperation, and to justice. But in every case, the value provided by law is so great, and the reverence for law can become so overpowering, that law may become self-stultifying and its achievements stultifying as well. Thus, stability is a vital aspect of social life. But a society can become too stable, too inflexible, incapable of changing to meet new circumstances. In particular, the laws of a society may be antiquated, representing social relations long out of date, leading to injustice and even oppression. Laws prohibiting women from wearing shorts on the street exist in some areas —not apparently enforced, however. An enforced law of the same character is the law in the state of Connecticut which prevents a physician from dispensing contraceptive information to anyone, a law which has only recently been over-turned.

A society can be too uniform. This may be one of the most difficult problems of contemporary life—the extent to which people live in similar houses, work at similar jobs, receive similar educations, dress similarly, and live alike. A young man looking ahead to his future life finds no major options available to him. The uniformity which a stable society needs can easily become so oppressive that no clear choices remain. A natural consequence may be the development among young people of alternative life-styles, something—anything—different from the surrounding conformity.

There cannot be too much cooperation or too much justice. This is because these are understood to be the beneficial states which we hope to achieve. But there can be an enforced cooperation, which produces too great a uniformity in life, and also the repressive qualities of over-enforcement. I do not wish to support this position—in fact, I lean in the opposite direction—but the conservative view that too great a regulation of the economy is destructive is an attack on enforced cooperation through law. Conservatives argue that an economy which is uncontrolled is more beneficial on the whole than one where cooperation is required.

As for justice, we have noted that an overenthusiasm for law can lead to virtual injustices. In particular, militant blacks argue today that the fortunes and circumstances of American blacks are so unique that they cannot be treated as equal to whites before the same laws. It is not necessary to agree with them in particular to grant the principle of their claim. Justice is founded on law. But a justice which looks only to law is a crippled one. Justice is represented as blind to express *impartiality*. But impartiality has two sides, and one of them must take into account special circumstances. We believe that a crippled child ought to be given special care, that a deaf child should be given exceptional training. A poor person may deserve exceptional treatment also—for example, special vocational training, even the guarantee of a job. I do not want to argue here that skin color alone is a circumstance which calls for exceptional treatment. But the principle of exceptions to law within a system of law is a secure one.

When the faults of law intrude, men can become desperate. When injustices prevail, when society becomes too uniform and too inflexible, law can be taken to be an essential evil. When the system of law which prevails is held up to be worthy because it is the law, yet is also clearly disadvantageous and even wrong in important respects, men lose their respect for law. The critical danger is that reverence for the law may be imposed and not earned. Substantive appraisal of law is fundamental. The law must merit our respect. Where the law is to be revered merely as such, we have the hidden oppression of Kafka's *The Trial*. The natural reply is that the law merits no such respect at all.

It appears that the law too is trapped in a state of dynamic imbalance. It is the primary instrument a society has for achieving regulation, uniformity, and change. Yet its ability to provide a means for change is always in tension with its capacity to regulate and to achieve uniformity. It will always fail in some respects. Yet it requires of the members of a society a rather high degree of conformity, for without respect and obedience, the law loses all its effectiveness, and all its benefits as well.

There is no obvious solution. A system of law which can be changed easily does not generate respect. Law gains respect in proportion to its stability and its endurance through time. On the other hand, a system of law which cannot be changed no longer is beneficial, and fails to merit our respect. Shall we live without law? That is the most absurd prospect of all. The only solution is no solution at all in a direct sense. It is to meet the problems of law as they arise, and to make changes where necessary. This is an arduous and complex process. It is one of the reasons why the political process is so complex and unsatisfactory to many people. Yet it has no obvious substitutes either.

(4) *Education.* The educational influence of law may be divided into three types. First, there is the indirect influence of law upon the activities of men. For example, to the extent that uniformity and stability are gained in a society, law not only regulates the activities of men directly, but modifies their actions through what they think and do. Men learn from what other men do, and are influenced by them. In an indirect fashion, law achieves an educational result by the indirect effects of men upon each other. Men often tend to do what others expect, and often imitate them.

Second, there is the more direct influence of law in its enforcement. The penalties accruing to disobedience of law make men fearful, and through their fear men come to obey the law rather habitually. In many people, obedience has an educational consequence in itself. It may be the fundamental principle of moral education that men learn moral habits by practice.

Third, law has a direct educational influence through the loyalty and respect which are generated in men for law itself. To the extent that men respect law, they obey it and come to believe in what it dictates. Here it is interesting that law only in part follows moral principles. The reverse is also common. What takes on moral force is what has been first enacted into law.

The educational force of law can be beneficial, and it can also be disadvantageous. To the extent that law exerts a control over how men think, it may stand in the way of its own reconsideration. Law is persuasive in its own right. And its greater influence can produce purity and inflexibility.

Conversely, a system of laws which is obviously unjust can teach a disrespect for law and a rebellious attitude. The educational effect of law is so great that, where loyalty is not instilled, disloyalty rather than neutrality is the likely result. This is not always clearly noted by legislators and politicians. It entails that a law for which there is only a weak justification is a great danger. And a law that many people will disobey is an even greater danger. Prohibition was such a law. It may well be that laws prohibiting the use of marijuana will prove disadvantageous in the same way. Marijuana might be harmful, and yet it might not pay to legislate against its use. Not, at least, if we are concerned about what such legislation and its enforcement may teach people. Especially, not where far greater injustices are allowed to exist without legal steps taken against them.

G. Custom

It has become clear throughout the preceding discussion that the formal or explicit social structures and institutions of politics and law rest upon a basis in the feelings and attitudes of the members of a society. Both politics and law work through explicit regulations which cannot be explicitly enforced in every stage. At some point, members of a society must simply follow regulations without the need for enforcement, because they are inclined to. This is a particular example of a more general trait of members of a society to develop patterned and habitual modes of behavior. The habits of conformity in response of human beings over time I will call "custom." It may be worth noting that the very word "ethics" is derived from the Greek word "ethos," which means *custom* and also *character*. In particular, we are concerned with what we call "customary" behavior and responses. Custom is what men *usually* do. Therefore it is repetitive behavior. It may be founded on law or on fear. Yet custom is always in part an expression of two features in addition to law and enforcement: (a) natural organic dispositions and (b) general patterns of response developed in the day-to-day activities of social life.

It is possible to see in custom the fundamental bond which holds a society together. Hume's moral theory is founded on the two elements of sympathy and custom. Men are disposed, either organically or in their social development, to form general patterns of action, to think and to feel in repetitive ways.

Charles S. Peirce saw that the ultimate basis of all meaning and all knowledge is habit—the patterned modes of response of human beings as they develop beliefs and act upon them. The twin notions of habit and custom—the one individual, the other social—are representations of the same principles. Men live in society and develop or learn repetitive modes of response and thought. Individually we speak of habits. But since most habits are developed in social contexts, learned from others and followed by others also, habits are usually also customs.

The notion of *custom* represents two traits combined: (1) the fact that men learn from what they do and from what happens around them, especially from other people; and (2) the repetitive, even conservative quality of all such learning. Recent theories of learning have been founded on a union of both these notions. To an experimental psychologist, learning is literally the development of repetitive modes of behavior. The measure of something learned is the disposition of the organism to repetitively respond to a given stimulus with the same response. Learning then is both habitual and customary—meaning that it is patterned and repetitive.

In addition, most learning is social in that it involves activities which men perform together. Custom represents all the general attitudes and learned responses transmitted from person to person, or developed in similar activities performed by different individuals.

Certainly there are habits of individuals which are not part of the customs of society because they are idiosyncratic. In addition, there are habits or responses developed by individuals which are not customary because they are intelligent or the result of inquiry (though inquiry itself is probably a matter of custom where it exists at all). We would not like to call a proved theorem in mathematics a mere matter of custom.

In any case, all societies are a matter of sharing, of joint efforts, of cooperation, of similarity of aims and activities. Members of a given society share genetic backgrounds, and inhabit a common territory. Far more to the point, they have a common language, a common loyalty to flag or ruler, a common love for some things. They work in common, dress in common, spend their recreation in common ways. We speak of many of these common traits of a people as "customs." In the sense in which the word is being used here, all joint patterns of response within a society which are learned and developed are custom.

Custom is analogous to politics and law in the ways it functions within social life. We may consider them in the same order.

(1) *Management.* The fundamental characteristic of management is its contribution to the making of decisions. The striking thing is that many decisions of human beings are not explicitly arrived at. It would be remarkable if all the important decisions of individuals within a society were the result of explicit mutual decision. Custom represents the full range of actions which are implicitly decided and yet which produce sufficient order and uniformity to be of social value. Men on line for the subway or for a store to open wait there calmly and without too much jostling or moving out of place. Lines would be worthless and even dangerous without customary ways of acting in them.

Hume argues that morals is primarily a matter of custom. He has a very powerful position, and for two distinct reasons. In the first place, most men do not weigh every moral decision that comes before them. Rather, moral actions are generally a matter of habit, of custom. We meet people in the street without thinking of whether we ought to kill them or not, and then deciding not to.

Instead, we generally ignore moral issues unless confronted directly by them.
Even when confronted by them, men usually respond in almost automatic ways. Only where a moral issue becomes paramount and unavoidable does a full moral decision arise which requires deliberation and careful thought.

Second, it is impossible for a man to deliberate deeply on every moral issue brought before him. In order to remain capable and avoid paralysis, a man must not view every moral situation as a complex one. The sheer fact of moral life is that a complex decision requires a considerable amount of time and effort, as well as of emotional energy. It is physically impossible to make every act a significant one, in requiring deep deliberation. To carry the point to an extreme, a man could never succeed in walking a hundred paces if every step required deliberation as to where he would place his foot. We can deliberate deeply on some issues only because others are habitual and customary.

The first point can, when taken to an extreme, lead to an acceptance of moral blindness. Men usually do not deliberate deeply on moral issues unless they have to. It does not follow that men ought never to engage in profound deliberations. The second point, however, reveals the absolute need men have for custom in social affairs. While they engage in great thoughts, social life must go on. Decisions must be made. Chances must be taken. Actions must be performed. Custom is the basis of all actions in social life which are not the result of deliberate choice.

(2) *Enforcement.* Literal and explicit means of enforcement of custom are rare. Occasionally, a town will be so aroused at one of its members as to join together in punishing him. Far more often, members of a society do no more than exert their collective wills and show their collective disapproval in open ways—by manifesting open contempt or refusing to speak to a wayward member. If what we mean by enforcement is an open policy of punishment, especially physical coercion, custom is rarely enforced.

But the enforcing power of custom is all the greater because it is not physical, because the contempt of other men can be an effective means of coercion. The strength of custom and its enforcement as well depend on three features of social life, going back to the very roots of social relations.

(a) The primary means for effecting customary behavior and developing standard responses in men is educational. All men grow up in society and are educated either implicitly or explicitly to conform to fairly standardized modes of behavior and feeling. Children learn by imitation, but also through training, through indoctrination, and through punishment. Generally, we tend to think of custom as founded in learning and therefore not as coercive. As contrasted with legal regulations, customary practices may be thought to depend on no coercive controls. This is an error. Only in the sense that a willful adult may flout custom and suffer no *legal* punishment is coercion lacking. But the coercions inherent in custom are in fact rather severe and pervasive.

In particular, education of a child is almost always coercive. Children learn by imitation and by rewards. But virtually no societies believe that education can be effective without punishment. Children are punished by beatings, by deprivation, certainly by manifest disapproval. Custom is in good part developed through what psychologists call "internalization." External forms of disapproval and punishment are taken into the individual person's modes of behavior, and become virtually automatic, unthinking. To Freud, internalization is the turning of aggression inward, thus founded from the very beginning on coercion.

(b) Children are dependent from infancy on the society into which they are born, and are educated almost automatically to the customary modes of social behavior. But as they become adults, the dependency in no way lessens. Rather, it changes its form. A newborn infant is literally helpless, and needs care to survive. Through this care it becomes dependent in two further respects on the adults who tend it. It becomes emotionally dependent on them, in that the emotions and actions of others exert a coercive and manipulative influence on it. In addition, social life is usually itself interdependent. The need of an infant for others for mere survival becomes less obvious, but exists throughout life. Most men in a complex civilization could not survive long without the benefits of the activities of others. A man who could not obtain the contributions of others would find life almost impossible. It follows, then, that men will automatically develop ways of acting which enable them to get along with others.

Emotional and physical dependency entail rather direct forms of social coercion. The disapproval of others is a powerful device for changing behavior, and for generating the conformity which custom depends on. The sheer need men have for others in order to gain their personal needs leads them to act in ways which promote such ends, to obtain both the aid and the approval of other people.

(c) The coercive results of emotional and physical dependency lead naturally to a deeper or more inward quality of coercion, the one Freud stresses in the notion of internalization. Not only must men act so as to avoid severe censure by others and to gain their cooperation, or else suffer both emotional pain and physical deprivation, but they come to fear the disapproval of others directly. The general views of society come in themselves to exert a coercive effect. Men act not in a deliberate appraisal of what others will tolerate, but under the shadow of fear that others will disapprove of them. We are speaking here of *shame* and *apprehension*.

Shame properly is felt only after an action which others disapprove of. But the fear or apprehension of possible shame is even more effective than shame itself, which, being after the fact, can have no direct influence on actions. Men conform to those modes of behavior which they believe are required to avoid shame.

Properly speaking, apprehension of shame is not a form of external coercion, but an inward one. It is the inward result in feeling of the external coercion of manifest disapproval and the punishing responses of other people. Nevertheless, the fact of such internalization in feeling is a pervasive trait of human life. Moreover, it is difficult to defend the position that shame and apprehension of shame are unmixed evils. In Emerson's famous essay on self-reliance, he remarks that

"Society everywhere is in conspiracy against the manhood of every one of its members. . . . Whoso would be a man, must be a nonconformist." These indubitable truths are obvious only if the nonconformity rests on a clear and pervasive custom in which even the genius follows the customary rules of social life. Total nonconformity is absurd. In addition, it entails the loss of all the benefits of social life

(3) *Benefits.* Custom may be regarded as the ultimate bond of social life. Only so many decisions can be dictated by a political leader. Only so much of life can be subject to law. In the rest of life, men work together on mutual projects, and cooperate in shared efforts. Custom provides the uniformity essential to cooperation which is not compelled by law or direct force. Since law and government both depend on the effectiveness of custom, all of the benefits which they achieve, and all of the benefits a society has to offer for its members, depend ultimately on custom.

Custom is the source of stability and uniformity in a society. What is shared by individual men, other than the sheer fact of geographical location, is the fruit of custom. Institutions have the forms they do in the customary practices which such institutions depend on. The church rests on the custom of worship and charitable contribution. The stock market rests on the custom of investment as well as the desire for gain. Even recreational sports, apparently the result of a desire for physical enjoyment, partake of a customary form. Golf is preserved as the game it is through custom. And the customs of a community lead to the building of golf courses.

The benefits of uniformity in a society are obvious. Equally obvious, though by no means effectively understood, are the faults of excess uniformity. Social life cannot exist without the uniformities men share. But too great a uniformity in life saps individual vitality, individuality, and strength of purpose. Emerson's essay on self-reliance stresses the deviance inherent in all major work. Society requires adaptability and invention as well as uniformity and cooperation. Custom can become oppressive and destructive, as small towns show in a most obvious way. The need for nonconformity in social life, therefore for the weakening of custom, will be considered in detail shortly.

(4) *Education.* Custom is the result of education, and is acquired in the natural process of growing up in a society, as well as in the explicit means provided for educating the young. Most of what men learn they acquire in a social setting, from their parents, playing with other children, in the classroom, and therefore is bound to involve the common aspects of social life we call custom.

In return, the social setting of learning is from the beginning imbued with the forms and characteristics of custom. In this respect, society is not only the result of the workings of custom, but also the means for transmitting customary habits of behavior to children. This need not be explicit as it is in the schools, but may be implicit in daily life. Custom is the great teacher of mankind, both in setting as it does the terms of social relations which the child encounters while learning, and in providing a model for children to follow in their own behavior.

The easiest way to make this clear is to ask ourselves, what else can a child learn except customary habits which he finds around him? And how can he do so? A child learns through imitation, through his own exploration of the world, in the classroom and eventually through books and reading. Unless from the beginning, his parents are unique and follow noncustomary modes of behavior, a child will imitate them and their customary actions. In exploring the world, he discovers how people act and how they expect others to act, and will tend to emulate those actions. The classroom is always a social setting, with its own customary aspects of integration. In reading, a child does encounter strange modes of behavior, and can follow them if he chooses—though he will usually come to see that they are not effective in his own social milieu.

There are only two ways of gaining not only an awareness of noncustomary ways of acting, but the sense that they are effective and legitimate. One is by being surrounded from the beginning with idiosyncratic behavior in one's parents, friends, and classmates. A nonconforming society will generate nonconformity—though only in acceptable ways. A conforming society will instill conformity in its children, either through sheer imitation or through coercion. At best, a counter-culture may develop, with its own customary norms.

The second way is the one Emerson seems to have in mind—the noncon-formity of genius, of effort, of struggle, mainly of mind. Through effort, men learn of new things by discovering or inventing them, and by demonstrating their effectiveness. Scientists make discoveries. Artists invent new works of art. Philosophers build new systems. Knowledge of the world gained through inquiry teaches us something new, and can lead to new customs and modes of action. Above all, new technological inventions change society and its customs in a rapid fashion.

Both of these ways of learning to behave in an uncustomary fashion are gained from the society itself. A society may embody a variety of customs and norms. Men are found who deviate significantly from others in dress or thought. Otherwise a child has no model to follow, and tends to conform to custom almost entirely. At best he may deviate in ways that lead merely to shame. The result is that even nonconformity must become customary if it is to be effective. The customs of mankind are the primary educational instrument, even where learning is thought to make a man free from the oppression of society.

H. Punishment

The rules and regulations of society are often enforced, either through forms *Bad* of legal punishment or through the implicit reactions of other men. As we have noted, enforcement of rules has some special problems which are worth considering in detail. Especially to a moral purist, if it is wrong to impose suffering on a person, it would appear that all forms of punishment are unjustified. What is required, then, is that the moral purist amend his rule so that it is wrong to harm an *innocent*

person, but sometimes right to punish a man who has broken a law. This is the
position Kant is led to. The sole basis for punishment is a principle of equality. We may see the most obvious fruits of this principle in capital punishment. A man who has taken the life of another *ought* to have his own taken in return.

The principle that *the punishment should fit the crime* is well established in most codes of criminal justice. Unfortunately, in the case of capital punishment, it violates the ideal of avoiding suffering. It is necessary, then, that we study the grounds for punishment, and determine their relationship to the ideals we hope men will live by. We begin, however, not with overt punishment, but with implicit and indirect forms of punishment—that is, with moral condemnation.

(1) *Condemnation.* Condemnation is the explicit and open expression of disapproval at something a person has done. We may say that his action was wrong, immoral, bad, even monstrous or evil. We may also say that the person who committed such an action is immoral, bad, monstrous, or evil. Obviously, the latter forms of condemnation are the stronger.

Moral condemnation has several functions. First of all, it is the expression by the speaker of his own emotional reactions, and may serve either to relieve the revulsion he feels at the act he is condemning, or to move him to some further action—for example, to undertake some kind of overt punishment. Second, condemnatory language can be extremely persuasive, in leading other people also to condemn the given action, and perhaps to join with the speaker in punishment. Third, condemnatory language is educative in several respects. It reveals to the man condemned the responses of the speaker, in case he did not know them. It also exerts a persuasive influence on the condemned man's own attitudes, due to his reactions to such strong language.

Finally, a point often overlooked, condemnation is in fact a form of punishment, and not always a mild one. At the very least, to publicly declare an action monstrous is to seek to influence the way other people regard the agent who performed it. He is punished by the collective scorn of other men. Sometimes this can lead merely to shame and contempt for oneself. But collective condemnation by everyone has far more serious consequences. We suffer disapproval, especially when it is obvious. Manifest contempt is very difficult for most people to endure.

In addition, moral language is laden with very strong emotions. To be condemned is, at least for most men, a hard experience to tolerate. Shame is generated by the sheer force of language, and by the revealed attitudes of the speaker. The man who feels shame suffers no small amount of pain. Most crimes are committed in secret not only to avoid punishment, but to avoid condemnation and loss of face as well. It is striking that many thieves steal from their friends, and are quite fearful of being caught and condemned by them.

Most people believe quite fervently that a man who does something wrong, especially one who breaks a law, ought to be punished for it. However, I have heard young men and women express a violent hatred for all forms of punishment, and of moral condemnation as well. The reasons for such antipathy seem to be two.

First, a result of either strong or weak relativism, is the view that each person decides what is right for himself. Therefore, no one else has the right to condemn or punish him. Second, there is the belief that punishment is itself an infliction of suffering on another person, and therefore wrong. In addition, though not a reason for holding such a position, there seems to be a heartfelt sense that people are too often condemned for what they do and are. Especially, an adolescent is almost constantly criticized by his parents. A natural consequence of feeling overcriticized is the view that people ought to stop condemning each other as much as they do.

In a moment, we will look at the grounds for punishment. But now it is worth asking whether the position that men should not *condemn* each other is a defensible one. We have already taken a hard look at moral relativism, and concluded that it is not a defensible position. In particular, a person is by no means an ultimate authority on what is to his own benefit, and certainly is not one concerning what benefits others. Thus, we may condemn a thief for his stupidity in stealing when he could get a job, for his lack of consideration in stealing from someone who has greater need than he does, or so ineffectively as to let himself be caught. Or we may simply condemn him for violating a law which he himself requires in order to be secure in society. We may condemn him for harming himself as well as others.

In addition, though condemnation is a form of punishment, and inflicts pain on the man condemned, we must consider its function as an educational device. A child brought up without a single word of condemnation might become a man wholly indifferent to others, harming them without provocation or concern. Can we justify avoiding condemnation where it can be shown that the result of silence is greater suffering than where condemnation is expressed?

Most important of all, what does it mean to believe that stealing is *wrong*, if that belief leads to no condemnation? Is a man tempted to steal willing to condemn himself for his temptation? If not, then the word "wrong" and the belief that stealing is wrong seem to have no content at all. If so, then we seem led to the position that stealing is wrong for one man, but not for anyone else. If we believe that no one ought to steal, then it would seem that the mere belief itself entails that we will condemn stealing where we find it. Certainly we may take circumstances into account, and perhaps not punish nor strongly condemn a man who has stolen bread for his children. But at least part of the force of moral principles is that they entail condemnation and even punishment. The very language we use reveals this fact. If the principle "stealing is wrong" is accepted, then an instance of theft *is* wrong. And to say so is to utter a condemnation of the act and even the thief as well.

We are led to conclude that holding moral beliefs entails a willingness to condemn actions as immoral, wrong, or bad. And since condemnation is usually a form of punishment, we seem committed to believe *in principle* that punishment is justifiable. But we are not obviously committed to any degree or type of

punishment by the mere acceptance of moral principles. Perhaps the young man
who will not tolerate even the expression of condemnation is rather convinced that
most forms of punishment, even open condemnation, are too severe.

In recent times, the conditions in many prisons in the United States have
been exposed in all their horror and inhumanity. Men are beaten, fed badly,
herded together in crowded conditions, thrown into solitary confinement for
indefinite periods of time, and on capricious and arbitrary grounds. Can anything
really justify the kinds of punishment to which prisoners are exposed, even for
major crimes?

Consider here an extreme case of actions which many people would condemn
—the war crimes of German officers during the rule of Hitler. Especially consider
Adolph Eichmann, who was one of the major contributors to the smooth functioning
of the Final Solution, the killing of millions of Jews in the concentration camps.
Can we possibly think of his deeds without severe revulsion and condemnation?
The very idea that we might have a strong loyalty to moral principles and not
condemn such atrocities as the concentration camps and the men who committed
them seems absurd.

Our condemnation is so great, in fact, that some extreme form of punishment
seems required. Not to punish a man for wholesale atrocities is morally reprehensible. Yet what punishment could possible be suitable for a man like Eichmann?
What punishment could fit the crime of wholesale murder? We cannot justify
torture. Simple death is too slight a punishment. In the case of crimes of sufficient
magnitude, no punishment seems of the appropriate order of severity. It might
follow that we cannot defend the principle of fitting a punishment to the crime.

We turn now to the major types and justifications of punishment.

(2) *Retributive Punishment.* The retributive theory of punishment is essentially the view that a man who commits a crime ought to suffer in a manner and
to a degree approximately equal to the moral gravity of the offense. The punishment shall fit the crime. The retributive theory certainly reflects a widespread
conception of punishment, and one installed at the heart of most systems of
punishment. A man who commits a crime ought to be punished for it, in a manner
commensurate with the seriousness of the crime.

There are several difficulties with a purely retributive theory of punishment,
at least so far as commonly accepted practices of punishment are concerned.

(a) Not all punishable offenses seem to involve moral issues. Laws are common
forbidding men from giving away secrets important for national security, and we
would expect penalties to be justified for a man who betrays such secrets. Yet it is
not clear that maintaining such secrets is a moral issue. A country may have
enforced laws concerning certain financial abuses, or traffic offenses, though again,
such violations are not usually taken to be of moral import.

(b) The wider problem raised by such matters is whether there is really a
way of determining the *degree* of a moral offense, or whether the notion is not
hopelessly vague. Sometimes it is far worse to tell secrets than at other times,

depending on the nature of the secrets and the critical circumstances. The Rosenbergs were sentenced to death for stealing secrets involving the atomic bomb and giving them to the Soviet Union. Clearly it was not the mere offense that led to such a sentence, but the nature of the secret. It seems to follow that a man who murders a great scientist should suffer a more severe penalty than one who murders a nobody.

The retributive theory suffers from the same defects as Kant's entire moral theory. A schematic principle of considerable persuasive force is made the basis of a moral system. But punishment is in practice a far more complex matter than strict equality can provide. In good part, this is due to the impossibility of weighing as equals crimes and punishment. A murderer kills a man quickly and without forethought. The victim never knew what was happening to him. The killer is now incarcerated for several months awaiting trial, and then for weeks awaiting execution. Are the two really equal in pain and suffering?

In *The Mikado*, Gilbert and Sullivan satirize the whole notion of fitting the punishment to the crime, by thinking up genuine comparisons. Obviously such extreme fastidiousness is not inherent in the retributive theory, which is not in practice consistent with its own moral principles.

(c) A related difficulty, though not perhaps a crippling one, is that the strict equality of crime and punishment does not make it easy to understand the rationale of distinctions between first degree murder and manslaughter. Both involve the destruction of a life. If we hold that the moral gravity of a crime obviously depends on the *intent* of the agent, then we complicate the problem beyond repair. For how could a retributionist justify any judgment he might come to concerning the greater seriousness of killing without premeditation as compared to stealing jewelry with premeditation?

(d) The more serious difficulty here is that we often believe that the circumstances of a crime may call for at most a very mild penalty. A young man who joins an older one in a bank robbery may be given a lighter sentence. All differences in length of sentence would seem to be ruled out by the retributive theory of punishment.

(e) A most striking example of this, worth separate mention, is the fact that a first offender is often given a lesser punishment than a chronic repeater. If a sentence looks only at the crime, then such a practice is without justification.

(f) This brings us to a general attitude developing in recent penology, that punishment should not look to the crime as much as to the criminal. A chronic offender reveals that he may be unredeemable, and is to be punished more severely than a first offender, who may have given in to temptation only this once.

Even more than considering the criminal rather than the crime in looking at the severity of his punishment, we should also look to the criminal to determine the actual results of punishment on him. Such a view is antithetic to the retributive theory, and if it has any force at all, entails a very different theory of punishment.

(g) Finally, if we accept even a part of the view that men who commit crimes do so because of circumstances over which they have no control—their poverty, lack of formal education, early training, emotional development, even their mental and emotional instability—then retribution seems quite unjust. If a man commits a crime and cannot help himself, then punishment seems inappropriate. If we suppose that almost all crimes have a strong component of lack of control in them, and are not wholly cases where a free and responsible agent willingly chooses to commit a crime, then retribution is not easy to defend. The facts are that few thefts are committed by middle-class, educated people. In general, it is the poor and deprived who steal. In particular, narcotics addicts steal to obtain money for drugs. Retribution seems harsh and unjust under such circumstances.

(3) *Utilitarian Punishment.* The utilitarian theory is that punishment is to be justified solely by the benefits provided generally by such punishment. There are three types of benefits which imprisonment may provide. (a) A well established system of courts and prisons has a strong *deterrent* effect on men who would otherwise commit crimes. (b) Imprisonment often teaches prisoners a lesson, not to repeat their crimes. (c) During the period of imprisonment, the criminal will be removed from society, and be unable to harm others. Capital punishment is an interesting case in that the second benefit of punishment is eliminated. An executed criminal will not learn from his mistakes. Because there is no prospect for rehabilitation, many people oppose capital punishment, especially since most studies show that capital punishment has no greater a deterrent influence than imprisonment. It appears unjust to such people that capital punishment should be employed *solely* to protect society from possible harm.

Act utilitarianism suffers from the severe drawback that it seems to justify both executing a man solely for the benefits of others, and imprisoning an innocent man. Suppose a town is panicked by a murderer. Maybe it would be generally beneficial to convict an innocent tramp found in the vicinity. We do not think that such an act would be right, even if it benefited society as a whole.

Rule utilitarianism appears far more defensible. The principle of rule utilitarianism is that a *rule* or promulgated principle is good only if obedience to the principle by everyone would be generally beneficial. Clearly the practice of imprisoning innocent men would have a destructive effect on society generally. Therefore, we must consider only a rule-utilitarian theory of punishment.

It is important to realize that on the utilitarian view, punishment is an evil to be avoided where it is not clearly beneficial to society as a whole. Nevertheless, if punishment is to be an effective deterrent, it must be fairly severe. In addition, the length of terms of imprisonment must protect society, and provide some lessons for the criminal.

Several criticisms are sometimes offered against the utilitarian theory of punishment.

(a) It would appear that all excuses should be ruled out on this theory of punishment, for the fewer the excuses permitted, the stronger the deterrent effect of the law. In other words, there is no utilitarian justification for excluding the insane or children from punishment. The utilitarian reply is that such a criticism is psychologically naive. In fact, allowing such extenuating circumstances strengthens the force of the law, since it strengthens our conviction that the law is just. Men might well become hardened to crimes and lawlessness if young children were punished severely. Finally, a rule that ignored extenuating circumstances would be extremely undesirable, promoting fear and insecurity. If all theft would be punished by imprisonment, even inadvertent failure to pay a debt, then the whole practice of lending money could be undermined.

(b) It appears also that *mitigating* excuses cannot be justified on utilitarian grounds. Would we not have more effective laws if no distinction between premeditated and impulsive actions were generally made? The utilitarian might well point out that actions on impulse would not be deterred by stronger penalties. In addition, it is beneficial for society as a whole to reveal a humanitarian concern for distinguishing a hardened and deliberate crime from an outburst of a man who is generally good.

(c) A more interesting view is that the utilitarian theory is led to view punishment as essentially a form of quarantine. A leper is quarantined for the good of society. A criminal is imprisoned for the good of society. The reply is obvious. A leper contracts a disease through no fault of his own, and we quarantine him in comfort (if we can) to recompense him for his personal sacrifice. But a criminal ought to be imprisoned in fairly harsh circumstances to deter him and others from crime. The utilitarian is committed no more than the retributionist to regarding imprisonment as comfortable.

All of these criticisms overlook the paramount function of punishment as an educational device. The most important benefit which punishment may provide in social life is to teach people what is important and what is not, which rules are to be followed and which are not. Some matching of the degree of punishment to the gravity of a crime is beneficial, for it teaches men of the heinousness of the offense. Excluding children and the insane from punishment, or taking premeditation into account, is beneficial in showing how central forethought and deliberation are to moral responsibility. The types of punishment employed are to be evaluated for their emotional and moral effects on the prisoners punished, as to whether they are taught the errors of their ways. When we take the range of educational effects of punishment into account, the utilitarian theory of punishment is far more justifiable than its critics seem to realize.

Nevertheless, the last criticism raises an interesting question. What right has society to act in such harsh ways to men, even criminals, solely for the benefit of other people? Is not the whole theory of imprisonment—utilitarian or retributive—morally indefensible, sacrificing one man to the interests of others? Here we come to the third theory of punishment.

(4) *Rehabilitation.* Hume's theory of punishment is strikingly different from either of the two views propounded so far. Essential to Hume's argument is the conviction that men act in ways determined by their past. (See below, Chapter

IX, Section F.) Punishment therefore can only be justified by its effectiveness in changing the character of the criminal. The sole function of punishment is to educate and remake character. The deterrent effect of punishment is a minor factor to consider. Young children and insane men are not be be punished because they cannot be educated by punishment alone.

Instead of taking Hume's theory literally, let us expand it on moral and utilitarian lines. A criminal is a man of poor character, who acts in ways that harm others and even himself. We recall Plato's principle: it is never right to harm a man. Imprisonment must not then be looked at as harming the criminal, but as *bettering him*. The only form of punishment which is justified is the kind we impose on children—a punishment to teach them right from wrong.

From this point of view, our entire system of penology is immoral and indefensible. Prisons do not improve or rehabilitate their inmates. They usually make them worse. It is a well known fact that young offenders learn from hardened criminals elaborate tricks of the criminal trades. Prison life is degrading and dehumanizing. It brutalizes men and makes them criminals with no hope of rehabilitation.

It is true that many prisons offer forms of vocational training and access to libraries. Rehabilitation is not unknown in prisons, and runs through almost all penal literature as an aim. But in practice, the retributive force of punishment tends to be primary. Criminals lose their citizenship and their human rights, and their humanity and decency as well. Such a result is a natural consequence of the continuum of means and ends. A man treated as if he is inhuman and with contempt becomes less human, less decent, and comes to merit that contempt.

There are two central difficulties with a purely rehabilitational theory of punishment. One is a moral one—the moral impulse which underlies the retributive theory. Men ought to be punished for their misdeeds. This is a moral dispute which is not easy to settle. Nevertheless, we may point out in criticism of retribution that that theory entails that it would be right to punish a criminal even if it did no one any good. I can only repeat my earlier remark that a rule or action that benefits no one cannot be defended as good or right.

The second difficulty is that not all criminals are capable of being rehabilitated. What is to be done with the unredeemable? The rehabilitational theory alone cannot tell us. A criminal who cannot be rehabilitated must be incarcerated to protect others. A murderer with no compunction at killing must be imprisoned and kept away from others. Perhaps an incurable criminal should be treated exactly as we treat the insane. That is Hume's view. The trouble with this conclusion is that we really ought to treat the insane as well as possible (which is not to say that we do so). After all, they are not to blame for their illness. Should we treat unredeemable criminals as well as possible also? We would lose the deterrent and some of the educational effects of punishment by doing so.

The rehabilitational theory also entails that we must use the most effective means possible to cure criminals. Suppose that effective rehabilitation were achieved by giving criminals several years of luxurious living, plenty of rewards, and no punishments. Suppose the pain of punishment were an ineffective means of conditioning. There is some evidence from experimental psychology that rewards provide far more effective means of learning than punishment. Would we then conclude that we should make the lives of criminals very pleasant if that rehabilitated them? Such a conclusion would completely eliminate the deterrent effects of punishment also.

The rehabilitational view regards punishment as wholly an educational device. In the next chapter we will take up the subject of moral education, and the function of punishment in such education. We may note here that if punishment has no educational value, then it is not defensible on the rehabilitational view. But we have seen that condemnation is not avoidable in moral affairs, and that condemnation indeed has a punishing character. In addition, the deterrent effect of punishment is well established, though not in all cases, and should not be completely neglected.

The rehabilitational view of punishment is a morally pure position, and like all such positions leans toward an indefensible extreme. However, in combination with the utilitarian theory it provides a very powerful theory of punishment. The utilitarian view provides the substantive judgment in terms of consequences, while the rehabilitational principle provides the moral or regulative basis of punishment. Here we subscribe to Plato's principle with a small qualification. The *primary* function of punishment is to rehabilitate and reeducate the criminal. Yet it is necessary to consider the deterrent effects of punishment also, though to a lesser extent, and also the protection society requires from a hardened criminal. Rehabilitation should be the ruling principle of prisons, and they should be made into far more humane and beneficial places. But the term of imprisonment should not be so short as to provide little deterrence or protection for society. The force of retribution may be preserved in strenuous and open condemnation of wrongdoing, though not necessarily accompanied by further and extreme penalties.

The strongest argument against the retributive theory of punishment and for the rehabilitational view is pragmatic and utilitarian. Our entire system of justice today is in a state of chaos and near collapse. Trials require time and money, especially time. Where so many arrests are made that there is not time for a careful trial for everyone, then a variety of injustices are produced. Almost no one who receives bail for an offense is convicted. Most defendants are offered short prison terms if they will plead guilty and avoid the expense and trouble of a jury trial. Innocent men are thus led to plead guilty, while the guilty are let free after short terms in prison. Both the deterrent influence of imprisonment and the protection of society are lost in the shuffle, while the rehabilitative effects of punishment are almost totally dissipated. Criminals return to society in a short while, no more fit either emotionally or in skills to be effective and productive members of that society.

If there is a solution to the chaos of our courts and our entire system of justice, it can only lie in the direction of increased rehabilitation, and the minimization of the painful aspects of prison. The alternative of seeking a greater efficiency in conviction could be achieved only by diminishing the protections afforded the innocent, a practice difficult to defend on moral grounds. But if prisons sought not to punish as much as to build character, and release were partly predicated on the prospects of living successfully in the outside world, many of the unfortunate aspects of imprisonment would be eliminated. Where prison life is inhuman and brutal, there is a strong moral imperative toward avoiding longer terms than can be morally justified. Where prisons are educational and provide the means for men to improve themselves, the length of term looks to the man imprisoned more than to what he has done.

This solution cannot be achieved through a few small changes in our penal system. It involves a complete reconception of the dispensation of justice and also of the functions of prisons. The magnitude of the task is overwhelming. And the will of most people to achieve it is small. Prisons function on the principle, "out of sight, out of mind." The average person knows little of prison life, and cares less. Yet prisoners have recently begun to protest conditions in prisons and have gained some publicity. And many citizens' groups have finally begun to direct their energies toward prison reform. The results of public concern may be impressive, or may turn out in the end to be of small significance.

A plausible theory of punishment is one with a completely indefinite term. Here a criminal rehabilitated in a short time will be released then, while a man incapable of change will remain longer. Ironically, such a view is unjust too, and here we see the beneficial side of the retributionist position. For a man could be sent to prison for life for a small crime, if he did not change. In a perfect world, where we could read his mind and be sure of his waywardness, this might be defensible. But in our imperfect prison system, we cannot justify imprisoning a man for an indefinite period, depending only on the opinion of a physician or prison warden.

Here is another instance of a tension which moral circumstances create which has no complete solution, only a compromise. The ideal of imprisonment ought to be education and rehabilitation, however long it takes. Yet too long a term can become evil in itself. We have developed the parole system, in which terms of definite length may be shortened upon signs of rehabilitation. Even prisoners have the right to know in advance the maximum penalty they face.

I. Moral education

We have noted throughout our discussion of social relations the educational influence of politics, law, and custom. Men are taught what they know by others, by the institutions surrounding them, through imitation and indirect influence. Custom exerts a powerful influence on the members of a society, often with no external controls or explicit aims. Societies tend to perpetuate themselves and their customs in the sheer fact of individual development in the context of social life. If a man grows up in a society with well defined social customs and norms, he will take them for his very own, and conform to such customs and norms.

The force of habit and custom is so great that it is tempting to view all individual actions as the working of such habits and customs, acquired from others or at least in affairs which involve others. It is extremely implausible that men are born with any fundamental moral attitudes or responses, though of course they are born with premoral emotional dispositions and feelings. A child acquires skills, habits, and also new affections, new loyalties, new feelings. The forms of adult life may be regarded as acquired. Whatever a man's moral dispositions are, they may be viewed as the results of conditioning, therefore the results of habit and custom.

This position is not refuted by the fact that men differ from each other in their moral convictions, nor even by the fact that some men seem to lack all moral conviction. In a complex society, moral customs are anything but monolithic. Different people belong to different groups in the larger society, and are bound to acquire the customs of the smaller group as well as of the larger. Where the customs and norms of a society do not form a monolithic and consistent unity, there is bound to be divergence among the people who acquire these norms, but with different emphases.

Thus, a standard norm of American life is the principle that men ought to work, and that laziness is a character deficiency, that wasted time is an evil. Yet work is also regarded as unpleasant, arduous, unsatisfying in itself, but required for the money it brings. Now, where advertising generates the conviction that life should be pleasant, that a man without a new car, a beautiful woman, and a house in the country is deprived, and where work will not provide these, then it is a natural conclusion that work is unjustified. The customary values of society here come into direct conflict. Laziness is wrong on one set of norms, and admirable according to another. Whether a man opts for one mode of life or another, both styles are customary to some degree in the larger society.

In general, Western societies tend to be strongly influenced by Christian principles, especially that the life of material affluence is a less valuable life than is a spiritual one. A young man who pursues a career of medicine in order to be wealthy is simply adopting one customary path. But if he instead opts for dedicated service, scorns wealth, and tries to find ways to better human life, then he is pursuing another value or ideal equally firmly entrenched in social life. Medicine accommodates both ideals. It serves the ideal of a selfish man, in that medicine has the highest status of any profession, and might be pursued for sheer personal gain. It also accommodates the ideal version of dedicated service. An individual physician makes of this conflict of ideals what he will. But in either case, he does not break totally new ground, but accepts one or another customary value, and combines them in proportions to his taste.

The upshot of this discussion is that we may regard moral education as a subject without relevance or interest. Moral education always takes place, through the working of custom and the influence of other people. Men acquire the values they find around them, though in different orders of priority, and to differing degrees. To the general question, how do men acquire the values they do? we answer: from others, from learning, from their experience, through custom and habit. No one simply invents moral values from scratch, or develops loyalties hitherto unknown. Men who advocate the continuation of tradition overlook the fact that all life continues the past and comes out of the past.

Clearly the issue is not one of how men gain the values they come to have, but rather, why do they not learn a *particular* set of values posed as given? When a traditionalist condemns the new morality, he has in mind a *specific* set of norms and a *specific* manifestation of them. The question of moral education is not the general question of how values are formed and transmitted, but how to teach children a specific set of values which adults wish to foster in them.

The larger issue continues to haunt the narrower one. One reason why moral education is so difficult to achieve may be that training children in a specific set of values is unreliable where those children are exposed to a great diversity of conflicting norms in the rest of their lives and even in the educational process itself. Thus, children who imitate their parents and acquire their values may sense the conflicting tendencies within these values, and merely reorder them within their own lives. It is by no means uncommon for parents to manifest respect for the Christian virtues of love and charity, yet live in a highly competitive, status-seeking, and selfish manner. They assume that the moral virtues which their children should learn are the Christian ones. But their children are also told to be realistic, to avoid the wrong side of the tracks, that the poor are shiftless and sinful. The obvious and expected result is that their children acquire not the manifest values but the implicit ones, and moral education seems to have failed once again— when in fact it may have succeeded perfectly in a wider sense.

There is a more fundamental issue than the diversity and incompatibility of values in a complex society, which may enable us to explain the problems of moral education. The specific problem is how to teach children what is right and what is wrong. The obvious question which must come up at some point is just what is right and wrong. Shall we assume that parents know this? There are several ways in which children may become convinced that in fact their parents do not truly know right from wrong.

First, children discover that their parents' values are both extremely diverse and incompatible with each other. If parents are *inconsistent* in their actions, it appears that they are not clear in what they are doing. Many people are indeed dubious about some important values. They cannot then expect their children to acquire clear values from them.

Second, the surrounding society contains many people whose fundamental values may conflict with each other. Under such conditions, it is a natural conclusion that important values are not settled or clear. In both these cases, children come to reflect within themselves the inconsistency and diversity which surrounds them.

Third, a child may come to the realization that his parents are unhappy and dissatisfied with their lives. A minister's son may sense the deep current of resentment his parents have at never having enough money, and come to believe that money is of greater value than service or God. If the values a man lives by are not great enough to preserve his sense of satisfaction with them, perhaps they should be abandoned.

Fourth, a child may come to the realization that the values he has been taught to follow are destructive to him and cause him a great deal of pain. He will therefore abandon them. A child in school who has been taught to love learning and books may find that the other children revile and even hate him. He may find it far easier and less painful to conform to their anti-intellectualism than to fight it.

The third and fourth ways in which a child comes to reject his parents' teachings are modes of substantive appraisal. He discovers that the values which his parents have espoused are unsatisfactory, either in their lives or in his own. The conflict among differing values in society is not always a conflict in promulgated aims, but also in styles of life. Certain values simply cannot fit in easily to certain modes of life, and must be rejected. Or else, the style of life the community demands must be rejected instead.

The central problem of moral education is posed in Plato's *Meno*. The dialogue opens with Meno's question: can virtue be taught? After considerable discussion both of what virtue is and how learning takes place, Socrates and Meno come to an impasse. If virtue is knowledge, then it can be taught. But, Socrates points out, if virtue is knowledge, there will be experts in morality who can be teachers of virtue. Yet no ordinary man will admit that someone else is more of an expert in moral decisions than he is. In addition, parents often do not succeed in teaching their own children what the parents consider right and wrong. It would seem that morality cannot be taught. And it follows also that morality is not a form of knowledge.

There are only three general methods for teaching morality. Let us consider them in the light of our previous discussion.

(1) *Habit*. According to Aristotle, virtue is acquired by habit, not through teaching. And the way in which habits are formed is by practice. We gain the virtues by exercising them first, and form the habits afterward. "The virtues we get by first exercising them, as also happens in the case of the arts as well. For the things we have to learn before we can do them, we learn by doing them, e.g. men become builders by building and lyre-players by playing the lyre; so too we become just by doing just acts, temperate by doing temperate acts, brave by doing brave acts."

There are two major strengths of the Aristotelian position. First, morality must often be a direct response to a moral problem. A man cannot deliberate on any and all moral problems which face him, but often must have an instinctive, intuitive, or habitual response to the problem posed. A man who finds a wallet in the street must feel the force of ownership, and his own lack of any right to the contents of the wallet. In particular, a virtuous man has a strong and clear sense of duty, at least in some definite cases. When we speak of a man with a strong sense of duty, or a strong conscience, we note his unequivocal and habitual response to certain kinds of moral issues.

Second, Aristotle is certainly correct that such habits are acquired through practice and imitation. A person develops habits of response by producing such responses. A child learns the habit of moral judgment by *first* imitating his parents' language and actions, and then finding the same language and habits becoming internalized in his own behavior and feelings. In terms of our earlier model, strong affections for certain modes of action are generated by undertaking similar actions, and by developing easy skills for acting in similar ways.

The habitual mode of moral training is probably the most widespread one in practice. Children are firmly told what is right and what is wrong, and punished for what they do wrong. The force of the punishment and of parental disapproval is great enough to bring such children to follow what is right in an automatic fashion. Presumably they will develop habits of responding in similar ways, which will become their basic values in adult life.

The difficulties inherent in this method of education are obvious. None of the aspects of social and moral life mentioned above can be dealt with adequately by so habitual and dogmatic a method of moral education. Where parental values do in fact conflict, children will develop conflicting habits, and may not come to reproduce in their actions or their loyalties the habits their parents explicitly proclaim. Where the social environment is filled with conflicting ideals, and conflicting requirements, children will acquire incompatible habits, especially those acquired at different times. Values in school and in the home may be quite disparate and apparently unrelated.

Far more important is a problem inherent in Aristotle's psychology. He seems to be claiming that mere *repetition* leads to the formation of a habit. So also, in many schools, drill and repetition are considered effective educational means. But current psychological evidence shows that habits are not acquired through repetition alone, but in fact the reverse is true: where habits are acquired, then there will be repetition. Learning occurs only where there has been a reward, only where the repeated act produces something pleasant or desired. An action must produce affection in order to be learned and repeated.

In most cases, parental approval for certain kinds of action, and disapproval of others, provide clear enough rewards and punishments. The affection of children for their parents, teachers, and peers leads to the acquisition of habits which all these people approve of. Yet it is important to realize that a habit acquired at home which produces pain and suffering in other social affairs may be abandoned. A value which a child's parents teach him will be eliminated if he finds that it produces too much suffering. A value which a child's parents explicitly hold will not be followed if they subtly reward him for activities incompatible with it.

The major problem of habitual moral education is that it provides no means whatsoever for dealing with moral conflicts. Where these are rare, as they are in some societies, this is of little concern. But where conflicts are frequent, then habits not only fail to provide a resolution of difficulties. They can also generate crises, paralysis, and suffering.

(2) *Social Interaction.* Piaget has argued that in the play of children, certain fundamental moral norms are developed rather directly and automatically. In early childhood, moral laws are parental commands, almost of supreme authority. A child understands right and wrong wholly in terms of parental approval and disapproval. The arbitrariness is fundamental. But in later play, a child discovers principles of fairness and equality. The very fact of cooperation produces a conviction that certain principles are inherent in and facilitate such cooperation. The only intelligible way to play a game is to let everyone have a chance. The only intelligible way to divide a pie is equally, and so forth.

For certain kinds of principles, those involving fairness, justice, and equality, direct social participation seems to be effective. The fact is that children have very strong emotional reactions toward other children, and are bound to develop habits of responding which are effective in social affairs. Piaget describes a procedure whereby moral principles are developed through social interaction and a substantive evaluation of means to effect such interactions. Clearly, however, not all principles can follow from such social relations. For example, a child cannot develop a loyalty to his parents in the mere fact of peer group relations.

(3) *Evaluation.* The habitual theory of moral education is not a method of education so much as it is a method of *indoctrination*. Compared to it, the method of social interaction is a truly educational theory, in that it grounds what is learned in the experiences of relations among people engaged in common tasks. We may generalize this procedure toward a full theory of moral education. Moral education is the *study* of what is valuable in terms of the agent's surroundings, the attitudes of others, his own feelings, and the variety of affections he possesses. In effect, a man learns what is good or bad by studying the most effective means for gaining his desires, fulfilling his loyalties, and realizing his affections. Here we conceive of moral *education* as precisely a method of *evaluation*. Instead of proposing a model where a person *first* acquires a moral education, and then evaluates his surroundings in terms of it, we may consider instead a method of evaluating the world in terms of needs, principles, and consequences, and acquiring a set of regulative, constitutive, and substantive principles on the basis of them.

A moral education is, when scrutinized carefully, not different in kind from education in any subject. The goal of education is not the memorization of facts *alone*, the acquisition of skills *alone*, but in the end to become a thoughtful and knowledgeable person in the subject studied. A student in physics first studies problems assigned by his teachers, memorizes certain laws propounded by his textbooks, and eventually comes to understand enough physics to perform productive tasks in an experimental setting. An education is successful when it leads to thoughtfulness, understanding, and insight.

A moral education is often thought to lead merely to a habitual and virtually automatic obedience to moral principle. But we have seen that moral principles often conflict, and obedience to principle can lead to a disadvantageous moral purity. A further step is required. A man must acquire not only loyalties and commitments, but the ability to choose among them in difficult circumstances, to appraise new possibilities, to deliberate with forethought, to take a long-range view where necessary, to reconsider past judgments and to learn from them. A moral education too must include thoughtfulness, understanding, and insight.

Practice and the acquisition of habits may lead only to automatic responses. A student can give automatic answers to questions on a physics examination, and not know very much about the subject. Physics is learned well only where it leads eventually to questions and investigations. Physics is more a system of inquiry than a system of facts and answers. A first-rate physicist knows the questions to ask more than he knows the answers to give.

Let us apply the same model to morals. Automatic responses are sometimes overly pure, thoughtless, and often mistaken over the long run. A man wise in moral affairs knows of the complexity of moral issues, and of the difficulty of obtaining answers. He recognizes the importance of moral conflicts and of hidden consequences. He realizes the dangers of oversimplification and also the dangers of procrastination. He understands the attitudes and loyalties of other people, and how they bear upon his own loyalties.

How does a man acquire the ability to inquire and the habits of deliberation? Here Aristotle's solution is perfectly correct. A man acquires habits through practice—though the practice must be rewarded and encouraged, not merely imposed. If we wish to develop in moral education habits of supreme loyalty to principles without deliberation or further appraisal, then we may encourage that, and discourage originality and the asking of questions. But if moral questions are acknowledged as complex, and both thoughtfulness and concern are desired, then from the beginning these must be encouraged as well. The analogy with other areas of education holds. A student taught facts and details, and discouraged from originality, will find it difficult after he has mastered all the necessary facts to think inventively and imaginatively about them.

The fundamental principle in all education, and moral education especially, is the principle of the continuum of means and ends. A student learns what he is taught and as he is taught it. It is fantasy to suppose that a student may first learn to repeat and to memorize, and much later do original work as well. If moral evaluation requires both commitment and also open-mindedness, then both must be encouraged from the beginning.

It is to be noted that a student cannot even begin to ask questions in physics until he knows something of the subject. The more ignorant we are, the fewer questions we can pose or even understand. The general problem of education is that we can pose questions only after we have knowledge. Yet we come to this knowledge only by posing questions, or else through memorization. But if we only commit ideas to memory in the beginning, how do we become able to pose questions? The answer can only be that we must also ask questions from the beginning, all through the period of memorization.

Meno poses to Socrates the paradox of learning. How can a man learn anything, since if he is ignorant he can ask no questions nor understand the answers, while if he has knowledge he cannot learn? The paradox rests upon a sharp distinction between learning and the knowledge that is learned. It rests on a sharp separation of means and ends, learning and knowledge. But in what sense are learning and knowledge the same? In inquiry, what is learned and what is investigated are the same. In physics, a scientist acquires knowledge by experimentation and analysis, by inquiry. The emphasis is on the inquiry, not on the end result, which is nothing but the conclusion of the investigation. A great physicist is not great because of the facts he can recite, but in the experiments and studies he has performed.

Analogously, in moral education, the emphasis should not be on what is right and wrong, but on questions and answers, on problems and difficulties. We begin in young children not with orders and commandments *alone*, but with the question of how cooperation and benefits can be gained. Certainly children must be prevented from harming each other and themselves, and rules are necessary. But such rules become effective as moral rules only where they function efficaciously in social affairs. This is Piaget's message. Even further, if men are to be equipped to make difficult moral decisions, they must learn to ask moral questions and to face difficult answers from the very beginning.

Of course, one result of such an approach to moral education is that children will learn quite early that there are few simple answers in moral affairs. But should they not be taught this, if it is true, and to the extent that it is true? Especially, consider the risks we run in pretending that right and wrong are simple notions, and that all men of conscience agree on them. In fact there can be only abstract agreement and great disagreement in particular cases. A child who has never faced a hard question in his thinking is quite vulnerable to a violent intellectual and moral challenge. A child who has dealt with complexity his whole life is equipped to face the challenge of a new difficulty, and to devote the effort necessary to at least partly resolve it. Children educated to think that there are simple solutions become panicked when the solutions cease to be simple—for example, in economic crises or war. The habitual mode of moral education can lead to a violent crisis where habits will no longer serve.

J. Nonconformity

In our preceding discussion of the value, extent, and power of the social dimension of human life, we stressed the bonds provided within society by politics, law, and custom. These ties generate cooperation and stability, and are often quite beneficial. Yet we have noted also that extreme conformity in a society can be quite disadvantageous to the members of the society. The benefits close social ties provide can become evils if they are too powerful. At least one of the differences between a democratic society and a totalitarian one is the degree to which the latter seeks a homogeneous and uniform quality throughout the entire society. Democracy may be rule by the majority. But a good part of its value resides in its heterogeneity and lack of uniformity.

The Western liberal tradition has developed from the principle that individuals have absolute rights. In the Declaration of Independence, these rights are defined as the rights to life, liberty, and the pursuit of happiness. Such a view goes back to Locke, who maintains that a government which violates such rights may be overthrown. This entire approach to revolution and politics suffers from an incurable vagueness. Just why individual men have certain rights and not others is not easy to determine. Indeed, the view that a man has any particular and unique right seems to hold that right to be an absolute good. If so, then men not only have the right to liberty, but an obligation to achieve it; not only a right to life, but an obligation to preserve it; not only a right to happiness, but an obligation to pursue it. If life, liberty, and happiness are supreme values, then anything we can do to attain them for ourselves or others is obligatory. Such an analysis is the antithesis of the view which maintains that individuals have particular rights which are unique to them.

The fundamental difficulty with the model of individual rights as opposed to the oppressive interference of governments is that we seem to postulate a theoretical disjunction between an individual and his society. We have already noted some of the difficulties of this view. On a purely theoretical level, the disjunction is absurd, because society is necessarily constituted by individuals. There can be no social benefits that do not benefit some men. There can be no social actions that are not actions of some men. There can be no social goals that are not goals of some men. There are no social interests which are not the interests of some men. A society may benefit one man instead of another, and that may be bad. But a society which benefits no one cannot be defended on any grounds whatsoever.

It follows that our criticism of societies which are too uniform has two parts. It is easy to see how a coercive society which strives to attain a monolithic uniformity might lead to the overt repression of some imaginative men. We are tempted then to say that social needs and individual needs may be in conflict, Society seeks uniformity and stability. Individuals need diversity and adventure. What we must do is to compromise the different interests of society and individuals.

The whole comparison is absurd. Men certainly may have conflicting interests and have to compromise among them. But society is no man and has no interests of its own. Society seeks no goals which are not goals useful to particular men. A certain degree of uniformity generates stability in social life, a stability which is beneficial to individual persons. We have seen that cooperation can increase productivity and strengthen individual abilities. In addition, men tend to share feelings and concerns, and a degree of sharing is emotionally satisfying also.

But too extreme a uniformity, and men will tend to lose their imaginative abilities and their capacity for original thought. Too great a uniformity can become coercive, and lead to the repression of some particular men. Custom is the binding thread of social life. But if it becomes too strong, it becomes a chain. This chain is unfortunate, however, not only because some men suffer under it, but also because too uniform a society loses its flexibility and adaptability.

It is no more correct to say that society requires strong bonds of cohesion than to say that society requires imagination, invention, and adaptability. Under some circumstances, it is generally advantageous to the members of a society to share a great deal. Under other circumstances, particularly in crisis or in periods of rapid technological change, too great a uniformity can be stifling, and inhibit the imaginative qualities needed for adaptation. Men gain from uniformity in life. They can also be harmed by too great a uniformity. Men gain from being separate and self-reliant to a degree, but independence can also be overdone.

What does seem to be true is that inventiveness and discovery are specifically individual traits. Cooperation and sharing are vital contributions to large-scale projects and achievements. But the development of something new is usually achieved by individual men. Here we can see some of the pitfalls of totalitarianism, especially in a society committed to major changes. For a totalitarian society stresses uniformity at the expense of invention. If it pursues inventiveness also, it may work against itself. On the other hand, a country founded on religion may neither pursue nor propose change. Such a society may consistently stifle all invention and imagination.

Can social homogeneity be justified as a supreme value? Only, it would appear, on the grounds of security. A rigid society with fixed traditions and norms is a secure one for its members. But not perfectly secure. For there are other countries, other men, and nature itself, all of which work their influence on a society, and make it change. The search for perfect security is vain. Worst of all, the rigidity that promotes great security can generate crises from small irregularities. In order to be flexible enough to meet the changes that are inevitable without collapse, a society cannot tolerate total conformity. Nonconformity and conformity are both of value to men collectively in social life. It is one of the most arduous political and moral problems to determine the most effective balance between them. Here too a dynamic equilibrium seems more plausible than a definite and permanent compromise.

There are two basic sources of conformity in society: coercion and custom. The first of these is by far the most obvious, and the issue over which supporters of different political systems vie with each other. Both law and political power together can be used to compel a uniform obedience from members of a society.

Three different issues are important in determining the right degree of coercion to be used in generating conformity within a society. First, there is the question of the *degree* of conformity which is desirable. Too extreme a uniformity within a society can be stifling, and weaken the imaginations of men. Too little uniformity, and society may collapse into chaos, with no common language, system of laws, or reliable expectations.

Second, there is the question of the *type* of uniformity achieved. In theory this might not be a fundamental problem. But in practice, a society which uses force to compel obedience must possess a ruling clique, men who are often not responsible to the same rules as other men. They may be richer. They may merely be above the law. But their uniqueness in a society otherwise highly uniform can be the source of instability. Particularly, the resentments of other men can be upsetting.

Third, there is the crucial problem of the means utilized to achieve uniformity through coercion. The use of power can be extremely destructive. Violence tends to breed further violence. For example, a country with a powerful army to preserve order and to repel invaders can itself become prey of that army if the latter chooses to take power. Another example, a large group of men hunted down for minor acts of deviation are forced to become outlaws, and may move toward major rebellion and even promote a successful revolution.

All in all, the dangers inherent in the use of coercive power to generate conformity are so great that advanced countries have been led to most elaborate safeguards against the misuse of power. Hobbes did not realize that too powerful a ruler would eventually find his own power turned back upon him. A country will gain a far greater stability if it establishes a small degree of coercive conformity, achieved by an absolute *minimum* of force, and relies on custom for all further conformity. A minimally coercive country is also a far more beneficial one.

Custom then becomes the great source of uniformity in social life. And since it is supported by no coercion and no particular body of men, its repressive qualities may be overlooked. A society of great uniformity and strong customs may offer its citizens quite literally security in their lives, tremendous liberty from external and arbitrary power, and a total opportunity to pursue happiness, and yet not make them very happy. There can be two reasons for this. First, the customs may be severely out of date, and not apply to contemporary life in a satisfactory way. For example, the custom of arranged marriages may be followed closely yet quite disadvantageously, in a society of great geographical and class mobility.

Second, a society can become too uniform, so much so as to obliterate all sense of personal identity in its individual members. Individual men seem to require a principle of differentiation beyond that of mere distinctness. In some societies, social classes provide uniqueness. In others, identity comes through vocation or family. But a society where families, houses, vocations, and economic classes all become indistinguishable in any important respects may be intolerable to its members. This cannot be fully proved on the basis of our present knowledge. But many recent events in the United States can be explained on the basis of such a principle.

QUESTIONS

1. A man is asked to betray his friends. Explain how an egoist might argue that he should not do so. Are these arguments defensible?
2. In what ways would a society in which everyone acted from self-interest be a good one? Would it be preferable to ours? Would it be different from ours? How?
3. Is it good to be altruistic? Discuss the issues raised by this question.
4. In what ways are the interests of the agent more important to his moral decisions than are the interests of other people? Does this justify egoism?
5. Is a man emotionally indifferent to the sufferings of another person obligated to help him? Why?
6. To what extent can a man extricate himself from his social surroundings? What benefits are gained by trying to do so?
7. Discuss the advantages and disadvantages of local versus centralized systems for the making of political decisions.
8. State the anarchist case against government and evaluate it.
9. To what extent do governments need to use force to govern well?
10. If we assume that either parents or the schools are supposed to teach children right from wrong, how do the educational effects of government, law, and custom affect this process?
11. Should we obey laws we consider unjust?
12. To what extent are laws dependent on fear?
13. How important is knowledge of other people to moral and political decisions? How is this knowledge to be obtained? How do law and custom contribute to our knowledge of other people?
14. Are all men equal before the law? Should they be? Is this principle essential to justice?
15. In what sense is custom the foundation of social life?
16. Should men deliberate on every moral issue which faces them? What alternative is there to this deliberation?
17. Do you think human life would be better if men did not experience shame or fear it?
18. Can torture ever be justified as a form of punishment?
19. Is it wrong to take away a man's right to vote after he is convicted for theft? Discuss from the point of view of different theories of punishment.

20. On what basis should we decide that a given punishment is too severe?
21. What would be the result if all forms of moral condemnation were eliminated?
22. What shall we do with chronic repeaters of criminal acts?
23. "Criminals should be treated as if they were ill. Only trained psychologists should work in prisons." Discuss.
24. How do we learn right from wrong? Are we taught it?
25. Can morality be legislated?

SELECTED READINGS

Works on egoism:

Hobbes, *Leviathan*, xiii–xxx. An important study of polity and social order also.
R. G. Olson, *The Morality of Self-Interest*, 1965, Harcourt Brace & World.

Works on politics and social organization:

Aristotle, *Politics*.
M. Weber, "Politics as a Vocation," *From Max Weber*, 1958, Oxford University. The entire book covers the range of political and social affairs. Well worth reading.
E. Durkheim, *The Division of Labor in Society*, 1933, Macmillan.
G. H. Mead, *Mind, Self and Society*, 1934, University of Chicago.
R. M. MacIver, *The Modern State*, 1926, Oxford University.
R. Pound, *Introduction to the Philosophy of Law*, 1925, Yale University.
J. Dewey, *Human Nature and Conduct*, 1922. An important treatment of custom.

On love:

Sartre, *Being and Nothingness*, Part III, Ch. III, I.
Plato, *Symposium*.
E. Fromm, *The Art of Loving*, 1962, Harper.
S. Freud, *Civilization and Its Discontents*.

VII. THE UNJUST
SOCIETY

A. Justice in an unjust society

One of the most striking themes of Plato's *Republic* is the implicit question of whether a just man can live in an unjust society. Unfortunately, Plato himself does not directly address the question, and we are denied his explicit answer. On the one hand, we have Socrates, who surely must be regarded as a just man, living in the imperfect society of Athens. On the other hand, we recall that Socrates is found guilty of corrupting the Athenian youth, and offered merely the choice of exile or death. His term of life as a just man in an unjust society must be regarded as limited. In the *Republic*, Plato develops the theory of individual justice solely in the context of as perfect and just a society as can be imagined, as if to say that without social justice, individual men cannot be expected to be just. On the other hand, the society described in the *Republic* is based on the existence of a philosopher-king as ruler. If an ordinary society cannot provide such a man, then the *Republic* is utopian and wholly unrealistic. Finally, Socrates' fundamental point throughout nine books of the *Republic* is that justice is a good in itself. It is always better to be a just rather than an unjust man, in any society whatsoever. A man who accepts Socrates' argument seems then to be committed to acting morally no matter what evil surrounds him.

The question of whether a just man can live in an unjust society is ambiguous. There are two distinct though interrelated questions which are implicated. The first is whether a just man can *survive* in the midst of injustice. Will he be put to death? Will he be corrupted? Can a man even learn right from wrong in an evil world? The second question is whether justice is the same in a just and an unjust society. Do exceptional circumstances call for exceptional deeds? Does an evil society require a heroic morality? Does morality in times of crisis differ significantly from morality in times of peace and stability?

The second question is the one we will devote the major part of our attention to. The first, however, is by no means irrelevant to the second, nor is it uninteresting in itself. Plato himself notes that the kind of person who would in a just society become a philosopher is, in an evil society, subjected to the greatest temptations possible, and is virtually certain to be corrupted by them. His very intelligence makes him a desirable tool for other men to use. In more modern terms, the brightest young men can succeed most easily in the worst of activities—advertising or politics. The temptations of material success totally overwhelm the possibility that a brilliant man might discover that not wealth and power but knowledge and justice are the greater goods.

There are four grounds on which we may doubt that a just man can be found living in an unjust society.

(1) In an extremely evil society, a just man will be jailed or killed. Let us take Nazi Germany as our first example. A man of secure moral principles would have opposed the regime, would have spoken out strongly against its evil practices, against the concentration camps, and would have been arrested and placed in a concentration camp himself. These camps were not filled with Jews only, but also with political prisoners. A just man would have been obligated to stand in political opposition to evil. Being just, he would necessarily have had to meet his obligations. He would most likely have died for his beliefs.

We might hold that a just man would indeed have an obligation to oppose so evil a society, but that his opposition should be kept secret. A secret opposition, coupled with covert sabotage of the workings of the government, might be more effective in accomplishing something worth while than an opposition which leads to nothing but one's own death. There were a few—unfortunately, *very* few— German soldiers who helped prisoners escape from concentration camps. In the end, such soldiers were usually caught and killed. The secrecy proposed should be thought of as a way, not to secure the life of a just man, but to improve his effectiveness in achieving good results. In the end, he will probably be killed.

Secrecy has its special risks, especially if it is directed toward self-preservation rather than effectiveness. There might be thousands of just men who oppose tyranny, who together could overthrow it, but all of whom remain silent from fear. Silence may lead not to greater effectiveness but to impotence. Here it becomes not a means to action but a temptation and a corruption.

A just man who openly opposes a tyrannical government will be taken and eliminated. He cannot survive in so unjust a society. Suppose, then, the just man withdraws in peace and solitude, and maintains his goodness in his personal life. To many people, such withdrawal is cowardice and even injustice. A man makes himself an implicit instrument of the state in not openly opposing it. Thoreau claims without qualification, "Under a government which imprisons any unjustly, the true place for a just man is also a prison."

The choices left to a just man amidst evil powers are all in vain. Either he remains just and is killed, or he capitulates to silence and compromises himself.

Compromise may be not half justice, but half evil. Take a man who from fear first remains silent, then joins the local party in uniform, next beats some Jews because he is afraid to appear different, and finally cooperates in their murder. He would not have been willing at first to kill anyone. But each step in fear and compromise makes the next one easier.

If secret opposition is justified in an evil society—and many men would argue that it is—then we move to the second aspect of justice surrounded by injustice: that morality is different during a crisis. For clearly in ordinary circumstances, evil is to be openly fought and condemned. Secrecy is seldom mere silence. It is usually half cooperation. A spy is most valuable when he has risen high in the enemy hierarchy. And he can do so only by being effective as an enemy agent. Secret opposition is really an opposition which rests on complicity. Is it right to commit small evil deeds in order to forestall major ones? That is the larger question this chapter will confront.

Finally, if the risks of a just man in an unjust society are not sufficiently clear in reference to Nazi Germany, let us consider the adventures of a just man incarcerated in a concentration camp. Fighting back means certain death. Cooperating and joining the Germans may enable a man to survive. Obviously the risk of death is very high in any case. But it is also true that the prisoners who aided the Germans often survived longer, and some came through alive. What is justice in such appalling circumstances? Especially, we know that if one man turns down the post of trustee, another will take it.

Turning away from such extremity, we look instead at an ordinary society, with its imperfections and temptations, and the continual need for compromise. Every society has its poor. How can a just man live comfortably when others are poor? How far shall we extend Thoreau's principle that while men are imprisoned unjustly, a just man should also be in jail? If there are slaves, shall a just man be in prison? If there is racial discrimination, shall a just man be in prison? Note that a man in prison makes a poor father. A man in prison cannot vote. Thoreau assumes that if all just men enter jail, they will triumph. This is simply not always the case.

In Athens, Socrates was condemned for his teaching. In Nazi Germany, men who opposed the state were jailed and killed. In a democratic society, men who oppose the social norms are sometimes jailed, if they refuse to fight a war. They may be jailed even for advocating opposition to the war. They may be jailed for breaking trespass laws to fight racial discrimination. They may be jailed for openly advocating a new form of government. Most often men who oppose the society in fundamental ways are neutralized. They are kept from political power, from jobs, and from the public news media.

Such neutralization is not death, though it is a form of exile. Just men in partly unjust societies do survive. They are left with their lives and their liberties. But their effectiveness as agents is destroyed. This is one of the great advances contemporary societies have made over past societies. Men can be so completely neutralized as agents that their personal convictions and actions have no influence.

Socrates was condemned because the Athenians thought he mattered. To an unjust society, a just man is an enemy. But in a complex modern society, he can be rendered impotent. The fate of a just man in a democratic but partly unjust society is not his death but the death of his beliefs. This is a very great advance in justice, one of the major reasons why democratic societies are only partly unjust.

(2) A more important question than whether a just man will be killed by an unjust society is whether he will be able to preserve his moral convictions. The strongest weapon of an unjust society is not its open and naked force, but its subtle temptations and its varied forms of corruption. A just man, after all, must live within society. The steps he takes in his daily activities may warp his moral convictions beyond repair.

We have already noted the corrupting effect of compromise in an evil society. Open opposition means death. A just man then opposes evil secretly. But every step into secrecy is a form of corruption. Everyone salutes *der Fuehrer*. Dare a man refuse? Everyone displays the flag on holidays. Dare a man show himself to be different? All the men in a town volunteer for the army. Dare one of them be different? In an evil society, to be different is to bring attention and suffering upon oneself.

But every compromise has its effects upon the moral strengths of a man. Once a man has done something he believes is wrong, in the interests of compromise, then he discovers that it is not so difficult to do. He learns to live comfortably with it. He makes excuses to himself. Worst of all, he comes to the realization that many things are more important than his moral scruples. They must be more important because he has chosen them.

Compromise can be and often is corrupting. Nevertheless, there is a fundamental difference between compromising a firm moral belief to obtain effectiveness in action, and compromising a belief that is neither firm nor clear. We are speaking of compromising a belief in a moral principle. A German may be opposed to killing and to the concentration camps. But he may compromise from fear or even to function in secret.

Consider instead a man whose moral convictions are formed within the evil society. Others tell him that the national destiny will be served by extermination of weaker races. He can rise in status and in wealth through becoming an obedient and efficient servant of the state. Most important of all, the basis on which people gain praise or blame is not their moral goodness, but their efficiency in achieving evil ends. How is a man to avoid corruption here?

In many societies, prestige and status depend on wealth and power. The pathway to either of them is a path of corruption. Wealth is acquired through business practices which are often shady and certainly inhumane. The great wealthy families in the United States were formed by men who were brutal in their dealings. If the rich are admired, and wealth is acquired in unchristian ways, how can Christian values be accepted as higher? As for power, it comes through politics, which is notoriously a field of almost total compromise.

Politics is the most obvious arena where compromise is a basic corruption. A politician can become powerful only by gaining votes. But votes are won on two fronts, neither of which rests on a secure morality. A politician must work within his party, with the loyalty of party workers by compromising with them and promising them favors. He must also tell the voters what they want to hear. After election, he gains effectiveness in office again through compromise. A bill he favors must be sold to other politicians. The fundamental principle of politics is mutual back-scratching. Is it realistic that a man of great respect for power will remain uncorrupted by the practices of political life? Rather, the means of political life which are compromises and half-truths become the ends themselves.

The principle of the continuum of means and ends makes it clear that where the means are unjust, the end will be tainted by that injustice. But in an unjust society, all the means are partly unjust. The society is unjust in that the powers that rule it are corrupt. The great dilemma is that to be effective, one must work with the existing powers which are corrupt, and be corrupted oneself. To remain morally pure, we must remain aloof from power, and impotent as well.

(3) The greatest corruption of injustice is not its control of power, but its appearance as justice. An unjust society does not represent itself as unjust, but as just. To a child growing up in a society, what the society represents as right and wrong *is* right and wrong. The most important reason why a just man cannot easily live in an evil society is that his education provides him with no means for the development of secure and defensible moral values. An unjust society educates its children toward injustice.

Moral education is the development of secure moral principles based on the teaching of one's parents, one's natural affections and desires, what proves satisfactory in one's life, and the norms of society. In many societies, there are a great variety of conflicting norms and regulative principles, which provide a variety of differing moral beliefs. But it is important to realize that many of the apparently separate elements of moral education can in practice support each other.

We take as our model here not a society like Nazi Germany, which changed in a short span of time from conventional norms to a very different set of norms. Rather, we take a partly unjust society which has remained much the same in its laws and values over several generations. What we find is that a child growing up in this society encounters the unjust social norms several times over. The teachings of his parents represent what they have come to believe is right and wrong. They live successfully in society, so their moral convictions are in general the same as the social norms. In addition, the institutions of society reward individuals who conform to them. A child growing up in a society founded on a work ethos will be taught respect for work by his parents, will find this respect around him, and will succeed in winning both approval and more tangible rewards wholly through hard work.

A materialistic society which fosters the belief that possessions are the goal of life supports that belief at every turn. A child grows up in a home with possessions,

and knows that his parents have struggled to gain them and take pride in them.
If he is poor, he is aware of the tremendous desire his parents have for possessions, and their sense of failure in lacking them. The child is surrounded by advertising and by possessions. He finds that the wealthiest men are most admired in his community. He discovers that occupations are ranked according to income. It is a rare person who can live in a materialistic society and remain uncorrupted by it.

At best there are two sources of alternative values. First, all societies are diverse in their values, though to differing degrees. A child does encounter some spiritual aspirations, though he usually realizes that they are of little practical importance. Second, there are indeed natural affections and desires, which must be at least partly satisfied. Sometimes they are not. All too often, a materialistic society satisfies precisely the simplest and most immediate needs, and provides at least sensory delights. If greater satisfactions would come from discipline or dedication, they may be wholly lost within the unjust society's pleasures.

Let us, however, suppose that the materialistic values deemed highest in an unjust society are felt to be unsatisfactory by a child within it. They do not meet his needs. How shall he develop alternative principles and values? There may be no source for alternative values but the values he has rejected. Under such conditions, a man will define new values wholly negatively. He will move to an opposite extreme. If possessions and middle-class life are insensitive and unjust, then a child becomes an ascetic, one who scorns all possessions, all work, all discipline, all comfort. Such a position is quite common among young people who scorn the middle-class values they consider empty.

The problem is that life is a complex in which many values intersect. An extreme version of life is not likely to be satisfactory. Both extreme materialism and extreme asceticism are likely to prove inadequate, either individually or politically. The child growing up in an unjust society is virtually certain to accept that society's values as his own. But should he reject them, then he will be led, not to a realistic alternative, but to an extreme negativism which is not defensible either.

Moral decision rests on a ground of principles and of feelings. Most of the time, the principles which are social norms are adopted by a member of that society without question. On occasion, a man may reject such principles strongly. The deeper effect of the unjust society on its members is found in the feelings they develop and expect. In particular, a society can lead its members to expect never to be satisfied, to believe in sacrifice and dedication. Eventually, men who have seldom experienced intense satisfactions become incapable of appreciating them or pursuing them.

In a materialistic society founded on inflated advertising claims, men are taught to judge their happiness by their immediate pleasures, by the beautiful women that pursue them, by their possessions, and by their popularity. The greatest source of corruption in Western society is its emphasis on immediacy of sensory pleasure, to the point where men come to expect ecstasy as their due, and judge all values ecstatically. In Plato's terms, the appetites can become so inflated as to make any clear judgment of a future value which involves a present sacrifice almost impossible.

(4) The last and most serious difficulty a just man faces in an unjust society is not of temptation or corruption, nor even of the formation of his values. It is the theoretical problem of what constitutes justice in an evil society. We touched on it in discussing moral education in an immoral society. The society will declare the highest values to be lesser ones, and lesser values to be great ones. Far more important is the question of whether the same kinds of actions are right in both a just and an unjust society. During war, a man must fight and kill, even though killing is wrong in a just society.

In the rest of this chapter, we will address the variety of arguments which are given to justify war, spying, and killing. It is a commonly held position that a just man in times of crisis must perform actions which would not be right at other times. If this is true, then moral decisions really do take on a mystical and other-worldly air. For all societies are imperfect. All societies have their injustices. Under what conditions, then, is it right to violate our moral convictions *in the name of morality*? Can a man believe that lying is wrong and still act as a spy in his country's interests?

The theoretical difficulty is related to the fact that moral principles are not separable from each other, but form a system. We noted in our discussion of substantive appraisal that a moral principle in itself cannot easily be judged as beneficial or not. Rather, a whole system of principles is found to be beneficial or disadvantageous. In particular, substantive appraisal is the evaluation of a system of regulative principles as to their effectiveness and benefit in a given social setting. For example, we may substantively appraise the tenets of Christian morality, especially charity and brotherly love, in a country at war. It would not seem to many people that charity and love are beneficial ideals in a time of emergency. The general problem is that substantive appraisal is always performed within the setting provided by the society which defines the relevant norms.

Consider the Eastern ideal of selflessness in a postRomantic Western society. Romanticism is founded on the principle that the unique individuality of a man is the foundation of all value. The strength of Romanticism is that it makes all governments look to individual men for their justification. Romanticism tends to emphasize idiosyncrasy and even neurosis as individuality. Men who are too much alike have lost their creative spark. The strength of Romanticism is considerable. It militates against too great a uniformity and homogeneity.

Nevertheless, once uniqueness of individuality is a dominant ideal, the notion of selflessness is almost unintelligible by comparison. The incorporation of a moral ideal from another culture into a given one may be impossible until significant changes have taken place in both, due to the complex interconnection of ideals, feelings, and ways of living.

A similar incompatibility may exist between the ideals of a just man and the values of an unjust society. In the *Republic*, Plato argues that a man without possessions, without family, without luxuries, and without many sensory pleasures will be happy. An ascetic and dedicated life in the service of the Good (for the philosopher), or even in service to a craft, is a happy one. Suppose Plato were correct. Could the average member of a materialistic society possibly accept or even understand his position? Clearly not, for it is alien to the values he has acquired in his social life. So also, if a man from the brutal period of the Italian Renaissance were brought back to life, he might well find a peaceful society with a reverence for human life quite far from ideal.

The point is not merely that a man may be so corrupted by an unjust society as to be unable to recognize what is truly valuable. It is that the very basis of the judgment of what is of value depends on social learning, especially the feelings men develop as they become adults. In a fundamental sense, what is good must be beneficial to someone. But if a society is so unjust that it develops an abhorrence in its members toward what is beneficial, they will not be benefited by it. A totally competitive society might be so successful that its members would be bored and unhappy in a world of peace and plenty.

It follows from this discussion that the determination of what is just or right in a society evil by the standards proposed is a very difficult one. It is especially problematic because if we were to be able overnight to change our society into the one we considered ideal, *it might not benefit the members of that society.* This is one of the most difficult problems for all revolutions, and one of the reasons why revolutions tend to require violence long after they have succeeded in their purposes.

B. Heroism

Shall we conclude that a just man in an unjust society must be a hero? If he compromises, he is led to corruption and weakness. If he is weak and afraid, the injustices will continue. Is not Thoreau right that a just man belongs in jail in an unjust society?

Two different cases can be made for heroism. Together they constitute a strong argument for it. Yet individually there is much to be said by way of qualification for each of them. First, our moral principles obligate us to conform to them. In the interests of sheer morality, heroism is required. Men may be weak, but their weakness is immoral. Second, Thoreau's argument is that if all just men would oppose tyranny openly, the tyranny could no longer continue. Let us look at each of these arguments a bit more closely.

(1) The view that a moral principle simply obligates us to follow it come what may, and regardless of circumstances and consequences, is another example of the moral purity which we have encountered throughout our analysis. We recall that such moral purity is particularly risky because it often leads to consequences which are extremely undesirable in terms of its own ideals.

We recall also that a man in an unjust society has a particularly difficult task of ascertaining just what is truly valuable when he is surrounded by false values. It is not so difficult to repudiate an evil. It is sometimes extremely difficult to discover an alternative that is much better. It is easy to say that war is evil and to oppose it. It is extremely difficult in a time of international crisis to find a way of avoiding war, or a satisfactory alternative to the difficulties which are everywhere.

A man who conforms to a moral principle regardless of circumstances and temptations will certainly be led into a heroic attitude. On the other hand, a man who conforms to a moral principle regardless of circumstances and consequences is morally pure and verges on the fanatical. A man who will not tell a lie to save an innocent man's life is a fanatic, not a hero. If he is regarded as a hero, it is a heroism easy to attain. Kierkegaard notes that there is a tragic heroism which consists in placing a moral law above everything. Agamemnon sacrifices his daughter Iphigenia to obtain favorable winds for the Greek ships to sail to Troy. He sacrifices his daughter for the glory of Greece. But, Kierkegaard notes, there is something greater than this, according to which a father's love for his child makes that sacrifice evil. At least, a hero who would commit a moral sacrifice for his ideals must be aware of the evil of his own actions.

Moral heroism is surrounded on all sides by dangers. Too close an acceptance of a moral law can bring us to fanaticism, where nothing matters but duty, neither love, self-interest, nor human lives. Too great a hesitation before a crisis and the time for action will have passed. Too quick action may be the result of blindness to particular circumstances. Too close attention to the price duty requires and we may never be able to act at all. The line for true heroism is very fine. Yet heroism is a broad and noble gesture, quite unconcerned with fine distinctions and subtle points of differentiation.

A German who opposed Hitler in 1941 would have done so with a vanishingly small chance of success, and a great likelihood of failure. Suppose he were married, with a family. To have spoken out against Hitler would have meant his death and the suffering of his family, with virtually no prospect of overthrowing the regime. This is a heroism that is fanaticism. It is acting according to duty where we cannot succeed, and where the price of failure is high. Duty seems absurd if it ignores the circumstances and consequences. Particularly, an agent must look ahead to the probability of his success or failure, and the price involved in each case. A man who fights evil by speaking out against it when he is weak and it is powerful, and who takes no steps to protect himself, is no hero, but a fool.

On the other hand, Hannah Arendt has pointed out that many Germans justified themselves after the Second World War by the argument that they could do nothing with any chance of success. The circumstances made opposition almost impossible, Yet, Miss Arendt notes, some Germans did try to oppose the Nazi regime. And, she notes as well, if many Germans had separately fought the regime, each believing himself alone, yet in concert, they would have succeeded in weakening it considerably. This is another version of the second argument.

(2) Thoreau claims that if all just men were in jail, the government could not long continue its unjust practices. We may divide his and Miss Arendt's

argument into two parts: first, that an unjust government would be forced to change if all just men opposed it openly; second, that silent opposition often works in practice as a tacit acquiescence in official policies. For example, a man against a war his country is pursuing, but who pays his taxes and speaks against the war only in private, in effect supports the war in two ways. He pays for it as much as anyone else. And he merges with the "silent majority" which the government requires for its own policies.

The second point is certainly correct, and requires no further qualification. All governments, however tyrannical, require the tacit support of the majority of their citizens. In return, men often find it difficult to stand alone in a vulnerable position. The more silent we are, the more silent we lead others to be. The more silence is coupled with obedience to law, the more custom generates a secure uniformity behind official policies, whether just or not. The major argument in favor of heroism is that anything less supports tyranny and injustice.

A further aspect of this argument is the temptation cowardice generates. We have noted this before. Suppose a man remains silent first, believing himself in a minority, but vows never to actively support injustice. Nevertheless, he will remain silent from fear and frustration. His silence and the silence of others like him lead to the strengthening of the tyranny, and the use of more severe means of repression. Eventually he is asked to join the army or to work for the government. Dare he now refuse? The earlier silence leads to a more desperate situation, where he must either actively join the forces of evil, or suffer extreme penalties.

As for the first point, that just men acting in concert against tyranny will succeed, such an argument has little foundation in fact. In the United States today, opposition to the Vietnam war has grown steadily through the past seven years, yet without forcing the end of the war. And the United States is not Nazi Germany, Spain, or Greece. If all Greeks today opposed the rule of the Colonels, would that lead to their overthrow? Not obviously. A military regime always controls the superior weapons. In addition, no tyranny is wholly without support among its citizens. The greatest danger is that open opposition might lead to nothing better than the imprisonment or death of the opposition.

Thoreau's argument that just men ought to oppose injustice where they find it, though the risks are great that the agent and all opposition may be destroyed, is an argument from *desperation*. Not to oppose injustice is in effect to support it, and to make it harder to eliminate later. Such an argument is a powerful one, but it involves a large number of risks. Desperation is always a precarious ground for action. We may summarize the moral issues relevant to the subject of heroism as follows:

(a) Heroism which is strict and unqualified conformity to a moral law may lead to moral purity which is no longer justifiable. Once we consider circumstances and consequences, then the risks and small probability of success seem to make some forms of heroism nothing but foolhardiness. Why get yourself killed while accomplishing nothing?

(b) In an unjust society, especially in times of crisis, early opposition is often far less risky and more likely of success than later. A man who postpones opposition to evil from fear or passivity may find the evil grown and the risks far greater later.

(c) In our earliest discussion of expediency, we noted that expediency is a lack of commitment to a regulative moral principle. This is exactly what moral cowardice is as well. Where a man's loyalty to principle is too weak, he will compromise it from fear of pain or death. The irony here is clear, especially in the light of (b). We compromise our principles because we are not deeply loyal to them, and because we are fearful of death. What we may discover is that the evil grows to become unbearable, worse than an honorable death.

(d) This brings us to the more general question of whether it is worth remaining alive at any price. To Plato and Aristotle, life in itself seems to have little value. What is worth while is a life lived well. From (b) we note again that a man becomes corrupted by evil. A man surrounded by good things might consider a life in jail not worth living. A man after several years of jail is far less likely to consider it worth dying to avoid. It does not follow that either is obviously correct. Rather, in evaluation we must take circumstances and feelings into account. And they tend to affect each other. This is the strongest reason for conceiving of moral evaluation in terms of realistic ideals rather than simple rules alone.

(e) Moral purity can lead to evil consequences. Countries often go to war from purity rather than prudence. Compromises are often the most effective solution to complex and unresolvable differences. But if compromise is sometimes and even frequently a good, then heroism has far less apparent justification. Of course, we may note the reply that one cannot compromise with evil. But in practice, no principle has caused more misery than that puristic one.

(f) Moral purity is a form of dogmatism. The only grounds for it are an unfailing commitment to a regulative principle. As soon as we consider consequences, however, we are forced into a modest fallibilism. It is never possible to be absolutely certain of the right thing to do. It follows that heroism is extremely risky.

(g) The most plausible ground for moral heroism is that of desperation. Where the powers that rule are evil, and we will by conformity live in misery, then opposition is risky but unavoidable. We should not overlook Hobbes' argument here. He maintains that chaos can be considerably worse than most tyrannical regimes. On the one hand, a desperate man has little to lose. On the other, the risks of desperate action are considerable. He may indeed lose more than he thinks, and harm others as well.

(h) Desperation is a frightening condition. A desperate man can do terrible things. It follows that desperation should be avoided, both on an individual and also on the social level. It is the society's responsibility to avoid conditions which generate the need for heroism. The same conclusion is supported by the fact that men are not inclined to perform heroic acts easily. The only way to avoid their falling easily into guilt is to avoid conditions which require heroism. Here the continuum of means and ends reminds us that where heroism is both required and practiced frequently, it tends to perpetuate the very crises which called it forth. Revolutions tend to remain in a state of crisis far too long. The way to avoid the need for heroism is to refuse from the beginning to condone it. All societies face the consequences of heroism when their soldiers come home from the war. There are always a few who have learned too well to kill, and learned little else.

All of these considerations make moral heroism an extremely problematical matter. There are many excellent reasons for avoiding it. There are also conditions which make it unavoidable. It seems impossible to find a rule telling us when heroism is or is not called for. Ideals, principles, circumstances, consequences, and the risks involved must all be taken into consideration. Here is a decision which a man must make for himself, which no one and no rule can make for him. All we can ask of a man is that he make his decision based on as full as possible knowledge of the circumstances, consequences, and values involved, both obvious ones and hidden ones.

There remains for consideration the problem of whether morality in times of crisis is different in kind from morality in times of peace and stability.

C. Crisis

The most obvious distinction between actions in times of crisis and actions in more stable times is the appeal to expediency to justify actions required in an emergency. *The end justifies the means.* Clearly, a man who subscribes to this principle without qualification has repudiated all other regulative principles of morality. Let us consider several crises, and ask whether the principle that the end justifies the means is plausible in each of them.

(1) If our country is at war, and fighting for its liberty at the hands of a nation that wishes to conquer it and enslave its people, many of us would agree that the duty of every citizen is to fight to repel the invaders. It is true that pacifists are opposed to any war, and will refuse to fight in any. All of us feel the temptation of pacifism, not least because it is a moral position which provides considerable security. A man who concedes that it is sometimes right to kill in war is left with the decision of when and how. A pacifist has no further decisions to make.

The problem of when to fight a war and how is not removed by the general principle that wars are sometimes justified. Can we settle the problem by the principle of expediency? It does not seem so. First of all, many men are more than willing to defend their country against attack, but are opposed to fighting in a war to enrich it. The crisis of a war does not lead them to a principle of mere expediency. Second, most people agree that *some* rules are necessary during war. Certain weapons are to be forbidden, such as biological weapons or poison gases. Torture and the killing of helpless prisoners is wrong. And it does not seem that such actions would be made right by the mere winning of the war.

On the other hand, contrast two wars, one in defense against an enemy who commits all sorts of atrocities in the field, the other against a neighbor over a disputed piece of territory. Many people would condone actions in the first case which would be indefensible in the second. Here it is not the war itself which matters, but the end sought and circumstances under which the war takes place.

Finally, we should note that, in most wars, it is seldom possible for the ordinary soldier to distinguish the two cases just mentioned. A war over territory is represented as a patriotic defense of the homeland. It follows that a man needs two protections if he is to be able to avoid evil during war. First, he needs as much information as he can get about the war and the political circumstances surrounding it. Second, he must avoid like the plague too expedient a conception of the morality of war. Without secure rules of war, a soldier will find it too easy to commit atrocities. Even in war, the regulative rules must be clear and rather strong.

(2) All countries have vested in their rulers emergency powers, which enable the summary arrest of citizens, jailing without a hearing, even military trials and executions. Canada recently resorted to its emergency powers after the kidnapping of a government official. Most men agree that governments require emergency powers of an exceptional character. During the Second World War, emergency powers were declared in Hawaii and enforced. The case of the tens of thousands of loyal Japanese-Americans who were interned during the same war is well known and little defended today.

But the very fact that the interning of a whole group of people on grounds of racial background is no longer condoned shows that sheer expediency is not thought defensible even during an unquestionable emergency. Shall emergency powers include the power to execute any individual on the judgment of a military leader? Few judges would think so. The Supreme Court has upheld the principle that men may be *detained* during a crisis, if it is thought that they might increase the danger to the country. But punishments may not be exercised on them during the crisis.

The notion that an emergency calls for special provisions is tempered considerably in many people's thinking by the need to consider the extent of the crisis, the nature of the crisis, whether the powers called for are truly bene-ficial or necessary, and so forth. Sheer success does not justify the means used, if the success did not require these means, and even where the success is not of utmost importance.

(3) In general, it is thought wrong for a man to kill another. Yet it is usually considered not only acceptable but right for a man to kill in self-defense. Does the end of saving one's life justify the killing? Apparently. But would saving one's life justify torturing another person? Would using a bomb that would kill several other people as well as the would-be murderer? To many people, the answer would have to be no. In some cases, it is right to do what would be wrong in other cir-

cumstances. But circumstances and consequences definitely matter. The end does not in itself justify the means.

(4) An even more obvious case is the right given to a policeman to kill a criminal. Clearly it is sometimes necessary for a policeman to use his weapons. But almost everyone including the police would agree that the use of guns should be controlled by rather definite rules and depends on circumstances. Police and their critics differ not on the principle of control, but on the exact rules and circumstances involved. In a sense, the consequences are of utmost importance in determining what is right. But they do not justify any means whatsoever. Very strict rules are required to determine what is right and what is wrong.

In all these cases, it is incorrect to say without further qualification that the end justifies the means. Rather, different circumstances call for different actions. But the regulative principles involved appear to be the same. Put another way, the principle of expediency suggests that no regulative principles govern crises other than itself. In practice, few people act or approve of actions of others based on expediency alone. Let us consider the difficulties inherent in sheer expediency.

(a) The idea that the end justifies the means in principle sets all regulative principles aside. Yet in two respects expediency depends on regulative ideals. First, the end can justify the means only where the end possesses considerable value. Clearly we have the regulative ideal in force that this end is a good and ought to be secured. But we have so far neglected the element of crisis. The principle of expediency is plausible only where we have a conflict among ends and means—the conflict inherent in the crisis. For example, national security is an important end to achieve. And we seek to gain it under all circumstances except where it will cost too many human lives. The crisis arises only because the two important values have come into conflict. One man may hold that preserving lives is an end worth any means. Another holds that national security is a goal worth any number of lives. Both men are moral purists.

Thus, moral expediency is not the antithesis of moral purity, but another form of that purity. An end can justify any and all means required to achieve it only if that end is a supreme one, and all other ideals worthless by comparison.

Second, we have seen that moral expediency in practice is not so extreme as we have just assumed. In all the examples discussed above, the end was to be realized through means regulated carefully by moral principles. If expediency is at all defensible, and is not an extreme form of the purity it opposes, it must rest on implicit regulative principles taken for granted. For example, it is expedient to fight a war using any means required *except* those prohibited by law, custom, or ordinary moral decency. During an emergency, anything is permissible *provided* it conforms as much as possible to the moral rules of peacetime. Killing all suspected persons might end the emergency, but it would be wrong beyond question if the emergency could be overcome without killing.

In other words, the principle of expediency is almost never followed literally or taken seriously. It is rather parasitic on all the moral principles it ostensibly rejects. The end of national security justifies any means used to gain it *provided*: (1) national security is the most important ideal involved; and (2) it can be realized in no better way than through the means used. Expediency is offered in place of all moral principles. Yet it is in practice nothing other than the position that a higher ideal may require the sacrifice of lesser values. Who would deny that?

(b) The purity of the principle that the end justifies the means leads to a dangerous half-truth—that history and the passing of time provide the only reliable test of an action. It follows that a man cannot and even need not try to determine what is right in advance. Moral decisions are too complex to settle definitely until all the facts and consequences are known. Therefore, a man can tell whether his actions are right only in terms of the final results. A war is shown to be justified by victory and by a satisfactory resolution. All means are risky. All means are both good and bad. Only time can tell.

The dangers here are obvious. On this argument, a man may do anything, leaving it to posterity to determine whether he was right or wrong—a posterity long after his own death. Only a believer in divine judgment would be swayed by the indefinite future. More to the point, the argument is an excuse for ignoring all present rules and information, since they cannot guarantee the future. It is an excuse for avoiding the use of intelligence. The argument should be turned on its head. Rather, a man can base his decisions only on the information he has before him and the principles in force at the time of his decision. If he cannot justify a course of action in terms of what he knows, it is irresponsible to appeal to posterity to justify him. Nevertheless, no action, however well grounded in available information and ideals, can be assured of success in the indefinite future.

(c) Expediency is, when taken literally, sheer desperation, and a rationalized blindness as well. In effect, setting all considerations of means aside leaves an agent with no basis whatsoever for his future expectations. If regulative principles have any substantive basis—and if they do not, they may be criticized for it—then conforming to them is likely to maximize the beneficial consequences. The man of expediency is actually a man of little vision, who repudiates those principles which have any chance at all of grounding his decisions. On the other hand, if expediency is but the tailoring of actions to circumstances given such circumstances, it is exactly what all moral decision is and must be.

(d) In its worst forms, the principle that the end justifies the means becomes a messianic vision. A revolutionary may believe that the new order can come about only by the destruction of the old. A phoenix will rise from the ashes. Such a view is a union of the two most dangerous moral stances: nihilism and purity. It suffers from the ills of both of them, especially the willingness to sacrifice any present good to a future miracle.

(e) The most pervasive difficulty of expediency is that it substitutes for all the substantive principles of moral life a schematic principle which has virtually no content, and can be used to justify anything. Expediency does not tell us what to do. Rather, it tells us that we may ignore all rules but itself. Yet what is valuable to us, and worth being expedient to gain, must be imbedded in one of these principles if not all of them.

The same point may be expressed more technically. The principle that the end justifies the means is fundamentally self-contradictory. Either it is no principle at all, and a mere slogan. Or else, it is a principle which will maximize benefits for men generally. Under rule utilitarianism, a moral principle is one which, if followed as a rule, will be generally beneficial. But the principle of expediency asserts instead that men should act to gain benefits without regard to any rules at all. It appears that the principle of expediency is a rule which is either rejected with all others, or else is justified by rule utilitarianism itself. But can we justify expediency on the grounds that followed generally it would be of benefit to everyone? I suggest not, and suggest moreover that no one has ever claimed expediency to be beneficial *as a rule*, but only as an exception.

The next question, then, is whether a departure from all rules is defensible. Can we justify acting at variance with a rule which has been justified substantively, perhaps by rule utilitarianism? Clearly not as a rule. This is no verbal quibble, but a fundamental point about moral principles. Obviously departure from a rule may be benefiicial on occasion. But we cannot justify that departure as a rule. A man may find a wallet in the street and keep it for his own benefit. He cannot argue that as a rule men should keep lost property.

Thus, we find that men of expediency in principle oppose principles bene-ficial to mankind. They therefore stand in the way of all progress toward making these principles the common practice of all men, and virtually prevent the achieve-ment of a better world. On rare occasion, it may be necessary to depart from a principle, at least where the foreseen consequences are deadly according to another moral principle. Except for moral purists, men generally agree that it is right to be intelligent about consequences, and not to follow moral principles unthinkingly. If this is all that is meant by expediency, it is inherent in all moral decisions which call for deliberation and evaluation.

The fundamental issue for a man who considers expediency instead of principled action is the true relationship between means and ends, and an em-phasis on the continuum they inhabit. The principle that the end justifies the means rests on a fundamental misconception—that we can in fact separate means and ends. In practice, men of expediency emphasize only those aspects of ends which they wish to and which apparently justify them. But the full consideration of justifying ends reveals the means still inherent in them.

Thus, the reason why certain actions are forbidden as war crimes is the effect they have on the entire course of the war. Torture, the killing of prisoners, and the use of poison gases corrupt the countries that use them. War itself does so. Life becomes of little value. And the war fought to preserve lives leads to its own antithesis.

In the case of a national crisis, the irresponsible use of emergency powers can lead easily to investing the authorities with so much power that they need never relinquish it. The democratic country which abandons its democratic protections during a crisis may find it very difficult to gain them again. The end of national security may be gained, but the end of democratic freedom may be lost.

What the continuum of means and ends shows is that we can realize an end which justifies means only where the means at all times preserve the real ends sought *as much as possible*. As soon as an end is postulated which is overly pure—winning the war but not preserving liberty and prosperity, keeping national security but not certain individual rights—then (1) it ceases to be capable of justifying the evil done to achieve it; and (2) the evil means are likely to bring about evil ends. The end does justify the means. But such an end will from the first be implicit in the means. And the means are justified only when they lead to a truly beneficial end.

This principle has been exemplified in all the concrete cases we have considered. War does indeed call for special activities. But where the war is fought wholly to be won, regardless of anything else, the winner may come to be not worth fighting for. A country preserves its values in the safeguards it provides during the crisis. The police show their respect for the lives of citizens by the infrequency with which they use their weapons. Where a group of people is treated with less strict standards of justice, what is shown is official contempt for them. In all these cases, though circumstances may require exceptional actions, the value of these actions resides in the principles still in effect.

It seems that we have concluded that there is no exceptional morality in times of crisis, but only exceptional circumstances requiring consideration and judgment. We turn now to specific cases to explore these issues more fully.

D. War

We have had occasion several times to refer to war, and to note both the purity of those who would oppose it under any circumstances, and the indefensibility of those who would gain peace by going to war. The subject of war, like all crisis subjects, tends to run to extremes—patriotism versus the horror of killing. Let us consider some of the relevant issues carefully.

Pacifism is a form of moral purity. Its weakness is that the pacifist possesses no intrinsic power to control events around him. He may refuse to kill. But he and others may be killed nevertheless. Suppose a country has but a few pacifists. Then, it may be argued, they could accomplish very little by fighting. But in not fighting, they follow their consciences, and serve as a symbol of morality for those who lose their principles in the midst of war. There certainly is something to this position. Suppose now that a country has many pacifists. If they refuse to fight, they may severely weaken their country's defenses. Here they may argue that with so many of them committed against violence, the enemy might win but could never conquer.

We move into the area of passive resistance as developed in India by Gandhi.
Men refuse to harm others, to use violence. But they also cripple the function of
the war and oppression by refusing to conform and by placing their bodies in the
path of tanks and guns. Peaceful resistance was quite effective in India. It is
difficult to believe that it would have been effective against Nazi Germany.

The strengths of pacifism are three. First, it preserves the symbolic force of
moral principles, and serves as a reminder to other men of the principles they hold
dear. There is a moving quality which nonviolent forms of heroism can have.
Second, pacifism may force the violent to confront their own moral priorities
openly. The British could not justify to themselves and the world using force
against men who would not fight back. Finally, pacifism not only has strength
but can be effective against an enemy of strong moral principles. This is its third
and most important strength. It is a mode of action which rests on the assumption
that the enemy is a moral agent with strong moral principles. Pacifism therefore
conforms to the imperative of the continuum of means and ends. Our goals must
be incorporated into our means, if the goals are to be attained. The pacifist
seeking a just society for all men acts throughout as if men are in fact just. It
cannot be denied that sometimes men are brought to justice by such an assumption.
It can also not be denied that there exist men and even societies who would be
quite unmoved by the example of others.

The man who would gain peace by starting a war is a purist of a different
stripe, one without the justification we have given for pacifism. The strength
of the position which advocates war is that wars are sometimes required by circumstances, if certain ends are to be achieved. When Germany invaded Czechoslovakia in 1939, Czechoslovakia had to fight or be overrun. A country may be
forced to defend itself against invasion by going to war.

The weakness of the position that war can bring peace is its complete
neglect of the continuum of means and ends. War is a nasty business, and cannot
be all good. A country at war suspends the rights of its citizens. It sacrifices the
comforts of individual life, even all ordinary pleasures, to achieve victory. A
government at war resorts to secrecy and to emergency powers. Facts are hidden
from voters, and even the elective process may be suspended. Most important of
all, a country at war kills the enemy, not only soldiers but civilians. A man at war
holds life very cheap, and the ability to kill very dear. War generates attitudes
wholly incompatible with the values of a moral society.

It would be unrealistic to argue that a country at war cannot turn to peace.
But it is worth noting that England and the United States, who found it rather
easy to demobilize after the Second World War, had never been invaded. Many
European countries hunted down German officers, and had a difficult time developing viable democratic political systems. A general distrust and fear of other
countries has pervaded Europe since the war, with little abatement. The hot war
became cold. The cold war has ruled the world for the past generation.

Let us consider war in somewhat greater detail. (1) A wartime economy tends to have rather special characteristics—emphasizing war goods, deemphasizing consumer products, and having an inflated work force. It is by no means easy for a country to move from a wartime to a peacetime economy without severe dislocation. (2) Soldiers are a relatively large proportion of the able-bodied working force. Whatever equilibrium a war economy has achieved, it will be thrown away by the return of the soldiers after the war. (3) Weapons of war are hard goods, and tend to be used, if not in one war, then in another. (4) War develops a mentality of sacrifice. A member of a war-torn society is likely to sacrifice too much, and give too great powers to his government. Or else he will demand special compensations for his sacrifice. And so forth.

The fundamental error in thinking of war is that it is conceived as a way of *meeting* a crisis. The truth is that war itself is a major and almost irremediable crisis. A country not at war, and not invaded, may look upon war realistically as a total crisis, calling for almost a complete reorganization of its economy, manpower, government, and laws. Certainly a country invaded by another is in a crisis in the first place, and may be forced to continue the crisis in the second place. But there is all the difference in the world between considering war a sensible response to a crisis, and a crisis in itself. War is never sensible.

Based on the continuum of means and ends, an intelligent and reasonable response to a situation is to begin as soon as possible to incorporate the goals sought into actions and circumstances. A hungry man goes directly to where he can find food. An engineering student who wishes to learn calculus takes problems in the subject and works upon them. The way to gain the trust of a man is to trust him, and to act in a trustworthy fashion.

By such a criterion, war is always unreasonable. It is the overt departure from the goals sought, whatever they may be, other than that of killing, looting, and conquering the enemy. War is the antithesis of peace. It is the antithesis of trust. It demands a special economy, unfit for peacetime, a special set of laws and official practices. Worst of all is what war does to the territory on which it takes place: death, destruction, devastation, misery, not to speak of overt torture and contempt for human life.

Can we ever justify war? Only on the condition that a crisis of greater magnitude precedes the war. There are several such crises we can imagine. A country is invaded. That is a crisis which might be met by going to war. (It is essential to note that a pacifist may deny the invasion to be a crisis of first magnitude. Going to war is always the greater crisis.) A country's people are starving, and have no prospects for supporting themselves. In addition, they are denied by a blockade all chance of improving their conditions. They might find it necessary to go to war.

Since war is a major crisis, it can never be regarded as beneficial to go to war, only as necessary to avoid some evils. From this point of view, a country need never justify avoiding war. Rather, the proof that a war is necessary should be of the strongest and most secure character. War is a *last resort*, and the word "last" is meant literally. A war is right only where no other alternatives of any sort re-

main, and the consequences to the people involved are extremely serious—death,
starvation, misery, slavery.

Unfortunately, patriotism intrudes in most considerations of war. Patriotism is a significant value, though it is overinflated. War and patriotism feed off each other—another liability of both of them. When war seems inevitable, patriotism becomes a necessity. Where patriotism is strong, it is easy to go to war. All too often, a government justifies war by arguments no stronger than it would use to raise taxes. It is often easier to go to war than to raise taxes. Too many people accept these arguments, based on the principle that a crisis calls for exceptional actions.

However, the situation is really turned around. There are indeed many things worse than war. But war is very, very bad. It is so bad that a country must be very sure that avoiding war will bring about something even worse. A nation needs to justify its creating a crisis, not avoiding it. A man must justify his killing another, not simply have to show that he *thought* he had grounds for doing so.

In conclusion, it does not seem that war can be justified by a crisis, but rather that war *is* the crisis to be justified. Unfortunately, except where the battles are fought on one's home grounds, the crisis is hidden. The same general slack supports war and capital punishment. As long as men can avoid thinking about them, they both can be permitted to continue.

E. Violence

Times of crisis are times of desperation. In times of desperation, men turn to extreme deeds of heroism and destruction, and feel that they are justified by the extremity of the crisis. The frightening aspect of such a sense of desperation is not the requirements of extremity, or the demands of a crisis, but the rapid degeneration of all moral standards in the midst of desperate actions. Some violence is justified by crisis. In no time at all, the situation degenerates to the point where any violent deeds of any sort seem justified. Where appropriation of property, murder, rape, and torture are all viewed as forms of violence, it becomes a matter of indifference whether one or another form is used. The worst danger inherent in violence is the decay of all moral standards in its presence.

In our time, violence has become the symbolic issue for a whole generation of youth. The violence of motorcycle gangs, of the police, and of bombs is present in domestic life. The violence of war is found on television screens in daily doses. A generation of young people became flower children and turned to drugs to escape violence. But the violence forced itself upon them. A group of young people engage in an orgy of killing. The news media engage in an orgy of words over it. Our political system is invaded by riots and clubs. Films wallow in gore. The fundamental problem for all committed young people is just when and where to use violence. Violence seems to have replaced sex as the immediate moral issue, except where it has been incorporated into sexuality.

A fair question is just *what* constitutes violence. Is it physical harm alone? There are forms of psychic and emotional violence which are more destructive than a slap in the face. It is often said that words do not harm, yet the anger which severe insults arouse, especially in public, seems to belie that claim. A man may be harmed by damage to his property, even by damage to other people. Must violence be intentional or willful? Accidental destruction can be extremely damaging. Is passive resistance a form of violence? Some people argue that standing in a man's way is committing violence on him. Others claim that the destruction of property is, after all, not harm to persons directly.

To avoid many of the irrelevant difficulties which stem from too narrow or too broad a conception of violence, we shall address a more specific question. What justifications can be given for causing a person suffering? Two answers are rather obvious. First, a criminal may be punished by imprisonment, which causes him pain. We have already addressed the question of whether it is justified to harm a man for what he has done, and found that the strongest case can be made for punishing a man to rehabilitate him. This is our second answer. A man may be punished in order to make him better, as a form of education.

The view that we are justified in causing a man suffering when he deserves punishment is much too simple, and requires qualification. First of all, although we may agree that punishment is justified, we are by no means ready to approve any and all forms of punishment. Some punishment may be too severe. We are forced to the realization that even where suffering is justified, too great suffering is still an evil to be avoided. Retributive punishment certainly must be matched to the crime. And rehabilitational punishment is not justified if it causes a man extreme pain.

Second, and more interestingly, even rehabilitational forms of punishment may fail to be successful in some cases. Yet a confirmed criminal must not be allowed to harm others. Punishment can also be a deterrent. It can in addition be a form of physical restraint, simply keeping an unsocial man from injuring other people. Here too, we are convinced that the form of restraint can be too severe and repressive. A criminal restrained for the good of others should not be mistreated. On the other hand, most people would be uneasy at making his imprisonment too pleasant, since it would not serve to deter others from crime.

We have noted several times Plato's principle that it is never right to harm anyone, even an evil man. Punishment is to improve him and make him good. We might accept this principle, though many people would not. Nevertheless, we will be forced at times also to cause a man some pain on no other grounds than to prevent injury to others. Once we grant such a principle, then we may be led to rather extreme versions of it. When is it justified to cause a man suffering? To benefit him and *also* to benefit others. But is it really right to harm one man to benefit another? It hardly seems so.

Let us for a moment lump together all forms of injury—violence, deprivation, even that of too little money. Any system of taxation in effect harms one man more than another by this definition. It is therefore clear that it is often legitimate to harm one man to benefit another. In fact, all moral and political life consists in the attempt to find a balance among needs and interests. A poor man may have special needs. A crippled one certainly has. It is acceptable to almost everyone to tax the affluent (to take their money) to help the poor and crippled. The crucial questions concern not the general principle, but the degree of injury, and far more, the type of injury. Too severe a taxation is not justified. Crippling a whole man so that he does not have his special advantage would also be absurd.

In addition to these last two considerations, there is a third. In determining what is right or wrong in cases which involve compromising injuries and benefits, we are seeking a general rule or principle, not looking to each case separately. Rule utilitarianism is far more defensible than act utilitarianism, at least where we are concerned with achieving maximal benefits for everyone in a society. We are looking for a *regulative principle*, It would not be right to force one rich man to give up his wealth to the poor if no other were required to do so. It would not be fair or just.

We ask again, when is it justified to harm one man to benefit another? The answer is, when the general rule of action which is applied in the particular case before us is more advantageous to men generally when followed than any alternative rule. For example, a graduated system of taxation provides a just means of distributing wealth more fairly and of helping the poor without unduly harming the affluent. On the whole, a graduated system of taxation is more beneficial than any other form. A uniform tax harms the poor more than the rich, which is neither fair nor beneficial to the poor. Finally, it can certainly be argued, and often is, that too severe a graduation would weaken the economy by depriving the rich of capital for investment, and harm everyone.

It is also justified to imprison a criminal who cannot be reeducated to become a useful member of society. Allowing him his liberty would cause injury to others. Yet clearly there can be little justification for the view that causing him severe pain benefits anyone. If prison life is too soft, some deterrence will be lost, especially for people whose life outside prison is particularly hard. On the other hand, if prison were not particularly easy, but simply decent, and men chose to live in prison rather than in a ghetto, then society might find itself forced to improve life outside prison. That would be a good thing. Finally, prisons have their costs, which must be weighed against the other considerations. A general balance of factors is required to achieve the most beneficial results.

We noted in our earlier discussion of utilitarianism that there is no general calculus of pleasure. There is no simple or routine way of adding benefits and subtracting injuries to arrive at a sum of goods achieved. It is foolish for us to pretend that we can simply balance the general good for society against the suffering of prisoners, and arrive at a numerical quantity. What we do instead is to sustain the function of the regulative principles we consider most important. In the case of imprisonment, the considerations of primary importance are the need to punish men for their misdeeds, the need to protect society from injury, and the need to avoid unnecessary suffering. In practice, the first two tend to predominate. But this is mainly because prisons are secret, and the average person does not know how prisoners are mistreated. Where facts of prison life are exposed, the outcry is often rather loud. The regulative principle that needless suffering is an evil to be avoided is very powerful for most men.

This brings us back to the more direct question of violence. It can indeed be generally right to injure one man to benefit others, provided that the injury is not too great, the benefit is significant, and the rules appealed to fair and just. The qualifications are of utmost importance. In particular, we note that the degree of injury must be controlled. Almost everyone would agree that certain kinds of injury are virtually prohibited in all cases.

We now can see the place of violence proper in our considerations. In addition to the general calculation of benefits for society as a whole, we must also take into account prohibitions against certain kinds of injuries. Torture, the infliction of extreme physical pain, the appropriation of property, are all generally forbidden, because to allow them to be used would be detrimental to society. Where men are tortured for political opposition, the entire political fabric of social life is weakened. Where ordinary criminals are beaten, there is harm done to them with little benefit to others, and a general suspicion engendered that life and suffering are unimportant. A society asserts its primary values in its regulative principles. If life is valuable, it may not be taken easily. If suffering is evil, it must be avoided at virtually any cost.

We now look to the most ordinary forms of violence. A man is angry, and punches another in the face. What we have discovered to our great sorrow is that permitting physical violence on such slight provocation tends to make people more violent. On the other hand, it is a well known psychological cliché that severely repressed forms of violence can become vicious and even less controllable. What we are led to is the realization that some forms of violence must be totally prohibited—those involving physical pain, striking or wounding others, and severe and costly damage to property. Other forms, especially verbal forms of violence, are more tolerable, though seldom desirable. And a malicious man who wounds others with words is worthy of contempt, but not of imprisonment.

The procedure at work is still a form of substantive grounding of moral principles. Certain principles regulate human actions effectively and beneficially. Generally, men can be asked to make small sacrifices for others. That is of great benefit to everyone. Some sacrifices, which involve severe personal injury, are not justified, and we make known firm regulative principles against physical violence. Killing and bombing of property are forbidden.

Does this mean that killing and other severe forms of violence are never to be used? To answer affirmatively is to be a moral purist, with all of the draw-backs of such purity. A regulative principle is one which rules our actions, until it comes into severe conflict with other regulative principles. When two *prima*

To most men, Hitler was an evil to be destroyed, even by violence.

But it is essential to realize that physical violence is an extreme. It is almost always bad. It is prohibited by a general rule, and that rule is one we hope all men will someday come to follow strictly. By the continuum of means and ends, we set forth toward a goal by incorporating it into our means. Violence will be overcome only through prohibiting it now, and obeying the prohibition. Any regulative principle can be set aside, if that is required, when it comes into conflict with another regulative principle taken to be of greater moral weight. The important thing to keep in mind is that a regulative principle disobeyed is always a moral crisis, and that disobedience of such a principle is to be avoided as much as possible.

It is difficult to grasp the nature of a moral decision that calls for a departure from a regulative principle. Certainly it involves a clear sense of the price being paid, and also a firm regret at doing what we must do. In practice, it means that violence will be used only where no alternative remains, and abandoned as soon as possible. Violence is like war, itself a crisis and a firm evil, to be entered into only where we are confronted by greater evils.

But now we may note the greatest evil of violence. Whenever it is used, it tends to encourage further violence. This is the fact whose oversight makes men resort to violence casually. Police violence encourages violence in return. Those who argue that extreme violence and force can repress the opposition look only at the short run. In the long run, the violence used is repaid. The members of a revolutionary group which casually uses bombs and kidnapping call down all the hatred of the powers that be upon them and anyone else who seems to challenge the authority. Extreme violence is a last resort. More important, it is to be abandoned as soon as no longer necessary. The regulative principle must be to *end* the use of violence. We cannot end the use of violence through frequent use of violence.

F. Power

Human relations are far too often power relations. Parents have power over their children. Employers have power over their employees. Governments possess greater power than their citizens, and have power over them. Often this power rests on superior force and the willingness to use violence. Such power we may analyze as we have analyzed violence in our last discussion. Violence is a last resort, itself a crisis, and to be avoided wherever possible.

When the question concerns individual acts of violence, many people would agree that violence is evil. Yet the same people are convinced that official violence is necessary for the stability of society. Hobbes' argument is an extreme form of this view. Men will live together peacefully only through fear. Without violent means to generate fear, a government could not rule well or peacefully.

The argument is simply unsupported by the facts. Authoritarian and tyrannical governments often provoke revolution and hatred. Hobbes' psychology of rule is inadequate. A far more effective stability is achieved through custom and management than through force. Indeed some uniformity and sharing of goals and activities are required in a stable and peaceful society. But education and custom, coupled with effective management, produce such a society quite successfully and enduringly. Violence leads to violence. Authority provokes counter-authority. Such a view is acknowledged by the frequent claim that a society is democratic not merely in government or constitution, but in its traditions and ideals.

It does not follow from the moral and practical superiority of custom and management that a government is never to use force. Rather, what follows is that the need to use force against its own citizens is proof of a crisis in government, one which cannot be resolved by force alone. Here we come to one of the most powerful justifications for the regulative prohibition against the use of force, even by governments. If force is a last resort, it may be used when necessary. But it cannot be thought to resolve any problems, either in a short or long run. For it is itself a problem, and its use generates a crisis. A government must remedy the *source* of the conditions which it has met with violence. If the poor rebel, they perhaps must be put down by force. But they must also be fed and their poverty ameliorated. The South seceded from the Union, and a war was required to preserve it. But what was also required was the transformation of the economy of the South into one no longer requiring slaves, and a modification of its government and social practices. Not enough was accomplished along the latter lines. The basic problems merely changed their form, quite unresolved by the war.

We shall put aside the problem of power where grounded in force. We have said enough for our purposes about force and violence. The more interesting form of power is that of sheer authority. Governments are thought to depend on power, whether or not they resort to force. Does not management use power over its employees? Is not a bureaucracy a structure which relates the superior power at the top with the power of lesser members in the system?

Strangely enough, a bureaucracy tends to minimize the powers of the head of the system. The rules laid down are so elaborate, and the steps required for any major decision so complex, that the nominal head of a bureaucracy is effectively hindered from acting at will, almost as much as any other member of the system. The great problem for a bureaucracy is that the system tends to absorb power from everyone, and make almost everyone impotent. The president of a large university has almost all the legal power, yet will follow the advice of the members of his bureaucracy. He has no alternative. He cannot accomplish anything if they would obstruct him. And he possesses few means of enforcement.

Power here is to be understood as the ability of a person to act and to achieve stipulated goals effectively. We note then that there are two general types of power: the power to accomplish one's goals, and the power over another person to inhibit his accomplishing his goals or to make him achieve one's own. Persuasion is a means of power. So is force. But so also is a harmonious and peaceful society in which people cooperate with each other. Such a society succeeds in maximizing the first kind of power, and of minimizing the second.

Unfortunately, men have usually lived in societies where they possessed only limited powers in the first sense, that of being able to achieve their own aims. Throughout history, food and other forms of wealth have been in short supply, and distributed quite inequitably. In past societies also, the second type of power—over others—has often been near maximum. A small number of members of a society possess great powers over the activities and even the lives and deaths of the larger number. Slavery is an extreme form of the second type of power.

The second type of power has its subtle forms. For example, parents usually possess great emotional powers over their children, and can manipulate them in all sorts of hidden ways, sometimes hidden from the parents themselves. On occasion, children can manipulate their parents, through tantrums or sheer outrageousness. Recent movements for women's liberation reveal unmistakably the variety of powers which are used to keep women in domestic subjection, ranging from vocational discrimination to the insidious expectation that a woman will receive her greater satisfactions in the home and as a mother. The family has often been a system of power exchange, and too seldom understood as such. In Western society, the man is usually the authority, and controls the wealth as well as the name of the family. In return, the woman too often repays her husband by spite, resentment, and, worst of all, taking out her impotence on her children, by manipulating them.

It is not implausible to regard the second type of power as a species of violence. It does violence to the goals and needs of the person controlled. It is a violence perpetrated by one person or group upon another. Like violence proper, power over others is extremely undesirable, and should be avoided. Unlike physical violence, this power is not something which can be relegated solely to situations of crisis, though it probably should be. It tends to perpetuate itself, and when used tends to encourage its further use, in a vicious unending spiral.

The objection will be raised that although physical violence is an unmixed evil, to be eliminated from all civilized life, the power of one man over another is a necessary feature of human life. How can orders be given without being grounded in power? How can parents educate their children without greater power? How can children be educated in school without the disciplinary powers of the teacher?

This argument stems from a confusion about the nature of power over men, which I will call "authority." A useful way to approach the subject is by consideration of Kant's second formulation of the Categorical Imperative. We recall that the first formulation is that all men should conform to maxims of action which can be made universal principles. Kant argues that the Categorical Imperative is a principle which stems from the rational faculty of all men, that all men are equal under the moral law, and most important, that each man both *legislates* the moral law (through his reason) and *obeys* it. It follows that every man is the end for which the moral law exists, and that no other end can be a moral one or a categorical one. Therefore, the second formulation is, so act as to treat all men as ends, never as means. We apply this to the subject of power, and we see that all imposition of authority on human beings is immoral, treating them as means to some end, even to their own good.

This second version of the Categorical Imperative is a powerful one, and captures an essential feature of our view of men as moral agents. Nevertheless, it can be objected that, in social intercourse, people cannot help but treat each other as means. We tell our troubles to our friends and look to them for help. Isn't this using them? In addition, even the second version of the Categorical Imperative is overly pure, since on occasion we must use people for social advantages.

Let us review the sense in which men are to be treated as ends. It is that they are the source of the moral law. In other words, men are to be regarded as *agents able to choose for themselves.* Now we see why authoritarian power is an evil. It treats men as objects to be manipulated by others, not as agents able to make choices. In asking for help, in telling our troubles to others, even in seeking flattery, we let the other person make his own choice to help us or not. Only where we have power over others do we treat them as means and not ends. It doesn't matter whether men actually *can* choose. What matters is that we treat them as responsible agents.

On occasion, we discover that a man is weak in conscience or intelligence. A criminal may be regarded as incorrigible, and jailed solely for the benefit of others. Even the second formulation of the Categorical Imperative may be too pure. Children too are not yet ready to be given full responsibility for their actions, and some authoritarian power is required.

But we recall the continuum of means and ends. The worst fault of authoritarian power is that it turns men into what it regards them as being. A child will not become a responsible agent unless regarded as such. Authoritarian power may be a necessity, but like violence, one to be used as little as possible. Instead, we seek the cooperation of responsible agents working together. An effective management functions best when all its members work efficaciously and conscientiously as responsible agents, not in obedience to authority. A government rules best through cooperation, not force or authority. A bureaucracy is a useful system, whatever its faults, in that it parcels out responsibility to everyone.

Unfortunately, it limits responsibility also. In the past hundred years, we may note an unbroken trend in modern technological society toward a diminishing of power in the first sense, and toward subtle and hidden forms of power in the second sense. Men literally have less power over their lives and choices in a complex technological and bureaucratized world. In addition, though slavery and tyranny may be absent in many Western countries, the forces of manipulation are complex and powerful. Modern society has achieved the destruction of overt oppression. With this decline in the power of one man over another, there has been no increase in personal power. Rather, hidden powers lurk in most social relations. Too many different activities are dominated by but a few corporate and government powers. Further, the complexity of life and its uniformity make individual choices less meaningful.

In conclusion, we should not overlook the subtle powers in social life. A fundamental regulative ideal which requires consideration at all times is that of diminishing the second type of power as much as possible, and of maximizing the first kind of power instead. Men must learn to choose for themselves, and to avoid being controlled by others.

G. Revolution

The substantive ground for the existence of a social order is the benefits which are provided to the members of that society. As Locke points out in his *Second Treatise on Government*, if that benefit is no longer available to the members of a society, they may be justified in withdrawing their support from it, and seeking to change it, even wholly rebelling against it.

Almost no one would deny the justification of men who live under a vicious tyranny which causes them severe suffering to revolt against it. Revolutions are sometimes justified. The view that they never are is insupportable, another venture in extreme purity. At the opposite extreme, we may ask if a man is entitled to press for a revolution whenever he is dissatisfied with the way things are going. For several reasons, this is too casual a view of revolution. First, the rebellion may not succeed, and may cause injuries without benefit. Second, the rebellion may make things worse. Third, and most important of all, a revolution is another extreme act, itself a full crisis. It is not to be undertaken lightly.

Here we come to the same conclusion we were led to concerning war and violence. All three—war, violence, and revolution—are morally prohibited, because of their extreme nature and dire consequences. What this means is that regulative moral principles prohibit war, violence, and revolution under ordinary circumstances. However, where circumstances are extraordinary—and this means where other regulative principles have been violated—war and revolution may become lesser evils. Where the enemy invades our homeland, and slaughters our countrymen, we may have to fight or be killed ourselves. Where a whole class of people are denied justice, denied equality under the law, and deprived of jobs as well, they may have to revolt against their oppression. Finally, once a conflict among regulative principles has been generated, it becomes a moral issue for all members of a society, not the oppressed group alone. The regulative principles of justice for all, and the right of all men to a decent and pleasant life, are essential to all moral decisions, for any member of a society.

The question is not, then, *whether* revolution is ever justified. Sometimes it is. Nor is the question whether we should tolerate even the slightest disadvantage before rebelling. Clearly a revolution is a violent and extreme act, and not to be undertaken lightly, or on slight provocation. A revolution may itself be far worse than any of the ills it would remedy. Even the view that the end justifies the means, which we have seen is simplistic and indefensible without qualification, cannot be defended if the end is not better than the means.

The critical questions are therefore just *when* a revolution is justified, and under what conditions. And also, *what kind* of revolution is justified, what means may be considered legitimate in overthrowing a government. All too often the rhetoric of desperation triumphs over the critical issues, and revolutionary sentiments are expressed to no particular end, while atrocities are defended as legitimate in desperate circumstances.

We will consider several factors essential to the determination of when a revolution is justified. But the more interesting question, which is not separable from the first, is just what kind of revolution we can justify. What means can be defended in revolution? Unfortunately, moral purity tends to overpower revolutionary rhetoric. Revolutions are often divided into two kinds, violent and nonviolent. Nonviolent revolutions are thought of as rapid changes without violence or force. They should be justified without difficulty wherever they are generally beneficial. Nonviolent revolution is rapid social change. Reform is gradual social change. The former is justified whenever rapid change would be more beneficial than gradual changes would be. Wherever a large group of men are suffering, it seems a good *prima facie* case that rapid changes improving their situation would be beneficial. If people are starving, then they ought to be fed, and without further delay.

The problems of rapid change are obvious. In making important changes quickly, a society changes in ways it cannot always foresee or control. If people are starving, they should be fed. But is it really better to dole the food out as charity, to find jobs for the poor, to educate them, or to redistribute all the available wealth? If ghettos are terrible, they ought to be destroyed. But then people complain about the exact form of destruction. Perhaps huge low-income compounds are even more dehumanizing than are the rotten conditions of the ghetto. Rapid changes may change too much too quickly and unwisely. Gradual changes often seem no change at all. Conditions remain as bad as ever.

The general problem of the rate of social change seems not to be a fundamental one. The reason for this is that we have granted the need for change, and are concerned only with how to accomplish it beneficially. We are not concerned here with great conflicts among ideals, but with the most effective means for the realization of our ideals. There are bound to be important differences of opinion, mainly because in areas of important political decisions we are more ignorant than knowledgeable. Nevertheless, though many men oppose rapid changes from fear or due to lethargic temperaments, it is difficult to grasp the regulative force of their opposition. Here it really is a problem of determining what is beneficial, without overriding any moral consideration other than that of general benefits.

However, in the case of a revolution which utilizes extreme forms of violence,

we are faced with a fundamental moral problem. We have a conflict between the
regulative ideals which prohibit violence and the regulative ideals of justice,
benevolence, and opposition to oppression which call forth thoughts of revolution.
The conflict inherent in all revolutions is a major crisis in the life of a society,
and can never be regarded lightly.

The degree of crisis is so great in most revolutionary situations that it is a
major drawback of most thinking about revolution that no finer distinctions are
drawn than between violent and nonviolent revolution. If all revolutions which
involve violence are equally difficult to justify from a moral standpoint, then
minor violence becomes extreme without challenge. What we must do is to
consider not *when* violent revolution is justified, but just what means are justifiable
in revolution. The following considerations are important in coming to such a
decision. They are all rather obvious, but often overlooked in revolutionary
considerations.

(1) Since revolution is in itself an extreme crisis, it may be undertaken only
where there is already a crisis in social life. Such a crisis must have two elements:
It must be a moral crisis, in that it involves the breaking of a moral ideal. It
must also be a crisis in that people are concretely suffering. The reason for the
first is that a revolution will always involve the neglect of some other regulative
ideal. People will be killed, others will suffer. The reason for the second is that
where no one is genuinely being harmed, moral purity alone cannot justify extreme
actions. For example, if a government regularly lies to its citizens, but in no ways
harms them (a benevolent despotism), a violent revolution may be extreme. On
the other hand, every effort to change such a society short of violence would be
justified by such lies. And where the despot responds by force to peaceful efforts to
change, violence may become necessary.

A revolution is therefore justified only where the society is already in moral
and physical crisis. Its evils must be real, and they must be *known*. We have here a
further point. Evils may be vaguely sensed without definition or clarity. If we are
to oppose to a vague evil a clear revolution with obvious forms of destruction and
suffering, it is difficult to justify the revolution. If men are not being unjustly
killed, how can a revolutionary justify the slaughter brought by the revolution?
In all revolutionary situations, there is a pressing need for educated and intelligent
men to analyze as accurately as possible the evils which exist. Where these ills are
merely inchoate and unrefined, we have at most a prerevolutionary situation. The
American Revolution, for example, was grounded in the concrete problem of
taxation without representation.

In addition, the ills of the society and the ills of the revolution must be
proportionate. It is foolish to pretend that a revolution brings no injury with it.
Its real prospects of harm must be laid against the real injuries which are to be
found in the society without revolution, and the revolution must be the lesser of
the evils. Here we come to the first condition determining the nature of the revolution involved. A revolution may be only so violent and destructive as can be

justified by the extreme nature of the evils it would overcome. A revolution in an enslaved country or a tyranny is more justified in being bloody and destructive than one in an unresponsive democracy.

(2) If a revolution is justified, it can be so only in terms of the end it achieves. Here the principle of the continuum of means and ends faces us with considerable force. It is not the postulated or imagined ends which will prove a revolution justified, but its real achievements. Revolutionaries tend to possess a phoenix mentality: destroy the old and the new will flower from the ashes. But real men in real societies are not mythical birds.

For example, a revolution is planned within a society with an oppressive government. The society has the variety of forms and aspects we have already mentioned: a government, customs, education, habits, regulative principles, institutions, and so forth. It is not too difficult to topple a government. It is close to impossible to withdraw from society, or to wholly transform it overnight. Many of its institutions will remain intact. Habits and customs will continue to prevail. The government may fall, but the revolution may gain none of its moral ends if they depend on changes in the institutions and customs of the society.

The greatest conservative force in a society is that embodied in the customary practices of groups of men, institutionally or in the statistical mass. Individuals can and do change, but the average tends to change very slowly. A revolution aims at major changes, not in government alone but in men and what they do and think. If a country is unjust in its racial discrimination, justice will not be served by changing the government alone.

It follows, then, that a revolution can be justified only on the basis of a clear sense of what ends it will accomplish, and a clear sense of the pathway to these ends. I do not mean by this that a revolutionary must be able to demonstrate beyond all shadow of doubt that things will work as he foresees. No one can quite foretell the future beyond all doubt. But he must have marshalled the evidence and the facts to show that the means of revolution have a good chance of success, and will achieve results that are concretely better than the ills of the present. Marx conceived of his socialism as "scientific" in contrast to "utopian" socialism, in resting on a clear sense of how socialism would come to pass out of pre-existing material and historical conditions. We may attack the truth of Marx's scientific principles. But it is impossible to attack the principle that social changes flow from pre-existing conditions.

Unfortunately, when we look to revolutions of the past, we cannot but be struck by the fact that they have almost never realized their own ends. When revolutions have succeeded, it has often been in unsuspected ways. Moreover, they have often brought many of the ills they condemned. This is no surprise, for men and societies do not change as rapidly as we might like.

The temptation, therefore, is to avoid considering the goal of revolution, and to let present ills alone justify the revolution. This is the phoenix mentality. History will in the end prove the revolution justified. But the revolutionary cannot himself use later events to justify his earlier actions. Revolutionary activity tends to become nihilistic and defiant of morality. In this respect it is like war. Nothing is more ironic than a revolution inspired by an unjust war, both leading to a total disdain for moral principles.

If the goals of the revolution are to be clearly conceived in advance, to justify the revolution, then most revolutionaries are unjustified in their claims and actions. In part, this is because it is very difficult to foresee the future. In part, it is a particular problem for a revolutionary in a half-good society. Where a government is oppressive and destructive in obvious ways, the goals of revolution are clear. Where a government is imperfect and vaguely at fault, it is more difficult to define the goals of a revolution which will lead to a society clearly better than what it would replace.

For example, the United States today is a racist society, engaged in a despised war, engaged also in imperialist ventures in many poor countries, and supportive of dictatorships and tyrannies throughout the world. The ills are numerous, and easy to detail. The country is affluent, yet there are people starving. Can a revolution obviously improve things? Certainly in some respects. Overt racism could be ended, albeit only by force. The war could be ended. Wealth could be taken from the affluent and distributed widely. But would the conditions of life be generally improved by these actions?

Consider merely one part of the whole. The education system in the United States is the most advanced in the world, and the model for most other countries. It is a true system of widespread education. Yet many Americans are functionally illiterate. Far worse than this, the system of education does not provide the upward mobility it should for the children of the very poor. The problems of the schools are tremendous and well known. No one really has the solution to them, and a revolutionary is no more ready to propose them or to achieve them than anyone else. The great danger is that the destruction of the established system will benefit no one and harm almost everyone.

The last argument is often generalized. Opponents of revolution argue that revolutions destroy without offering concrete alternatives. Such an argument can be used to prove that revolutions are never justified. We move again to a form of moral purity. Where specific ills are severe enough, a revolutionary can indeed propose concrete and superior alternatives. Instead of tyranny, democracy. In place of a society divided between rich and poor, an equal distribution of wealth. Instead of war, peace. If the concrete evils of a government are clear enough, it should be overthrown. However, where the ills are vague and undefined, and the goals of a better world are only felt and not seen clearly, then a revolution may not be justified.

The main problem for a revolutionary is that the regulative principles of morality are basically conservative. That is, moral principles regulate what men ought not to do, and do so fairly specifically. But ends of action are often rather unclear, and can oppose regulative principles only to a small degree. If a revolution means death and destruction, this is evil and prohibited. It may be justified to achieve a more decent life for most men, but that is again rather vague. It is more likely to be justified if the society to be overthrown is morally repugnant and causes its members extreme suffering.

In Karl Marx's later writings and in the writings of many of his followers, we find a disdain for moral principles. Marx saw that such principles could be a barrier to a better world. Marxist revolutionaries tend to dismiss moral principles as relics of the society which must be overthrown. Yet, in his early writings, Marx shows that the impulse which moves him is truly a moral one. The sense of a better world, of a world without alienation, is a moral one, and is governed by regulative ideals. Marx is correct that such ideals are often conservative, in the sense that they prohibit revolution for the sake of revolution. But a revolution can be justified only by these or similar ideals.

(3) In addition to the evils to be overcome and the goals to be achieved, a revolution must be justified in comparison with other alternatives. Here the means become of paramount importance, for the particular kind of revolution undertaken is justified only if it is the best of the alternatives. In addition, the main impulse to revolution is usually the conviction that there are no alternatives left, other than destructive revolution. Revolution is often the result of the desperation men feel where there is no way out.

Revolutions tend to move of their own momentum. Once begun, they prohibit all consideration of alternatives. Yet if we can speak of a revolution being morally justified, that justification is always grounded in the testing of alternatives. It follows that a revolution can be legitimately undertaken only where there is no better alternative, not only at the beginning but *throughout*. Here we find the major consideration for the determination of the violence needed. At *all* times during a revolution, the means used must be the best available—best in terms of the goal sought, and best in terms of moral principles which are taken to be regulatory. Once the revolution becomes so bloody that no moral principles are effective, it can no longer be justified in moral terms.

The consideration of alternatives also leads to an important distinction— between revolutions within democratic societies and revolutions against tyranny. Not all revolutions are the same, either in violence or in aims. A revolution against tyranny may have no recourse but extreme violence. No other alternative may be possible. A revolution against the unjust practices of a democratic government may have many alternatives available, later on if not at the beginning. The democratic heritage and institutions accommodate more reasonable and democratic procedures. For example, suppose a democratic government to be taken over by a military coup. A revolution might be initially violent, but become democratic again almost immediately once the coup had been reversed.

(4) Finally, a revolutionary must look to the prospects of success a revolution has. It is foolish to undertake an effort guaranteed to lose, especially when the failure may make things worse. Desperation promotes the view that *anything* is better than what exists at present, when in fact things can be made far worse.

The worst fault of desperation is that it leads to a complete misuse of the resources available. For example, a revolutionary concerned with success in the United States today would realize the need for a large support from labor and even the middle class, and seek ways to achieve such support. But the needs and values of the prospective supporters would then be effective in determining the revolutionary program. Yet we find instead that the rhetoric of self-styled revolutionaries often seems directed at the alienation of as large an opposition as possible. Militant blacks speak openly of killing whites and police. Student revolutionaries make bombs and beat up other kids. Nothing is worse than a failed revolution.

The preceding discussion enforces the view that revolution is a crisis, and should be undertaken only under extreme provocation. In addition, a revolution should be tailored to the circumstances, should have well defined goals, should rest on a clear sense of the evils to be eliminated, and should develop its means accordingly. These means should be kept as morally justified as possible, and should avoid the ills the revolution opposes. Finally, a revolution should be born of intended success and the improvement of human life, not of sheer desperation.

The revolutionary will reply that I have made revolution impossible with my conditions. Suppose that we have a democratic society which is unjust, extremely materialistic, and destructive to many of its members. Suppose that by the above criteria a revolution is not justified, but that things are very bad. Unfortunately, the world is a more difficult place than we wish. A just man alone in an unjust society may know that things are very bad. But he is impotent to improve them. Suppose he talks to people and they don't listen. Suppose he blows up bridges and cafes. How in the world will that improve the situation? All too often a revolution is proposed where nothing else will work, though it will not succeed either. Sometimes we have to concede the difficulty of improving the world, though we should not stop trying. Sometimes all the alternatives available to us are bad ones.

The principle of the continuum of means and ends does offer us an alternative to revolution in the circumstances just described, perhaps the only alternative with a chance of success. In effect, ends are realized through means which incorporate those ends from the beginning. If there is an unjust war, men may work for peace by refusing to fight. Here means and ends merge. Unfortunately, refusing to be drafted may lead to jail, and demands personal heroism. It is difficult to be heroic and not succeed. If the society is racist, groups of people can set themselves the task of individually avoiding racial discrimination. If the society is too materialistic, some men may avoid the pursuit of material affluence.

But suppose all of this is being done, and to no avail? Desperation seems the obvious result, and desperation can breed violence and destruction, if not apathy and resignation. Here we must note that there are two levels on which the discussion of political alternatives can take place. First, we may be concerned with what an individual is to do in the face of frustrating and evil conditions. The best conclusion we can offer is that he be intelligent, far-seeing, knowledgeable, and firmly moral, and make his own decisions for himself. Hopefully, he will choose actions which have a high probability of success. But if he is sufficiently desperate, as many blacks seem to be today, we cannot expect him to endure frustration without breaking.

Second, and much more important, we may be interested in the obligations of a government or other social institutions to a desperate and frightening situation. Here it is worth noting that the moral advice to a desperate man not to revolt because he has little chance of success may be useless if he is too desperate. The advice not to act is one of the causes of his frustration. What is required is for society and its government to respond to the sources of the desperation, and to try to ameliorate the ills which have produced it. We have been discussing what an intelligent and moral citizen ought to do in the face of injustice. We should also consider what an intelligent and responsive government ought to do in the face of desperation.

The temptation of government is to repress opposition, even in a democracy. The casual revolutionary encourages oppression. On the other hand, where desperation breeds revolutionary thoughts, the solution lies not in repression, but in responsive change on the part of the society as a whole. The arguments we have given against revolution are not complete without a further realization. Revolutions are indeed to be avoided. But it is not individuals alone who are responsible for avoiding them. In fact, individuals are relatively impotent in most political situations. It is the government of a society and its leaders who bear the final responsibility for avoiding the destructiveness of a revolution. In the next full chapter we will take up the question of the kind of society which is required to avoid the ills which lead to revolution.

H. Withdrawal

The temptation in the face of desperate circumstances is to withdraw from them. If a man is surrounded by evil and unable to do anything to eliminate it, he may prefer to have nothing to do with it, to withdraw from it, and to live in isolation. One of the great traditions of goodness consists in a peaceful withdrawal from the cares of the world, the preservation of a good life in quietness. Holy men have throughout history been men apart from the pressures of active confrontation. Christian saints are often hermits, who live alone in the wilderness. Monasteries offered a secure social order, but one well apart from the rest of life. Small groups of men have from time immemorial founded small communities of life apart. Through withdrawal, men have sought to develop a better society from the beginning, instead of seeking to change the society that they were born into.

There are two reasons for seeking a life of isolation. The first is that we gain a greater security, both emotional and physical. The impulse here is akin to that of the anarchist we have discussed several times. The source of pain in life is usually other men. By withdrawal from human society, a man keeps himself

secure in person and in feeling. Epicurus represents the best life for man to be one
of tending one's own garden. A life of pleasure, free from pain, is the best life.
And it must be quiet and controlled. Peacefulness demands disengagement.

The temptations of this view are considerable. Many ordinary people find
the prospect of a life of struggle too appalling to contemplate, and regard their
families and friends as the source of whatever secure pleasures a man can have.
Withdrawal does not necessarily entail complete isolation. Some smaller community may be maintained. It seems a tacit view of many men that the problems of
society arise with a certain size. Smaller groups are more secure. Oddly enough,
the family, which is a small social unit, is today probably the source of the greatest
tensions and unpleasantness.

On the whole, most men require social contacts with not many but with just
a few people. In friendship and love we find the greater emotional satisfactions,
though also on occasion the greater pains. Withdrawal understood as the building
of smaller communities for personal satisfaction has much to recommend it for
many men. Obviously, there are some men who glory in fame, and desire to be
known to everyone. Smaller communities do not appeal to everyone.

More problematical is the general dependence of smaller communities on the
larger society. In times of war or terror, a small village is completely vulnerable.
Smaller communities seem to presuppose a stable political world. But in real life,
such stability can be gained only through a concern with mankind in general.
Withdrawal from the larger world seems founded on either self-deception or
hypocrisy—the blindness of assuming that the rest of the world will let us be
without difficulty.

The second reason for withdrawal is that of a moral purity. Life in society
is a continual compromise, and filled with unbearable political alternatives. A man
becomes desperate at having no solution to the problems which surround him, and
escapes into isolation. Saints are so often represented as hermits because of the
prevalent conviction that to live among men is to be corrupted by them. A just
man cannot live in an unjust society. If societies cannot be made just, then just
men will live apart from the company of other men.

This form of withdrawal is another form of moral purity, and possesses the
usual faults of such purity. In particular, we are addressing the desire to avoid
compromise which leads to withdrawal. But the compromises required are not
dissipated. They are present by neglect. If men are starving, and we cannot help
them by political action, then our withdrawal will not feed them either. If a war
is taking place, withdrawal does not end the war or the suffering. Withdrawal is a
form of selfishness. Perhaps it would be better if men were more selfish, and less
ready to harm others by pretending to help them. But it is selfishness, and cannot
pass for a moral purity.

If complete forms of withdrawal are not easily justifiable, it does not follow
that we cannot learn a great truth from the impulse to seek isolation. The principle
of withdrawal is that men cannot easily succeed in benefiting either mankind as a

whole or even themselves by large-scale political actions. Great demonstrations dissipate energies. Men are far more effective in their smaller communities, and they usually receive greater satisfactions there. Except for the great political leaders, men require, not an entire society for their community, but the love and respect of just a few other people. Even more to the point, men are more effective in smaller rather than larger organizations. Large institutions swallow us up anonymously. A small community preserves a sense of personal identity.

It follows that, for most men, an impulse to withdraw, not entirely, but to life in a small subsociety within a larger one will always go hand in hand with the moral imperative to consider all men in our actions and decisions. The main impulse to overcome selfishness is not love for mankind but love for one or two other people. The main source of loyalties to others, even to the point of self-sacrifice, is not nationalism or patriotism, but family love. For most men, society means positively and concretely just a few other people. The larger society is but the organization and interconnection of the larger variety of small communities and groups.

It follows, I believe, that a society which overcomes its smaller groups, either by enforced conformity or repression, or even by a tacit homogeneity, weakens itself. The impulse to identification with a smaller group is a fundamental one in human life. This is what community means in concrete terms. The larger society has the obligation to preserve the character of distinct communities amidst the larger community, so that individual men may at least in part succeed in satisfying their need to develop closer ties to just a few people. This is the subject of the next chapter.

I. Politics

By now it should be clear that there are no simple alternatives for a just man in an unjust society. It is almost impossible for a man to develop a firm and reliable set of moral principles in a society which despises them and rewards evil. German children during the Nazi regime simply could not have been expected to understand what was wrong with their government and with their own values. A truly unjust society offers little room for a just man to develop his understanding of what is valuable. A truly unjust society offers little room for a just man to live within it.

But let a man be assumed to be just in an unjust society, and we see again that it is almost impossible for him to find a satisfactory course of action with firm prospects of success. Withdrawal in despair may save him, but it does not ameliorate the evil which surrounds him. To remain engaged, however, is to risk personal suffering or death and impotence as well. For an unjust society has all the power in its hands. A just man is weak and helpless by comparison. To gain power, he must wrest it by force from his oppressors. He must become as evil as they in order to have a chance of winning against them. But a just man knows that good seldom comes from evil, and can never be counted on doing so.

Finally, there is the ultimate irony. A child growing up in a completely unjust society cannot learn of justice, and will not form defensible moral principles. He will not oppose the injustice of his society with his own secure moral principles. Where we find a just man in an unjust society, we already have found a society mixed in its values. Socrates was condemned by the men of Athens because they understood far too well that he represented values they respected—truth, honesty, integrity, and reason. But they knew also that these genuine values could destroy something else they also considered valuable—belief in the traditional gods.

Wherever the problem arises of what a man of conscience will do when surrounded by official evil, the evil is a mixed one. It is necessary to distinguish a good man accosted by an occasional evil from a man who is surrounded by nothing but evil. Where only evil exists, it will perpetuate itself.

It follows, then, that we have two different types of confrontation of justice and injustice. We have first a man who confronts actions which are evil by all moral principles, of almost all men. It may not be possible to defeat such evil, for it may be too strong. Yet there is no doubt that it is evil. Such evil may be opposed and should be opposed. Such evil may require war or revolution. (We assume that the decision to go to war or to revolt is made carefully and wisely.)

Contrasted with this is the complexity of social life where mixed advantages and disadvantages are found in a bewildering array. Almost all courses of action have major drawbacks. All alternatives benefit some people and injure others. In such a society, men form their conceptions of right and wrong in a situation of conflicting values. All goods are mixed. All fundamental values are confronted by other ultimate goals. All regulative principles are qualified. Here we find no consensus on right and wrong—not because men disagree *in general* or *in principle*, but because they cannot find out what they should do *in particular*. Everyone agrees that murder is wrong, but we are not equally sure about capital punishment, abortion, or war. Everyone agrees that war is evil, but we disagree as to whether there are viable alternatives to war. Everyone agrees that no one should have to suffer poverty, but we disagree on how to eliminate it. Everyone agrees that it is wrong to steal, but we disagree on whether severe punishments should be enforced.

Where fundamental values and ideals stand in almost permanent conflict in social life, we find the arena of political decision. The difference between political and moral decisions is not one of kind, but of degree. All such decisions are essentially the same: a choice among conflicting regulative ideals to attain maximum benefits for all men, based on sufficient knowledge. In a later chapter, we will study the details of such decisions.

But the average man confronts major moral conflicts only on occasion. His regulative principles serve him adequately and habitually most of the time. Custom can be an effective guide to conduct in ordinary life except in times of severe crisis. It is worth noting that an important difference between adolescence and adult life is the degree of stability in the latter. Young men and women are forced into severe confrontations far more often than their parents, for they have not made their life choices yet. The area of sexuality is a clear example of this.

Happily married adults have few sexual crises. (Unhappily married adults have many.) Adolescents are continually confronting sexual rules.

The domain of political decision is one of constant struggle and challenge. All of the requirements of society, including conflicting moral imperatives, clash continuously in political decisions. For this reason, political decisions are extremely complex, and require special efforts and dedication to resolve. There are no simple political decisions, and it is sad when people think there are. One of the primary sources of desperation is the conviction that political decisions ought to be simpler than they are.

In earlier chapters, we noted the rather common view that political and moral decisions differ, the first directed toward expediency, the second toward purity of ideals. Such a distinction is not defensible. Moral and political decisions are the same in kind. But since a moral individual has fewer responsibilities for others than a political leader, he can delude himself into thinking that he can be truer to his ideals. He can do so only because his actions seldom matter very much. Where a man's ideals would lead him to injure many others, he enters the political arena.

What has happened with representative government is that men have relinquished their moral responsibilities to deal with all the affairs of life to their political leaders, keeping only the semblance of control through the vote. They then come to the discovery that few major issues are brought before them, even indirectly. The greatest skills of a politician are used to avoid genuine issues. Such a dispersal of responsibility makes ordinary life far simpler for the average man, who prefers not to have to solve every moral and political crisis which arises. The consequences are the development of a government rather unresponsive to the needs of its members, and also an increase in the powerlessness most men feel in political affairs.

Aristotle and Plato both regard the sphere of politics as an extension of the moral sphere. Our considerations have supported that view. One of the results of separating the political and the moral is the development of a moral purity that is wholly useless for major political decisions, and is justly spurned by politicians. Yet the same purity then becomes the model for conventional morality, and supports both self-righteousness and fear of compromise. Ordinary men may be admired for their purity provided they are not given the reins of power. The belief follows, and horribly, that men who hold the political reins of power should not be men of strong principles.

A further consequence of separating the moral and the political is that ordinary men become unable to deal with crises, since they encounter them so seldom, unable to cope with opposing positions and conflicting views. The political arena is always rather remote, and affords the possibility for men of remaining ignorant of it. The ideal of being well informed is rarely appreciated. Yet all men who vote are convinced of the justification of their beliefs.

If there is a solution to this problem, it lies in the development of a society in which moral and political affairs are merged once again, and where the complexity of political decisions is made part of everyday life. What is required is a society in which the variety of options which a political leader must face are realized constantly, even held to be a fundamental value. We turn now to the consideration of the pluralistic society.

QUESTIONS

1. Is a life in the company of other people necessarily a moral corruption?
2. "It is wrong to compromise with evil." Discuss.
3. Under what circumstances can secrecy and even lies be justified? Discuss from the point of view of an individual during a crisis and also from the point of view of the government.
4. Is it possible to be a moral politician?
5. Is it always right to be a hero in a good cause?
6. To what extent can cool and deliberate choices be made during wartime? Discuss the moral implications of this issue.
7. What function do strict rules of war serve, especially since war is so horrible anyway?
8. Is there something paradoxical about the claim that it is sometimes right to be expedient?
9. How can it be argued that pacifism is morally wrong?
10. Discuss the advantages and disadvantages of having a professional army to fight a country's wars, rather than drafting civilians for that purpose.
11. What kind of argument can be given to justify going to war to defend another country against attack?
12. To what extent are our daily social relations power relations? Must they be?
13. "A revolution is never justified against a democratic government." Discuss.
14. A major principle of revolutionary tactics is that of openly challenging government officials, making them retaliate with violence. Many people are made politically conscious by being subjected to this violence themselves. Discuss such tactics from a moral point of view.
15. Is it true that a man owes his first moral obligations to his family and friends, and should not compromise himself by political actions?

SELECTED READINGS

The following are all works on crisis morality, involving war, revolution, turmoil, and betrayal:

H. Arendt, *Eichmann in Jerusalem: The Banality of Evil*, 1965, Viking.

R. Wasserstrom, *War and Morality*, 1970, Wadsworth.

S. Freud, "Thoughts for the Times on War and Death," *Collected Papers*, Vol. IV.

R. V. Sampson, *The Psychology of Power*, 1966, Pantheon. A fascinating book on little recognized power relations.

Locke, *Second Treatise on Government*. The classic work.

Works on revolution and morality.

Lenin, *State and Revolution*.

K. Kautsky, *Terrorism and Communism*, 1920, George Allen & Unwin.

L. Trotsky, *Terrorism and Dictatorship vs. Democracy*. A reply to Kautsky.

F. Fanon, *The Wretched of the Earth*, 1965, Grove.

Other works on political power:

F. Neumann, "Approaches to the Study of Political Power," *Political Science Quarterly*, Vol. LXV, No. 2 (June, 1950).

M. Weber, "Class, Status, Party," *From Max Weber*, 1946, Oxford University.

VIII. THE PLURALISTIC SOCIETY

WE HAVE noted that there are two fundamentally different approaches to moral education. One emphasizes the regulative aspect of moral principles, and is founded on authority. The other emphasizes the substantive aspect of principles, the benefit moral principles are intended to provide, and the difficulties which arise in the making of moral decisions. In our last chapter, we noted that major decisions which involve moral principles, especially those of a political nature, are always tremendously complex and difficult, and often involve elements of crisis. The emphasis on the substantive aspect of moral principles, when coupled with the extreme complexity of moral decisions, suggests that society should be organized to maximize the likelihood of resolving such complexity and settling moral disputes in beneficial ways.

Two models of social organization seem to dominate most political thought. The first and most common is that of a government which in its wisdom pursues the policies which are most likely of success, as if a government were an individual capable of making a moral decision. Here we find the governmental control over most phases of life rather complete, and all social forces mustered to the service of the policies decreed by government officials to be the best. This model tends to be derived from that of crisis. During a war or other emergency, all available resources must be dedicated to resolution of the crisis—for example, to winning the war.

The model is further supported by the view that moral and political problems are susceptible to resolution through the discoveries of science—in this case, the social sciences. In physics and chemistry, we note that scientific research tends to promote a considerable degree of uniformity of conviction, to conclusions which are *true* or *correct*. If we assume that a society rests on scientific procedures and discoveries, we are led to the assumption that a particular policy can be found which is truly the best, and which everyone ought to follow. In effect, such a model leads to a general uniformity in style of life and also in norms and values. More accurately, it assumes that such a uniformity is both desirable and effective in moral and political life.

The further pressures which tend to promote such a conception of political organization are considerable. We have noted the impulse behind all moral convictions toward universality. *Everyone* ought to follow the same principles and to have the same values. It follows that variety in social life on important values is a source of instability and of conflict. Disagreement tends to evaporate, and with it comes a felt security of conviction.

Yet too great a uniformity can lead to a blurring of the distinction between tyranny and democracy. Where tyranny is successful, it will achieve a monumental uniformity under authoritarian rule. Where democracy becomes uniform in character, it also tends to be authoritarian and to emphasize conformity—though by custom rather than decree. The uniformity of conviction and style may be thought more fundamental than the source of government power. If moral issues are truly as complex as we have understood them to be, then massive uniformity and agreement are quite artificial, and tend to misrepresent the nature of moral decisions.

In particular, uniformity in moral policy tends to become a form of moral purity. Either certain principles are followed without exception, virtually without the consideration of consequences or circumstances, and especially without considering the particular persons involved. Or else, a species of political expediency is pursued as an ultimate policy without concern for the particular persons whose sufferings are of utmost moral importance. I have in mind in the latter case the neglect of a minority who have not organized so as to be able to claim political power.

The second model of political organization is derived from the principle that although men may eventually come to agreement on the regulative principles of moral and political decision, the complexity of such decisions requires the availability of a continual plurality of options. Because men differ in their emotional constitution and in their scale of ultimate loyalties, their specific moral decisions will differ, though their regulative ideals may be the same. We have seen how men who agree on the principle that murder is wrong may nevertheless differ in their attitudes toward capital punishment. Where such difference of conviction is taken as fundamental, we come to a model of a pluralistic social organization.

In our discussion of the complex nature of most political decisions, especially in times of crisis, we noted that the greatest need was for a society which is highly responsive to the need for change, and also highly responsive to the needs of its members. Revolutionary aims become significant where men are desperate with frustration. The two sources of this frustration are a sense of deprivation and suffering, and an inability to do anything about them. We have noted that a revolution is justified only in times of clear and extreme crisis. It follows, however, that a society which would avoid being overthrown must find a way to meet the needs of its members without generating extreme crisis. The first model of social organization, a monolithic conception of social welfare, avoids crisis just so long as it is successful and resolves its basic problems. As soon as unresolvable problems arise, however, such a society is thrown into fundamental crisis. It is monolithic, uniform, and founded on the principle of a best solution, though where none can be found. A pluralistic society can be responsive to its members without encouraging total solutions.

Most important of all, the first model tends to overwhelm the diversity of individuals in a society with a uniform policy, as if the decisions of the ruler might serve for all men. The second model takes as fundamental the plurality of persons and therefore the plurality of obligations within social life, assuming that no one person or group, however brilliant, can promote a complete reconciliation of individual interests. The first model stresses a tight and uniform society in which each individual has a place. Plato's *Republic* is certainly founded on this model. The second stresses a heterogeneous and diversified society with a great deal of flexibility, which affords individuals room to make their own decisions and their own mistakes, provided these do not overly harm themselves or others. The first model may not depend on coercive powers of any sort, but only looks to uniformity in life as a great goal. The second literally aims at heterogeneity and diversity. It is the second model to which we now turn.

A. Freedom of speech

The most complete account of the value of freedom of speech is found in John Stuart Mill's great essay, *On Liberty*. All too often we find lip service paid both to the right to free speech and to Mill's essay, without a concrete connection between the two. All too seldom is Mill's argument taken seriously, though it is one of the most powerful cases for an absolute right to a freedom that has ever been made. We have noted several times that Mill develops a theory of act utilitarianism, though he seems to move also to a rule utilitarianism. *On Liberty* is a wonderful example of the kind of argument which can be given for a rule on utilitarian principles. Yet Mill does not speak of utilitarianism in his discussion of liberty.

Mill's argument has two distinct poles. First, he makes a case for freedom of speech in connection with the truth of the positions espoused. Second, he makes a case for freedom of speech in terms of its larger impact on social life. It is worth considering both of these arguments in some detail.

(1) We assume to begin with that speech is aimed at gaining truth, or at least at making it clear. Such an assumption allows Mill to attack directly the opposition to free speech which maintains that the truth has already been discovered, and that all opposing views should be banned. It is worth noting that some uses of language have little relationship to truth or falsity, and would not seem to come under Mill's argument in any way. The Free Speech movement at the University

of California several years ago was a movement based on the right to utter obscenities in the name of free speech. There is no protection of such a freedom to be found in Mill's arguments, and we will not consider that freedom in our discussion. As we will see, Mill's second argument does raise some issues relevant to the freedom to use obscenities in public, but not in a way which enables us to reach a definite conclusion on that subject.

It is worth noting also that freedom of speech is protected on Mill's arguments only where truth and falsity are at stake, not action. The issue is how to arrive at truth and avoid error. Where a man exhorts a mob to lynch a man, there is no issue of truth or falsity, but of how to act. Deliberation and thought are ruled out by circumstances. It is often held that freedom of speech is protected only where it can be maintained that deliberation and study are appropriate. Thus, freedom of speech might not be protected where the speech itself was a dangerous action—for example, shouting "Fire!" in a crowd.

If speech is directed at achieving truth and avoiding falsehood, then Mill's first argument has three parts.

(a) Let us assume that the controversial opinion is *true*. Clearly it is unsupportable that authority should have the right to suppress a position which is correct. But, as Mill points out, any controversial position *may* be true, and an authority which would suppress it assumes its own infallibility. To the reply that such suppression is merely the exercise of judgment on the part of the authority, Mill simply points out how often true positions have been suppressed throughout history. A false opinion should be refuted, not suppressed. The first argument in favor of free speech is that the position suppressed may be true.

(b) Suppose instead the controversial opinion is indeed *false*—though we cannot be sure of it infallibly. Mill argues that it is not enough to *believe* what is true. It is necessary to understand it and to be able to reply to criticisms of it. Here Mill attacks both intuitionism and authority as grounds of belief. Men who believe without test lose their faith easily under fire. Convictions are made far more secure when they are criticized and when their proponents have to refute these criticisms and attack proposed alternatives.

For many years, the United States has had a mortal fear of the Red menace, and many people oppose giving Communists the right to speak freely, as if their opinions heard openly could corrupt those who heard them. Mill reminds us of Socrates, who also was convicted of corrupting the youth. Young minds are far more likely to oppose evil if they come to understand it openly as such, than if they encounter it in secret and unopposed. Mill's basic argument here is that it is not enough to *believe* what is true. It is necessary to understand it and to be able to defend it. Open argument and discussion *strengthen* conviction in what is true.

(c) More likely than either of the former assumptions is that the controversial position is a mixed one—half true and half false. History must by now have taught us that most established beliefs are half-truths. Suppression of a controversial position literally denies us the chance to amend our errors and to come closer to a fuller truth. We note that, in the sciences, freedom of inquiry is preserved at all costs, for progress in science is possible only through discussion and the resolution of controversy.

But we may add to Mill's argument the conviction which our study of moral decisions has brought, that moral issues are especially complex and difficult to resolve. Here we see most clearly the need for open discussion. For all significant moral issues depend on a conflict among regulative principles, with no simple or obvious solution. Only the free and open discussion of the variety of options can lead us to a fuller conception of how to live well.

We note in response to this last point that moral decisions are not decisions of a purely intellectual character, concerning merely a theoretical truth, but deeply affect how men live and act. Moral controversy is bound to have the greatest impact on the lives of men. And the greatest impact of all depends on the freedom with which the controversy proceeds. Mill tacitly acknowledges the continuum of means and ends in his argument. In addition to the principles upon which controversy may be waged, the very fact of open discussion instead of suppression has vital moral consequences. This brings us to Mill's second argument.

(2) The suppression of all views which oppose the established position generates a complete uniformity of belief and of life, especially if we include moral principles as we must. Here Mill asserts as a fundamental value the individuality which is to be understood as diversity, fertility, and inventiveness. Mill himself makes this point as well as anyone can.

> It is not by wearing down into uniformity all that is individual in them-selves, but by cultivating it, and calling it forth, within the limits imposed by the rights and interests of others, that human beings become a noble and beautiful object of contemplation; and as the works partake the character of those who do them, by the same process human life also becomes rich, diversified, and animating, furnishing more abundant aliment to high thoughts and elevating feelings, and strengthening the tie which binds every individual to the race, by making the race infinitely better worth belonging to. In proportion to the development of his individuality, each person becomes more valuable to himself, and is therefore capable of being more valuable to others. There is a greater fullness of life about his own existence, and when there is more life in the units there is more in the mass which is composed of them. As much compression as is necessary to prevent the stronger specimens of human nature from encroaching on the rights of others cannot be dispensed with; but for this there is ample compensation even in the point of view of human development. The means of development which the individual loses by being prevented from gratifying his inclinations to the injury of others, are chiefly obtained at the expense of the develop-ment of other people. And even to himself there is a full equivalent in the better development of the social part of his nature, rendered possible by the

restraint put upon the selfish part. To be held to rigid rules of justice for the sake of others, develops the feelings and capacities which have the good of others for their object. But to be restrained in things not affecting their good, by their mere displeasure, develops nothing valuable, except such force of character as may unfold itself in resisting the restraint. If acquiesced in, it dulls and blunts itself in resisting the restraint. To give any fair play to the nature of each, it is essential that different persons should be allowed to lead different lives. In proportion as this latitude has been exercised in any age, has that age been noteworthy to posterity. Even despotism does not produce its worst effects so long as individuality exists under it; and whatever crushes individuality is despotism, by whatever name it may be called, and whether it professes to be enforcing the will of God or the injunctions of men.

It is through the free spirit of individuals that originality and especially genius can inhabit the world of men. No one can deny the need for these in human life.

Unfortunately, Mill notes, men are mostly moderate in their wants and in their minds, and tend to distrust stronger forms of individuality. Especially, we find that the strength of custom and habit is so great as to virtually suppress the variety of forms which individuality takes. When custom becomes too strong, individuality perishes, and so does progress. What has protected Western society in the past from static decay has been the tremendous variety in lives of men. But even in Mill's time,

> they now read the same things, listen to the same things, see the same things, go to the same places, have their hopes and fears directed to the same objects, have the same rights and liberties, and the same means of asserting them. Great as are the differences of position which remain, they are nothing to those which have ceased. And the assimilation is still proceeding. All the political changes of the age promote it, since they all tend to raise the low and to lower the high. Every extension of education promotes it, because education brings people under common influences, and gives them access to the general stock of facts and sentiments. Improvement in the means of communication promotes it, by bringing the inhabitants of distant places into personal contact, and keeping up a rapid flow of changes of residence between one place and another. The increase of commerce and manufactures promotes it, by diffusing more widely the advantage of easy circumstances, and opening all objects of ambition, even the highest, to general competition, whereby the desire of rising becomes no longer the character of a particular class, but of all classes. A more powerful agency than even all these, in bringing about a general similarity among mankind, is the complete establishment, in this and other free countries, of the ascendancy of public opinion in the State. As the various social eminences which enabled persons entrenched on them to disregard the opinion of the multitude gradually become leveled; as the very

idea of resisting the will of the public, when it is positively known that they have a will, disappears more and more from the minds of practical politicians: there ceases to be any social support for nonconformity—any substantive power in society which, itself opposed to the ascendancy of numbers, is interested in taking under its protection opinions and tendencies at variance with those of the public.

The combination of all these causes forms so great a mass of influences hostile to individuality, that it is not easy to see how it can stand its ground. It will do so with increasing difficulty, unless the intelligent part of the public can be made to feel its value—to see that it is good there should be differences, even though not for the better, even though, as it may appear to them, some should be for the worse. If the claims of individuality are ever to be asserted, the time is now, while much is still wanting to complete the enforced assimilation. It is only in the earlier stages that any stand can be successfully made against the encroachment. The demand that all other people shall resemble ourselves grows by what it feeds on. If resistance waits till life is reduced *nearly* to one uniform type, all deviations from that type will come to be considered impious, immoral, even monstrous and contrary to nature. Mankind speedily become unable to conceive diversity, when they have been for some time unaccustomed to see it.

Mill does not neglect the problem that men of strong individuality can sometimes harm others. Society must indeed defend men from each other through law, principle, and custom. But the ruling ideal he is espousing is that of *minimal* moral control, to achieve *maximal* diversity in individual life. The ultimate source of all value is the feelings and thoughts of individual men. To weaken the strength of their individuality is to weaken the value of human life.

Many people fear chaos and social instability far more than they fear uniformity and mediocrity. To such people, Mill is arguing forcefully that too great a uniformity may be the first step toward a decay that will be far more destructive than what these people fear. The rebellion in cultural forms in the United States of the late 1960's and early 70's may be viewed as a violent revulsion against the uniformity of middle-class life and established norms. Mill does not ignore the social requirement of order and stability, but rather views it as already achieved and no longer threatened. The greater threat is to diversity and individuality.

We may perhaps reach a compromise between Mill and those who fear instability, by postulating as two regulative ideals which often conflict, *both* that of individuality—diversity, originality, difference; and that of social harmony—uniformity, cooperation, tradition. Mill's argument is directed at what he sees as the greater danger—the elimination of individuality. Social cohesion is well established, and can be continued through a minimal form of constraint. We have seen in the past few decades both the greater need for government control of individual life to gain individual benefits, and also the danger that such controls will nullify differences among individuals. The reconciling of two such opposed ideals is one of the great problems for both political and individual life.

We may summarize Mill's entire position by noting that he defends liberty in speech not only because it leads to truth, but because it also leads to diversity and individuality. The ideal of individuality forces us to consider a pluralistic society, for a monolithic society is destructive to originality. We turn now to a more detailed discussion of this individuality.

B. Individuality

It is important that we realize that the diversity and originality which Mill ascribes to individuals are not values for such individuals alone. We note again that the Christian dichotomy between egoism and altruism, between concern for oneself and concern for others, is fundamentally misleading. It suggests that a man may be either selfish or generous. What is left out is the realization that human life as a whole, and especially in its social qualities, requires individuals who are original and varied in their thoughts and attitudes. The sacrifices a man is supposed to make to others may weaken his value to them. It is this most of all which drives Nietzsche to oppose herd morality, and to dwell on the need for superior individuals.

The fundamental principle is that societies are composed of individuals. No one would deny it. But the complete ramifications of this relationship are often overlooked. In particular, societies do not act: men do. Societies do not invent: men do. Societies do not have obligations: men do. Most important of all, societies do not make decisions or judgments of value: men do. The qualities societies possess are consequences of the decisions, actions, and values of the individuals who comprise these societies. Of course, individual decisions and values are in part determined by social customs and institutions.

It is common to think of individual and social interests standing in opposition, as if societies could have interests distinct from the needs of their members. A more accurate description would be that individuals in a society have opposing needs, for separateness and also for sharing, for originality and also for community. An equally accurate description is that societies themselves have opposing needs, if they are to serve the interests of their members, for harmony and co-operation, but also for change and development.

In several earlier chapters, we studied the benefits society offers its members. We saw that men both desire the company of other men, and are benefited by the goods that are provided through cooperation. The sharing of activities can strengthen the powers of men, and can also make these activities more enjoyable. Individuals gain *as* individuals by some degree of cooperation and community. However, we noted also that every benefit provided by community could be overdone, and would then become a disadvantage.

Suppose we ask now, what benefits do individuals provide society? An immediate problem comes to mind. That is, that society does not have goals or receive benefits. Only men do. It follows from this that individuals may be judged in terms of what they offer to society only to the extent that this society in return benefits its members. A society which provides a necessary security from attack to its people may endeavor to find a better leader for defense. But a society which oppresses its people and causes them suffering cannot properly speak of an individual serving it. What sense can be made of the notion that an individual serves a collective order, other than that men are so served? In the writings of Italian fascists it is possible to find the view that men should serve the State. The view seems to be that a strong state is somehow good, independent of any individuals it is good *for*. Such a view is a strange and virtually indefensible one.

We must first determine the benefits which a social organization provides the individual members of a society. Clearly a society provides the pleasures of community, a strengthening of abilities, and also is an object of loyalty. Now, how can individual men contribute to each of these? The pleasures of the company of other people are varied, but in general seem to depend on the strength of the individuality of the people involved. It is true that men desire the approval and even the love of others. But as Sartre has pointed out, approval and love are the less valuable when the person who approves of us is less a strong and free individual in his own right. For a man without an original thought to approve of us because everyone else does so is no compliment at all. A musician complimented by the crowd receives no pleasure, compared with the praise he may receive from a master.

It follows, then, that as men become more alike and less varied in their abilities and qualities, their emotional responses become more predictable, more ordinary, and less valuable. An individual gives other men pleasure by approving of them, but only where that approval is a sign of respect from one worthy individual to another. This is one of Nietzsche's favorite themes.

Second, the abilities of men are strengthened through the discoveries which are made by individual men. Here Mill's defense of free speech is of direct relevance. When a society suppresses invention and originality, all its members suffer. They are themselves repressed, and they are also denied access to the views which might have helped them. The argument is obvious when we consider the contributions of the physical and social sciences. Were a society to suppress originality in these fields, all men would suffer, for science is one of the greatest sources of power, through knowledge.

In general, technological societies have learned the folly of suppressing controversial scientific opinions. Yet such societies have not seen the greater folly of suppressing controversial moral and political beliefs. The argument is the same. Where unpopular views are suppressed, men are deprived of the opportunity to consider alternatives.

As for the third benefit of society, its value as an object of loyalty, we are led to the difference between a loyalty which is blind to the faults of its object, and a loyalty which seeks to improve its object. As soon as we realize that social loyalties are values for *individuals*, then once again we need open controversy and diversity. Blind patriotism may involve a blindness to the truth also.

We may summarize this discussion in the following terms. What individuals contribute to society is provided by the strength of their minds and the variety of their abilities. Such a principle is embodied in the common view that a society's strength resides in its superior individuals, its great men. In this respect, society is not only a benefit to individuals, but individuals enable a society to serve its functions well. From this point of view, individuality is a quality of social life— that of variety, diversity, and inventiveness.

Put another way, individuality is not opposed to sociality, but to homogeneity and too great a uniformity. Too uniform a society is inflexible and blind to change. Individuality is the quality of a society adaptable to new things, and able to meet new adventures. A closed and static society is unsuccessful as a society. It is particularly vulnerable to new technologies and unexpected happenings. A static society might be pleasing to all its members, yet it would make them extremely vulnerable to the impact of novelty. Individuality in Mill's sense, of diversity and uniqueness, originality and inventiveness, is a benefit both to men and especially to a stable and adaptable social order. Customs tend to become rigid and unyielding. A variety of individuals in a pluralistic society can oppose the hardening of custom by fresh points of view.

What is the exact proportion of variety and uniformity required for an adaptable and harmonious society? Such a question is senseless. It has no answer, for the exact proportions cannot be measured. It has no answer, for the proportions necessarily vary with time and from society to society. It especially has no answer for there is no answer fit for all times and places. Rather, the proportion required can be maintained only in a dynamic equilibrium. Societies move through the development of unyielding customs to too great a uniformity, and must then find ways to loosen the bonds of conformity and to open men's minds. Perhaps too great a tendency will then develop toward nonconformity and disharmony, toward chaos and distrust. In response, a new trend will develop toward harmonious cooperation and customary conformity.

Nevertheless, Mill is correct that within a functioning social order, the only extreme worth fighting against is too great a conformity. Where there is too little agreement, society falls apart. Yet such a prospect is extremely remote and unlikely for established nations. It was a great possibility in Hobbes' time, when each town was a small society of its own, barely able to survive. In modern times, nations are so securely established through custom and tradition as well as force that the prospects of too much individuality are beyond expectation. It is the ties of conformity and mediocrity which are to be fought.

Can there be too much individuality? In Mill's sense of individuality as originality and inventiveness, diversity of outlook and intelligence, probably not. Even in rebellion, the rebels take on a similar form of dress and talk. It is ex-

tremely difficult to achieve a truly novel point of view, and to be original enough
to make a genuine contribution to thought or life. Emerson's essay on *Self-Reliance* also rests on the difficulty of being unique. It is so difficult that it requires a heroic effort without fear of going too far toward uniqueness. Men who fear individuality fear not originality but specific kinds of difference, especially a concern for oneself that neglects the rights and needs of other men.

There cannot be too much individuality. There can only be the wrong kind of individuality, an individuality not in thought or belief, in outlook and contribution, but in selfish and heedless action. When individuality is opposed to sociality, it can become absurd and also destructive. Individuality, as a dimension of social life, is in fact *an involvement with others*, by making an original and diversified contribution to them. As Mill points out, what we need are secure moral rules which protect other men from direct injury, and leave men free to find their own styles of life. Unfortunately, as Mill points out, custom can be so overpowering as to lead to almost total conformity even where no force compels it. In the end, Mill's position is that differences among men are valuable in themselves, and should be encouraged at great expense, provided that only minimal protections are maintained. Individuality is an ultimate ideal in human life.

If individuality is an ultimate ideal, then we can understand the convictions shared by many people that men have certain absolute rights to their own persons and lives. The Declaration of Independence defines our rights as to life, liberty, and the pursuit of happiness. But it must be noted that a country may take the lives of its criminals, or demand the lives of its patriots. A country also places some restraints on liberty, at least where one man would harm another. Finally, the right to pursuit of happiness is not worth much if happiness is made unavailable through customs and circumstances.

It is almost impossible to define precisely the absolute rights individuals must possess in a society which respects individuality. No one can guarantee the right to happiness or even to pleasure. Has a man an unqualified right to his body? An ill man may be taken against his will to a hospital. A soldier may be ordered to kill the enemy. A criminal may be jailed for his past misdeeds. Has a man an absolute right to his own life? Capital punishment has been practiced since the beginning of time. Has a man an absolute right to *take* his own life? We restrain a suicide attempt if we can. The justification given is that most suicides are the result of illness and imbalance. In practice, however, a suicide attempt is always prevented first, and analyzed afterward.

Mill defends the attractive thesis that individuals ought to have the right to do anything at all, however destructive to themselves or repugnant to others, provided they harm no one else. Such a principle has to many people a surface implausibility. Certainly it is not obviously right to allow men to harm themselves. Yet I believe this principle to be as well founded as any regulative principle can be, at least so far as law and enforcement are concerned.

The grounds are completely substantive. We may grant without ado that drugs, alcohol, and cigarette smoking are harmful to a person who uses them. Yet such harm may be far less than the results of prohibitive legislation would be. We have noted the abortive attempts at prohibiting the use of alcohol. Laws which interfere with personal activities tend to become oppressive, and also to make men contemptuous of law. Homosexuality may generally be despised. Yet it would not follow from this that it should be prohibited by law. On the other hand, laws may be desirable to prevent either homosexual or heterosexual acts of aggression.

We might say, then, that we have discovered an absolute right of individuals to engage in any activities whatsoever that harm no one else. However, the phrase "absolute right" is a dangerous one to use. Rather, let us say instead that we have discovered a regulative principle: men shall not be prohibited through law from engaging in any activities which harm no one else. I say "through law," for we really ought to try to talk a man out of jumping out of a window if we find him about to do so. In addition, like all regulative principles, this one is likely to conflict with others. If we find a man shooting heroin, is it really right for us to turn away? If we find a drunk in the street, though it was his choice, shall we ignore him? We may have found a regulative principle which should be observed so far as law is concerned. But as moral individuals, we cannot ignore the harm men do to themselves. At some point, we are morally obligated to interfere. Once again, the issue addressed is too complex for a single principle to resolve.

The reason why such absolute rights cannot be defended without qualification is that absolute rights are moral principles which are overly pure, and circumstances and consequences may force us to qualify them, *though only where other regulative principles are concerned*. One of the most plausible is the rule that an innocent man must never be punished to benefit others. Almost no one would advocate that we do so. Yet in time of war, we can imagine choosing to execute an innocent man to preserve the morale of troops in the front lines. What if the certain alternative were the death of everyone? If we refrain, it is because of the awesome risk involved in guessing the future. A degree of moral purity protects us against the foolhardiness of trying to guess what will come when we do not know.

Individuality may be regarded as one of the greater ideals which carry moral weight. The lives and also the uniqueness of men are values to be preserved at *almost* any (though not quite any) cost. The sense we have that men have absolute rights is a reflection of our acceptance of this ideal. The reason why we cannot quite define these rights is the inherent vagueness all ideals possess. Nevertheless, the strength of this ideal is a central feature of all moral and political judgments. When it is weakened, by either the use of force or even the rigidity of custom, all moral values are shaken.

Thus, where law results in the poverty and suffering of a few, and a uniform life for the rest, men seek individual liberty in strange ways. They turn to drugs and break the law, as if that were a path to individuality. They claim that drugs can improve the personality, and make a man more inventive and original. If young men and women may look ahead to a life called good, which contains a

dullness of homogeneity and few genuine options because there are so few important differences, they may disdain the entire prospect offered them. Such a
reaction tends to support the sense that individuality is truly a fundamental value.

We must therefore add to the strong bond which men feel for one another,
and which underlies all communal life, the other desire, for personal identity and
uniqueness. Unfortunately, these are not clear notions. For if mere identity and
uniqueness were desirable, we could satisfy our need through our social security
numbers. The identity which is needed is not a mere label, but part of activities
within a social community. Men seek uniqueness in their involvements with others,
and in their activities and abilities.

Both community as sharing, and individuality as difference, are ultimate
values. How they will be harmonized in a given society or for a given individual is
not determinable in the abstract. For some men, small intimate communities
provide a sharing which is also individuality, to the degree that a variety of
communities exist which are genuinely different from each other. For others, large
heterogeneous and loosely-woven groupings may provide both a general mode of
sharing and room for a variety of individuals within it. But in all cases, the need
for union must be tempered by diversity and difference. Each society must
develop a plurality of alternatives within it. Even more plausibly, the wealth of
different societies in the world may afford its own plurality. Many people fear that
there is a world trend toward technological uniformity, and that all countries are
developing toward a single norm. That is a fate terrible to contemplate.

C. Community

We noted just above the possibility of achieving an adequate balance of
community with uniqueness through small intimate groupings. The impulse
toward a utopian communal life has always been present in larger societies. The
complex and tormented life of ordinary man is thought to be resolved by a simpler
existence. But complete isolation is extreme and unbearable to most men. The
alternative of a small social community, modelled on the large family, seems
attractive to many. Life is simpler. The number of people to be dealt with is
small. The variety of options is small. Everyone can know each other fairly
intimately. The temptation is to imagine that such a communal life can be
deeply satisfying on the one hand, yet provide a unique sense of identity for its
members on the other.

The variety of benefits which communal life can provide is rather great. Let
us note just a few of them, with their associated drawbacks.

(1) A morality founded on a general concern for mankind is a difficult one.
Freud claims that it is unnatural for men to love all men, and natural to love but a
few. A small community in which everyone knows everyone else fairly intimately
is a more natural moral unit. Morality is supported by close ties and genuine
concern. Instead of abstract rules of interrelationship, men can live by direct and

open personal relationships. Friends and acquaintances can achieve a far greater honesty and openness in their actions toward each other. The anonymity which is required of men to endure urban life is replaced by a genuine concern for all the people around.

The positive prospects for communal life are obvious and many. There can indeed be found families which achieve a great closeness and mutual respect. However, the intimacy of family life can also bring with it special strains, which cannot be relieved by developing new social relationships if the community is too small. Families can develop jealousies and hatreds. Feelings run particularly strong in large families, both positive and negative. A small community may gain the benefits but also the ills of forced intimacy. In particular, family members often learn to avoid honesty, as destructive and debilitating, without compensating benefits.

(2) A small community achieves a degree of isolation from the rest of the world which can afford some prospect of ideal relations. Utopian communities are marked by the sense that within the smaller scope of interrelationships in a community isolated from the larger society, a greater moral purity can be achieved. Monastery life rests on the same principle: that large size is an important element in making decency and integrity impossible.

On the other hand, small towns testify to the destructive aspects of such isolation. Separation can lead to narrowness. Members of a small town may come to feel trapped, unable to leave, yet unable to endure the narrow norms of the community. Isolation has its virtues. But the agility of the larger society to replenish its stock from outside may be lost.

(3) Smaller communities tend to develop styles of life which differ from community to community. The benefits here are that individual members of different communities gain a sense of personal uniqueness through their community. On the other hand, within each community, styles of life are likely to merge and become uniform. Again, small towns show how narrow are the prospects for variety in a smaller community. If individual diversity is to be achieved through communities, it must be coupled with a great degree of mobility. Such mobility, however, would militate against the intimacy of the ties generated within the community. The strength of custom within a community can be very great. Such communal life may destroy the prospects of originality in its members.

(4) The impulse toward the intimacy of communal life can be drawn from a desire for a *new* kind of community. We find the impulse toward utopianism almost always grounded in a new sense of human relations. In Israel, many people discern the prospects of a new society, founded on intimate communities which overcome the flaws of the small family by a larger yet not very large communal relationship.

For example, children brought up in a family with only two adults as authority figures are exposed both to a very narrow range of adult norms and to a strong proprietary sense of ownership of children by parents. An alternative which is already established on many Israeli *kibbutzim* is the communal rearing of children. In its extreme form, not practiced literally anywhere, children are a community asset, and are tended by any and all adults, brought up in common, and with no sense of belonging to a particular set of parents. Plato describes such a communal mode of rearing as a way of avoiding the narrowness of family life and the strong emotional ties which may be harmful to children.

In many respects, though it is somewhat early to be sure, the *kibbutzim* have developed a new kind of man and a new mode of relatedness. The loyalties of adults brought up in a communal setting are strongly communal. They have a lesser sense of personal idiosyncrasy, yet may also have rather strong personalities by conventional standards. The common mode of education and upbringing is bound to create a greater uniformity among the members of the community. In addition, members of a kibbutz are less selfish and competitive than are members of other societies.

An interesting and similar prospect can be found described in *Walden II*, by the behaviorist psychologist B. F. Skinner. Skinner postulates a small community where children are conditioned against the stronger and destructive emotions, such as jealousy and hatred. Such a community realizes a uniformity of ease and tranquillity, and a general sense of well-being for everyone. Obviously the members of such a community will be rather alike, since they will not differ from each other in the violent emotions we often consider essential to personality. In addition, the intense competitive drives and overweening ambitions that have led to great achievements and also to overpowering frustration will be gone. The members of Skinner's community paint and write, in a quiet and moderate way, which they presumably find quite satisfying.

Such a conception of communal life is a major alternative to urban life. If it is to be adopted, several questions must be considered. (a) Is it a viable alternative? Skinner uses current psychological principles for his basis. In a sense, then, he is quite practical. He does not deal with the larger problem of whether many such communities could be conjoined in a complete society. (b) Is the elimination of the violent emotions an unmixed good? Competitiveness, ambition, hatred, and envy are certainly destructive. Yet many great things have been achieved by men who suffered them. Would we want a uniformly peaceful world, or would it be dull and unsatisfying? (c) Is the goal of human life the contentment and peacefulness Skinner assumes, or are there not other equally valuable goals which his community would be unable to achieve?

This last question is the fundamental one. Are there a small number of ideal values whose realization would mean complete satisfaction? Or are there not many human ideals, which are often in conflict, which can be realized only in part, and at the price of some of the others? I suspect that for mankind as a whole, the latter alternative is the true one. Men are alike in many respects, but also different. Any static achievement of ideals may well prove unsatisfying to many men. It does not follow that no adequate communal life can be achieved, only that it depends on a pluralistic realization of alternatives and benefits. Skinner's fundamental error consists not in the assumption that psychology may provide the answer to human needs—it well may—but in the other assumption, that a uniform goal of human life will serve men satisfactorily.

Nevertheless, the whole subject of new communities and alternative social relations ought to make it clear that we have no final solutions at hand, nor any specific way of life to offer for all or even most men. And the only conclusion that can be defended here is that a variety of options must be tried, and a pluralism of styles of life always maintained as alternatives.

D. Privacy

The impulse toward community exists on all levels of social life. It ranges from family ties to patriotic nationalism. We have noted Mill's forceful arguments against uniformity and the suppression of individual differences. It is worth at least a passing mention of a value that is not only vanishing in modern life, but whose passing is mourned by few people—the value of privacy.

It is important to be clear that privacy has never been available to many people. It is the purest type of elite value. Where large families live in limited space, privacy is impossible. The very poor will never be able to afford privacy. In addition, many people who can afford space of their own find a strong pressure without and also a strong need from within themselves to join their neighbors in constant activities, and to avoid a privacy which appears to them a kind of loneliness.

Nevertheless, there was for many years an ideal of privacy which people who lived in overcrowded conditions hoped for. The desire for community in the past few years has made this privacy appear no longer an ideal. Young people live during college in dormitories which afford no privacy. When they leave college, they live with three or four roommates, and have no privacy. A whole generation of street people has grown up, who live in public on the streets.

The value of privacy is tied intimately to the value of individuality. There are two basic reasons for this.

(1) A public life is necessarily a life of compromise. We have seen enough in our discussion of the varying needs of people to be sure that in public relations, people are forced to accede to a very great extent to the needs and wishes of others. Family relations are a strain because members of a family must continuously keep the needs of other members in mind, in almost everything they do. The virtues of community are many, and there is ample justification for the compromises necessary to social life. But if a man is to develop himself uniquely, distinct from others though among them, he needs a place and a time for privacy. Thoreau is one

of the most noble men in the American tradition. His nobility is part and parcel of the qualities that enabled him to live alone at Walden Pond for three years. Only a man capable of such isolation could advocate civil disobedience with such power.

(2) Individuality is to Mill difference and originality. But originality is always a private matter. An original idea made public ceases to be original, partly because others share it, but far more because they modify it from their own points of view. Certainly original ideas should be shared. They are meant to be appropriated by others and modified by them. But they are born in privacy and isolation. The inventor withdraws for a time into his laboratory. The artist works alone in his studio. Eventually they emerge and present their achievements to the world. But their creation is an individual and private thing.

Obviously privacy can be overdone. Kafka wanted his writings destroyed after his death, and the world would have been the worse had his wishes been followed. Complete privacy is usually impossible, and seldom productive either of things or even of original ideas. Yet the pressures which surround modern life are not toward too great a privacy, but against its very existence. Apartment houses are built with very thin walls. Virtually everyone owns a telephone, which is used by unconscionable salesmen to harass people in their homes at will.

Modern society is complex, and suffers insecurities from within and without. A consequence of this has been that the last vestiges of privacy have been invaded by officials of the government in the name of efficiency and security. Telephones are tapped. Dossiers are compiled on private citizens for legal political activities, at the mere whim of officials and law enforcement agencies. All members of modern society are checked and cross-checked in a central registry. Clearly, there are advantages to such surveillance. Hardened criminals find it more difficult to escape detection. Taxes are collected more effectively and accurately.

Yet it is not implausible to argue that totalitarianism and lack of privacy go hand in hand. Where a government keeps all its citizens under close watch, and allows them no privacy, it moves toward controlling them at will. It is true that surveillance is not directly a form of control. But it is absurd to ignore the ease with which it can become so. The continuum of means and ends warns us to realize that means used have a strong tendency to generate ends like themselves. In addition, knowledge of surveillance strikes fear into most men's hearts, and deters them from lawful actions they might otherwise have performed. Even intimate communities modelled on the family, where privacy is almost totally lacking, have a repressive quality unless individuals can leave at will and suffer no penalty.

Privacy is a sphere in which a man can do whatever he wishes, where he is responsible to no one but himself. The smaller is the private sphere, the more a man is forced to conform to the demands of others. The greater the sphere of privacy, the greater the chance a man has to develop his unique manner of life.

Too much privacy can be debilitating to an individual, and socially harmful as well. Too little privacy affords communal ties and an escape from loneliness, but at considerable cost. We have once again a problem that has no simple solution.

QUESTIONS

1. Should a government seek to define the best way of life for the members of the society over which it rules? Should we look to the experts who are knowledgeable in economics, in political affairs, and in international affairs, to provide the basis for political decisions? Discuss the issues involved here.

2. How should a pluralistic society be developed to meet the needs of the poor and unskilled who are now on welfare? Or would welfare be unnecessary in a pluralistic society? What would be the difference?

3. Should a Nazi be allowed to advocate in public the killing of Jews? How about during the Second World War?

4. Should a man be allowed to solicit actors for pornographic films as a right to free speech? Is hard-core pornography protected under the right to free speech?

5. Is academic freedom a good? Does it depend on educational institutions avoiding controversial positions, at least as official policy?

6. Should nihilists who profess the destruction of everything good, and who institute riots and violent demonstrations, be put in jail?

7. Is it possible to have a just and yet pluralistic society? Can there be individuality where there are no major differences of social or economic class?

8. Mill believes that a society may reach a point of so great a uniformity that differences and deviations are no longer possible. Is he correct that such a point can be reached? Have we reached it?

9. What are some of the problems connected with the principle that men should be allowed maximal liberty to do what they wish, provided they do not harm each other?

10. Should we encourage minor forms of neurosis and even insanity as types of individuality?

11. Were the hippies and the beats before them the most individualistic people of their generation?

12. Has a man an absolute right to freedom of speech?

13. Can we achieve individuality by simply acting differently from everyone else?

14. Are two heads better than one in art, science, or morals?

15. Should everyone be required by law to spend one hour of every day alone and with no distractions?

Works on the problems of democratic social life:

L. T. Hobhouse, *Liberalism*, 1945, Oxford University.

R. H. Tawney, *Equality*, 4th ed., 1952, George Allen & Unwin.

G. Myrdal, *An American Dilemma*, 1944, Harper.

D. Riesman et. al., *The Lonely Crowd*, rev. ed., 1950, Yale University.

H. Brown, *The Challenge of Man's Future*, 1954, Viking. The last decade's long-range view.

C. A. Reich, *The Greening of America*, 1970, Random. The latest optimism.

Nietzsche, *Thus Spake Zarathustra*.

J. Ortega y Gasset, *The Revolt of the Masses*, 1932, Norton.

J. Schumpeter, *Capitalism, Socialism, and Democracy*, 3rd ed., 1950, Harper.

F. Engels, *Socialism: Utopian and Scientific*.

L. Mumford, *Technics and Civilization*, 1934, Harcourt Brace & World.

M. Weber, *From Max Weber*, 1958, Oxford University.

IX. DECISION

THE VARIETY of issues we have considered in our discussion, and the complexity of human life, should make it clear that moral decisions are complex also. Their complexity has several dimensions, some of which we will now review.

A. Evaluation

A moral agent finds himself in a moral situation when he is called upon to make a decision and to act in some way, and where some regulative principle has application in determining what he ought to do. We have already noted the elements which enter into the making of a moral decision: the circumstances of the situation, the consequences which will be brought about through action, the principles which constitute the situation a moral one, and the feelings of the agent in determining what is satisfying and to what he owes his loyalty.

The simplest moral decision is one which involves a single *prima facie* obligation, and where no conflict among principles, ideals, or loyalites is involved. Here we may go so far as to say that decision is not made "by" the agent, but is determined by the situation itself. A man finds a wallet containing money in the street, and has no need for the money himself. *Certainly*, he ought to return it to its owner.

A somewhat more complex situation is involved where several principles come in conflict, but where one of them holds priority over the others. A physician may lie to a dying old woman to spare her pain, though he believes that lying is in general wrong. In such cases, certain precautions must be taken by the agent. He must not act from hidden motives which would compromise his decision. For example, a physician who lies to a patient merely to spare himself embarrassment may not be acting rightly. His decision is not justified unless he has at least coped with the temptation of his own feelings. The problem of self-deception arises here and will be discussed shortly.

A full-scale moral situation is one where several moral principles conflict, all of which command the agent's ultimate loyalties. As we have seen, a moral action is one which is regulated by a moral principle which permits no exceptions. The substantive value of the principle is grounded in its being accepted as a regulative principle commanding obedience without exception. Yet a man can find that two such principles conflict, in a situation where at least one must be disobeyed. A father may feel an unquestioning obligation to protect his son from harm, only to discover that the boy has committed a burglary. The father also believes that a thief should be punished.

In such a case, it is simplistic to assume that an obvious choice can be made between two *prima facie* obligations. The choice is anything but obvious. What the father must do is to determine what course of action will prove most satisfying to him and to everyone concerned. He must take into account the need to achieve a rule for action, for if he violates rules with impunity, it may be impossible for others to trust him. A man for whom no rules are binding is almost impossible to trust. It is easy to trust a man who follows a rule of protecting his friends.

In addition, the agent must have a rather clear sense of the prospects for the future. It is of no benefit to protect one's son against punishment, if by so doing he is made a thoughtless and irresponsible person, who constantly gets into trouble. Finally, in choosing the course of action to follow, an agent tests his decision in his own feelings and loyalties. A father who fails to protect his son may hate himself forever for it. A man who does protect his son may be disappointed in his son's actions in the future, and regret his earlier actions. Regret is the practical test of a moral decision, subject to the qualifications we will make shortly.

We may summarize the variety of decisions as follows: Regulative principles are the means for resolving moral difficulties. Strict loyalty to principle can sometimes lead directly to action. However, the agent must know enough of the circumstances and the consequences of action to avoid unfortunate results. Where several principles conflict as *prima facie* obligations, a man must choose among them. Sometimes such a choice is straightforward, and requires nothing more than a principle of order among *prima facie* obligations. Sometimes two ultimate principles conflict directly. All a man can do is to make the best choice he can, based on what he knows of himself, the circumstances, and the consequences. In all cases, the decision may fail. The consequences may prove disastrous. The agent may despise himself for his weakness. He may find that he cannot live with what he did. Through failure, men make substantive appraisals of their decisions and the principles to which they are loyal. Enough failure, and men may be brought to reconsider the moral principles they live by. In evaluation, taking the prospects of failure into account, a man can do no more than to achieve a course of action that makes his success as likely as possible.

B. Failure

The complexity of moral decisions, especially where there are ultimate conflicts involved, entails that moral actions always include a risk of failure. A man's actions may be aimed at gaining some good, and lead only to pain and suffering. His actions may benefit no one, especially himself. It is worth noting the varieties of failure in human actions.

(1) The consequences of a course of action may be unfortunate. A child may tell a lie to escape punishment, only to be caught in the lie and punished even more strenuously. Suppose, however, we are dealing with a moral purist, who disdains any concern for the consequences at all. Then it seems that he will not admit to having failed no matter what the consequences of his actions may be. Such an attitude is a bit like Peirce's *method of tenacity*. Nothing can possibly prove a man wrong in his belief, for he holds to it no matter what.

Failure may be avoided through ignorance, where a man never discovers the results of his actions. It may also be avoided by obstinacy, by refusing to admit any chance of being wrong. It is difficult to see why such obstinacy should not be despised as much in moral affairs as it is in the realm of science.

(2) A special kind of consequence worth particular mention is that of the reactions of other people. In particular, a man may be convinced of the error of his ways through punishment, or even by the disapproval shown by others. To someone who is very responsive to what others think, the reactions of other people may be a consequence of great importance in showing him whether he has failed in his actions or not. Here too, a man quite indifferent to what others think cannot be led to believe he has failed merely because other people disapprove of what he has done.

(3) A course of action may lead to a sense of frustration or dissatisfaction. A man who obeys a moral law may come to regret having done so. He may feel that he has not been benefited by his scrupulousness, and neither has anyone else. If it is supposed that evaluation looks to beneficial results, a man may come to believe that a past action was not good if it gives him no satisfaction, even the satisfaction of having been loyal to his principles.

In every case, the mark of failure for the agent is felt regret. A man who has felt no regret or dissatisfaction cannot be held to have failed by his own standards—though of course, he may have failed by the standards of others. It is worth repeating again that the views of other people affect us, are "internalized," in Freud's language, and are therefore a potent force in judgments of failure or success in moral action. But where there is no internalization and no dissatisfaction, there is no proof of failure to the agent himself.

It follows from this that where one man is strongly convinced of another's wrongdoing, he may have no choice but to condemn or punish him. And we may see that the strength of the condemnation might well be thought to match the wrongdoing, so as to make the agent regret his mistakes. A selfish man will learn that selfishness is wrong only through the reactions of other people. Either he will lose the respect of other men, and will not gain the ends he desires, or he will be punished, and will learn that other men despise him for being selfish. Without the reactions of others, a man cannot learn that selfishness is wrong. For its evil rests on how other people respond to it.

A moral decision is a complex choice among a variety of elements and factors. Such a complex choice may always prove mistaken, and lead to regret. Where a man of strong character makes a firm choice, nothing may be able to cause him regret. Where a man is blind to others, and ignores all consequences, nothing will be able to make him regret his past actions. Both cases are examples of dogmatism in morals, and are extremely common. A dogmatic person cannot be shown his errors, for he dismisses all demonstration. Even punishment may strengthen his resistance and stubbornness.

If dogmatism is to be avoided, we must rely on moral education, not alone on argument and persuasion. Where moral principles are thought secure against all doubt, then regret becomes rare, and men follow their principles blindly, no matter what harm results. Substantive evaluation is undermined by extreme dogmatism. Nevertheless, it is worth noting how often, even in the face of apparent dogmatism, we have proved to us individually and even collectively that we have failed in our past decisions. Regret is a potent emotion in human life, and fortunately, for without it men could not learn from their mistakes.

It may be objected that too easy regret tends to paralyze us, and to make us unable to act in times of crisis. Sartre certainly suggests in *The Flies* that remorse is an affliction that paralyzes the will and turns men into cowards. Heroes are firm and strong-willed. Even in the face of disaster, a man must be able to stand by his principles and moral convictions.

The objection is correct. Two extremes haunt every moral decision, and undermine our ability to learn from the past while acting with conviction. On the one hand, a man who follows his principles without question or doubt can become so morally pure as never to be able to recognize his errors, and may act with moral conviction only to bring great harm to himself and others. Moral purity can be blind and foolish. On the other hand, too great a willingness to admit the dangers of action can be paralyzing, and, far worse, can lead a man to compromise himself and his principles easily, even to his own disadvantage and the disadvantage of others.

The solution lies in a double loyalty, to principle in action yet also to substantive evaluation of those principles. The regulative principles to which a man is loyal must be followed wherever he can do so. They are respected substantively as the most reliable ideals of action available to him. Even where fundamental principles conflict, a man can do no better than to formulate an alternative principle of action. We follow Kant's Categorical Imperative here, though emphasizing consequences and feelings also. An action must obey a general law. This principle or law is obeyed wherever possible. That is what morality means. But in addition, the principle is tested by its results. And where these results are extremely disadvantageous, the principle may be amended or abandoned. On the one hand, a man can avoid guilt only by doing what he is convinced is right—which means following some regulative principle. On the other, he can avoid too great a purity only by keeping an open mind to the dangers of following a rule blindly.

The arduousness of complex moral decisions is so great that regret is almost certain to be felt often by an open-minded and sincere agent. Usually such regret is experienced in either personal and intimate relations, such as love and family, or in political affairs. In both the very public and the very private domains of life, we must struggle to learn to couple firmness of character with openness and flexibility. It is too much to expect that all of us will find the exact proportion of such characteristics satisfactory both to ourselves and to others. It is far more likely that we will struggle constantly with errors and mistakes, confronting our failures and learning from them, but never quite enough. In times of crisis, failure will be unavoidable and desperately important.

In a sense, every moral decision is a contribution to the future. By our failures, we teach the men who follow us what is to be pursued and what should be avoided. In a deeply implicit sense, we all bear a responsibility for the future. We are ancestors and they are our descendants. We have the responsibility for teaching them right from wrong, through our moral decisions, both our failures and our successes.

Unfortunately, men are capable of learning very little from the past. We may note again that the moral realm requires politics for its service. A secure and flexible society can avoid individual failures becoming very serious more than can a rigid or unjust society. Through education, a society can instill a reverence for the lessons of the past. Still, in living people cannot but make mistakes, some of which may affect their entire lives and also the lives of others. All we can hope is that we can make such errors less frequent, and that their consequences will be less serious than they might have been.

If failure haunts every moral decision as a possibility, then it is clear that no honest and open-minded approach to moral decisions can expect to avoid failure altogether. It follows that the goal of decision can only be to *minimize* the prospects of failure, and to *maximize* the prospects of success. This is the force of substantive evaluation of moral principles. Principles are intended to be the rules for action which are most likely to succeed, which are least likely to end in regret.

In addition, it is important to note that moral decisions depend heavily on the agent who makes them, and in two important respects. First of all, where a moral decision rests on a conflict among *prima facie* obligations, a priority of values is called for. It is essential to realize that the interrelationship of the most important values in human life is bound to differ from person to person with differences in character. Intellectual persons will find knowledge and understanding of greater value. Active persons will find strength and sincerity of greater value. Individuality resides in individual differences, and these differences show themselves in subtle variations on the most important values in life. All men may agree on which are the ultimate values. But they may differ on just how such values are related to each other.

Second, moral decisions look ahead to the possibilities of regret. But such possibilities depend on the real feelings of the moral agent. A man implicitly tries to foresee future prospects for his own reactions and attitudes in his moral decisions. Loyalties, commitments, loves and hatreds, all come together in a man's feelings toward the choices he must make, and his reactions to the consequences of his actions. The greatest difficulty is that a course of action transforms the agent, often in unforeseeable ways. He may then come to regret a former decision, regret it because of new feelings within himself that developed over the years.

It follows, then, that we simply cannot expect moral decisions to be the same for all men in similar circumstances. Two different men in like circumstances nevertheless are different. Often these differences are not important. The weakness of extreme relativism is that it overemphasizes the importance of individual differences for moral decisions. Sometimes there are important differences, though the general rules to be followed may be the same for all men. But in extreme crises, men may have to act differently, depending on their abilities and feelings. In times of war, a quick and skillful soldier ought to behave differently from a discoordinated one.

There is a truth to moral relativism. Differences among persons can make a difference in their actions and in their decisions. What is right for one man *may* not be right for another. But we must emphasize that in most cases this is at best a logical possibility. When we look to the facts and consequences, the general regulative principles of morality tend to produce similar kinds of action. Only in crisis, where the agent's special characteristics are of special importance, may men find that they must do different things.

Morality is an attempt to find principles which may govern most conditions of life for all men as they live together. To the extent that social life is valuable, the attempt is successful. But there are always crisis conditions where moral principles are ineffectual in generating actions in common. The same ultimate loyalties may lead different men to differing actions. Not only are we forced to admit the possibility of such differences. Sometimes we acknowledge them as just and right. It would be wrong for a poor actor to become a double agent.

It must be remarked, however, that in evaluation we seek principles of conduct which everyone can live by. If we overemphasize differences among men, we may make the discovery of these principles impossible. Individual differences may lead to different actions and decisions. But the goal in such decisions is to reach a common set of moral ideals which everyone can follow. In the end, we may well find it necessary to admit to a variety of different ideals, reflecting different personality characteristics. Yet over all such ideals there may rule principles of cooperation, reverence for life, tolerance, and even respect for differences, which are the greater ideals on which social life rests.

C. Reevaluation

A dogmatic person may avoid all regret through sheer blindness. Regret cannot serve a dogmatic person as a test of failure. It follows, then, that moral dogmatism is wrong. Its result is that men act blind to consequences and to the harm they do to others. Reason calls for open-mindedness not as an abstract virtue, but due to the benefits which open-mindedness brings with it. Throughout history, dogmatism has received the worst possible substantive evaluation. Unfortunately, through its willful blindness, it manages to survive all attack.

Where an open-minded person encounters failure, it is necessary to him to *reevaluate* his past actions, at least in thought if not in what he does. Evaluation is a decision as to what is right or wrong, a decision which leads to action, a decision based on regulative principles. Throughout our discussion of moral decisions, we have noted the impulse toward general rules. But no general rule can be a final principle which leaves no questions. Principles clash with other principles, and may lead to unfortunate consequences.

In every case where a man has formulated a principle and acted upon it, but is subsequently led to regret his actions, he has not only evaluated his actions in the first place, but *re*evaluated them thereafter. Regret is a test of values, and allows a man to modify them prior to further action. For example, the man who protects his son from arrest though he is a thief, and who discovers that this protection encourages his son to further crimes, may regret his deeds. This regret leads him to the conviction that a man ought to be punished for a crime. Perhaps he will punish his son himself, or even turn him in to the police.

The more interesting point concerns, not the principles involved, but emotional loyalties. A father certainly owes his son protection and loyalty. Here we have a father whose interpretation of loyalty is unquestioning protection. Let us exaggerate the description, and say that this is a loyalty with no moral standards other than itself. In his regret, the father comes to see that his interpretation of these loyalties is destructive, not beneficial. It follows that he is condemning his own emotional reactions. He should have been loyal to his child by teaching him a firm respect for moral principles.

A complex moral decision is a choice among a variety of principles and feelings a man has within a moral situation. His regret at failure subsequently is a regret, not merely at a slight miscalculation, but at his entire scale of values and priorities. Extreme moral regret calls for a genuine reorganization of a man's values and feelings. His deepest loyalties have failed, and must be reconsidered. Reevaluation can be extremely painful, where it requires a man to transform himself in fundamental respects.

In this sense, a man is tested by his failures, and is changed by them if he succeeds in reevaluation. We see this in action where a man undergoes psychotherapy. His failures in everyday life have led him to seek professional help to make rather basic changes in his personality. Quite apart from psychoanalytic experiences, men sometimes change in important ways when they suffer major reversals. We have seen that virtually all the affections and emotions a man has enter into the principles and ideals to which he is loyal. If he cannot choose among them satisfactorily, even for himself, then he must find a way to change.

One of the most common sources of failure is ambivalence. A man who does not know what he really wants, because he always desires conflicting things, cannot be satisfied. An ambivalent man must either learn to live with his ambivalence, or overcome it through some psychic change. In effect, he must learn what he really wants. Unfortunately, men deceive themselves as to their feelings and desires, and may be led to regret almost everything they do. This is a major source of failure in evaluation.

D. Self-deception

Psychoanalytic theory embodies a view which has important consequences for moral theory. Freud claims that men not only lie to others, they also deceive themselves. Men not only err in the means they choose to help them realize their goals. They err in the goals they are aware of having.

Such a view is important because it addresses a general problem which is implicit in most moral theories, yet which is seldom dealt with directly. The problem is that of explaining the fact that men often do not do what is right. Why is there so much evil in the world? Why have we not succeeded in making the world a better place?

There appear to be several reasons for evil in the world. Let us consider a few of them. (a) The world is a difficult place to live in, and requires great efforts for men to find food and shelter. No doubt there have been places and times where men had little to eat, and famines and droughts were frequent occasions. Yet not all the evil of the world is due to nature. Men are often the source of destruction. (b) Men have conflicting interests. To some extent this is true. But we must explain why men have not learned through time to get along by compromise and adjustment. (c) Men are creatures of emotion, not reason. Here we have the classical theory of weakness. Plato argues in the *Republic* that men pursue what they think is good, but are led astray by their appetites. Christianity views the body and its appetites as the source of sin.

Plato's theory may be interpreted as a theory of self-deception. As we have seen, Plato assumes that men pursue what they believe to be good. All evil is the result of ignorance as to what is truly good. But why do not men know what is good? Their appetites are too strong, and overwhelm their understanding. In Spinoza's terms, an immediate object appeals to us more than does a superior but remote good. The general principle is that a man's emotions blind him and mislead him as to what he truly desires.

From the point of view of psychoanalysis, Plato's theory of self-deception is rather naive, and in a particular respect. This is that Plato seems to assume that men form a clear idea of the objects they desire, and are only mistaken about whether they desire them or not. Spinoza points out, however, that most of our ideas are confused, in that we do not clearly grasp the objects of these ideas, their causes or consequences. Following Spinoza, psychoanalytic theory raises the question of whether men are not deceived also as to the nature of their own actions.

For example, a man finds a wallet containing a large sum of money, and

Decision decides to keep it so that he can make a down payment on a house. First, however, he will have a drink to celebrate, gets into a poker game, and loses all his money. On the classical model, we would have to explain his actions as a falling into a temptation, overcome by his desire to gamble. On the psychoanalytic model, the man also does not know *why* he is gambling. He rationalizes his actions in terms which are rather misleading and misled. For example, he thinks that he intends to win enough money to have enough for himself yet also to return the sum in the wallet. He *really* is showing off to his friends how rich he is. But if he is really rich, he can afford to lose the money without pain. So he loses it.

To take a more extreme example, a man studies to become a concert pianist— not because he loves music, as he thinks, but to bask in the glory of fame. When he falls short of world fame, he will be unhappy. To take a more common example, a boy enters medicine, not because he likes the idea of tending the ill nor because he is fascinated by the workings of the body, but because his parents want him to. Sometimes a man simply does not know why he acts as he does. What this means is that he rationalizes to himself, and obscures his true intentions and motives.

From the standpoint of psychoanalysis, a man deceives himself when a part of him hides its intentions from another part. Self-deception is a strange notion. For a man can lie to another only when he knows the truth in the first place, and falsifies it. A man must therefore both know and not know his true feelings if he deceives himself about them. Psychoanalysis handles this by a model of a person as a multiplicity of parts, one part deceiving the other.

Even more important, Freud postulates a censoring mechanism, which can prevent undesirable thoughts from reaching consciousness. Thoughts which are repressed in this way are usually censored to avoid the pain which consciousness of them would bring. A man deceives himself to avoid the torment of being honest with himself. In *The Iceman Cometh*, Eugene O'Neill portrays a whole tavern full of men and women who live on pipedreams, pretending that they are just waiting until "tomorrow" to do something worth while. In the meantime, they get drunk. They do not want to do anything else, as O'Neill shows by bringing upon them a character who offers them the chance. They are terribly disturbed by the threat to their self-deception.

The notion of self-deception is a problematic one. So too is the idea of a person composed of psychic parts, each of which can have goals and desires. The idea of a *person* acting degenerates into a mere sum of parts acting and their results. Many philosophers and psychoanalysts have tried to develop an analysis of self-deception that is not so problematic. The strength of Freud's position is that there does seem to be in the human mind a mechanism at work which keeps certain unwanted emotions or thoughts from reaching consciousness. Such a mechanism is quite common, even in ordinary experience.

For example, Freud argues that men forget simple things, often under the pressure of strong emotion. Many people find that they have forgotten important appointments, where a considerable strain was involved in meeting such an appointment. Loosely speaking, an appointment may be forgotten because the agent didn't want to remember it. But once forgotten, it offers him no chance to decide for himself what he really wants.

The importance of self-deception for moral theory is considerable. We recall that a man makes a moral decision by determining what is most important for him to do, considering the circumstances, consequences, and principles to which he is loyal. The mark of failure in decision is found in regret. The test of whether a decision has been justified or not comes afterward, in results which are or are not satisfying. In the end, a man must evaluate his actions in terms of whether he finds the results satisfactory, and he finds them satisfactory or not in feeling. Where a man heroically sacrifices himself for others, it is his love for them or his loyalty to duty which may move him to heroism. But afterward, it is the same love and loyalty, coupled with other feelings, which afford him a test of his sacrifice. If he acted from good intentions but succeeded only in injuring others, then he has failed. Where a man dies in action, of course he cannot reevaluate his own decisions. Others do so instead. From the point of view of moral regret, death is sometimes easier than remaining alive. Still, it is perfectly intelligible that we may consider a policeman too self-sacrificing, and look for a way to make others more careful in the future.

Normally we suppose that a man who gains the goal he seeks will be pleased by it, and will not regret what he has done to achieve it. Such a conception of the relationship between intention and action seems to be inherent in most theories of moral decision. Unfortunately, it appears to be too simplified a view. Plato's criticism is that men often seek what they *think* is good, only to find when they have it that it fails to satisfy them. For example, a man may go to considerable lengths to win the love of a woman, only to find that he no longer loves her once he has gained it. Many fairly affluent middle-class people find that they are bored by their lives and their wealth. The popularity of psychotherapy among the prosperous shows how often people are dissatisfied afterward by what they thought in advance would make them happy. This regret is also a form of reevaluation, the judgment that past choices were wrong. Unfortunately, we may regret a course of action without knowing of a better alternative.

A man may not be satisfied even with gaining his own ends if, as Plato argues, these ends are not *really* good. In addition, men are complex creatures, and often desire many contradictory things at once. When a man desires two different things which are mutually exclusive, he will be dissatisfied no matter which he gains. This ambivalence is very important in human life. All forms of psychotherapy may be viewed as attempts to enable ambivalent people to settle their ambivalences in some way, and to choose what they really want. Ambivalence may in itself prevent any satisfactory realization of a man's goals, and lead to nothing but regret. People who find nothing satisfactory, and think nothing is right that they can do, are quite common.

Decision   Finally, add to ignorance and ambivalence a mechanism by which a man literally deceives himself as to his true aims, and we see how difficult it is in human life to achieve satisfaction. For example, a student in college comes from a home in which everyone is a gifted and successful professional. He fears that he may prove to be the only failure in the family. In particular, he is afraid that he may prove to be the only stupid one. Such a person may find it impossible to put any effort into his studies, and may fail his classes and examinations regularly. But in every case, he knows securely that he has not really tried his best. And since he has not tried, he has never shown what he is really capable of. This student really wants to be a success—or, more accurately, really is afraid to be tested and found a failure. One solution is simply never to allow himself to be tested fully, by doing no work. Such a student is extremely unlikely to know what leads him to do so poorly in his studies.

Let us take another example. A girl gets married, not, as she thinks, from love and a desire to have a home of her own, but unconsciously because she wishes to escape the control of her parents. She may achieve her wish satisfactorily. But it is more likely that she will (a) come under her husband's domination instead, (b) resent him for not being exactly the kind of man she wants, or (c) resent her marriage and motherhood because she is not ready for the responsibilities of a home.

Where a person deceives himself about his true wants, it is likely that he will regret his decisions based on what he thinks he wants. Such regret can lead to bitterness, and the development of violent but hidden resentments and hatreds. Under such circumstances, parents take their fears and anxieties out on their children. Men take their hidden frustrations out on their wives. Friends cause each other to suffer. Yet the hidden aspect of all these actions often makes the agents themselves unaware of the harm they cause. Worst of all, even when aware of what they do, they are not conscious of why they do it, what they wish to accomplish in a hidden sense, and therefore continue to do it.

It is important to understand that an action is not a mere movement, but includes its aim within it. We have noted this several times. The point is that a covert aim constitutes an action. But it is not an action fully within the agent's control. For example, a man who punishes his son cruelly for telling a lie, because the father himself is a frequent liar and despises himself for it, may succeed in teaching the boy only the value of never getting caught. The man *thinks* that he is teaching the boy not to lie. He may really be punishing himself, and the boy may learn also how to punish his father.

We may now see the results of self-deception in moral decisions, and explain also the justification many men feel is possessed by a strict adherence to duty. Men are complex creatures who do not always know what they do. If their deeds are to be evaluated in terms of satisfaction or regret, but men deceive themselves about their own aims, then regret is highly likely. To avoid regret, a plausible suggestion is that men formulate clear moral principles and follow them strictly.

To some extent, such a practice is a legitimate means of avoiding the insecurities of personal decision. But we have seen over and over that too strict a moral purity can bring consequences which are regrettable. We may gain some security through strict performance of our duties, but never quite enough.

Nevertheless, following principles has its value for actions of a general character, which involve other people who have no special relationship to us. For this reason, it is usually easier for us to treat strangers well. Only in times of crisis, when the issues are made exceedingly complex, are ordinary moral principles useless in moral affairs. But in intimate relationships of family and friends, the emotional strains are always complex, and ordinary moral principles may generally be of little value. A woman may desire courtesy from her children, but she may need far more to be loved and also to be needed, needed in ways that lead to discourtesy. In a close family, the Golden Rule is useless most of the time. Parents should not treat their children as they treat themselves, but sometimes far better, sometimes more strictly, almost always differently. For this reason, the problems which arise because of self-deception reveal themselves more often in personal relationships than in impersonal ones. But the same kinds of problem can arise in all moral decisions.

One of the most difficult and urgent of all social problems of contemporary life is that of the care for the aged. There is an increasing number of people alive in their seventies and eighties. But the family has changed so that parents cannot easily be accommodated in the lives of their adult children. The problem is a difficult one to deal with on an individual level. It is a vital problem for society as a whole.

But each individual's solution to the problem is likely to be contaminated by deep and hidden feelings. Some adults resent their parents, yet cannot admit this to themselves. Their resentments may bring them to more cruel indifference than is necessary or even justified. Other children find the world a harsh and cruel place, and prefer the security of self-sacrifice in caring for their parents to coping with the world on their own. Unfortunately, aged parents eventually die, leaving a middle-aged spinster who has no reason or strengths to remain alive. Finally, the individual fears, frustrations, resentments, and sense of guilt which almost all voting adults face with respect to their parents severely contaminate social policy.

To this point, we have considered self-deception only as a source of failure in action, and as a cause of regret. Yet there is a common form of self-deception whose function is to avoid regret and a sense of failure. We turn now to a discussion of rationalization and the giving of excuses.

E. Rationalization

Not only are people capable of self-deception concerning their aims and intentions, but they are capable of misrepresenting circumstances and even consequences. All facts require some degree of interpretation. But a person interprets the facts according to his own needs and values. Facts can be misinterpreted and misrepresented. A man may so completely falsify the results of his own actions as to be incapable of regretting what he has done. Such a misrepresentation we will call *rationalization*. A person rationalizes what he sees. He excuses his failures. All in all, people find extremely clever ways of avoiding a sense of failure, or at least of bringing it to full awareness. The pipedreams of O'Neill's *The Iceman Cometh* not only are a falsification of what the various characters intend to do tomorrow, but they are a way of avoiding regret at having failed. If a man will set everything right tomorrow, then it doesn't matter how lazy he is today.

There is a particularly extreme conclusion which may be thought to follow from the notion of rationalization. Once we grant that some men falsify their perceptions and misrepresent events according to their needs and values, then we may consider the possibility that all human judgments are but rationalizations. Karl Marx argues that all political understanding of the workings of a society is contaminated by class loyalties and the structure of that society. It may be thought to follow that there is no truth in any description of political events, only interpretations imbued with class commitments, with ideology, with the speaker's fundamental values. Such a position leads naturally to extreme scepticism and extreme relativism. The same arguments we considered earlier apply here with little modification. The position that all claims are but rationalizations is self-stultifying. We have no choice in any case but to collect evidence and to draw our conclusions on the basis of it. There are still logical and illogical inferences, justifiable and indefensible conclusions. Not just anything follows from anything else. A modest fallibilism is the only defensible position. Men rationalize frequently and cleverly. But some truths are well confirmed. Nevertheless, no truth is immune to criticism.

The ability of men to rationalize, however, does point up a fundamental weakness in the view that failure is shown most directly through regret. A man may be able to rationalize his actions and their consequences to such a degree that he never admits regret, even to himself. It is always the fault of someone else. The consequences could not have been foreseen. Above all, many people are always ready with the excuse that they couldn't help themselves. Strangely enough, an admission of weakness, which ought to be avoided and even condemned, can serve some people as an excuse by which they apparently manifest regret, but really make no effort to change.

It is important, then, that we qualify our interpretation of regret as a sign of failure. Regret testifies to failure only where the regret looks to a change in oneself or one's values. This is the reason for calling the stage of regret "reevaluation." It is a new moral decision, to avoid making the same error again, by either learning from the error, becoming stronger, avoiding temptation, or the like. We note, then, the remarkable ability of men to manifest regret, but to make excuses which so completely rationalize their past actions as to call for no change in their conduct or attitudes.

This distinction may serve us as a definition of rationalization. Many excuses which people give are perfectly acceptable. For example, we accept a man's claim that he didn't know what was happening: it all happened so quickly. Nevertheless, our expectation is that a man who offers such an excuse is asking for release from blame, but understands the importance of knowing what is going on. If he merely offers the excuse with no intention of trying harder to find out what is going on around him, we have a mere rationalization, which justifies action from ignorance.

Consider the excuse a man makes that he was drunk, and thus couldn't have avoided the accident. Such an excuse is not acceptable, though it is true that he couldn't help himself once he was drunk. For a man can avoid getting drunk and should if he is planning to drive an automobile. The excuse in effect explains the accident away, and appears to call for no change in the agent's conduct. We note that he can give no excuse for having become drunk in the first place.

It is important that we understand the nature of excuses. In order to do so, we must appeal to some theory of blame, condemnation, or punishment. A retributive theory of punishment has no room for excuses, properly speaking. For example, a man pleads self-defense in killing another. This is no *excuse*. Rather, it is an exception under the law. On a rehabilitational view, however, an excuse may be given and accepted to modify the punishment. For example, insanity is certainly an excuse. It is not right to commit murder, even when insane. But we accept insanity as an excuse for eliminating punishment.

The arguments in this book have tended to support a modified rehabilitational theory of punishment. From this point of view, excuses are attempts to mitigate punishment, by making the rehabilitational value of punishment less. For example, a man who commits assault in the throes of extreme provocation and violent emotion may not be punished severely, on the grounds that he is unlikely to repeat such an action. On the other hand, an excuse which looks to mitigate punishment, but which in no way speaks to the required changes in the agent, is a poor excuse. When believed by the agent to be a justification which requires him to change nothing of himself, to become neither more knowledgeable nor firmer in his loyalties, we have rationalization.

A rationalization is therefore a device which serves two purposes, that of an excuse to avoid punishment, and that of justifying the man who gives it in avoiding any effort to change. It cannot be denied that many men are adept at rationalization and self-justification. And the result of their rationalizations is that they come to regret almost nothing of what they have done. A notorious example is that of officials in Nazi Germany who, almost to a man, denied responsibility for murders and atrocities. There was always some excuse—obedience to orders, efficiency, fear, or the like. In a vague sense, it is quite possible to admit having done something wrong, yet to have a sufficient number of excuses as to make one's own judgments, decisions, even actions perfectly justified. It follows from such excuses that punishment is inappropriate, and that the guilt or remorse which might lead to changing the agent's values is also inappropriate.

Punishment looks to changing a man for the better. Excuses are attempts to avoid both punishment and change. It follows that legitimate excuses require no change on the agent's part, while rationalizations are nothing but specious arguments to avoid a confrontation with the requirements of change. To accept an excuse is to agree that the wrongdoing involved calls for no changes on the agent's part.

In the face of extreme rationalizations, there can be only two responses. The fundamental one is the realization that there is no solution except through education. It is the function of moral education not only to instill in members of a society a strong loyalty to principles and ideals, but to teach them also habits of appraisal and reappraisal which make it possible for them to learn and relearn from their experience. In a society where rationalization is frequent and both personally and socially destructive, moral education has not been successful. Self-deception and rationalization are to be eliminated only through an education which places no premium on them, and which rewards instead honesty and an open-minded willingness to learn from experience.

But where moral education has in the first place not succeeded as well as it might, then the second response to rationalization can only be through punishment. This is required by a rehabilitational conception of punishment. A poor excuse or a rationalization are attempts to evade both punishment and change. And where they succeed, they become reenforced. It follows that when we strongly feel that other men have done evil things, we are forced to find ways of punishing them, except where their excuses are good ones.

It does not follow in the least that the appropriate punishment need be severe or injurious. Punishment here is intended as a form of reeducation, to teach men both that certain actions are wrong, and that certain excuses do not relieve them from blame. It may even be argued that the primary function of punishment is to eliminate rationalization. For where a person does not rationalize, and feels genuinely remorseful, it is difficult to see what further purpose rehabilitational punishment can serve. Often probation boards look precisely to such a sense on the part of a prisoner before releasing him on probation.

There is a particular type of excuse which has a remarkable character. It consists, as we have noted, in admitting the evil of an action, but also claiming that one couldn't help oneself. In its most common form, it is an admission of weakness. It is sometimes an admission of being a certain *kind* of person, a being who couldn't help but do that sort of thing. For example, a man may note that he knew of the concentration camps and of their horror, but was simply afraid. "I am not a hero." Such a claim actually has the force of an excuse, though in fact it is an admission of wrongdoing. A man may also admit that he is an *angry* person, to explain and excuse his malicious insults to another.

Sartre seems to take this kind of excuse as a model for all excuses. And, struck by the peculiarity of this mode of excuse, he is led to repudiate the validity of all excuses. Whenever a person claims that he is a particular *kind* of person,

Sartre argues that he is giving an excuse and lying to himself. A man can always change himself. Sartre clearly has in mind the excuse, "I am that kind of person, and couldn't help myself." He attacks the second half of the statement. But we must note, before taking up this subject, that a man may not wish to change, because he is a heroic and decent person. The claim "I am a responsible person" can be used to support responsible actions, and to repudiate excuses. Is a person lying to himself if he feels that his ideals are so important to him that he *must* follow them? Such a view seems to undermine any sense of moral decision altogether. Sartre has been criticized on such grounds.

The type of excuse which depends upon the notion that a man "could not help himself" is an excuse to avoid blame. We do admit that an insane person is not responsible for his actions, because he acts under some kind of compulsion. Perhaps no one who must act in a certain way is responsible for what he does. We move now to the subject of moral responsibility.

F. Responsibility

The problem we have just posed is whether a man who *must* do what he does is responsible for his actions. It is commonly believed that a responsible agent chooses to act as he does. And if he can choose one action, then he can also choose not to do it, or to do something else instead. When a man cannot choose among alternatives, he is not a free agent, and thus not a responsible one.

An even stronger version of this position rests on the notion of duty and obligation. A man cannot be obligated to do something if he cannot do it. In a version promulgated by some philosophers, "ought implies can." A man who cannot swim is not morally obligated to save a drowning man by swimming out to him. A man who cannot read is not obligated to have read an important sign.

At least one reply to this particular approach to obligation is to accept the inability of a man only as an excuse, and not as a release from obligation. A man has a *prima facie* obligation to save a drowning man, but if he cannot swim, he cannot meet that obligation. If he is a hundred miles away, he cannot meet it either. And if he is swimming out to save one man, he cannot save another. The point is that a man may indeed have *prima facie* obligations he cannot meet, and must choose among them. The doctrine "ought implies can" may arise from ignoring the distinction between *prima facie* and overall obligations.

Nevertheless, such issues are peripheral to our major concern. The fundamental problem is that we often accept the principle that a man who is not able to perform a given action is not to be blamed or held responsible for not performing it. An insane man is thought under a compulsion, and held not responsible. But, it is argued, men are biological creatures who follow the laws of nature. What a man does follows from his nature lawfully. A man is determined to do what he does. It follows from the principle of causal determinism that no one is responsible for any of his actions. We have studied in some detail the apparent incompatibility of efficient and final causation. We now come to a different problem for efficient causation: it makes moral responsibility unintelligible.

The principle of causal determinism is not an easy one to formulate. Clearly human beings are complex creatures, and the number of influences on a single person affecting his actions is quite large. Spinoza, who is a strict determinist, admits that the number of causes which affect any finite thing is infinite. For our purposes it will suffice if we postulate a given set of laws of nature L, and the state of the entire universe U_1 and U_2 at two given times T_1 and T_2. The causal determinist presumably believes that the conjunction of L and U_1 logically entails U_2. The exact state of the universe at a future date follows strictly from the laws of nature and an earlier state. Events therefore cannot be other than they are, not at least based on a definite past. And human beings are therefore not able to do other than they do. They are not, therefore, responsible agents.

It is worth noting that it is not possible today to prove the thesis of causal determinism as stated here, and probably will never be. The state of the entire universe is of too grand a scope even to contemplate as an object of scientific study. Nevertheless, many psychologists accept a principle of determinism in human affairs, for they believe the task of science is to predict the future from the past. It must be granted that to deny psychological determinism is to put an obstacle directly in the path of psychological explanation as it is usually conceived. Perhaps the entire issue in the end comes down to whether we are justified in placing obstacles in the path of scientific progress.

The issue of determinism is rather more complex than we have shown so far. The main argument for determinism is the scientific one, grounded in the successes of the sciences in providing explanations of events in terms of efficient causes. The main argument against determinism in human affairs is the sense of freedom people feel they have, to act as they wish, and to make their choices as they wish. Spinoza is forced to agree that men do feel free, but claims that this is but the result of our ignorance of true causes. A man may feel free to go down either road at a fork, but in fact the choice he makes is determined.

Let us note a variety of complicating factors.

(1) A man may be compelled by brute force to perform an action against his will. For example, he may have his arm bent by someone stronger, and he may be forced to bow his head. Under this type of compulsion, there is no blame. A man may be compelled by a violent physical need, when starving or under drugs, to commit a crime. He may even have a sense of inner compulsion. Sometimes we do not blame a man who acts under this kind of compulsion. But often men act with a sense of total freedom, and make their choices with no sense of compulsion. If determinism is a form of compulsion, it exerts its force not upon the conscious will of the agent, but unnoticeably affects his choices. Some philosophers deny any compulsion here. Nothing *makes* a man do what he does, even under determinism. He is free and responsible, even when following the laws of nature. Laws of nature are not compulsions, but expressions of how men do act, even when they are free.

(2) Recent discoveries in physics, especially on the quantum level, support the view that the future does not follow strictly deterministically from the past. Charles S. Peirce and Lucretius both maintain that there is in addition to causal relations a principle of randomness in things. Determinism might be false, not where men are free agents, but in a random fashion. But a man who acted randomly would seem to be no more responsible than one whose actions were completely caused.

(3) Determinism cannot be demonstrated conclusively. Neither can it be refuted. If determinism is a form of compulsion, it is a very special type. The strongest argument for determinism is that science is committed to it as a guiding principle. It is noteworthy that many philosophers have recently argued that psychology must be reconceived, in nondeterministic form. For they deny that the purpose of psychology is simply the prediction of the future. Psychologists, it must be noted, have not yet been convinced by such arguments. The philosopher's main point is that human actions are *purposive*, and must be understood in terms of final causation, not efficient causation alone. We have already discussed such matters.

All of these issues complicate the issue of determinism severely. What is most problematic about the entire subject is that the connection between determinism and responsiblity becomes more and more tenuous as we qualify our conception of determinism. Where determinism is regarded as a compulsion to act in a certain way, it seems clearly incompatible with moral responsibility and blame. But where determinism is merely an expression of the lawfulness of human behavior, it is not quite so obviously incompatible with determinism. And what is especially confusing, we can postulate a lack of lawfulness which is certainly not compatible with responsibility—randomness or caprice.

This last point can be generalized to lead to a remarkable conclusion. Let us postulate that moral responsibility and strict causal determinism are incompatible. To the extent that a man's actions are a causal result of his past, he can do no other than he does, and is not responsible for his actions, We turn now to Hume's argument that *in*determinism and responsibility are incompatible.

Hume argues as follows: In holding a man responsible for his deeds, we are concerned with praising or blaming him for his actions. Let us reject causal determinism. We are therefore postulating that a man's past does not determine his present or his future. For two reasons, then, we are not justified in condemning a man for what he did in the past.

First of all, a man who performs a misdeed must be held to be the same person who is now to be blamed. For example, a thief is brought to trial seven months after his apprehension. Now, where there is causal determinism, we are justified in supposing the later man to be of the same character as the earlier one. But, Hume claims, we cannot even speak of the character of a man without presupposing that the past is connected with the future, and determines it. If a man were a thief, but there were no connection of any causal sort between past and future, we could not hold him blameworthy later. Unless a man is in some way made what he is by his past, then there would be no difference between an unredeemable criminal and a virtuous person. Both would be as fresh snow, totally indifferent to their past deeds. It is because we know that a man of poor character will continue to be of poor character that we can speak of blame and responsibility.

Second, if we ask ourselves what the function of the notion of responsibility is, we see that responsibility serves solely to justify punishment and condemnation, or praise and reward. We then ask, when are these justifiable? Clearly, if there were no causal determinism, then nothing we did today would have any effect on a man's future actions. It follows that punishment would lose its entire justification. In short, Hume argues, causal indeterminism is also incompatible with moral responsibility.

Hume's arguments have been criticized on two grounds. First, Hume assumes as alternatives only strict determinism or total indeterminism. We may grant that complete indeterminism cannot justify responsibility, but conclude instead that human beings are a mixture of determinism and indeterminism. There is sufficient determinism to ground our expectations that punishment will affect a man, and that a man's character will remain somewhat the same through time. But there is enough indeterminism to free a man from strict conformity to the past. The problem for this position is to present an intelligible analysis of the relations between the deterministic and indeterministic elements of a man's life.

Second, Hume assumes that a person's character depends on causal relations between his past and future self. But the past of a person need not *cause* him to act as he does in the future, so far as his character is concerned. It is sufficient that there be a continuity through time, and a man may *choose* to act in a coherent fashion throughout his life, and to have a certain character, without causal laws. Obviously we are speaking of intentions here, and look once again to final causation as an alternative to efficient causation.

Hume's critics are left with a major problem. This is to define a sufficiently orderly world to make sense of character and continuity through time, and to do so without strict determinism. And on the other hand, they must interpose indeterministic elements without having them collapse into sheer randomness. This is another version of the problem of rendering final and efficient causation compatible in one world.

The strength of Hume's position rests on the fact that he addresses the question of responsibility directly, and does not worry about determinism or freedom in the abstract. The general problem is whether we can justify praise or blame, on what grounds and in what circumstances. In reality, the theory of responsibility is a theory of condemnation and praise. If there were strict causal determinism, would punishment be justified? Obviously, rehabilitational punishment would, and retributive punishment would not. We came to that conclusion without concerning ourselves in the least with issues of freedom and causal determinism. If there were complete indeterminism, would punishment be justified? Not for actions that rested on no ground. Hume is correct that punish- ment and blame look to character and to continuity through time.

Putting the entire issue of freedom and determinism aside, let us consider only the actual function played by the concept of responsibility in moral affairs. It seems that there are two functions, and two notions of responsibility corresponding to them. The two of them are expressed in ordinary speech when we characterize one man as a *responsible* person, but punish a second when we hold him *responsible* for certain misdeeds. The two functions of the concept of responsibility are (a) we wish to *hold* a man responsible for what he has done; (b) we wish to *praise* a man for being a responsible person.

What does it mean to call a person a responsible man? It means that he is the kind of person who accepts obligations and meets them. An irresponsible person is one who ignores others, who denies his responsibilities, who acts selfishly and unthinkingly, or who is weak and unreliable. In this sense, a responsible person is a dedicated moral agent, who acknowledges responsibilities and does his best to meet them. An irresponsible person is one who either denies his obligations or, though he acknowledges them, does not meet them.

When we hold a person responsible, in sense (a), we condemn him for failing in his obligations. This sense is primarily a sense of blame. Although a person may be irresponsible in the sense of (b), and deny his obligations, another person may call him "irresponsible," and hold him responsible in sense (a) for not meeting them. It seems fairly clear that there are two related but distinguishable senses of responsibility involved. There is the general sense of responsibility which consists of having obligations. There is a more particular sense of responsibility which consists of doing what one ought to do.

(1) *General Responsibility.* It is worth distinguishing between calling a person's action "wrong" and calling him "irresponsible," though often such condemnations may both apply to the same action. A person may deny that he is obligated in any way to another man. In calling him ''irresponsible,'' we mean to emphasize that he does have such obligations. Probably what he will do, having repudiated such obligations, is also wrong. But a man may also accept an obligation, yet act wrongly with respect to it. For example, a father may disown his son on little or no provocation, We may call him irresponsible. We mean that fathers owe their sons protection and support, if not love and concern. Oddly enough, the son may manage quite well on his own. An irresponsible act may not be wrong, if it turns out beneficially. This notion of responsibility looks to intent and attitude, not so much to ends and results. On the other hand, a father may accept responsibility for his son's welfare, but spoil him rotten. We might well call the man's doing so *wrong*. But he is not an irresponsible person.

The general sense of responsibility, then, is that of having and trying to meet moral obligations. Another way of putting this is that a man of general responsibility is one who is loyal to regulative principles, and who struggles with moral issues. But it is essential to all moral decisions that men be loyal to principle and evaluate their actions. It follows that all men are generally responsible for what they do and fail to do. What this means is no other than that we demand of them that they ought to meet their obligations. Put another way, men must make moral decisions, and may be condemned for failing to do so.

We have noted that a man may be condemned for denying his responsibilities to his children. A man is generally responsible for taking care of his children. But we also condemn people for ignoring things, for their lack of knowledge. For example, a German may be blamed for not knowing of the concentration camps. An American is sometimes blamed for not knowing of the mistreatment of blacks in the South, or of atrocities committed in Vietnam. We call all men generally responsible, and may blame them for ignoring evil in the world which they might have tried to prevent or ameliorate.

For how much are men generally responsible? It is extremely difficult to say. If ignorance is no excuse for general responsibility, then men often need to know of remote events both in space and in time. Is a politician not generally responsible for knowing of the historical results of past wars? To the extent that a man can learn from history, is he not generally responsible for doing so? To the extent that an economist may learn from a variety of facts and theories, is he not responsible for knowing them, if he is to guide his country's economic practices?

The greatest complication of all is that general responsibility looks only to the acceptance of responsibility, and the making of a relevant decision. It does not look to the specifically best actions a man ought to perform. For example, a father is generally responsible for his children—but not generally responsible for doing anything in particular. He is responsible for their support, but not at any particular level. General responsibility is essentially a responsibility to *try*, a responsibility to seek the most effective and beneficial course of action. It is not a responsibility to act in precisely a determined way.

We have noted that the facts relevant to a given moral decision are complex and varied. It is impossible to say precisely what is not relevant. Even worse, there are a tremendous variety of facts which are indirectly relevant. Where a man chooses to address one obligation, he in effect chooses to ignore many others. Where a man chooses to support his family, which is a responsible choice, he cannot work for the poor or fight for his country. General responsibility looks to an indefinite range of facts and circumstances. We can never know until far too late whether we ought to have considered something that we did not know about. General responsibility acknowledges the complexity of moral decisions, and rests only on the general imperative that we know enough to make our choices responsible ones.

It follows, then, that general responsibility is more a responsibility *to* things than *for* them. General responsibility is the responsibility men bear *to* make moral decisions, *to* know enough for such decisions, *to* consider the evidence and deliberate using it, and *to* meet events of experience with strength and conviction.

Several themes in past moral traditions touch upon this notion of general responsibility. In Christianity, for example, we find the doctrine of original sin. A man is to blame for having been born, for Adam's eating of the apple. A man is to blame for what he could not help. A man is in sin first, no matter what he himself did. We hold men generally responsible even for obligations they do not wish to accept.

In Dostoievski's *The Brothers Karamazov*, we find a modified version of original sin. Dmitri Karamazov has a dream in which he sees a starving child, and thereafter keeps saying that we must do something about the child. We are all guilty for the starving baby. What he means may be interpreted as the responsibility all men bear to eliminate starvation, pain, and suffering. All men must become brothers. But it is to be noted that neither Dmitri nor Dostoievski ever quite say how we are to go about it.

Finally, in recent existentialist writings, we find a general notion of anguish or dread. In Sartre's writings, all men are responsible for accepting their total freedom. And the sense of this responsibility is anguish. In Kierkegaard, dread is the acknowledgement of impossible obligations, impossible because absolute imperatives conflict with each other. According to the notion of general responsibility, a man is responsible in the sense of having obligations. But in this sense, *prima facie* obligations are frequently in conflict. We can meet only a small number of our *prima facie* obligations. We can help only a few people in a lifetime. And we have obligations to ourselves also. Dread and anguish seem to follow from the notion of general responsibility.

However, it would be a mistake to suppose that general responsibility commits us all to permanent suffering, as does the doctrine of original sin. For the suffering of original sin can become so great as to overwhelm all the good men do for each other. When general responsibility leads to suffering, it has to be condemned. Put another way, general responsibility is the basis for condemning men for what they do and fail to do. But condemnation is not something to embark on lightly.

General responsibility seems to be the condition of being a moral agent, obligated to make decisions. Sometimes we condemn men for failing in their responsibilities. But far more often we accept their excuses, even their ignorance. The reason for this is obvious. General responsibility is so wide that no one could meet all his general responsibilities. It would be cruel and also disadvantageous to punish people for all their lapses, especially from ignorance, by default, or from a minor lack of judgment. We would come to a point of diminishing returns very quickly. Therefore, we condemn people for weakness, for serious omissions, for cowardice, for extreme cruelty, for extreme indifference. But we neither punish nor even blame people who err in ways anyone would, who are insane, under extreme pressure, or, sometimes, under violent emotion. Punishment and even blame are actions to be themselves justified by their consequences and benefits. In a great many cases, punishment and even spoken blame can do no good, and can achieve only harm.

One solution to the problem of responsibility, then, is that we totally ignore the question of whether there is or is not causal determinism. Rather, we postulate that all men are generally responsible for their obligations. But we blame them only when this blame can be beneficial. Will blame teach a man something? Will it educate others? Will it generate extreme resentment? A sense of paralysis? Rebellion? In other words, we acknowledge men to be generally responsible, merely because they are men, because they are moral agents, because we expect them to make moral decisions. But we excuse men for what they do where accepting that excuse will be generally beneficial.

(2) *Personal Responsibility.* The second sense of responsibility is precisely a sense we use when we praise a person. General responsibility is the ground for blame. We condemn a person for failing in his obligations. In some general way, a person is responsible for doing the best he can. But in a more particular sense, a person is praiseworthy when he actually accomplishes something worth while.

Of course, we could blame him for not doing so. But since in almost all cases where one man fails, another might instead have done what needed to be done, this kind of blame is fruitless. For example, if one man does not serve on a jury, another will. If one man does not become a doctor in the jungle, another might. We would have to condemn almost everyone for such lapses, which is absurd and not beneficial to anyone. But if a man does indeed go to work in the jungle, we may praise him especially for being so responsible a man. This is a sense of accepting a *personal responsibility* for acting in a good way.

Personal responsibility is shown by doing the right or good thing. Probably we should add as well that the act is good by no accident but by design. We praise a person for being responsible when he does what he ought to. A father who supports his children may be praised for it. He has personal responsibilities, and he meets them. He meets them by his own personal actions, and he meets them well.

It is worth comparing this notion of personal responsibility with another strain in the tradition of moral theory. In contrast with the view that a free and responsible man must be able to do and also not do what he does, we find in a variety of philosophers a rather contrary position. We recall Plato's model of the soul in three parts. A just soul is under the rule of reason. A tyrant, Socrates argues in the *Republic*, is not free *because* he is ruled by his appetites. A man who commits an evil action is compelled by something within him to the act. He is therefore not free, and not responsible. This type of approach entails that a responsible action is always a good one. A man who does what he ought to do is a responsible man.

Kant comes to the same conclusion. A man who follows the Categorical Imperative acts according to a law which is given by his reason, and also obeyed by him. Obedience to moral law is at once a giving of the law and also a following of the law. Kant argues that to obey a law that one has legislated for oneself is a free and responsible action. A responsible man therefore follows the Categorical Imperative.

However, in our discussion of moral decision, we have seen that because men differ in their loyalties and in their feelings, a decision which is right for one person may not be right for another. Moreover, a man may make a careful and deliberate decision, yet the future may prove him wrong in terms of consequences he could not have foreseen. It would be extremely frustrating to make personal responsibility a matter of doing the right thing when there are so many intangibles.

An alternative, then, is to think of a man who is personally responsible as one who acts carefully, deliberately, from knowledge, and also with firm conviction. A personally responsible man is one who acts in a *way* which seeks to maximize his prospects of success. He may still fail, but only due to events which are beyond his powers of control. Personal responsibility may be thought of as the application of an open-minded method for making moral decisions. And it is worth praising when encountered. Unlike Kant, I cannot believe that any moral decision can be assured of success in advance. There are two different ways in which we may praise men for their actions: We may praise them for having done the right thing, as we see by the consequences. We may also praise them for having made their decisions in the best way they could. A personally responsible man is praiseworthy in the second sense.

Our entire discussion of responsibility has looked to the responsibility of individuals in their particular actions. We may note in conclusion that the subject of individual responsibilities is severely complicated in our time by a very different problem from that of determinism. This is the relationship between individual responsibility and collective action. Many courses of action may be successful only where many individuals cooperate together. Only in collective action can effective political power be generated. But if a group commits an evil action, how are we to assign individual responsibility? Shall each member of a lynch mob be punished? Should every German have been put to death after the Second World War?

The problem is almost unresolvable in general terms. Each case calls for a separate decision. Yet the principles involved seem clear. Where a group has committed an evil action, we may condemn and blame all of them and each of them for that evil. But when the question of punishment is considered, we must look beyond the sheer fact of evil to the benefits of punishment. In this sense, collective action generates no new principles. But the determination of concrete goods and ills is always far more complex. Unfortunately, the main reason for this is that the execution of a single murderer can never have very bad consequences for most other people. But the execution of everyone in a country for its atrocities seems very bad. It may be argued that such anomalies should make us far gentler in punishing individual criminals.

QUESTIONS

1. In what sense is a simple moral decision not made "by" the agent? In what ways does a complex decision call for the use of the agent's special qualities?

2. How can we avoid the problem of moral purity, since any moral decision must follow a regulative principle?

3. A man embezzles money from a bank, is never caught, invests it and lives modestly and well for the rest of his life, and never suffers remorse. In what sense is his embezzlement wrong? In what sense is it a failure?

4. Can a dogmatic man literally avoid feeling regret for anything he has done? If so, does this make his actions right?

5. Can a man be so open-minded as to be unable to make up his mind?

6. Give some detailed examples where the different characters of two different agents ought to lead them to different moral decisions.

7. If we deceive ourselves as to our true motives and goals, how can we possibly make a valid and defensible moral decision?

8. Is it a poor excuse for a Nazi to give that he was only obeying orders?

9. If a man acts in a manner determined by his past upbringing, is he responsible for his actions?

10. Discuss the problems which arise in trying to define causal determinism for human beings.

11. Discuss the problems which arise in denying that men are causally determined.

12. Should we always condemn a person who fails to meet his responsibilities?

13. In what sense is a responsible person a deliberate and careful one? In what sense is impulsiveness incompatible with responsibility?

14. Is it irresponsible not to give all one's money to the poor? Would it be right to do so? Is a man who does so responsible?

15. A town has lynched a tramp for a crime of which he is innocent. Is every individual in the town responsible? What should be done to the people in the town as punishment?

SELECTED READINGS

On self-deception:

S. Freud, *Outline of Psychoanalysis*.

Sartre, *Being and Nothingness*, Part I, Ch. Two. A critique of psychoanalysis and a different view of self-deception.

F. Dostoievski, *The Brothers Karamazov*.

On freedom and determinism:

Aristotle, *Nicomachean Ethics*, III.

Spinoza, *Ethics*.

Kant, *Fundamental Principles of the Metaphysics of Morals*, III.

Hume, "Liberty and Necessity," *An Inquiry Concerning Human Understanding*, VIII. **303**

H. Bergson, *Time and Free Will*.

F. Dostoievski, *Notes from Underground*.

S. Morgenbesser and J. Walsh, *Free Will*, 1962, Prentice-Hall.

X. IMPORTANT VALUES

AN INTERESTING and useful application of our discussion may be found in the consideration of several of the most important human values. The list is far from exhaustive. I have made no attempt to find all such values. Nor is the list presented in any particular order of priority. Rather, it is my opinion that such values fall in a different order of priorities for different people. And this is all to the good, for differences in character and style are an asset in human life. Nevertheless, the values discussed are all important, and would all seem to be part of a life lived well. Perhaps an overarching regulative ideal for human life might be to achieve as many of these values as is humanly possible under the conditions in which we live. Such an approach is akin to the Greek view of the Good Life. We aim for the realization of all the excellences life has to offer. Yet, forgoing Aristotle's bias toward the contemplative life, we may be dubious about the supreme value of a particular style of gaining such excellences.

Finally, it is worth mentioning that in crisis situations, and especially in an imperfect world with unjust societies, it will be impossible to gain all of these values at once. It then becomes necessary to choose one or another as supreme, and worth sacrificing the rest for. Such a choice should be recognized for what it is: a choice among evils. Where all our greatest values cannot be significantly gained throughout the years of our lives, we have failed to live a good life. The mark of an unjust society is the necessity for frequent crisis decisions, where only ills can be achieved.

All the values given are intrinsic values. They are good in themselves. Yet we recall Aristotle's claim that all virtues lie in a mean between undesirable extremes. Every value mentioned has extremes which are undesirable. Not only does it seem important to gain all of the values mentioned, but it is necessary to qualify each of them so as not to compromise the others. In this sense, each value is intrinsically good. But each is a means with respect to all the others as well.

A. Life

Certainly life is one of the supreme values. Never to have been born is to lack every value and every chance for value. Enjoyment, love, work, and knowledge all vanish into nothing without life. Life can be filled with pleasure and with achievement. And without this life, no prospects of value remain.

Yet it does not follow that life has a value apart from the other values it makes possible. In Plato and Aristotle we find a strong impression that it is not life which possesses value, but a life lived well. Life provides the possibility of value, and it may be argued that it possesses no value of its own.

A moment's thought of the continuum of means and ends and we see that we have been construing the value of life in unclear terms. Life is an intrinsic value. It is also an instrumental value, since it makes other things possible. Most important, it is an intrinsic value and an instrumental value in the same respect. Life is not good in itself, if it contains no joy or achievement. It is good *because* it makes other values possible. Yet clearly it has its own qualities to offer. "While there's life there's hope" expresses the intrinsic quality of life. The future always remains pregnant with the possibility of new values.

Too many of the other values we will consider are dependent on life. In this sense, the value of life looks to them for its significance. Life ceases to be good when it affords no chance of other goods. It loses its savor. So if it has no value then why should evil by it be wrong.

The love of life is a great strength. It can also be the source of the greatest corruption. A man may sacrifice everything he considers worth while in order to remain alive. Life has its greatest value when it is a means to other goods. It has its least value when it becomes extreme. In particular, when a man chooses to remain alive at any cost, he chooses life without other values. Though there remains the bare hope of improvement, such a hope may have no ground in fact. A life in miserable poverty may have no value. A life of constant illness may lose all value. A life of pain may be unendurable. The value of life is the hope which remains for gaining the other values.

Some men commit suicide, when life is no longer enjoyable, or where their personal honor has been destroyed. Often suicide is unjustified, in the sense that life might have been improved. But suicide testifies to the fact that mere life can lack value. Other men are willing to sacrifice their lives for a cause, for others, even from a sense of honor. They too demonstrate that life gains its value through the manner of living and its fruits. Biological life is a value in possibility and in hope, not in the mere activity of organic processes.

Finally, there are certain values which are directly part of life, and tied intimately to it. In particular, I am thinking of health. To those who suffer illness frequently, nothing is a greater boon than good health. Unfortunately, to a healthy child, nothing may be taken more for granted. And ill health is far more common than it need be. Life loses much of its value when coupled with disease or a crippling injury.

If life is valuable, then death would seem to be an evil. And to many people, death and life stand opposed both in concrete terms and in value. If life is good, then we must avoid death at any cost. The great religions have made much of the fear of death, and the problem that all men must someday die. Some religions rest on a firm commitment to life after death, as if death can be dealt with best by eradicating it. In return, some existentialists argue that the expectation of death can imbue life with a pregnancy and urgency that can improve it, and can make human actions all the more poignant.

If life is a good, does it follow that death is an evil? On the Greek view mentioned, life is a good in being lived well. And as Nietzsche points out, living well and dying well are often the same. A variety of points may be made on this subject. (1) An organism begins its way to death from the moment it is alive. Life and death are two faces of the same process. We have seen that life makes other values possible. Death too, while it remains ahead, make those values possible. (2) In this sense, death is the *completion* of life. (3) Where a man has lived well, in the sense of having accomplished worth-while things during his life, he dies well, satisfied with his achievements. (4) The lurking fear of death may be a sense of having wasted one's life. (5) A man who dies poorly may undermine a good part of his achievements during his life. A rich man who dies with an outrageous will can make his children hate him and each other. (6) Would immortality be a blessing? Only where both health and intelligence remained intact, and the other values of life could be enhanced. Certainly a longer life would be a good for many people. For others, a longer life of illness or poverty would seem only to lengthen the torture. Life without death would seem to offer only the eventual prospect of misery—boredom, senility, weariness. (7) Death remains as the final possibility of life, whereby all suffering may be ended. In this sense, it adds its own value to life.

Life and death, illness and health, are among the most urgent of our social problems. We seem never to resolve them completely. New issues intrude which require new rules and guiding principles. Old issues remain with us in new forms, never losing their poignancy.

Among the older issues are disease and starvation, which are ameliorated but never quite relieved. Twin evils haunt us on either side. We have too few physicians and exorbitant medical costs. Or we may train too many incompetent physicians. The United States once had the greatest medical system in the world. Yet medical care is in a state of crisis today. There are too few physicians. The poor receive a care that is entirely inadequate.

Newer problems stem from changing sexual norms and a remarkable increase in the incidence of venereal diseases. Laws prohibiting abortion have been re-pealed in many states, leading many people to fear a total disrespect for life in the new attitudes toward abortion. On the one hand, we find people who seem to regard an abortion as no more serious than removing a wart. On the other, there are people who regard abortion as genuine murder. In dealing with subjects on which feelings run very strong, we must somehow struggle to find social policies which reconcile the different needs and attitudes in a beneficial way.

Finally, a whole nest of new problems lurks ahead in the area of health and biology, problems we have barely begun to discern. Heart and organ transplants have brought to the fore a new type of medical decision. Medical science is so advanced that a few people can be saved from death at incredible expense, and also at considerable risk. Heart transplants make the surgeon's reputation. Are they justified? At what risk of killing the patient? At what cost? Is it justifiable for a hospital to spend thousands of dollars to save one life, when it could instead help hundreds of others who are not seriously ill? How long should a person's body be kept alive when he is unconscious and unable to function? We have heart transplants instead of medical care for children who suffer from lead poisoning. And emergency heart care instead of a balanced diet for everyone.

Biological sciences are beginning to move into the field of directed genetic development. If we can manipulate individual development genetically, should we do so, and to what extent? Shall we turn out better looking people? Develop resistance to disease? Musical and scientific geniuses?

All of these problems demonstrate that, so far as the greater moral problems are concerned, we are far from secure and from settled. Nothing testifies to the need for an open-minded concern for evaluation more strongly than the problems we have yet to resolve, old and new.

B. Security

It is sometimes said that men need security. Yet also we know of men who find quiet and stability confining, and who climb mountains, drive racing cars, and seek sources of excitement. Security is a great value in life. Yet it can become extreme. Where a man sacrifices everything else to security, he may discover that it was not worth the price. Particularly, he will discover that perfect security is impossible.

The greatest value of security is reliability or stability. Men need to know what to expect from others, and what will happen in the world around them. Security is knowledge of the future. In this sense, science provides knowledge and control. and security as well. Ironically, science also breeds technology as a means of control, and technology is often the source of change.

Perhaps the most complete form of security is the security of thought we call peace of mind. A man torn within himself is insecure with respect to both the world and himself. Peace of mind is a security within oneself. Perhaps it depends on both knowledge and external order, to the extent that external dangers require an alertness incompatible with inner peace. But peace of mind is mainly an internal harmony wherein we remain content with ourselves. Unfortunately, even this peace can degenerate to an extreme of smugness and dogmatism.

The major source of security is custom. Where social life is orderly and well structured, men act in similar ways. We then obtain the security of knowing how they will respond and how they will act. Where habit and custom are strong, we may expect other men to think as we do, to act as we do, and to respond as we do. All of this provides a greater chance of cooperation and sharing.

Yet the dangers of custom are obvious, and have been discussed many times. Where custom is too strong, it can be oppressive in a variety of ways. Notably, it can inhibit originality of thought and difference of outlook, and it can lead to a dull world with too great a uniformity. Above all, the patterns of custom may provide little enjoyment or knowledge. Custom has little value when it does not lead to other values of life. Here too, security is valuable in itself, but only when it is instrumentally valuable also. Security always requires a balance with its complement: variety.

C. Variety

We have already spoken of variety as an important value. It provides interest for life. It also may breed originality of thought and action. Men who are too much alike think alike also, and lack the urge to originality which social life requires. Variety is the salt of life.

Yet it can be too strong. Variety can collapse into chaos, into disharmony, into insecurity. Social life depends on some degree of order. Most important of all, too great a variety in a single person's life may also inhibit originality of thought. For originality is a disciplined control of the past in order to add to it for the future. All too often, the encouragement of sheer difference leads to no more than triteness and shallowness. Originality is the control of variety, a control which rests upon a secure basis in custom and tradition.

In this sense, security and variety are complementary values, not separable from each other, nor valuable apart from each other. Moreover, together they look to the other values in life. For where they provide no enjoyment or dignity, they have no obvious value in themselves.

D. Enjoyment

A life without pleasure has no value. A man who enjoys nothing values nothing. Enjoyment is a fundamental and undeniable value. Yet we have seen that most forms of hedonism, which regards pleasure as the aim of all human activity, are indefensible. The reason for this is simple. Enjoyment is a supreme value when realized through other valuable activities, and a far lesser value when sought as an ultimate goal. A man who looks for pleasure may find only boredom. A man who looks for worth-while activities which develop his mind and skills will also discover the greater enjoyments life has to offer.

Enjoyment is not something in itself. The closest thing to pure enjoyment is the stimulation of the pleasure centers of the brain. Yet most of us would not regard this as a good. Rather, enjoyment is to be viewed as a characteristic of activities done well. An athlete enjoys hitting a home run, or surpassing his last feat. A poet enjoys his work, though it may involve effort and strain, even hours of frustration. An activity is not valuable where it is completely dissociated from pain or effort, but is most enjoyable when it is part of effort and dedication.

We may repeat the point of the continuum of means and ends. All activities are to be viewed as both means and ends. An instrumental good which has no direct value in itself—which provides no enjoyment—is not much of a value. A value good *only* as a means can be debilitating and destructive. Enjoyment is essential to all intrinsic goods. Like life, it is itself no value without the activities with which it is joined.

E. Love

Love is a value in two senses, which correspond closely to means and ends. In the most obvious sense, love is a satisfying feeling. It is good to be in love, to care for another person. And it is also good to be loved, to know that one's wishes matter, that one's hidden feelings may be shown honestly. Men have a strong desire to love and be loved.

The sheer desire for love can be extreme, and lose its value. Love can haunt every activity and every waking thought, and interfere with every task and every skill. Love can involve great torment, and lead to great suffering. Love can lead to a will to possess another person, to actions which are repressive and cruel.

Love is therefore good only when it both satisfies the emotional needs of the lover and leads to activities beneficial to the beloved. A parent's love for a child is a good when it envelops and protects the child, and leads him to a rich and satisfying development. It is repressive and ugly when it stifles him, and denies him the opportunity to develop to the fullest extent. Love can inhabit activities of shared experiences, of deeper trust, of intimacy and concern. Love can lead to generosity and to giving, to a widening of experiences which involve more than just one point of view. Yet it can also lead to insecurity, to resentment, to repression, and even to hatred.

F. Other people

Other people are themselves valuable, in the respects in which social life is valuable. Cooperation can be enjoyable. It can provide security. The thoughts of others may reenforce our own, or may provide a variety of different ideas. Life can be more secure with others. More can be accomplished. In this sense, social life is valuable as a means to all other values.

In addition, insofar as men care for others, love them, or simply desire their company and approval, all the values we have mentioned and will discuss subsequently may be regarded as values for other people. That is, not only are life and security values for each of us separately, but they are values for everyone. Just as a man can lead a good life only where he gains many if not all the important values in life, so social life requires that all men gain the very same values. In other words, all the goods we are discussing are to be thought of as goods for all men, others as well as ourselves. Where these goods are provided for everyone, we have a good life individually and socially.

But where only a few men acquire most of these values for themselves, we have an unjust society. We recall our earlier discussion of a just man in an unjust society. Here we ask, can an individual man lead a good life in a society which does not provide a good life for everyone? It should be clear that no individual in such a society could gain *all* the values we consider important.

Probably the most important requirement for successful group relationships is that of trust. Other men are helpful only where there is trust. It is often said at these turbulent times that the family is no longer a viable social unit. Yet the intimacy of family relations contributes to trust. Large groups make any personal trust difficult to obtain. There is a general trust which is no more than reliable expectation. Custom can provide this. But where trust depends on loyalty and sensitivity to another person, it can be achieved only in direct and personal confrontation.

G. Knowledge

Knowledge is one of the obvious intrinsic goods. It is a good in itself, and may also be valuable as a means. Developing one's mind and abilities is also a good. And intelligence too is a good—though it is not always within a person's control to attain intelligence. Do we not have here a good which requires no qualification, which is a supreme value regardless of all other values?

Properly understood, knowledge is an unmixed value. But this is because it is already a union of means and ends. In order to be clear about this, let us recall Mill's argument concerning freedom of speech. We suppose that the established view is correct. Nevertheless, Mill argues, to suppress a controversial position merely because it is false weakens the established position. Not only do we need to know the truth. We must be able to defend it against attack.

Mill's argument may be generalized. There is a claim to knowledge which is indistinguishable in form from dogmatism. On occasion, a true position may be dogmatically asserted. Yet would we consider a dogmatic truth knowledge? If so, then this knowledge is indeed a mixed value requiring qualification. Dogmatism may lead to thoughtlessness, to lack of originality, even to a weakness in understanding. A parroted dogma, even when true, is not fully understood.

Knowledge is an unqualified and unmixed good only when it is the fruit of investigation, when the evidence is known and the alternatives have been criticized. Knowledge is an unqualified good when it comes from open and free

inquiry. But free and open inquiry is precisely a union of means and ends. It is the
development of means for solving problems, and the entertainment of theories which continually serve to resolve new problems. An outmoded theory is an end which has no function as a means. A mere device for solving a problem has no status as an authoritative conclusion. Only the two together are knowledge. Knowledge and inquiry form a single enterprise, in which means and ends are conjoined. Here knowledge is intimately related to social life, to originality, and even to peace of mind. Where knowledge produces the peace of mind which is dogmatism, it is only a qualified value.

H. Performance

The Protestant work-ethic is an extreme version of a great value—that of doing something well. The work-ethic suffers violently where it leads to labor without enjoyment, and to effort without satisfaction. It is difficult to understand what is valuable about diligence without reward. It is perfectly understandable that where men are forced to labor for their sustenance, the value of relaxation should seem great.

But mere relaxation has its flaws also. A yearning for originality and creativity is often evinced even by those who despise the work-ethic. Men have minds and talents which are to be used, and used to create, to produce, to achieve.

Plato's *Republic* is founded on the principle of productivity. Not work, but achievement is the value. To Plato, men are fulfilled through their abilities as developed and realized in activities which involve high standards of performance. The stress in Plato is on the standards of achievement. The goal is not work for its own sake, not mere effort, but effort devoted to excellent things. Plainly and simply, it is a great thing to do something well. Athletes invest hours and hours of their time in practice, to enable them to surpass their past achievements by just a little. The yearning for perfection is the value of excellence carried to its completion.

Performance is often confused with competition. Yet they are very different. The value of performance is the value of achievement—that is, of doing something well, of meeting high standards. Competition is no more than surpassing others. Performance emphasizes far more a surpassing of oneself. Where others are weak, competitiveness may lead to weakness of performance. Performance emphasizes the highest standards men can define. It is worth noting that even criminals may seek to attain high standards of achievement in their crafts.

Performance is doing something well. Some actions are transitory, and leave no permanent mark. For example, an athlete may run faster than anyone else ever has. But that event passes, and is no more than a note in the record book. Some performances are also productive, in that they involve making things. Making and building have special virtues which are worth noting. In particular, since they involve an object made, such as a work of art, they can be means to other things.

Here we may add to sheer performance the value of productivity. Productivity itself can lead to work with no standards, to mere strain. But the union of productivity with standards of excellence leads to art, to the crafts, even to the sciences. The value of all of these as means is obvious and almost without limit. The value of them as ends is also great. Nothing is a greater satisfaction than completing a project by oneself, to high standards of perfection, and producing something which others can appreciate. Home gardeners, cabinet makers, even stamp collectors, all know the great satisfaction of achievement.

The dangers of performance are obvious. Too high standards of perfection may lead to paralysis and self-hatred. Sheer productivity can be effort without satisfaction. A whole generation of young men and women seem to have become aware of the evils of performance and work carried to an extreme. Unfortunately, they may lose the genuine value of performance and productivity in their extremes of revulsion.

To Plato, life is not worth living if it does not involve making a valuable contribution to the world through the development of one's abilities. Such performance is the greatest satisfaction a human life can have. Perhaps Plato's view is exaggerated, especially where hard work interferes with the other pleasures of life. Yet it is worth noting that the special and enduring values of knowledge and mind require diligence and effort, while the casual pleasures of the body may pall in sheer repetition.

I. Self-respect

Finally, all the varieties of activities and goods in life have their value only as lived in a single life, and only as they contribute to the sense a man has of his own value. A person who has few skills may despise himself for it. If he is a perfectionist, and can do a great deal, but will not believe it, then his self-contempt will undermine everything he does. A man may take pleasure from play and from sex. But if they make him despise himself for wasting his time, such pleasures are far from good.

We sometimes speak of a man of *integrity* or *dignity*. In one sense, such a man is honest and trustworthy, a responsible person. He can be trusted to do what has to be done. In another sense, such a person is comfortable with himself, in the sense that he has a firm sense of what is important and what is not, *for himself*. Among all the values which are important he has found an order of priorities he can live with. Therefore, he is seldom insecure about what he ought to do, seldom ambivalent about what he really wants.

Even a man who lives a life of pleasure can be thought of as honorable and sincere in the sense described. By this I do not mean a person who lives *solely* for pleasure, sacrificing all the other important values of life to it. Rather, take a man who looks for enjoyment in everything he does. He looks to athletic pleasures and sexual pleasures. But he respects the needs of others, seeks out some field of knowledge, develops his abilities, and is fairly secure in mind and body. Such a person, living harmoniously within himself through the variety of important things and activities in his life, though all directed toward pleasure, possesses integrity and even dignity.

Self-respect can degenerate into smugness. Honor can become a fetish with the most destructive of qualities. Dignity can be a form of pompousness and inflexibility. Integrity can decay into lack of feeling. In all these cases, the greater value of inner nobility collapses in its disdain for the other values of life. Sheer love of oneself may blind one to everything else of importance. Self-respect is a firm value only where it is based on other values.

Self-respect, then, may be thought of as an assured sense of the variety of important values in life, a respect for all of them, and a willingness to act toward them with patience and love. A man of integrity knows what is important, and lives accordingly. He also has a sense within himself of his own balance of values and actions. Self-respect is here no value in itself, but a value through the other good things it makes possible. In this respect it is one with all the other values.

QUESTIONS

1. List some values other than those discussed which are also important and valuable to the same extent and in the same ways. Discuss some of them in detail.
2. Is each of the values discussed in the chapter represented in some moral principle? If so, state and discuss the principle. If not, why not?
3. Explain in some detail the connection between the important values of this chapter and the continuum of means and ends.
4. Is it possible to have all the good things in a single life? How? Describe such a life.
5. Is it right to sacrifice any important value to some others? When and why?

SELECTED READINGS

A variety of views on the good life in concrete form:

Plato, *Republic*.
Kant, *Metaphysics of Morals*.
Lao Tzu, *The Way of Life*.
Bhagavad-Gita.

Important Values

G. Allport, *Becoming*, 1955, Yale University.

B. F. Skinner, *Walden II*, 1960, Macmillan. Two psychologists' very different treatments.

J. Dewey, *A Common Faith*, 1934, Yale University.

E. Shirk, *The Ethical Dimension*, 1965, Appleton.

H. Fingarette, *The Self in Transformation*, 1963, Harper.

H. Hesse, *The Glass Bead Game*. A profound literary treatment of a variety of noble lives. Especially the three lives at the end are worth reading.

XI. CONCLUDING REMARKS

WE HAVE ranged over many ethical and philosophical problems in these pages, and, I fear, have arrived at no port of safety. To some readers, our counsel will seem one of despair. To others, a bewildering confusion. In these final pages, I can but try again to order a discipline and a practice whose complexity wearies the heart, yet also gives savor to life.

The key element in the moral decisions we have studied is that of complexity, and the primary danger is one of failure. All moral decisions are risky. To the extent that they look to facts, all moral decisions can fail. Dogmatism is indefensible given the circumstances of moral life, and increases the peril. Yet open-mindedness can be flabby, and may betray a lack of moral commitment. Moral decisions are treacherous. Yet we must be loyal to some principles, strong in our convictions, and flexible enough to change with circumstances.

If it were not so important, the arduousness of moral life would be laughable. The comic sense of life finds much to mock in the moral stance, which is tragic yet absurd, paradoxical while indistinct, yet in which reside so much dignity and splendor.

Confusion is inherent in morals. Ethics demands difficult and bewildering decisions from us. Yet the relativist and the nihilist go too far in their despair. For we have seen that moral decisions can be arrived at deliberately and defended rationally. Most important of all, we may look to the ideals described in the last chapter, as a completion of the moral life.

The elements of moral decision are the principles upon which it is based, the human feelings implicated, and the factual conditions which surround the circumstances of decision. All of these are complex. And all of them change in time. We may, then, look to counsels of desperation for our motive force, and cynically dwell upon the vanity of life.

Yet despair worsens the conditions of life. And desperation proves the most destructive of grounds of action. Within and among the complexity of moral decisions we may wend a way by deliberation and forethought, and by the cultivation of principles which merit our loyalty. Dogmatic loyalty too leads to deleterious consequences. So we temper our loyalties with adaptability and open-mindedness.

We come, then, to see the greater value of open-mindedness, reverence for life, flexibility, consideration for others, self-respect, and intelligence. The very complexity and peril of moral decisions require of us a commitment to the most efficacious means of life, and the most stringent yet flexible means for bettering our condition. Complexity breeds order, in defining a pathway among the vicissitudes of life.

The sense of a pathway is a persuasive metaphor. But it is fundamentally misleading by undue emphasis on the singleness of the way. The moral life becomes repressive where it is monolithic. Rather, we may instead conceive of the ideals or greater intrinsic values as flexible landmarks, among which we make our way, but through which no single path can be found. The ideal human life possesses many or all of the primary values, but in no specific ratio, and in no fixed manner.

In the last chapter, we explored some of the ultimate values of life. These are the ideals men have discovered through experience to be essential to a life lived well. We have seen that they implicate each other. Any one ultimate value is good in itself precisely to the extent that it serves to enhance the others. Where it is pursued alone, to the detriment of other important goods, it loses its value, and harms those who give themselves to it.

The continuum of means and ends, then, is the ruling principle of intelligent moral decision. Crudely, it calls us always to look beyond the immediate ap-pearance of good to interconnections and remote eventualities. It calls us to be open-minded and far-seeing. In detail, it leads us to grasp the interrelationship of all the great values in human life.

The ideal life, then, is a life which encompasses many or all of the important values. In what proportion? No precise answer can be given to this question. For there is a central truth to the principle that a man must make his moral decisions for himself. We may discern the means and methods essential to responsible moral decisions. We may discover the greater values in all human experience. But the choice among and within these values is left to the agent himself. For not only may he order such values in the light of his personal character. He must also live the rest of his life as a consequence of the order he has imposed on it. The variety of individuals and their personalities imposes a variety among the ultimate ideals. And this variety leads also to a dynamic and ever-changing process, as men are influenced by their own choices and the choices of others.

Each man chooses among the important values for himself. Yet he may order them unwisely and short-sightedly, as the consequences of his actions may show. We spend our lives defining and redefining a principle of life, never quite having completed it, continually discovering the need for change. Yet this makes of life a project never quite finished, and imposes a challenge without which life can be dull. And in the end, death is required to mark the only end to the project of life which can be realized. For a life lived well, death is a consummation and not a threat. That is the final and greater truth Socrates gives us.

INDEX